THE BODY OF WAR

NEXT WAVE:

New Directions in Women's Studies

A series edited by Inderpal Grewal, Caren Kaplan, and Robyn Wiegman

THE BODY OF WAR

Media, Ethnicity, and Gender
in the Break-up of Yugoslavia

Dubravka Žarkov

DUKE UNIVERSITY PRESS
Durham and London
2007

Printed in the United States
of America on acid-free paper ♾
Designed by Amy Ruth Buchanan
Typeset in Dante by Tseng
Information Systems, Inc.
Library of Congress Cataloging-
in-Publication Data appear on the
last printed page of this book.

TO MY SISTERS,

whose love kept me safe

AND THEIR CHILDREN,

to grow wise and kind

CONTENTS

Acknowledgments ix
Introduction 1

PART I. THE MATERNAL BODY

1. The Whore against the Mother of All Serbs 19
2. Pictures of the Wall of Love 43
3. Troubles with Motherhood 69

PART II. THE VICTIMIZED BODY

4. The Body of All Serbs 85
5. All the Bodies of Croatia 102
6. Sexual Geographies of Ethnicity 116
7. On Victims and Villains 143
8. The Body of the Other Man 155
9. Troubles with the Victim 170

PART III. THE ARMED BODY

10. Soldiers of Tradition 191
11. Troubles with Arms 212

Notes 233
Bibliography 257
Index 281

ACKNOWLEDGMENTS

This book depended on support of many people. I mention first those who were willing to talk to me about their lives, which were changed by the violent disintegration of socialist Yugoslavia. I thank them for trusting that I would do justice to their words.

Without the support of my mentor Willy Jansen, colleagues, and the staff and fellow students of the Center for Women's Studies in Nijmegen, the Netherlands, where I stayed between 1994 and 1999, I would have never been able to finish the research on which this book is based. I mention many of them in individual chapters, which they have kindly read. They gave comments, criticism, and suggestions on which my work grew; they provided interesting texts, references, and information, or simply kept asking how my work was progressing. Willy patiently took care of my visas and residence permits, while the secretary of the center took care of my constant hunger for copy cards. My colleagues shared their time and thoughts with me, as we worked together and planned to work together, and joined me in life's many ups and downs. Their unwavering support and encouragement, their human warmth and intellectual openness made the center a friendly, inspiring, and motivating place to work in, and Nijmegen a town I love dearly. They have spoiled me forever. I gratefully acknowledge my indebtedness to all of them, and wish to give special thanks to Willy Jansen and Ria Janssen. No amount of cakes will ever repay my debts to you.

Numerous other colleagues from many different universities and institutes, many women from nongovernmental organizations, and many anonymous readers of journals and books, based in the Netherlands, Germany, the United Kingdom, the United States, India, Serbia, Croatia, Bosnia, and Slovenia have read my work and encouraged it by inviting me to take part at their courses, seminars, trainings, and conferences, or to write for them. All of them have forced me to sharpen my thoughts and think deeper and further. I am deeply grateful to them all. If I am not mentioning any particular names it is only because these ten years of cooperation would require several pages of names, and I would still run the risk of missing some.

I also thank the NWO (Dutch Organization for Scientific Research) for financing my research; Duke University Press for publishing its results, and editors Ken Wissoker and Courtney Berger and the anonymous Duke readers for their work, support, and enthusiasm; and Matt Salusbury and Rada Drezgic for laboring over the language and the contents of the book. They all appeared at moments when I was ready to give up, and helped me carry on.

But most of all I thank my parents, Ana and Miroslav Žarkov; my two sisters and their families—Jadranka, Stefan, and Nikola Petrović, and Maja, Miloš, Uroš, and Milan Milanović; my family from the Netherlands, Arie, Thomas, Mineke, and Wybran Brouwer and the extended Brouwer family; and my dearest friends, Anissa Helie, Edda Kirleis, Indira Simbolon, Kathy Davis, Helma Lutz, Rada Drezgić, Tanja Djurić, Jasmina Vujatov, Djula Šodolović, Mira Oklobdžija, Željko Rakić, Dragana Obradović, Stefan Dudink, Halleh Ghorashi, and Marga Altena. They have been with me during all the years I conducted my research, the years I hoped to write a book out of it, and the years I actually wrote it. They have sometimes despaired how long it all took, sometimes wondered how quickly it went. But they have believed in me when I doubted and doubted when I was too confident. They have invested energy and labor when I had none left. They have endured my absences as well as my presences, laughed and cried many goodbyes and welcomings. They saw me move from the then-Yugoslavia-now-Serbia-and-Montenegro to the Netherlands, and many times within the Netherlands, and then they have gone themselves to many far and near places, for a short while or for good, while I stayed behind missing them. Some are no longer among the living. I thank them all. Without them, none of this would have been worthwhile.

INTRODUCTION

We all know what a chastity belt is, don't we? But, what could a chastity *border* belt possibly be?

This surprising concept was all nicely explained in an article with the same title, published in the Serbian weekly *NIN*, in March 1990, one year ahead of a violent war that caused the Socialist Federal Republic of Yugoslavia to disintegrate.[1] "Chastity border belt" was the name given to the stretch of land along the state border that—according to the article—needed special protection against illegal intruders. This stretch of land was in the north of the country, separating the Yugoslav republic of Slovenia from neighboring Italy. The article implied that Slovenians were not taking seriously their duty of protecting Yugoslav borders and symbolically defined Slovenia as a chaste, but not very trustworthy maiden, in need of proper protection, control, and defense (March 25, 1990, 18–20).

In 1993, while the war was raging through Croatia and Bosnia, the Croatian weekly *Danas* wrote about the changing political fortune of Vojislav Šešelj, the leader of an ultranationalist party in Serbia. The article made fun of Šešelj's Bosnian origin, discussing his posture, blond hair, and blue eyes (insisting that Bosnians are supposed to be dark) as well as his ever-changing political alliances (sometimes with and sometimes against Serbian president Milošević). But the article's title mocked, first and foremost Šešelj's manhood. It read: "Is Šešelj a Spy or a Woman?" The question is repeated in the article, which imagines Šešelj in a woman's dress, insinuating that, since nothing is certain with him—from his political allegiances to his mixed ethnic origin—his manhood may also produce some surprises (March 26, 1993, 29).

The evocation of female chastity in a newspaper article about the state borders and the questioning of the masculinity of a politician in an article about his ethnic origin and politics may have been quite coincidental. However, there seem to have been too many coincidences of this kind in the Yugoslav press in that period: texts in which the bodies and capacities of women and men acquired some surprising new meanings; in which the states and their national and ethnic groups became personified or symbolically represented as female or male bodies; in which the notions usually associated with norms of sexuality or assumptions of "proper" manhood and womanhood were suddenly associated with matters that concern state territory, daily politics, and—last but not least—ethnicity.

What was happening? Why were female and male bodies vested with such meanings, and why were they linked to notions of gender, sexuality, and ethnicity? What do these meanings have to do with the bloody war as a result of which the Socialist Federal Republic of Yugoslavia disintegrated—a country once known for worker self-management, participation in the nonalignment movement, and its beautiful Adriatic beaches? To what extent were these newspaper articles that mocked and accused, and many others that threatened and incited, really directly responsible for the brutality by which the former neighbors treated each other's bodies during the 1991–1995 period?

This book offers a perspective from which these questions might be answered and asserts that there was no coincidence in the vesting of female and male bodies with meanings that relate gender and sexuality to ethnicity, nation, or the state.[2] It was no coincidence that these images were in the press long before the war and during it, a war whose most notorious strategies focused precisely on the violation of the female and male bodies.

To the contrary, this book asserts, both the images in the press and the violent strategies of the war were vested with a very specific power: the power to produce ethnicity. The living and the symbolic bodies of women and men were the primary sites of this production. The war itself was the mode of production—*the wars*, actually, in plural. For there were two wars through which ethnicity was produced in former Yugoslavia: the "media war" and the "ethnic war." The former started long before the actual fighting was even imaginable, and its traces are present to this day. The latter raged from 1991 to 1995, in Slovenia, Bosnia, and Croatia, and since then has been flaring up and burning in larger or smaller fires, many times, in different places in the region.

In this book I argue that ethnicity was produced through the representational practices of the media war as much as through the violent practices of the ethnic war. In other words, I do not define the ethnic war as a war between ethnic groups (as common sense would have it); rather, I perceive both the media war and the ethnic war as wars that produce ethnic groups.

Separate, never collapsible onto each other, yet constitutive of each other, these two wars aimed to make ethnicity the only mode of being, to obliterate and obscure everything that could cast a shadow on its omnipotence.

From Media War to Ethnic War

It remains uncertain who was first to use the term "media war," but at the end of the 1980s the expression was commonly accepted by the national media, the public, and politicians.[3] The term referred to the direct and intensive engagement of the media of the different Yugoslav republics in forging nationalist politics, defending the leaders and the politics of, supposedly, "their own" nation and republic, while at the same time fiercely attacking leaders, politics, and general population of other nations and republics.[4] Various medieval figures suddenly started being referred to as if they were contemporaries, and contemporaries suddenly claimed more or less symbolic ties to medieval heroes. In almost postmodernist fashion, history stopped being linear and progressive—past was not past, future was not future, everything was happening here and now, and on the pages of the press.

The main condition that made the media war possible, probable, and effective was the closed, divided, and exclusive discursive space that existed during the late 1980s and early 1990s, in which the inflow and exchange of information between republics was greatly reduced (by controlling access to broadcasts and publishing from other territories), and within them was censored. However, this tightly controlled and restricted media space within a single republic indicates that the main target of the media war was not the audience on the other side of the republic's border, but the audience within its own, closed space. Ivan Čolović (1994) was first to point out that the media war was not only a mode of hostile communication between the quarreling parties, but primarily a mode of "auto-communication," with its most fundamental role to foster the cohesive and mobilizing power of an ethnically defined group (163).[5] I take his analysis a step further, and assert that the media war was about *production of ethnicity*, with notions of femininity and masculinity and norms of sexuality as its essential ingredients.

It was apparent that in mid-1980s the media in former Yugoslavia started covering stories that they had not covered before. The concern with which the media suddenly started addressing the so-called women's issues, especially issues regarding reproduction and sexual violence against women, was striking. Given that previously only feminist groups or official women's organizations would engage in discussing such issues, their sudden media prominence was a novelty, as was the framing of the discussions. References to childcare, maternity leave, abortion rights, legislation on rape, sexual morality, and so on, were now discussed (in political bodies as well as on the pages of the newspapers) in light of the population growth, traditional values, and historic dreams of, or historic injustices against, a particular ethnic group.[6] Family values were redefined and reasserted in terms of ethnic and religious values. Ethnic groups declared themselves endangered and started counting their population.[7] The *white plague* (a popular term that was coined to describe low fertility rates and negative population growth in Vojvodina and some parts of Serbia proper) became the most feared disease, and women—especially professional women and women who had abortions—were branded the main culprits (Drezgić 2000). Accused in speeches by religious and political leaders, in newspaper articles and TV interviews, in popular booklets and street posters, women were called to come to their senses, give up paid jobs, and raise children for the nation. Equally significant, men were summoned to account for their capacity to control their women, or defend the graves of their forefathers. And while the lives of women and men were brought into the stories of the nations, the reverse was true as well: nations and territories were referred to as raped or pregnant, as virile or virginal; states became mothers or stepmothers.

Within this atmosphere of media hostility, life for many people in Yugoslavia went on more or less as usual. The country's economic decline worried many families more than political speeches. And while there were some far-sighted individuals who warily talked about approaching war, for most others the "war" was just a word politicians used to scare each other. So for many Yugoslavs the actual fighting came as a surprise, although the process of secession and violent disintegration that started in 1991 was preceded by diffused violence and sporadic, low-intensity armed conflicts during 1989, 1990, and the first half of 1991. In Croatia, armed clashes between the Croatian majority and Serbian minority started already in 1989. In 1991 they escalated into a full-blown insurgency of Serbs from the Knin region in Croatia. Violence also followed a demonstration by Albanian students in Kosovo in January 1990, who demanded the end of the state of emergency in the province that had been declared by the regime of Slobodan Milošević the previous year.

Nobody, however, perceived these conflicts as an overture to a war. Not even when, early in the morning of June 27, 1991, tanks left their military barracks and rolled onto the streets of Ljubljana and other Slovenian cities, following the Slovenian and Croatian declarations of independence from the Socialist Federal Republic of Yugoslavia two days earlier.[8] Within two weeks the tanks had to withdraw from the streets, and Slovenians celebrated victory. Later that summer Croatia was engulfed in war, and in April 1992 fighting started in Bosnia. While the independence of all three former Yugoslav republics was recognized internationally (Slovenia and Croatia in January 1992, and Bosnia in June 1992), this meant nothing in terms of prevention of the violent disintegration, that would last until the Dayton Peace Accords were signed in December 1995.

At the beginning, this disintegration was called "civil war." But this term soon disappeared from use, and the term "ethnic war" was widely accepted both inside Yugoslavia and by the international community. This characterization was supposed to indicate that in different regions different ethnic groups were fighting each other and proclaiming their right to sovereign control of a specific territory that was also defined in ethnic terms. What made the ethnic component recognizable to Yugoslav citizens, and those familiar with the country, was the growing nationalism of different groups throughout the 1980s. As a political force nationalism had appeared earlier, as both a bottom-up (in 1968 in Kosovo) and a top-down (in 1971 in Croatia) movement.[9] But the term "ethnic war" was to a great extent part and parcel of Eurocentric, Orientalist, and Balkanist[10] perceptions of the Balkans—both within and outside of it—that slowly but surely became the main frame of reference for Yugoslav disintegration. With these discourses an entirely new country emerged, marked by a "history of ethnic hatred";[11] with people in search of a new father figure;[12] and with irreconcilable civilization, cultural, and religious differences among the national groups, as well as from the rest of Europe.[13] These characterizations came from nationalist politicians and academics within Yugoslavia as much as from outside. A few Yugoslav and international authors struggled to explain that both the rise of nationalism and the war were due to the fact that Yugoslav socialism already incorporated nationalism, in its administrative and political demarcation of ethnicity-based republics and its system of political representation.[14] But most important, they argued that the power struggle of communist elites since the Second World War was also organized along republican-ethnic lines.[15] Thus, political processes leading toward war had already produced ethnicity as the main carrier of political power, as the most significant social category, and as the most privileged identity, resulting in decentralization without democratization, and finally, in the creation of ethnodemocracies (Sekelj 1990).

Thus, not surprisingly, ethnicity did become the ultimate explanatory factor of Yugoslav social reality, the nature of its people as much as the nature of its disintegration. The bloodier the war became, the easier it was to call it, and its violent strategies, "ethnic." The fact that the war itself, the violence it unleashed, and the representation of this violence in media, were actually producing "ethnicity," was obscured or denied. As a history of heterogeneity was replaced by a "history of ethnic hatred," there were neither discursive nor geographical spaces for nonethnicized realities.

In his analysis of the war in former Yugoslavia, Robert Hayden (1996, 2) concluded that nationalism in the Balkans "has not been only a matter of imagining allegedly 'primordial' communities, but rather of making existing heterogeneous ones unimaginable." This unimaginability of heterogeneity was, according to Hayden, pursued by two strategies. One—evident in the political manifestos and constitutions of the newly established states—shows the reinterpretation of the historic and cultural evidence of heterogeneity in each of the states, and redefinitions of the majority ethnic group as the only rightful proponent of the state's sovereignty, excluding, thus, all others who lived in the same territory. Street names were changed, national heroes and novelists of "wrong" ethnicity were expunged from school curriculums, language was "purged" of "foreign influences," and people not belonging to the majority ethnic group were excluded from citizenship. Where the lack of constitutional rights or political and cultural intimidation did not persuade the minorities that they should move out, another strategy was used—direct violence. This violence obscured and erased heterogeneity and mapped the national territory in blood and bones, creating one of the most abhorred practices—and as some would say, one of the most accurate metaphors[16]—of our time: "ethnic cleansing." Sexual violence against women was one of its key components.

Accurate facts and figures about sexual violence and the rape of women during the wars in Croatia and Bosnia will never be known with certainty, regardless of the numerous fact-finding missions.[17] What has become certain, however, is its systematic and deliberate nature. A United Nations Commission of Experts determined and documented patterns that, according to its report, "strongly suggest that a systematic rape policy and sexual assault policy exists, but this remains to be proved" (United Nations 1994b, 11). Although the remark "but this remains to be proved" could render the finding indeterminate, the evidence presented indicated that rape and sexual assault were related to the policy of the ethnic cleansing, as conducted by Bosnian Serb forces. Out of 1,100 documented cases of rape, about 600 occurred in detention, indicating that they were neither random nor opportunistic (ibid., 12–13). While rapes in detention were also practiced in camps run by Croats and Muslims (ibid., 10), the U.N. Commission showed that in the case of Bosnian Serbs it was a consistent policy.[18] It was less known at the time that men too were sexually assaulted, and that this assault also had systematic nature.[19]

Ethnicity was produced through these violent practices of the ethnic war, as much as through the representational practices of the media war. The acts of violence were at the same time acts that defined both people and territories in ethnic terms. Furthermore, it was obvious that media war was not letting up, as news about sexual violence hit the TV screens and the pages of the press, and became media stories. These stories—whether cautious and impersonal, or full of pathos and fiery—became yet another way to assert ethnic inclusions and exclusions, to define ethnic groups and territories, to mark those who belonged and those who did not. In short, both the act of violence and the act of representation were engaged in producing meanings, and the struggle to control these meanings was as fierce as the struggle to control territories.

This is why I grant the same epistemological status to the meanings produced through the violent practice and the meanings produced through the representational practice. The images in the press are not approached as secondary to the reality of blood and flesh. To the contrary, the media war is seen to be as productive of ethnicity as the ethnic war, albeit by different means: instead of physical violence it uses words, photos, and cartoons. Still, the word and the deed cannot be collapsed into each other. Textual and visual images in the press can never be equated with the actual violence, nor can we draw a direct link between the media war and the ethnic war. Rather, I argue, notions of femininity and masculinity, and norms of sexuality and definitions of ethnicity, create the links between the media war and the ethnic war, and mediate the relationship between the words and the deeds. The meanings given to the words and pictures are derived from the same gendered, sexualized, and ethnicized practices from which the violent acts receive inspiration, justification, and/or sanction. Marked by daily politics and the web of cultural practices, violent acts and newspaper cartoons and articles draw from the same pool of widely shared assumptions about manly and womanly proprieties or about sexual moralities.

This does not mean that there is only one meaning attached to any particular violent or representational practice. Competing and conflicting meanings are produced through dominance, subordination, exclusion, and marginalization; the shifts and ambiguities in meanings reflect changing domains of power. In the context in which the primary difference is marked by ethnicity, ethnicity will inform both the act of violence and its media representation, and other differences will be obscured. In other words, the act of violence and its media representation are both produced within, and contribute to the same discursive and material reality, even if by different means.

Introducing gender and sexuality into the equation, I want to destabilize ethnicity. I want to show that without notions of masculinity and femininity, and norms of (hetero)sexuality, ethnicity could have never been produced, and the practices of the two wars would have remained unintelligible. We would make little out of the stories of state borders and threatened territories were they not conveyed through familiar gendered and sexualized imagery. What made both the media war and the ethnic war so powerful, so effective in mobilizing people's sentiments, and ultimately so deadly, is the familiarity and the casualness of notions that gave meaning to the bodies of chaste maidens and men in dresses.

The Fe/Male Body: Gender, Sexuality, Ethnicity

In this book the body—female and male—stands central. Both the violent practices of the ethnic war and the representational practices of the media war in Yugoslavia rested upon the symbolic and physical capacities of male and female bodies. Bodies were vested with gendered and sexualized meanings that made ethnicity appear transparent and unambiguous; that treatment reified ethnicity, turned it into an empirical fact, or obscured it altogether. This is a good enough reason to focus on the bodies. But there is another one—my attachment has always been to feminism and its political concerns with and theoretical perspectives on the *female body*. When I started this research, I did not think much about the *male body*; the material itself forced me to reconsider and to give an account also of the male body as it was treated in this conflict.

In Western feminism, the female body was always a central, if not *the* central, political and theoretical issue.[20] Theorizing on the female body, initially as a site of power and dominance, and later also as a site of autonomy and subjectivity, is a major "moral and political battlefield" (Fuss 1989, xii) of Western feminist thought, ranging from the investigations of the links between the embodiment, sexuality, and subjectivity to the essentialism-constructivism debates and discussions on sexual difference (Davis 1997b).

One outcome of all these debates is that the category of the female body has, to a certain extent, undermined gender as the central category of feminist analyses and has defined gender only as a point of departure.[21] Criticism within and outside of Western academia made that point clearly. While notions of femininity reflect social and cultural constructions of the erotic and reproductive possibilities of the female body, it has become increasingly clear that there are other, equally significant relationships in the body politics of different societies. Heterosexuality is a case in point, recognized as a significant organizing principle of social life. From the famous work of Adrienne Rich (1994) to studies on the relationship between feminist theory and lesbian knowledge, heterosexuality is introduced into Western feminist study of the body, albeit with struggle, as a new significant dimension of theorizing the female body.[22]

However, many of the debates on the body have suffered from "ambivalence towards the material body and a tendency to privilege the body as metaphor" (Davis 1997b, 15), creating a gap between social and cultural representations of the body and "embodiment as experience or social practice in concrete social, cultural and historical contexts" (ibid.). Kathy Davis argues that bridging this gap meant, first, accepting that women's experience of their bodies, social and cultural practices implicated in the female body, and symbolic meanings and representations of the female body are *all* produced through multiple social relationships defined by class, race, sexuality, and ethnicity, as much as particular sociopolitical contexts, such as racism, colonialism, or nationalism.[23] Second, it also meant that feminism has to concern itself with the male body too. Otherwise, as Davis (1995, 19) notes, feminism will reinforce the oppositional dualism of the body-mind split, which keeps only women and femininity trapped into bodily matters.

I follow Davis on both accounts, attempting not only to bridge the gap between the metaphoric and material body but also to show that lived experiences and symbolic representations constitute each other. This means that I analyze practices toward and meanings of both the female and the male body. The male body may have different roles to play as a site of production of ethnicity, but they are no less significant than the roles of the female body. Furthermore, I approach the fe/male body as gendered, sexualized, and ethnicized all at the same time. Finally, I take the context of the two wars, ethnic and media, as a concrete social and historical setting within which both the practices toward, and the symbolic meanings of the female and male bodies are produced.

Thus, there are a few assumptions about the relationship between gender, sexuality, and ethnicity that guide my analysis of the fe/male body. First, I understand gender—and thus femininity *and* masculinity—as constitutive of other social categories and power relations. In a war perceived as an ethnic war hardly anybody is just a man, or just a woman. Rather, a person is a Serb man, or a Croat woman, and so on. Manhood and womanhood are ethnicized and gendered at the same time. In stating that gender and ethnicity constitute each other, I do not assume a neat, balanced or fixed relationship. Rather, I hope to show that these categories produce each other in ways that are often ambiguous, contradictory, and conflicting.

Second, I presume that femininities and masculinities are not simply symmetrical, parallel, or complementary, nor are their practices and meanings produced only, or always, in relation to each other. There are aspects of masculinity, for example, that acquire meanings in relation to other masculinities, as much as in relation to femininities. An image of a Croat man will be juxtaposed to an image of a Serb or a Muslim man, as well as to an image of a Croat woman, which in turn will be related to an image of a Muslim woman, as well as to an image of a Croat man. Each of these masculinities and femininities, and the variety of their relationships to one another, will be thoroughly investigated.

Third, norms of sexuality constitute different femininities and masculinities, and the hierarchical relations between them. The hierarchy, however, does not refer only to heterosexuality—with female and male sexualities and sexual capacities (from that of desire to that of procreation) being hierarchically related to one another, differently sanctioned and controlled. It refers also to the sanctioning and positioning of homosexuality, vis-à-vis heterosexuality, and their relations to different masculinities. Thus this book analyzes intersections of different masculinities and homo/heterosexualities with ethnicity.

These assumptions impact upon my conceptualization of ethnicity. As is already clear from the previous section, I do not approach ethnicity in the way of classic (foundationalist) scholarship[24] or the early constructivists.[25] While appreciative of diverse and rich feminist, black, and (post)colonial studies that place identity politics in the center of their analysis of ethnicity,[26] I am wary of the straightforwardness of this politics. Thus I follow the footsteps of the scholars who go beyond oppositional duality and assume that gender, ethnicity, and heterosexuality—while different constructions of power and subordinations—are not separate or cumulative but rather mutually constitutive domains of power.[27]

This means first that I perceive ethnicity in a similar way to gender—as a relation and a category of *power*, always concerned with living individuals or communities, but never reducible to them. Thus I do not ask, "What is ethnicity?" because ethnicity seems to be many different things in many different places: black (but apparently not white) in Britain, Turkish (but not German) in Germany, and Muslim (but not Christian) in Bosnia. I ask rather, "How are specific realities *ethnicized*?" Through what workings of power are specific color and religion, specific individuals and communities, specific traditions and histories, and specific bodies defined as ethnic?

Linking ethnicity to gender and heterosexuality furthermore allows for a reconceptualization of nationalism. For, if ethnicity is produced through gender and heretosexuality, then nationalism is too.[28] Consequently, while ethnicity appears as the central category of so-called ethnic nationalism—as the marker of the ultimate Self-Other dichotomy—I insist that this centrality itself is produced, and that gender and heterosexuality are implicated in this production. In other words, the Other of nationalism is never *only* ethnic, but also always gendered and sexualized, albeit in ambiguous and conflictual way: a (female) rape victim is always female and ethnic at the same time, but her ethnicity and her femininity may bear different significance in different contexts; a man belongs to the ethnic Self only if both his heterosexuality and his masculinity are unquestionable; what will question them, however, may be very different, in different contexts. In all these cases, the physicality of the ethnicized body can hardly be separated from the symbolic meanings vested in it.

Feminist authors have already pointed out that the female body has symbolic functions, that it often epitomizes many different, if not contradicting and conflicting meanings. Sharon Macdonald (1987) argues that the "duality of gender metaphor" constructs the female body as inherently ridden by dual oppositions, making it an apt metaphor of dualities both *within* gender hierarchies (virgin/whore) and *between* them (mother/warrior, peace/war, passive/active, self/other, inner/outer).

Much of this capacity of the female body to epitomize duality and oppositions rests on the epistemological status of femininity in Western philosophy, where masculinity gives meaning to the universal and abstract, while the status of the feminine is linked to the particular and specific. However, femininity can also embody the universal. Marina Warner (1996, 12) notes that the "female form" used in monuments throughout the Western hemisphere "does not refer to particular women, does not describe women as a group, and often does not even presume to evoke their natures." To the contrary, it is emptied of the particular and made "hollow" (in the case of Statue of Liberty, even literally) in order to create a transparent metaphor of the universal, be it freedom, homeland, courage, resilience in the face of adversity, or unconditional love.

I would suggest, however, that hollowness and transparency are always only partial and that epistemologically, the universal and particular in the feminine do not only oppose each other. They also constitute each other. The universal claim (of liberty) serves as a marker of the particular difference (between those who are free and those who are not), while the ambiguity of the female body allows it to recall the universal and still remain specific (pointing to the United States as a "land of free"). Thus, it is not only duality that marks the female form, but also ambiguity: the capacity to be universal and particular at the same time.

It is precisely this ambiguity of the female body that is significant for the nationalist representations, because, as Jan Penrose (1993) argues, a nationalist claim is in itself an ambiguous claim: it relies on a general category of nations in order to establish specific and distinctive existence of a particular nation. This paradoxical position in which a national particularity cannot be established without universality of the concept of the nation means that it also cannot be represented without incorporating both the particular and the universal at the same time. Penrose (ibid., 44) further argues that "visions of people and place as discretely bonded entities" produce symbolic geographies of the nation; these symbolic geographies are, moreover, always racialized and ethnicized.[29] The female and male bodies implicated in this production are thus not only gendered, but also racialized and ethnicized.

Analyzing nationalism and war in former Yugoslavia, Rada Iveković (1993, 123) points out that feminine particularity is allowed into the universal only when representing masculine ideals and values. She argues that the fact that women embody universal ideas "thereby serving to justify them, doesn't mean that what is embodied, the principle or mechanism, is a 'feminine' one. . . . What is symbolically 'embodied' in the female figure can still remain a male ideal, activity, or experience."[30] However, saying that the female body represents masculine ideals and experiences implies, first, that specific ideas are essentially feminine or masculine and, second, that feminine experience is erased from these representations, remaining forever subordinate to the power of the masculine.

I question these assumptions in this book, showing that the representational capacities of both the female and the male body lie precisely in integrating specific lived experiences, of specific women and men within specific political and cultural contexts, with supposedly universal meanings; that is, meanings that in the European and Northern and Western tradition have figured as universals—civilization or humanity, for example. Thus, I show that specificity and particularity are attached to both the female and the male body, albeit in a different way. Furthermore, I contest the essentialist assumption of feminine innocence in matters of war and violence, and analyze it rather as one of the gendered narratives of war, to which many have contributed, including feminists. I will analyze international and local feminist theorizing on the fe/male body in war, and its implications on local feminist activism against the war in former Yugoslavia, starting from the assumptions outlined above.

My analysis of the productive power of the two wars is organized around three symbolic categories of the fe/male body: *the maternal body, the victimized body*, and *the armed body*. The choice of these three symbolic categories follows the theoretical concerns expressed above. But it was primarily led by the fact that the bodies of women and men—with all their powers and vulnerabilities—were the very site upon which the two wars were fought: fierce or broken, cowardly or perverse, mute or too outspoken, naïve or treacherous, hidden or starkly present, the maternal body, victimized body, and militant body were ascribed meanings through acts of violence, as much as through words, photos, and political cartoons. The power of a media image and the power of a violent act both depended on the different capacities of the female and male body for conveying their messages. It is the embodiment—lived and symbolic at the same time—that enabled ethnicity to be produced. Thus, this embodiment will be my guide in tracing back critically the process of production.

The Structure of This Book

The three parts of the book follow the three symbolic bodies, the maternal, the victimized and the armed, ending each time with a discussion of the controversies that each of these bodies raises in feminism.

The first part of the book is dedicated to the maternal body. In it I concentrate on two case studies: the media representations of two public actions of women, in which the participants defined themselves explicitly as mothers. One is the 1987 protest against a statement about rapes and prostitution by an Albanian politician from Kosovo—probably the most significant case for the flare-up of the media war. Another is the protest against the Yugoslav national army (JNA), its detention of soldiers who had completed their service, and its mobilization of new recruits in late August and beginning of September of 1991. The protests involved all the Yugoslav republics except Slovenia (because the Slovenian war for independence from the rest of Yugoslavia had ended in July, with the JNA withdrawing and de facto accepting Slovenian secession). In these two chapters I analyze articles, illustrations, cartoons, and photographs published in the main Croatian and Serbian weekly and daily after these two events, and I search for meanings of gender, sexuality, and ethnicity vested in the imagery of the maternal body. While the female body is central to this analysis, I also highlight the role of the different male bodies juxtaposed to the maternal body. In the last chapter of this section, I debate the ambiguities in the feminist analysis of motherhood and protests, in the light of similar protests in Latin America and South Asia.

The second part of this book deals with the victimized body. I focus on two different aspects of victimization. First, in chapters 4 and 5, I analyze the construction of *symbolic collective victims* in the Serbian and Croatian press, where gender and sexuality played a somewhat different, but still crucial role in producing ethnicity. In the Serbian press, the victim was "the Serbs"—the people. In the Croatian press, the victim was "Croatia"—the state. This difference in the representational strategies of the Serbian and

Croatian press will prove to be relevant for the practice and representation of sexual violence against both women and men, addressed in chapters 6, 7, and 8. The section closes with a problematization of the overpowering presence of the victimized female body in feminist studies on war in Yugoslavia. While acknowledging the vicious nature of the sexual violence against women in violent conflicts, I search for an analytical framework that would allow for a different conceptualization of violence in relation to both femininities and masculinities, drawing on studies of conflicts in South Asia and Rwanda.

The last part of the book deals with the armed body. An examination of the media imagery of female soldiering is followed by an analysis of the invisibility, in feminist discourses in the former Yugoslavia, of the women soldiering between 1991 and 1995 in the national armies and paramilitaries of Serbia, Croatia, and Bosnia. The absence of the armed female body from feminist texts is taken to indicate the meanings of gender, sexuality, and ethnicity for feminism, and is related to the presence of the victimized body. In the concluding chapter, I deal with feminist discomfort with female militancy and women as perpetrators of violence in the context of shifts in feminist theorization of war. Following South Asian feminist analyses of female militancy, I argue for a conceptualization of violence wherein it will be seen neither as inherently masculine nor as only gendered.

PART I.

THE MATERNAL BODY

1

THE WHORE AGAINST THE MOTHER OF ALL SERBS

When in 1987 women flooded the streets of towns and cities in Kosovo and Serbia proper, marching militantly (as the Croatian press stated) and claiming peacefully (as the Serbian press stated) that they were mothers under the threat of rape, few could imagine that the issues of rape and motherhood would become central in the violent conflict that would tear socialist Yugoslavia apart only a few years down the line.[1] Yet it should not have been a surprise. For there is hardly a war—let alone a war in which identity politics stand central—where the maternal body is irrelevant. For this is the body vested with the power to give birth to the nation. As such, it is both vulnerable and powerful, a potential target of attacks and a focus of protection, a fierce defender of its honor and its offspring. Thus, the maternal body, both symbolic and lived, is the body within which both victimization and militancy found their place.

It is this birthing role of the maternal body, and the apparent ease with which it was accorded both vulnerability and militancy, that are central to my discussion of the production of ethnicity in media representations of the women's demonstrations. For the writing of the press was not only different, with Serbian and Croatian papers offering very different pictures of the events to their readers; it was also curiously similar, with both the Serbian and the Croatian press using the same representational strategies to define the maternal body and link it to ethnicity. These differences and similarities are symptomatic of the representational capacities of the female body in all its ambiguities, of all the threats and promises it held for the nation, and of the discursive—and ultimately, mortal—practices through which it would be claimed and appropriated, as maternal body.

In 1987 Kosovo—a region that (following Slobodan Milošević's rise to power) marked the start of this region's disintegration and will probably also mark its end[2]—was one of the main foci of the "media war." And the maternal body was one of its main sites. As the least developed region economically, Kosovo had the highest illiteracy rate (of which women comprised the majority), the highest unemployment rate (with more women not working than men), and the largest number of dependents (with more women dependent than men).[3] Large amounts of economic aid were regularly distributed to Kosovo from the federal budget as well as that of other republics (Zolić 1986, 258). But Kosovo remained underdeveloped, its economic underdevelopment being regularly linked in political discourse to cultural factors (Mertus 1999, Vickers 1998). Not surprisingly, in the gendered narratives of socialist modernity, the Albanian women of Kosovo, uneducated, unemployed, and with numerous offspring, became a metaphor for backwardness throughout socialist Yugoslavia and especially in Serbia.[4] Regularly described as supporting patriarchy and tradition themselves, they were at the same time represented as victims of the patriarchy and tradition of their men. Mothering was essential in these representations. Throughout the 1980s the images of "overreproductive" Albanian women were pitted against images of "underreproductive" Serb women. Then in mid-1980 images of "sexually aggressive" Albanian men started to appear in the Serbian press, following discussion of the rapid ethnic homogenization of Kosovo.[5] Both a divisive political issue and a recurrent theme in the media, the ethnic homogenization of Kosovo was explained as the result of the relatively high fertility rates of the Albanian population[6] and the rapid emigration of non-Albanians, primarily Serbs and Montenegrins. Both processes were widely believed in Serbia to be a result of a conscious strategy by the Albanian political and religious leadership to make Kosovo "ethnically pure." Ironically, this strategy, renamed "ethnic cleansing," was the one that would be used by Serbian forces later on, in Croatia and Bosnia. The emigrations of non-Albanians from Kosovo were commonly referred to as "forced expulsions," the result of systematic intimidation that ranged from arson and the destruction of crops and livestock to attacks on people, and finally to the rape of Serb and Montenegrin women.[7] It is through these discussions of population growth and sexual violence that the maternal and victimized body came together in the media war in the mid-1980s. But what fixed their place of significance in the production of ethnicity was an alleged statement by a politician, uttered at a dining table, as a joke.

The Statement

On October 9, 1987, Yugoslav dailies reported that Fadil Hoxha, one of the highest ranking Albanian politicians from Kosovo, a member of the Socialist Federal Republic's collective presidency (established after Tito's death),[8] had made some "unacceptable" and "offensive" statements regarding the political situation in Kosovo and Serbia. According to the media reports, the statement had been made a year earlier, during one of the semiofficial lunches of the reserve military commanders of Kosovo, Serbia, and Macedonia, known as "gatherings of brotherhood and unity," and traditionally held in Kosovo. As the highest ranking political-military guest at the dinner, Fadil Hoxha had been asked to address the other guests at the table in an informal manner. His address was reportedly about critical political issues: conflicts between the political leaders of Kosovo and Serbia, the security of Albanians in Serbia and of Serbs and Montenegrins in Kosovo, the "forceful expulsion" of non-Albanians from Kosovo, the separatism and irredentism of Albanians in Kosovo, Serbian nationalism, changes in the 1974 constitution, demographic differences and population policies in Kosovo and Serbia, and the rapes of Serb and Montenegrin women from Kosovo by Albanian men. The element of his address that prompted the most reactions was about the rapes. He reportedly stated that the problem of rapes of Serb women by Albanian men in Kosovo would be solved if more non-Albanian women worked as prostitutes in Kosovo's taverns.

After Hoxha's address was reported by the media, a flood of reports followed about letters of protest and meetings of numerous institutions and organizations who condemned his words. Within days the protest spilled from meeting rooms into the streets: Serbs and Montenegrins began demonstrating publicly in cities and villages across Kosovo. In some towns in Serbia demonstrations were also held by people who had migrated from Kosovo during the previous decade.

A week later, Hoxha issued a press release. He confirmed that he did talk about all these issues, but not in the manner that was reported. He defended himself by explaining that the alleged "solution" for the rapes was actually offered jokingly. An even stronger outrage seems to have followed his press release, in the Serbian media and public, where the "statement of Fadil Hoxha"—meaning the alleged "solution" for the rapes—was consistently denounced. And "the statement" became "the Statement."

Two weeks after the first leak of the lunch speech (on October 22, 1987) the presidency of the Central Committee of the League of Communists of the Socialist Federal Republic of Yugoslavia suggested that he could no longer remain a member of the League of Communists nor could he continue to hold his high political functions. Hoxha was dismissed from all his functions, and the media soon lost interest in the entire event. But during those two weeks of October–November 1987, the events surrounding the Statement were often top news, with main daily and weekly newspapers from both Serbia and Croatia reporting on the happenings.

Women's mass street protests against the Statement were one of these happenings. They are significant for two reasons. First, they were probably the first massive, political actions in socialist Yugoslavia in which women participated in noticeable numbers. There are no independent sources by which one could corroborate the true extent of women's engagement, but their presence was obviously substantial enough for the highest political bodies to address it. The presidency of the League of Communists committee explicitly stated in its report that the anger of the public, and of "women specifically," was justified, adding that the incident was being misused by Serb nationalists for their own political ends. No feminist action—and there were some, in the late 1970s and 1980s—ever received such high support. Second, these demonstrations marked the first appearance of maternal politics in the region. Demonstrating women proclaimed their motherhood for everybody to know and hear.[9] The second time maternity became politicized—albeit in a different way—would be in 1991, with the beginning of the violent disintegration of the country. Each time, the maternal body would be the site of the media war. Each time, notions of femininity and masculinity intersected with norms of sexuality in order to produce ethnicity. I will address the issues raised by the 1991 events in chapter 2, and the troubles that maternal politics poses to feminism in chapter 3; here, I will examine the media representations of the Statement and the women's demonstrations, in search of the role of the maternal body in the media war. For this was not just any maternal body—it was a body with qualification. While women openly defined themselves as mothers, the Serbian press focused on two points of this motherhood, which were written on the women's banners: "We are mothers of the sons of Serbia" and "We are mothers, not whores."

It is precisely these two qualifications of the maternal body—its clear ethnic connotation and its clear sexual-moral distinction—that became significant for the production of "the Serbs" and "the Albanians" in the media war in the Serbian press. They were not only central but also directly linked to victimhood. In the Croatian press, on the other hand, the maternal claims and the maternal body were largely ignored. In their place came militant women.

The Croatian Press

The Croatian daily *Vjesnik* published a handful of articles, all consistent in both form and style during the entire time of reporting: most were five to six inches long, factual, dry, and to the point, and they always appeared on page 3 of the paper. Almost all the articles were about sessions of different political organizations that addressed the Statement or about the demonstrations, though only one was from the site of a demonstration. Most of the articles consisted of quotations from the discussions and conclusions of these organizations, usually without editorial interventions or comments, and came accompanied by a handful of photographs, most of which were also taken at the political sessions. These reports rarely described the women as demonstrators or mentioned the slogans written on their banners.

On October 9, 1987, *Vjesnik*'s first report on the events (reprinted the next day) quoted the alleged words of Fadil Hoxha, without comment: "There are individual cases of rape in Kosovo. I think that in the private taverns in Kosovo it should be allowed that women from other regions of Yugoslavia are brought in, so that the individuals who rape women of other nationalities can live out their frustrations that way. Albanian women will not do that, but Serb and other women would, so why not allow them?" (3). Hoxha's press release was quoted by *Vjesnik* a week later in a similar manner, in a short column, again without comment:

> In my wish to note that the reasons of these cases [of rape] are not only nationalist, but also pathological, I said half-jokingly that some of the causes may have been due to sexual frustration. Following upon that idea I said that we should perhaps be more tolerant toward some liberal behavior of some waitresses in private taverns. At that point I explicitly said that these are the waitresses who, in the majority of cases, are not from the territories where they work, meaning that they come from other municipalities. I did not talk about their nationality or their territorial background. I do think, however, that I have con-

> nected this anecdote in a rather crude manner with the problem of rapes, although my intentions were quite the opposite. . . . I did not think that I would be misunderstood. . . . I wish to stress that I do understand the justified and prompt reaction of the public, women in particular. (October 18, 1987, 3)

Vjesnik's single report from the demonstration did mention both the women and their demands. It noted, "The same demands that were put forward in previous gatherings and demonstrations of Serbian and Montenegrin women were repeated here—that stopping Albanian separatism and its precursors is long overdue and that 'women should judge Fadil Hoxha'; open calls were made for fighting and weapons, and insults were voiced. From such statements, however, some women distanced themselves" (October 19, 1987, 3).

An October 22 article about the report from the League of Communists committee (the longest of all the articles covering the incident, also appearing on the page 3 but announced in large bold letters at the front page) marked the end of *Vjesnik*'s reporting about the Statement and the demonstrations that followed it, although the name and the fate of Fadil Hoxha would still be mentioned there from time to time.

THE ABSENT ONES: THE MOTHER AND THE WHORE

Where is the maternal body in the articles in the Croatian daily? The dry, factual, almost uninterested style used in the short reports all but hides it. The style suggests that the articles simply gave information. But interestingly, this information is mostly about the sessions of various political bodies that discussed the events and not about the events themselves. The numbers of the demonstrators are mentioned (three hundred on October 18, five hundred on October 19), but there is only one report that mentions the slogans, banners, or actions of the women during the protests. Furthermore, the events surrounding the Statement, the demonstrations of the women and the sessions of the various political organizations, are not related directly to any other issues, such as other political or economic problems in Kosovo or Serbia. The main concern of the political bodies, most often mentioned in the reports, was the danger of public disorder, specifically in relation to "gatherings on a national basis" and to Serbian nationalists' misusing the protests of women. There are a lot of quotation marks in the texts, around statements from the meetings. The issue of rapes of Serbian and Montenegrin women by Albanian men is mentioned once, in connection to the Statement, and that is within quotations, too.

So, apparently, no story developed in *Vjesnik* about the Statement. Presented were the facts: briefly and to the point. At first glance, the reports seem to be just what good journalism should be: factual and neutral. A closer reading, however, shows that this handful of short, dry reports give the impression that the event was not all that significant and thus did not merit development as a story. Nevertheless, many of the highest political institutions held sessions debating the events, and these sessions were reported in *Vjesnik*. Thus the message about the story's insignificance is ambiguous, for it is difficult to render insignificant an event that at the same time causes political activity at such a high level. The resolution of that ambiguity lies in the representational strategy of *Vjesnik*—in which the Statement and the subsequent demonstrations were confined to and existed mainly within the meeting rooms of the political organizations that discussed them. An interesting shift of space occurs with this strategy: Fadil Hoxha's words were spoken in a political meeting room, taken to the streets by demonstrators, and brought back into the political meeting rooms. In the process, the women demonstrating in the streets were all but erased from the picture.

The significance of space in this representation is manifold. The fear of public protests, of streets as a political arena, has been a part and parcel of socialism. People were welcome onto the streets only to cheer their leaders, not to criticize them. The legalization of the workers' right to strike in many socialist states was a problem, in part because of the socialist fear of people's expressing their political opinions through street protests. This does not mean that there were no public protests, but rather that they were often downplayed or discredited. The situation with regard to the Statement is even more complicated, because the demonstrations were largely characterized as being on a "national basis." Almost every report on political meetings quoted in *Vjesnik* contained these words, adding expressions of fear that "gatherings on a national basis" were potentially dangerous in a situation when national divisions were already pronounced. For a society that praised itself for resolving the "national question" and living with the ideology of "brotherhood and unity," what could be more unsettling?

What seems to have been even more unsettling was the fact that there were neither workers nor proverbial "people," let alone "brothers," on the streets, but women. If streets were not a space for the political activity of the workers and the people, they were even less a space for the political activity of women. And if they were not a space for women, they were certainly not for mothers. The maternal space and place is indoors, at home.

The space for political activism for women, as for everybody else, was also indoors: this time, in the meeting rooms of political bodies. The socialist project of women's emancipation opened that space for them. But the ambiguities of women's presence in politics, especially in public, remained, despite slogans about women's equal participation in all spheres of social life.[10] By placing the protests back into the meeting rooms, *Vjesnik* addressed the socialist fears of people on the streets. By largely ignoring the presence of women among these demonstrators, it implied that politics and the streets are neither a place nor a space for women. But when *Vjesnik* did acknowledge that there were women on the streets, yet another level of representation appeared.

In the reports in *Vjesnik* neither the word "mother" nor the slogans "We are mothers of the sons of Serbia" and "We are mothers, not whores" are ever mentioned—not even in the report from the site of the protest. Instead, the phrase used consistently is "Serb and Montenegrin women." The report states that "Serb and Montenegrin women" called "repeatedly" for "Albanian separatists to be stopped," if needed with "fight and arms"; they used "insults" (though the reader was not told which ones) and insisted that "they judge Fadil Hoxha." *Vjesnik*'s depiction then is of militant, arms-seeking, and insult-throwing women. The note that "some women distanced themselves" from the militant demands adds a bit of relativity to the representation, but does not alter it substantially.

Besides representing the women as militant, *Vjesnik* reports that they were manipulated by Serb nationalists. It is worth noting that neither the women nor their demonstrations are called nationalistic—only "manipulated by nationalists." Thus here the women appear as political dupes, without agency of their own, as simply succumbing to Serbian nationalism. And at the same time, when their agency is recognized, it is characterized as a militant one.

This ambiguous relationship between political agency and militancy would continue in Croatian media representations of maternal protests and would mark the ambiguity that the maternal body brought into the production of ethnicity. For here, clearly, the absence of the word "mother" was a representational strategy that separated the discursively maternal body from militancy. This move, however, simultaneously separates the maternal body from the body of the woman, leaving the latter linked to a (problematic and largely denied) political action and to ethnicity. It is the very absence of the maternal body from the representations in *Vjesnik* that marks its relevance for the production of ethnicity, for here the maternal body is imagined as being essentially different from the bodies of the demonstrating women. Thus the reference to "Serb and Montenegrin women" and the absence of the word "mother" mean that the streets are not the space where the Mother can be found. Nor is it Serbhood or Montenegrinhood. It is the absence of the word "mother" that produces the ethnicity of the Serb and Montenegrin women.

The absence of the word "whore" in *Vjesnik* further sustains this interpretation. One could argue that, because it was a quality paper, the editors in *Vjesnik* would not use the word deliberately. But one could look at it differently. Not incidentally, in the Serbo-Croat language a brothel is called a "public house" (*javna kuća*).[11] Furthermore, the word for "prostitute" associates her with streets: *uličarka* means "woman of the streets" (from *ulica*—street). Thus, by either ignoring the women on the streets or bringing them inside, into the meeting rooms, *Vjesnik* forecloses the discursive space within which the word "whore" could be mentioned, and at the same time, it implicitly defines the streets as the place of the Whore.

THE PRESENT ONE: THE WOMAN

In contrast to the dry and factual journalist style employed in *Vjesnik*, the Croatian weekly *Danas* developed a considerable story about the events. A cluster of articles and photographs spread over six pages and published on October 27, 1987, illustrates its approach to the story. Two well-known commentators on the social and political affairs of socialist Yugoslavia contributed to the feature: the feminist Slavenka Drakulić[12] and the journalist Aleksandar Tijanić. Unlike the daily, the weekly analyzed the situation in Kosovo. Unlike the daily, where the only mentioned nationalism was Serbian, the weekly dedicated much of its space to Albanian separatism, the plight of the non-Albanian population in Kosovo, and the overall political and economic situation in the southern Serbian province. However, the representational strategies of the daily and the weekly were very similar, with *Danas* making it much more explicit by creating the figure of the Woman. Womanhood and motherhood appeared as two distinct moral places, and the female protagonists of the demonstrations were dissociated ethnically from "mothers."

In this cluster of pieces published in *Danas*, only the article by then already famous Yugoslav and Croatian feminist journalist Slavenka Drakulić had women's protests as a central issue against which the rest of the analysis developed. The other articles focus much more on Kosovo as a source of potential problems for Serbia and Yugoslavia, and on Fadil Hoxha as a symbol of the certain type of politics in Yugoslavia—characterized by voluntarism among those with political power and opportunism among the politicians. The article by the other noted journalist, Tijanić, mentions the Statement in support of this argument, while women and their protests are not mentioned at all (ibid., 10–12). He states the many grave reasons for which Fadil Hoxha should have been removed from politics long ago, but remained because his departure would have undermined the position of other politicians in Serbia and Yugoslavia. Tijanić lists some of the phrases used at the demonstrations ("calls for the 'military rule'" and the "close-to-lynching shouts 'Hoxha hang yourself, otherwise we will hang you'" [12]), but he does not mention explicitly either the women or the demonstrations, speaking instead of "Serbian public opinion" (11).

An editorial with the title "Tragic Reality" appears in the same *Danas* feature, in a box taking up a quarter of the page. The text consists of statements by the Slovenian member of the Communist Committee presidency, taken from one of the political sessions, and is accompanied by his photo. Within the piece, the women's demonstrations are mentioned by name but also assessed as a problematic way to seek a political solution to the problem:

> The migration of Serbs and Montenegrins [from Kosovo] is a painful issue. . . . It is an anachronism in this century to call for ethnic cleansing [of non-Albanians from Kosovo], but so is the call for the arms [by the demonstrators]. . . . The reasons that Serb and Montenegrin women and their children are going to the streets cannot but touch every honest citizen of this country, but it needs to be seen where these methods of gathering lead us, and what is at the end of all this. It is absolutely true that Albanian nationalists and separatists have employed dangerous provocations and serious excesses to hamper political stabilization. Serb nationalism is also obviously in expansion. . . . Today, we have an old situation in the public arena and in the media: divisive views and assessments of the situation in Kosovo, and differences between the Albanian- and Serbian-language media in Ko-

> sovo and between the media in Belgrade [i.e., Serbia] and the media of other republics, both in the space they dedicate to Kosovo and in the content of their coverage. (Ibid., 9)

This broader context of political problems is the background against which the women and their protests are presented as manipulated and militant in other articles in the same issue, in particular one titled "Punishment Arrives Too Late to Kosovo"[13] (ibid., 7–10), the lead article in the feature. In this piece, the "political happenings [surrounding] Serb and Montenegrin women" (7) are discussed explicitly in the first half of the text. The second half is about the complexities of the situation in Kosovo, Serbia, and Yugoslavia. Analyzing the situation, the authors (two journalists) state that calls for political accountability among those responsible for creating the mistrust between Albanians and Serbs in Kosovo are late in coming, for the gap between the two groups already threatens to turn into an abyss (8).

Writing about the demonstrations, the authors quote two political sessions in which the manipulation of the protests is mentioned explicitly. The demonstrations are depicted in a very graphic way, using the rhetoric of filmmaking: the demonstrations were "directed," and looked "as if in a set" (7); "the hidden dark forces" sitting in "nearby taverns" are mentioned as "awaiting for their couriers" to come from the "overheated halls" and inform them about the performance of their puppets; the two terms that are used to characterize the women as puppets, *bukače* and *narikče* (8), are particularly telling.

Bukače and *narikače*, are taken from political language and traditional culture respectively and are in the feminine grammatical form; together, they classify the women as puppets of the political process. A bukača is someone who makes noise (from the noun *buka*, noise), meaning anything from instigating, provoking, and making a fuss to rocking the boat and whistle blowing. The word was often used in socialist parlance, frequently to insult and belittle political opponents, and discredit criticism of the official politics. In that context the noun was usually used in its masculine gender form—for men were supposed to be political subjects—while here it is rendered feminine.[14] A narikača is a woman whose function it is to lament at funeral rituals in Serbia (from the verb *naricati*, to lament). The narikača follows the deceased, weeping on behalf of the family. In the ritual, through her laments, she tells the glorious story of the deceased and expresses the grave loss felt by the family. The ritual, which used to be both highly poetic and performative, is still performed here and there, in a hugely reduced form, but the term—which occurs only in the feminine gender, for only women perform the ritual—is preserved, and most often used in a pejorative way.

Besides this depiction of the demonstrations and the participants, a couple of the other phrases shouted by the protesting women ("Women should judge him," "Shoot the rapists") are reported in the article. It is also noted that the Yugoslav national anthem was sung. The article also gives the slogans on the banners carried by women: "We want freedom," "Down with Fadil Hoxha," "We demand peace for our children," "We are not whores but mothers, women, sisters." This particular article in *Danas* is the only one in the Croatian papers to mention the slogan with word "whores" (7). The text is also accompanied by a photo in which the same words could be seen on a banner carried by the women. Further, the calls for military rule are reported, as they were shouted by demonstrating women in front of one of the military barracks: "We ask for freedom," "Long live the Yugoslav National Army," "Our sons will protect us," "Freedom or military rule," "Give us the weapons," "Down with the political leaders," "We give our lives but we do not give Kosovo," "Better death than slavery" (8). Besides invoking the metaphors *bukače* and *narikače*, noted above, women protestors are also described explicitly, and graphically: "Loudly and with bile, [women] expressed their fury (often with words not common for the fairer sex), demanding the head of Fadil Hoxha" (7). The aggressiveness of these images of the "fairer sex" is countered by one image of "trembling voices and glittering tears in an overcrowded hall filled with emotions" (8). This sole image of tearful women—the lamenting ones (narikače)—is, however, lost in the overall representation of the militant and aggressive—those loudly instigating violence (bukače).

In *Danas*, women are not only militant, aggressive, or manipulated; they are themselves manipulators. The authors note that Serb and Montenegrin schoolchildren were forbidden by "their parents" to attend school and were taken to the streets to carry banners and shout slogans, "thrown into the first rows, and used for political purposes" (8). The significance of the gender-neutral word "parents" is that it again, dissociates the Mother from the Woman, as the women who manipulate their children for political ends are denied the right to be called mothers.

Like *Vjesnik*, *Danas* is also consistent in writing about "Serb and Montenegrin women" (and sometimes, "parents"), and never associates words

"Serb and Montenegrin" with word "mothers." Interestingly, *Danas*, unlike *Vjesnik*, gives some justification to the cause of the demonstrating women, both implicitly, through the analysis of the overall political situation in Yugoslavia, Serbia, and Kosovo, as well as explicitly, in the statement of the Slovenian politician quoted above (9). However, its representational and linguistic strategies still separate this politically problematic, aggressive, and manipulative womanhood from motherhood, and link womanhood to ethnicity. Thus, *Danas*, like *Vjesnik*, renders absent the maternal body while producing Serbian and Montenegrin womanhood.

These multiple separations of motherhood and womanhood, and their diverse positioning vis-à-vis political action and militancy, as well as vis-à-vis ethnicity, that are used in the reports on Hoxha's statement would remain representational strategies of the Croatian press in the years to come. The same strategies would be used by the Serbian press. When I first began to analyze the Croatian and Serbian press, I was puzzled with this representational strategy. But it became apparent that this particular juxtaposition and separation had a major function in the production of ethnicity. Precisely because the femininities and sexualities of these two symbolic female bodies were imagined as opposites, they would become instrumental in production of the Self and the Other ethnically, defining invariably the Self through the maternal body, and the Other through the body of the woman.

The Serbian Press

It is not difficult to imagine that the Serbian press would have very different representations of the Statement and the events surrounding it. While it too would separate the Mother from the Woman, it would claim motherhood in the production of Serbhood, rendering it not only vulnerable and victimized, but ultimately the very symbol of the plight of the nation. Unlike the Croatian press, the Serbian press would give its readers not only a story about the Statement but also an epic narrative of national suffering, within which the maternal body—with all its distinctions—would be absolutely central.

On October 25, 1987, two weeks after the news of Hoxha's statement first appeared in the press, the Serbian weekly *NIN* published a three-page cluster of articles about it, with several accompanying photos (12–14). The same issue also published one separate column on the topic, with an illustration (4). The texts in the cluster are relatively short, compared to those in the Croatian weekly *Danas*. The longest occupies about three columns. The others are within it, in three boxes. The first box is a reprint of the conclusions of Communist Committee presidency, with a photo of three smiling Albanian politicians from Kosovo, Fadil Hoxha being one of them. Another box was written by a well-known female journalist and political analyst, Slobodanka Ast. Her piece is both analytical and critical with regard to the events, and in its form and content it is closer to the critical-analytical articles in *Danas* than to the other three pieces in *NIN*. It is worth noting this cross-republic similarity, as it attests that the media war as a process went through different stages, and that in the early days, especially before the actual violence began in 1991, it was still possible to find texts with quite different political perspectives side by side within one newspaper, or to find similar political perspectives in the press across the region.[15]

Under the title "Power and Powerlessness of Politics," Ast writes about the political situation in Kosovo, Serbia, and Yugoslavia, echoing themes addressed in *Danas*. She warns that the "spontaneous taking of things in one's own hands" leads to "quasi-democracy," and that "inflamed words, demagogic rhetoric, unbalanced statement, and cynical 'anecdotes' produce—in the stormy space of Kosovo—only hysteria that can lead to the worst" (*NIN*, October 25, 1987, 13). Ast further asserts that it is not wise to do politics "in the name of the people" when both support of, and consensus among "the people" is lacking. She affirms that the demonstrations were spurred by Fadil Hoxha's statement, but says that shouts such as "We want freedom or military rule," "Hang Hoxha," "To Belgrade," "Take up arms," and "Hoxha, kill yourself, otherwise we will kill you," cannot be excused. She never explicitly mentions women among the demonstrators, nor does she mention the slogans about motherhood, "We are mothers not whores" or "We are mothers of the sons of Serbia." That absence makes for another similarity between her text and the texts in *Danas*.

The last box, a short quotation from a speech by a male politician who addressed one of the gatherings of women, introduces a style of writing quite different from Ast's. It is a style that would be used in the Serbian daily *Politika* in abundance: dialogical, passionate, and filled with pathos: "While we discuss, the enemy works on the confrontation of nations and minorities. ('We will not allow it'—the masses answer.) The League of Communists does not support dark thoughts and the assaults on dignity. But we cannot accuse all the Albanians. It would be a pity to solve things this way, because uninational gatherings are not good. We should remain dignified and should not call for the dark forces"[16] (ibid., 12).

The enemies and dark forces, the assaults and dignity mentioned here are given a very prominent place in the Serbian coverage of the Statement that I have examined. And so are the women demonstrators and their claims. Reading the Serbian press one could easily gain the impression that only women were demonstrating, and that all they cared about was to make it clear that they were not whores, but mothers—mothers of the sons of Serbia, at that.

MOTHERHOOD, MORALITY, AND VICTIMIZATION

The main article with which *NIN* started its reporting, and within which all the boxes were placed, sets the atmosphere for the above quotation. The headline asks, "Why Do Women Protest?" and the text immediately offers an answer, variously phrased: because Fadil Hoxha had "offended Serb and Montenegrin women in an, until now, never recorded manner" (12); because Fadil Hoxha's statement was a "heavy and unprecedented attack on the morals and dignity of a Serb and Montenegrin woman" (12); and because the statement was an "official invitation to Albanian chauvinists and separatists to freely assault women of Serb and Montenegrin nationality" (14). The "unseen bitterness" (12) of Serb and Montenegrin women, the "bitter protests of the hurt women" (13), the "glass of bile that spilled over for the bitter women" (13), and their "anger" are all mentioned in describing women's feelings about the statement. According to the text, these feelings were not only about Hoxha's words, which in themselves were "assaults on dignity of Serb and Montenegrin women" (13), but even more so about the "rapes and assaults on Serb and Montenegrin women [that] continued" (13) in Kosovo. One of the participants in the demonstrations is quoted saying, "Nobody will come back to Kosovo as long as rapes and assaults on Serbs and Montenegrins continue. I call upon all the women of Serbia and Yugoslavia to rise and wash away the stain of insult that Fadil Hoxha inflicted upon us" (13–14).

Thus, the text makes a clear and explicit connection between Hoxha's statement, the rapes, and the overall political situation in Kosovo, making the connection also apparent in the quotations of demands of protestors: "At all costs we must stop the blind assaults of Albanian chauvinists on women and girls, in which the perpetrators get 50 to 60 days of prison as the only punishment" (13) and "It was requested that Albanian separatist molesters who attack the honor [the 'face'] and the life of Serb and Montenegrin women be stopped" (14).

The names of the towns and cities in which the demonstrations were held were listed, as well as the number of demonstrators (and where the Croatian press earlier said there were hundreds of demonstrators, the Serbian press claims there were thousands). The minutiae of the protests were described: the routes of the protesters through the city, the places where they stopped to sing the national anthem or to shout slogans. The many different slogans written on the banners were also noted: "Kosovo-Serbia," "We give our lives but we do not give Kosovo," "Down with Fadil, the traitor," "Women should judge him" (13); "We are not whores but mothers of the sons of Serbia," "We ask for freedom," "Peace for our children" (14).

At the point where the journalist noted that in the capital city of Kosovo women stopped in front of a military barrack, there is an editorial interpolation into the text. The journalist had omitted to quote the particular words shouted there, and the editor of the text has added a half sentence in brackets, as follows: "(at that spot women shouted "We want freedom or military rule"—editorial remark)" (13).[17] The text of "Why Do Women Protest?" shows what would become one of the main representational strategies in the Serbian press on this occasion, and on many others. Women in this article appear neither manipulated nor aggressive. Rather—as all the quotations above repeatedly emphasize—women were gravely insulted and thus justifiably outraged. Their anger and bitterness are not represented as aggressive or militant but rather as understandable, caused by an insult to their "honor," "dignity," and "face." In short, they are represented as victims. That approach is also adopted by the Serbian daily *Politika*.

Unlike the Croatian papers that I examined, and a few texts in the Serbian weekly *NIN*, the Serbian daily *Politika* quotes at length from the interviews with women demonstrators and had its journalists at almost every spot where the protests were going on. There are no interviews with men, nor is the reader told whether there ever were any male demonstrators. Women are represented as the main, if not the only, protagonists of the demonstrations, as much as the main victims. The slogans from the banners carried at the demonstrations as well as women's demands and statements are quoted extensively, and photos accompany many texts. Hoxha's statement is itself quoted many times in different versions.[18]

Like the Croatian daily *Vjesnik*, the Serbian daily *Politika* also wrote about the sessions of various political bodies and their conclusions. Unlike *Vjesnik*, however, it reported many individual discussions and reactions at length, particularly these of women. In many of the reports the concern for women stands central, and mention is made of the need for protection of the "moral and physical integrity of women, regardless of their nationality and geographical area where they live and work" (October 17, 7). The reports also express anger and demand protection of the women of Kosovo, whose security was "endangered after Fadil Hoxha [uttered] the statement" (October 14, 10).

The emphasis on women in jeopardy and in need of protection appears several times; one article, for instance, notes the banner slogan "Fathers and brothers, protect our honor" (October 19, 7). Another banner, however, is reported as carrying the words "We will defend our honor in blood" (ibid.), indicating that not all women felt that helpless, and that, if protection was needed, they might be ready to protect themselves.

It is worth noting that *Politika* never recorded any of the calls for arms mentioned in the Serbian weekly *NIN* and in the Croatian daily *Vjesnik* and weekly *Danas*. But it repeatedly recorded that women gathered in front of the monuments of the victims of fascism, or other places associated with World War II, singing the national anthem or partisan songs. It also reported the banner with the words "Better death than slavery"—a famous slogan from the early days of antifascist struggle. In doing so *Politika* connected the demonstrating mothers with the antifascist movement and the ideas of brotherhood, unity, and Yugoslavism, while at the same time connecting Albanians—and Albanian men in particular—with fascism; a strategy that the Serbian press would use in the future too.

Unlike *Vjesnik*, *Politika* never saw aggression, chaos, or political danger in the demonstrations. To the contrary, the characterization repeated many times in headlines, subheads, and articles alike was that the protests were peaceful, dignified, and without excess: "About 4,000 women of Serb and Montenegrin nationality started peaceful demonstrations" (October 17, 7); "gatherings and protest occurred without excesses" (October 18, 7); "Members of the League of Communists were given the task to take care that the protest proceeded with dignity and without provocations"; "We should remain dignified and not call for the dark forces"; "The League of Communists does not support any dark thoughts and attacks on dignity"; "protest with dignity and without provocations" (all October 19, 7).

The insistence on dignity, peacefulness, and order is a significant element of representation in the Serbian daily *Politika*. For these attributes are not only descriptions of the demonstrations, but also of the *demonstrators*, and are the building blocks of a link between Serbhood and a very specific morality. This is the morality of the victim whose dignity and honor are insulted by the words of one particular Albanian man, as much as by the violent deeds of many Albanian men. The victim is a woman who is placed primarily within a family context by quotations from speeches and in the banners and slogans that define her as a mother. Ethnic references are often omitted in *Politika*, and the words "people" and "women" often appear unspecified ethnically; Yugoslavia is recalled, indicating that it is not only Serbs and Montenegrins who are offended and threatened, but simply everybody who adheres to moral principles based on honor and dignity. In this representation the *potential* victim is there to indicate the gravity of the offense against the *actual* victim—Serb and Montenegrin woman/mother/wife: Hoxha's statement is "disgusting and offensive to all the people and the Yugoslavs"; it "strikes the honor and the dignity of women and of the family"; "There was a lot of bitterness and justified revolt, all caused by the statement, which attacks the honor and dignity of women and the family" (all October 18, 7); "I joined the revolution at the age of 14. . . . [Hoxha] spits in my face with his statement, which he says was told as a joke. One cannot joke about that"; "Women were spat at in their faces"; "Whether he said something like this about an Albanian woman or a woman of any other nationality, I would grab his throat the same"; a report adds, "[The] sharp protests of women of Serb and Montenegrin nationality, who are increasingly joined by their husbands and children, continue" (all October 19, 7).

In these representations Serb and Montenegrin women stand dignified in defense of their own and their families' honor. Beyond that, they stand in defense of the honor of all Serbs and Montenegrins in Kosovo, and all other potential victims. But clearly, the only ones insulted and victimized according to *Politika* are Serb and Montenegrin mothers, wives, and daughters. They are the only real victims.

This story about dignity and victimization in the Serbian daily (and to an extent, also in the weekly *NIN*) defines very clearly the protagonists: the aggressor (individually, as Hoxha, and collectively, as all Albanian men from Kosovo), the weapon (rape, assault, insults), and the victim (first and foremost Serb and Montenegrin women, and then all the Serbs and Montenegrins from Kosovo). It defines also the "weapons of the weak": "dignity," "honor," and "face." Paradoxically, in this representation, the victimization is what brings the moral victory. Serb and Montenegrin women are rendered victims precisely because of their ultimate and superior morality. Nothing defines this victimized but superior morality of the Serb and Montenegrin woman better than the juxtaposition of two words: "mother" and "whore." And no other distinction in the Serbian press is as central to producing ethnicity as the distinction between the maternal body and the body of the whore.

The Whore against the Mother of all Serbs

"We are not whores but mothers and sisters of the sons of Serbia and Yugoslavia" (*Politika*, October 17, 7); "We are not whores, we are mothers" (ibid.); "We are not whores" (October 18, 7); "Mothers are not whores" (in a photo, ibid.); "Our mothers did not give birth to us to be whores" (October 19, 7); "Our mothers are not whores" (in a photo, ibid.).

The persistent repetition of these slogans characterizes most of *Politika*'s articles about Hoxha's statement. The power of the word "whore" overwhelms all the "cool-headed" political arguments, economic explanations, and critical analyses. Clearly, the word "whore" was chosen because of its moral weight. It is a moral concept. As a concept, it was grabbed and thrown back into the face of the initial offender, Fadil Hoxha, and into the face of all Albanian separatists, and all the politicians in Serbia and Yugoslavia who had ignored the plight of Serbs and Montenegrins in Kosovo. It was used to pass a moral judgment on the whole world. And the judge was represented by another moral concept—the Mother. The gap between the two—the Whore and the Mother—is an abyss. It is the difference between the two worlds and their moral orders. It is the difference that produces ethnicity.

The most stunning definition of the Whore as a moral concept was actually offered by the Serbian weekly *NIN*. Separated from the cluster of other articles, just after the introductory pages and before the letters to the editor, a commentary appeared in a regular column, "The Word of the Week." The column was written by a renowned linguist and theater director, Jovan Ćirilov. Every week he would give a short semantic analysis of a word that had become (in)famous in the cultural and political life of that week, discussing the roots and the meanings of the word from the linguistic point of view, but also briefly commenting on the event or cultural and political context in which the word had became so important. On October 25, 1987, the word, and the title of the contribution, was "Whore."

Ćirilov begins his commentary noting that one of the, until recently, most influential politicians in Yugoslavia had "discovered his psychotherapeutic potentials." In the "typically phallocratic manner of a *Homo balkanicus* [he] showed concern for the sexual health of the male population," "concluded that sexual frustration is the cause of rape," and proposed a "solution." "The unexpected 'Freudian' thus insulted at least half of the population of our country, suggesting that all the women of Yugoslavia are potential prostitutes" (4).

After noting that once upon a time the word "whore" used to be uttered with "half a voice," Ćirilov continues with two paragraphs of history of the word and the profession—from the Chinese dynasties to ancient Greece and Christ and Magdalene. The concluding paragraph refers back to the political situation in Kosovo: "If Fadil Hoxha were Charles Bodlieur, maybe he could allow himself to say, with the poetic imagination of decadence, that 'love has an affinity to prostitution.' But here, at this moment, in the boiling climate of conflict, in the world of patriarchal traditions, just after a good lunch, jokingly, it is most terrifying to utter whatever variant of the words spoken on the last year's 'gathering of brotherhood and unity'" (ibid.).

The significance of Ćirilov's commentary is that it raises the voice that utters the word "whore." By being in the title and having the whole text organized around it, the word is brought into the daylight. More significant, in this text, the whole event around the Statement is contextualized by that single word. In *Politika* the event was already contextualized within a moral order. Words such as "dignity," "honor," and "face" were there as a moral background against which the word "whore" appeared. Ćirilov's column follows the same pattern, but with an illustration that was published with it, the contextualization of the morality comes in a somewhat ambiguous way—the Whore is linked not to ethnicity but to universal femininity.

For the representational strategy that juxtaposes the Whore and the Mother to work, both have to appear as generic, universal symbols. Only as a symbol of ultimate immorality of the untamed and undomesticated female body with nonprocreative, commercialized sexuality, can the Whore sustain its opposite—the ultimate morality of the maternal body and its procreative, marital sexuality. Only after the ultimate morality of the maternal body is defined beyond ambiguity, can she be appropriated ethnically. So there she is, the Whore, with closed eyes and gentle, if seductive smile, and unmistakable insignia on her breasts.

According to Hoxha's Statement, this body was an ethnic body: the body of the Serb and Montenegrin woman. But what the illustration offers is something else: the Whore who gives her body for money, the ethnically unspecific, but utterly feminine, eternal Whore. The strange shyness in the eyes that avoid the gaze may well be arrogance, a complete disregard for the moral judgment of the viewer. What this illustration tells is that the Whore does not really resent what she is. There is no forced prostitution here, no sad story of poverty or abduction. The "woman of the streets" is depicted in this illustration, the woman defined entirely and only by her specific sexuality: the body of the Whore is not *for* sex, it *is* sex itself, sex for money, public and available. No, no, the women shout from the pages of *Politika*, we are mothers, not whores. In this slogan, the maternal body is defined in direct opposition to the body of the Whore: for giving birth, not for sex and money.

Through the photographs and commentary about the banners carried by the demonstrators the reader is reminded, however, that the women are not just any mothers, but "mothers of the sons of Serbia and Yugoslavia." The Son is both the proof and the product of the maternal body and its procreative heterosexuality, it is the very point of distinction with the Whore. The body of the Whore cannot, by definition, produce Sons, for the Whore has a nonprocreative body, a body for sex, and not for giving birth.

If the Serbian newspapers were only telling a story about the dignity and honor of Serbs, the story would have ended there, with the clear distinction between the two moral orders, symbolized in the bodies of the Whore and the Mother. But this was not an end. In *Politika*, a clear and direct line connects the verbal insult of Fadil Hoxha against Serb and Montenegrin women to the physical attacks against not just all Serb and Montenegrin women, but specifically Serbs and Montenegrin women living in Kosovo. The numerous examples of rapes and attempted rapes, cited by the participants of demonstrations and speakers alike, were contextualized within the Albanian separatist campaign, and always as one of the gravest assaults that Serbs and Montenegrins living in Kosovo, as a group, had to endure: "the rapes of girl minors are persisting" (October 17, 7); "Rapes [are] the main means by which the Albanian separatists' plan of an ethnically pure Kosovo will be realized" (October 18, 7); "Women want to know whether

РЕЧ НЕДЕЉЕ

КУРВА

Један од доскора најутицајнијих југословенских политичара изненада је открио своје психотерапеутске претензије. Бринући се на типично фалократски начин homo balkanicusa о сексуалном здрављу нашег мушког дела становништва, констатовао је да су сексуалне фрустрације узрок силовања, и предложио је, на банкету, да „будемо толерантнији према неким либералнијим понашањима неких радница у приватним кафанама".

Овај изненадни „фројдист" тиме је увредио бар половину становништва наше земље, сматрајући све жене Југославије потенцијалним проституткама, новог, социјалистичког типа. Иначе, овај облик скривене проституције по кафанама био је познат још у доба кинеске династије Сунг (960–1126.н.е.).

Пошто су поједини сведоци тврдили да је из овог предлога да се баве „најстаријим занатом на свету" политичар у униформи искључио припаднице своје народности, ек-

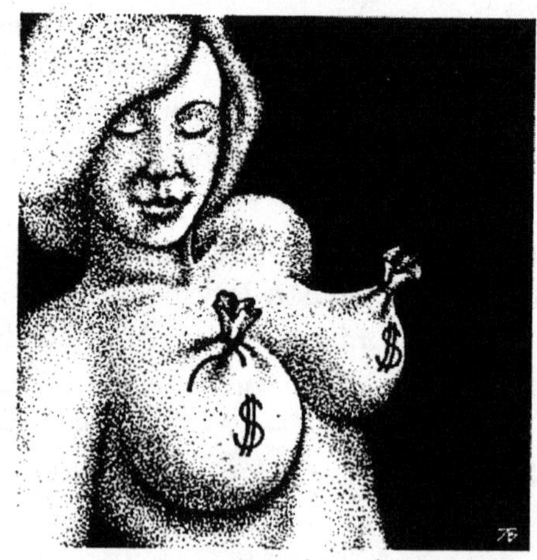

сплодирале су демонстрације у Приштини, где је запажен транспарент: „Ми нисмо курве, него сестре и мајке синова Србије и Југославије".

Illustration for the article "Whore," *NIN* (Serbia), October 25, 1987, 4.

they will be protected or whether we are going to emigrate from Kosovo collectively" (October 19, 7); "the real terror against children and women of Serb and Montenegrin nationality has been going on for seven years now" (ibid.); "Hoxha's statement about rapes in Kosovo represents an element in the strategy of Albanian nationalists and separatists" (October 21, 9).

In the above representations, the Albanian separatist-rapist is the symbol of all Albanians: monsters without morality. But this is not all that *Politika* wants us to see, that Albanians belong to a lesser moral order than Serbs. For, after all, the story about Fadil Hoxha, even if seen in moral terms only, has its due end in the Serbian press: he was punished for insulting both women and the Serbs. Thus, if the story were only about an ethnic definition of dignity, Serbs would have been vindicated. The texts in the Serbian daily and weekly could have been victorious: he got what he deserved. But instead, it brought up ongoing questions: "How long will this go on? Are we going to endure?" (*Politika*, October 19, 7).

According to the repeatedly quoted banners, women demonstrators who asked these questions are the "mothers of the sons of Serbia." In a logical order of things, that would mean that these sons have two mothers: the Serb women demonstrating against sexual assault by Albanian men, *and* Serbia. In the symbolic order of things, it means that the sons are mediators between the two birth-giving bodies: the body of the demonstrating mothers, and the body of Serbia. The consequence is that Serbia mothers, and more specifically, that she mothers Serbs. The metaphoric Mother is, thus, not so much Mother Serbia but the Mother of all Serbs: the sons who are explicitly claimed in this mothering, as well as all the raped daughters, all the insulted and assaulted Serb and Montenegrin women, all the demonstrating children and husbands, and all the threatened families. And while the *dignified* Mother of all Serbs is the embodiment of the story about the higher ethnic morality, the *raped* Mother of all Serbs is the embodiment of the narrative of ethnic suffering.

This narrative of ethnic suffering redeems the demonstrating women, forgiving them their political action and presence on the streets. For they are there for the higher good—to defend their family as well as Serbhood. Their motherhood frames all their actions and their claims. Furthermore, their femininity and their sexuality are unquestionable, regardless of their public political engagements, because they are defined not only by their morality but also by their vulnerability. Their maternal bodies produce ethnicity precisely because ethnicity and maternity are defined in the same way: under attack, suffering, but with impeccable, superior morality.

The multiple and shifting links among femininity, sexuality, and maternity and their militancy and vulnerability in the press makes clear that the maternal body is an ambiguous category that has to be jealously guarded for the production of the ethnic Self, but that continuously requires very specific representational strategies. The fact that both the Croatian and Serbian press used similar divisions and associations in their representations points to shared notions of femininity, sexuality and ethnicity, as well as shared assumptions about the gendered nature of (sexual) violence.

While the representations of the female body in the Croatian and Serbian press were similar, the representations of men—and male bodies—were quite different. In the Croatian papers men appear as politicians in many photos; their words are quoted in reports; they are the manipulators of the Serb and Montenegrin women, separatist Albanians from Kosovo or politicians from other regions of socialist Yugoslavia. While they display quite different political positions, one thing unites them—they were all political subjects. As much as women are ignored as political subjects in the Croatian press, all men are equalized by it, and ethnicity does not appear to have a substantial impact. In the Serbian press, on the contrary, men are clearly defined as *ethnically* different, and the ethnic Other—the Albanian Man—is defined in classic Orientalist manner, in opposition to Serb and Montenegrin women, his body the very symbol of the aggressive and violent sexuality that spares neither young girls nor old women, nor even Orthodox nuns, as other media in Serbia had reported. In a few years, after the violent disintegration of Yugoslavia began, this would change, and the Croatian press would turn its gaze toward the ethnic male Other, while the Serbian press would start looking inward, defining, and defending the male ethnic Self.

2

PICTURES OF THE WALL OF LOVE

Only four years after the events described in the previous chapter, in summer 1991, women were on the streets and in the press again. On June 25, 1991, the Slovenian parliament declared Slovenia's independence from the Socialist Federal Republic of Yugoslavia. Two days later, on June 27, tanks belonging to the Yugoslav National Army (JNA, Jugoslovenska Narodna Armija)[1] left their military barracks and entered the streets of Slovenian cities, only to be forced to withdraw within two weeks, leading to de facto recognition of Slovenian independence. This southward withdrawal aided the concentration of military forces in Croatia, whose leaders too demanded independence. Within a month full-blown war was raging in Croatia, engaging JNA soldiers as well as a number of volunteer paramilitary units from various associations, while the political leaders of the federal state, the republics, and the JNA negotiated. As the towns and villages of Croatia were burning, thousands of people in Serbia, Croatia, and Bosnia went out into the streets to express their concerns with, and rejection of, the violence. Among them were parents and, more specifically, mothers of the soldiers drafted into the JNA, who called for the release of their sons from the army.

The public protests and actions of these parents and mothers became the focus of the media. As in the fall of 1987, many of the women's speeches and public addresses, the banners they carried, and the slogans they chanted were explicitly based on the pleas and demands of motherhood. As in fall 1987, it was not only mothers, nor only women, who demonstrated. Nevertheless, the press and politicians quickly named all these actions "mothers' protests." The storming of the Serbian parliament in Belgrade in July 1991 and of the Bosnian parliament in Sarajevo in August 1991 were such actions. And so was the action for the return of soldiers. Its clear claim to motherhood, its organization and coordination, its multiethnic and cross-republic intention and reach, and the interest it stirred among the press, politicians, and feminists alike, set it apart from the protests of 1987, as well as other actions organized during the summer of 1991.

Through the newspaper coverage of the women's protests, the maternal body became once again the ultimate site of the media war. Marked again by both militancy and vulnerability, it was jealously guarded for the production of the ethnic Self. The body of the woman was again juxtaposed to the maternal body, transcending ethnicity and becoming an enemy in its own right. However, unlike in 1987, in 1991 the ethnic war was raging. There was suddenly a country that was disintegrating, and a country that was about to be made. A former and a future country, both now claiming territories, drawing borders. The maternal body became a focus of *these* claims. Its powers and vulnerabilities were now not only the symbol of the nation, but also of national geographies, of a land and the ways the land was lost or gained.

The Croatian Press

The Wall of Love was an action organized by the Committee of Mothers for the Return of Soldiers (known as the Mothers' Committee). With its headquarters in Zagreb, and sister organizations all over Croatia, Bosnia, Serbia and Kosovo, Montenegro and Macedonia, it was one of the best-organized wartime committees. In August 1991 it was busily planning two actions. One, building "live walls," made up of women besieging military barracks simultaneously in different cities and towns across different Yugoslav republics. The action was supposed to last until the soldier-sons were sent back home. These "live walls" were supposed to symbolize the love of mothers for their children, as well as their demand for peace—thus the name of the whole action: the Wall of Love. All citizens were invited to join, and many feminists and women-centered groups answered the invitation. But, as the "live walls" started forming on August 29, 1991, an increasing number of Croatian politicians—from local leaders to the then Croatian president Franjo Tudjman[2]—took over the task of giving speeches, welcoming protesters, and participating in the organization of demonstrations. As a consequence, public manifestations of the Wall of Love in Croatia started resembling any other patriotic propaganda gathering. Women's actions in other republics had almost the same fate.

The second action of the Mothers' Committee was a convoy of buses aiming to take women from different republics to the JNA headquarters in the Yugoslav (and Serbian) capital, Belgrade. Mothers vowed to stay in Belgrade, besieging the headquarters with another Wall of Love for as long as their demands were not met. All the buses set out on August 29 and were supposed to reach Belgrade at the same time, so as to increase the pressure on the military leaders by the very numbers of participants. The Mothers' Committee from Serbia, along with Serbian feminist and antiwar groups, was supposed to welcome the convoys and join in besieging the military headquarters. But when the convoys arrived in Belgrade the Serbian Mothers' Committee did not join in. On the contrary: together with politicians from Serbia and the JNA leaders it accused the women participating in the convoys of destroying Yugoslavia. Only a small group of women from Serbia—mainly feminist antiwar activists—joined the action. Women from Kosovo, prevented from leaving by police, did not even reach Belgrade. Women from Macedonia split into two factions, one of which left the gathering. Groups of women supporting the JNA confronted the women from the convoys, organizing counterdemonstrations.

On September 2, 1991, the Croatian convoys of mothers returned from Belgrade with none of their demands fulfilled. Furthermore, women, who had started out as mothers unified by their love for children and claiming peace, ended up divided along ethnic lines. Soon after, the Croatian press lost its interest in the event. But between August 29 and September 2, 1991, the daily *Vjesnik* and the weekly *Danas* had been full of texts, photos, graphics, and illustrations about the Wall of Love. Three symbolic female bodies appeared central to those press representations: the Fierce Mother, the Mother of Tears, and—the Woman. These three bodies carried three stories: about the birth of a new, independent country; about the brave defenders of its territory; and about its brutal enemies. All part of the same, gendered narrative of war and nationhood, these bodies and these stories were defined in ethnic terms, marking, in turn, those who belonged to the new country, and those who did not.

THE FIERCE MOTHER

Already on the first day of its coverage of the march on Belgrade (August 30, 1991) *Vjesnik* placed the maternal body in the core of its narrative of war and the birth of the nation. Its front page carried a full-width headline: "Croatia at War for Defense of Freedom." Below it were two photos: one of the demonstrations, labeled "Mothers," with the caption "Peace protest across Yugoslavia"; another of a ruined house, with the label "Vukovar" and the caption "Defenders are not giving up, even in the ruins." Beneath the photos, there was another, even larger headline, "Parents' Movement Destroys Army, Generals' Fury Destroys Cities," and two articles: aligned under the photo of the demonstrations a piece about the JNA destroying Croatian cities and villages in eastern Slavonia and under the photo of the ruined house a piece about the mothers' convoy.

These two themes appeared together again in the days that follow, under the same or similar headlines, with photos and articles about the women's demonstrations and the war destruction placed always side by side. It is worth noting that the word "parent" disappears from the articles and titles within a day, to be replaced by "mothers."

This intertwining of the stories about the Wall of Love and war destruction would be one of the main representational strategies in *Vjesnik*, recognizable not only in the editing of the photos and texts, but also in the use of language and narrative styles of the texts, especially this first day. Both stories on the cover page consist of a list of names of cities and villages through which the convoy of buses passed, or which were attacked by the JNA; both give the time sequences of battles and convoy travel, with descriptions of events and the attitudes of the protagonists. The same words—such as "bravery," "determination," and "discipline"—are used to describe soldiers defending cities and mothers progressing in buses through Croatia toward their gathering place in Zagreb, or toward Belgrade. The mothers even earn a look of surprise and unwitting respect from Serbian police, as they break through the cordons and march steadily and undeterred on foot, when ordered to leave the buses. Later articles also mention the suffering and pain of civilians in the attacked cities and of mothers worrying about their sons. They also invariably note the "stained blazons," "cruelty," and "aggression" of the JNA generals attacking Croatian cities and of the civilian Serb population and Serbian police attacking or threatening the convoys as they passed. This representational strategy symbolically merges the plight of the mothers' convoys with that of the destroyed cities and the civilians and defenders under attack, while at the same time it juxtaposes the JNA, and explicitly the JNA generals, to the themes of destruction and demonstration.

At first sight these representations have nothing to do with ethnicity, as there is an explicit statement that the mothers come from different ethnic backgrounds. An article published in *Vjesnik* the same day notes that among the women waiting to board the convoy in Zagreb one holds a ban-

HRVATSKA U RATU ZA OBRANU SLOBODE

knin ne potpisuje primirje, str. 3 — **tko napada policijsku postaju na plitvicama, str. 3**

srbija pere ruke od armije, str. 9 — **razmjena uhićenih u petrinji, str. 14**

INOZEMNO IZDANJE

Zagreb 41000
Avenija bratstva i jedinstva 4
Telefoni 333-333 i 666-666
Dežurni urednik 661-681 i 661-682
Telex: 21121 vsk
Fax: 041 661-650
Direktor: Dražena Slade Šilović
Glavni urednik: Hido Biščević
YU ISSN 0350-3305
Godina LII. broj 15785

Vjesnik

POLITIČKI DNEVNIK

Austrija 10 ATS, Belgija 35,00 BFR, Francuska 4,50 FFR, Italija 1500 ITL, Nizozemska 2,00 NLG, Njemačka 1,80 DEM, Švedska 8,00 SEK, Švicarska 1,70 CHF

Petak, 30. kolovoza 1991.

Pokret roditelja ruši Armiju, generali u bijesu ruše gradove

Armija će poduzeti sve, procjenjuju u vukovarskom zapovjedništvu Zbora narodne garde, da »svoj osramoćeni obraz spasi«, jer je, prema priznanjima iz armijskih redova, na pomolu ono što se Armiji dogodilo u Sloveniji.

REDAKCIJSKI IZVJEŠTAJ

I nakon razgovora hrvatske i vojne delegacije na Brijunima mira nema, a ratni sukobi u istočnoj Slavoniji i Baranji i dalje eskaliraju neviđenom žestinom. U Borovom Naselju više nema čitavih zgrada, sa zemljom je sravnjena i osnovna škola, oštećen je kombinat »Borovo«. U Vukovaru teško su oštećene brojne stambene kuće i zgrade, osobito one uz Dunav. Nakon četiri dana bombardiranja potpuno pust grad pruža stravičnu sliku. Četiri dana stanovnike su agresori tukli teškom artiljerijskom vatri iz minobacača, haubica, tenkova, višecijevnih raketnih bacača, zrakoplova »galeb«, »mig«, iz ratnih brodova.

Tijekom srijede vođene su žestoke borbe u kojima jedinice u uniformama Jugoslavenske armije nisu uspjele zauzeti nijedan cilj. Na vukovarskom frontu Armija je do srijede izgubila trećinu svoje tehnike. Ukupno je na vukovarskom području Armija angažirala više od 150 različitih borbenih oklopnih sredstava, ali je uspjela postići samo neviđena razaranja. Najžešće borbe vođene su na Mitnici, prema Sotinu, odnosno u jugoistočnom dijelu Vukovara. Sotin je u srijedu žestoko bombardiran, a iz toga smjera prema Vinkovcima se kreće velika kolona izbjeglica.

Armija će poduzeti sve, procjenjuju u vukovarskom Zapovjedništvu Zbora narodne garde, da »svoj osramoćeni obraz spasi«, jer je, prema priznanjima iz armijskih redova, na pomolu ono što se Armiji dogodilo u Sloveniji.

Napaćenim Borovčanima i Vukovarčanima treba pomoći, odvesti im hrane, uspostaviti s njima bolje komunikacije, jer užasan problem predstavljaju prekinute telefonske veze s Vukovarom. Hrabre borce treba opskrbiti svim što traže. Oni čak niti ne traže pojačanje u ljudstvu, nego samo traže da se imaju s čim boriti protiv surovog agresora. Stoga je u vinkovačkom općinskom čelništvu organizirana dostava kruha za Borovo Naselje. Šesto vekni kruha i nešto pereca ispečeno je u vinkovačkoj pekari i pod okriljem noći kamionom poslano u Borovo Naselje, gdje je situacija daleko najteža i čijim je stanovnicima hrana najpotrebnija.

Borbe se vode i oko Osijeka i u njima je ranjeno još devet pripadnika oružanih snaga Hrvatske. Četiri teško ozlijeđena zadržana su na liječenju, a pet ih je otpušteno kućama. Krizni štab u Osijeku i dalje stoji pri odluci da se armija može kretati samo za potrebe opskrbe i to iz vlastitih izvora, te u kad se prevoze ranjenici. Agresoru se i dalje obustavlja isporuka hrane, struje i vode.

Na barikadi kod Šida majke su odlučile, krenule su put Beograda pješice, probivši živi zid koji su napravili milicionari kao od šale – Odbile su sastaviti spisak svojih imena i imena svojih sinova – U 15 sati autobusi su napokon propušteni

IVANČICA KNAPIĆ
Beograd

Do granice sa Srbijom mještani su dočekivali majke cvijećem i pjesmom. Pripadnici MUP-a Hrvatske, koji su osiguravali kolonu od 27 autobusa punih majki iz Zagreba, Čakovca, Varaždina, Siska, Osijeka, Vinkovaca, Dubrovnika, Livna... do granice Hrvatske i Srbije, upozorili su nas da je moguća negostoljubivost sa suprotne strane.

NEMA PARKINGA? Pripadnik srpske milicije rekao je da imaju naređenje da nas osiguravaju do Beograda »jer neki građani Srbije prijete majkama«. Od 11.30 do 12.15 sati milicionari su obrazlagali da čekamo još šest autobusa iz Sarajeva. Nakon prosvjeda, prvobitna susretljivost milicionara pretvara se u: »ne možete dalje bez osiguranja«. U 12.15 sati majke obznanjuju da one kreću bez pratnje, da se ne daju izigrati. U to stiže svježa informacija da nas ne mogu primiti u Beogradu, jer ne mogu osigurati parking. Žene kreću revoltirane, predosjećajući da je to tek početak otkrivanja pravih likova iza anonimnih prijetnji da neće stići do Beograda. U 12.45 sati zaustavljaju nas na autoputu kod Šida. Postavljene su barikade od nekoliko automobila milicije i kamiona punih zemlje.

NA VLASTITI RIZIK: Komandir srpske milicije rekao nam je da ponovno čeka naređenje i da nas neće pustiti. Na pitanje – može li reći da ćemo krenuti za pola sata? – odgovara otresito »u Beograd nećete ići ni za pola sata, ni za pola dana, ni za godinu dana«. Majke više nitko nije mogao zaustaviti, odlučile su pješice krenuti u Beograd. Milicionari su pokušali napraviti živi zid ali majke su ga probile. Šokirani hrabrošću majki nisu znali što da rade. Ne želimo ni pomisliti da su možda imali naređenje da primjene silu. Majke su mirno krenule put Beograda, vezane zajedničkim ciljem – osloboditi sinove. Nakon 10 minuta pješačenja, kada su uvidjeli da majke ništa neće spriječiti, milicionari dozvoljavaju prolaz autobusima. Odlaze ispraćene riječima da idu na vlastiti rizik. Tijekom vožnje primjećujemo vojnike u vozilima, koji pozdravljaju, trube i mašu majkama. U 14.15 sati ponovo nas dočekuju ista lica kod naplatnih kućica autoputa, dvadesetak kilometara od Beograda.

»SAMO SMO VAS ČUVALI« Uz riječi dobrodošlice komandira milicije, kažu da je sve što su majke prošle za njihovo dobro jer Šešelj prijeti, a oni su ih samo čuvali. Kaže da možemo dalje, ali tek kada se sva imena majki i očeva koji su u autobusima, zajedno sa imenima njihovih sinova i brojevima vojne pošte u kojima služe, napišu na papir i uruče im se. Majke na to ne pristaju. Ponovo kreću pješice. Rečeno im je da pred Generalštabom u Beogradu nema nikoga, već da će ih generali uz ručak primiti na Topčideru. Oglušuju se o prijedlog i nastavljaju put pješice. I ponovo je dozvoljen prolaz autobusima. U 15 sati krenule su put Beograda. Što ih čeka u Beogradu, nakon takvoga puta, jako dobro znaju.

Front page of *Vjesnik* (Croatia), August 30, 1991. The headline over the two photos reads: "Croatia at War for Defense of Freedom"; the two-line headline under the newspaper name reads: "Parents' Movement Destroys Army, Generals' Fury Destroys Towns."

ner reading: "Name: Ljiljana; nationality: Serb; homeland: Croatia; occupation: mother" ("Our Children Want to Live," August 30, 4). Furthermore, the defenders of the cities are not referred to as Croats, but rather as "Croatian," that is, of Croatia, and the names of the towns—attacked or visited by mothers—clearly denote Croatian territory. Thus the ethnic references do not come through the naming of the *people*, but rather through the naming of the *territory*. However, the same is not true for the JNA generals—they will be explicitly named as Serbs.

Besides the front-page text and photos, on the first day *Vjesnik* dedicated its entire fourth page to the Wall of Love, using the same banner headline style ("Generals, Our Weapon Is—Love") and below it, photos and articles about the Wall of Love and a copy of the Mothers' Appeal. One of the articles describes minutely the demonstration of 100,000 Zagreb citizens in front of a military barracks around which the mothers had formed the "living wall of peace": the protest started at noon, heralded by factory sirens, car horns, and church bells. Many workers were given the day off to be able to participate. Banners read "Generals murderers," "Give us back our sons" (also visible in the accompanying photos), and "Mothers are stronger than generals." *Vjesnik* states that "Croatian, Slovenian and Muslim[3] flags, as well as the flag of the European Union were waved." At 1:00 P.M. the "magnificent gathering" in front of the military barracks started with the singing of the Croatian national anthem, and then the secretary of the Mothers' Committee addressed the audience:

> To the generals she sent the message not to try to withhold from the mothers what is most sacred to them—their children. "We will not allow you to manipulate their lives and we will fight with our last breath. You will not deter us with the power of your weapons, [because] the weapon of mothers is stronger, and this is our eternal concern for [our children's] life. This gives us the strength to struggle, and if needed, we will give our own lives for the lives of our children. Wherever you have gone you have left madness, ruins and death behind. . . . Could you ever have a clear conscience after this? Could you ever look any mother in the eye?" (Ibid., 4)

The mayor of Zagreb was quoted speaking about "criminal and imperialist war" and the JNA's "Serbo-communist leadership." His message to the gathered women was quoted: "The whole of Croatia is with you now, and be sure that [your action] will echo throughout the world. Every protest brings us closer to our common aim, which is freedom. Thus, do continue your protest, but with dignity, in contrast to barbarity, the fortress of which is just in front of you" (referring to the military barracks in front of which the gathering was held). The next speaker talked on behalf of the mothers of Vukovar, demanding that the JNA leadership be replaced and asking President Tudjman of Croatia not to negotiate with the Yugoslav military but with the European Community: "Otherwise, we will burn Vukovar, so that the army goes up in flames with us."

In all these articles, the determination with which the mothers demand and defend their children is constructed in direct opposition to the cruelty and barbarity of the JNA soldiers and generals, the proof of which is already given on the front page of *Vjesnik* in the articles and photo of a ruined Croatian house. The mothers and the JNA generals are two opposing powers, and their opposition is enforced consistently, in articles published in both the daily *Vjesnik* and the weekly *Danas*. Through this opposition the "Fierce Mothers" are produced. They journey through the ruined country to claim their most precious possessions—their sons. They are like crusaders fighting for a just cause, brave and determined, they come from everywhere, and all go in the same direction, with the same goal. They resist the JNA just as the Croatian cities and their brave defenders do, despite the destruction. They are defenders too, epic figures, whose advances across the destroyed cities and villages map the country's territory into a new cartography: enemy land where they are opposed, homeland where they are welcomed: "Up to the border with Serbia, citizens have been greeting mothers with flowers and songs" (*Vjesnik*, August 30, 1). Through this epic journey the Fierce Mother maps the motherland, and claims it for herself. Thus, even though not all the mothers are Croats, the Fierce Mother is Croatia: determined and powerful in its resistance, undefeated albeit under siege.

The distinction between the Fierce Mother Croatia and the JNA generals could not be greater. They inhabit two different worlds, as the piece "To Brussels for Justice" (September 1, 5) shows. It describes how mothers came back from Belgrade to Zagreb to be greeted by several thousands of citizens and the mayor of the city. The mayor informs them that President Tudjman of Croatia has encouraging news: the mothers are invited to Brussels in order to show the "civilized world [that] Yugo-generals are withholding from them [their sons]." The article is accompanied with a graphic: a dove with a bough of peace encircled by twelve stars, the emblem of the European Union. Above it is the headline: "Give Us Back Our Sons." The same graphic accompanied the piece "Love Is Stronger than Anything" (September 2, 5), about the return of the mothers from Brussels, where they had "informed the civilized world about the failure of negotiations in Belgrade."

In these pieces the civility of the Fierce Mother Croatia and the barbarity of the generals are further contrasted, establishing at the same time clear identities for both. The latter are defined through the ethnic and political references to Serbhood, Yugoslavism, and communism, on the one hand, and through barbarity, cruelty, and aggression, on the other. The former are associated with Europe as the place of civilization. Claiming ties with Europe, the emerging new country claims a new, European identity, and a clear historic and geopolitical break-up with the former Yugoslavia, leaving behind its communist history and the barbarity and primitivism by which Europe defines the "symbolic continent of Balkans" (Bakić-Hayden and Hayden 1992).[4]

This symbolic distancing from the JNA in this Croatian daily was not a rejection of militarism altogether, but just a rejection of this particular military. One's own military was glorified, and the Fierce Mothers' epic journey itself was represented rather like a military conquest, with mothers being greeted with flowers, flags, and applause throughout Croatia, just as a liberating army might be; and being resisted, opposed, and treated like an enemy army in Serbia, with huge forces of police being mobilized to stop them. Although praised for their disciplined and civilized ways, for their motherly and nonviolent manners, the Fierce Mothers are represented as potentially dangerous, and *Vjesnik* warns that they should be feared, for their just fury is a threat to the enemy: "We will burn the city," one mother is quoted as exclaiming. This was a threatening and powerful exclamation. And as the army of the Fierce Mothers marched, the fervent flames of their love and fury became one with this threat, a dire warning to those who threatened the most precious fruit of their maternal bodies—the newly mapped motherland.[5]

THE MOTHER OF TEARS

There is another maternal body in the Croatian papers, however, besides the powerful and threatening one of the Fierce Mothers. It is the body of sorrow and helplessness, introduced by the article "Be Afraid of Mother's Curse," which appeared on the first day of *Vjesnik*'s coverage of the Wall of Love (August 30, 4). It deals with the same gathering of women around the military barracks in Zagreb mentioned earlier, but in this article, the text is different: "mothers shed endless tears," "unified by love for their children"; one "cried desperately," one had "a grimace of anguish," and yet others would "burst into tears while speaking." The reporter exclaimed at the end of the text: "thousands of mothers continued tirelessly to tighten the ring around the Command . . . with the message: 'Generals, beware of a mother's curse and mother's tears.'"

A piece "You Can Go Home" (August 31, 14) conveys the same image of "mothers' tear-stained faces" as it tells about ill-treatment of demonstrators by the JNA military officials as they left Belgrade (ibid.). The article ends with a short paragraph describing a conversation between the reporter and a young man he encounters in the courtyard of the Guard Hall (one of the buildings housing JNA in Belgrade). The young man has just been released from the military, which he served in Belgrade. He came to "rescue his mother" from the Guard Hall, because he had heard that she was held there with the other mothers.[6] This brief paragraph reveals a world of difference between the Fierce Mother and the crying mother. While the former is a powerful and brave mother, determined and unstoppable, with the main task to rescue her son and bring him safely home, the latter is broken by defeat, overpowered by grief, and dependent on the son to come to her rescue. Thus the Mother of Tears was created.

It is interesting to note that on the first day of coverage in *Vjesnik*, the pieces appearing on the front page depicted only determined and powerful women. Other pieces published on the same day depicted both determination and tears, sometimes within the same stories. But, as the reporting proceeded, the Fierce Mother disappeared from the pages of *Vjesnik*, and the Mother of Tears became more and more prominent. The same happened in the weekly *Danas*.

In the article "Belgrade Does Not Believe in Tears"[7] (*Danas*, September 3, 1991, 9–10), the determined women are all but replaced by the image of the helpless, crying mothers, drowning in their sorrow. The atmosphere among the mothers in the Guard Hall in Belgrade is described as one of chaos, disagreements, and disillusionment. The closing sentences tell that the Wall of Love was being brought down "without the use of force," and that the "dispirited and sobbing mothers entered buses" to go back home without a single one of their demands having been fulfilled. The photo accompanying the text shows women sitting in the Guard Hall, many of them crying, with the caption "The cry without reply: mothers of soldiers from Croatia in the Guard Hall."

In the story about the Mother of Tears maternal body is again metaphorically linked to the ruins of Croatia, albeit in a different way. While the Fierce Mother shared courage, determination, and resistance with the destroyed Croatian towns, the Mother of Tears shares their pain and suffering. Just like the towns, she is broken and in need of defenders and protectors. All the fury, courage, and determination have melted into tears of pain. The only threat left is that of a mother's curse, but would anyone fear it? Whatever the answer, one thing is clear: if the Fierce Mother was the metaphor of Croatia determined to gain its independence, the Mother of Tears is a metaphor for martyred Croatia.

Furthermore, the Mother of Tears inverts the previous gender narrative of war. Instead of the Fierce Mothers ready to die to save their sons, the sons will (die to) save their mothers. Thus, while the metaphoric role of the Fierce Mother was to map the motherland and thus establish the borders of the new country, the metaphoric role of the Mother of Tears is to surrender the war to the sons—to men.

This message is particularly well conveyed through the press photographs, in both *Vjesnik* and *Danas*. While they started by offering images of both the Fierce Mother and the Mother of Tears, the latter became more prominent as time passed. The photos published in *Vjesnik* (August 30, 4) on the first day of coverage offer an interesting additional image—a single vertical figure of a praying woman, the unmistakably iconography of a female saint. Elements recognizable from popular prints of female saints in the Christian tradition are here: a woman on her knees, her hands folded in prayer, a row of candles in front of her, in the place of crucifixion. She is the embodiment of all female endurance and faith. The crying mother rescued by her son and the praying mother merge in this figure, sharing suffering as well as a possibility of salvation through the son/Son. A huge spread of photos published in *Vjesnik* a day later (September 1, 4–5) further reinforces the shift in the narrative. On one page, the single photo of a crying mother, with a boy on her shoulders, his hands folded in prayer, accompanies two articles about the Wall of Love. On the opposite page, nine large photos cover more than half the page, running from top to bottom. In each of them Croatia lies in ruins while male soldiers fight the war. Separated from this cluster, on the same page, there is a photo of two old seated women,

snik ZAGREB Petak, 30. kolovoza 1991

vim lancem mira okružile Komandu 5. vojne oblasti u Zagrebu

enerali, naše oružje je – ljubav«

je počeo točno u podne, oglašavanjem tvorničkih i automobilskih sirena. Zvonila su zvona, a mnoga poduzeća su stala s radom

Majke ne dopuštaju da se manipulira s njihovom djecom i poručuju generalima da će se za svoje sinove boriti do posljednjeg daha

ROMEO IBRIŠEVIĆ

The headline over the four photos reads: "'Generals, Our Weapon Is—Love.'" *Vjesnik* (Croatia), August 30, 1991, 4.

reminiscent of the images of refugees. The arrangement on these two pages reinforces the mutual exclusion of these images: soldiers and mothers, war and tears.

THE WOMAN

The maternal metaphors in the two main Croatian papers were continually positioned not only against the JNA generals but also against the Woman. As in the Serbian press in 1987, politics was at the heart of the distinction between the Mother and the Woman. Mothers' actions were continuously defined as outside politics, while those who engaged in politics were denied maternal feelings, and—as in 1987—sons.

In the piece "Some Mothers Are Interested in Politics" (*Vjesnik*, August 31, 1991, 14), a journalist reports that the sole purpose of the mothers who went to Belgrade was that "of liberating their sons." They could endure all the hardship simply "because the mothers were determined not to turn their peaceful gathering into political protest." These mothers are then contrasted with a "group of women" from one Bosnian village who came to protest against the mothers' gathering. The reporter continues: "As we are informed, on Thursday the inhabitants of this village stoned the bus of the mothers from Šibenik [Croatia] on their way to Belgrade. The group was made of Serb women exclusively. Only two of them have sons in the military" (ibid.). Thus, there are mothers from Croatia, and Serb women. A clear ethnic difference follows the difference in maternal status. Maternal-ethnic differentiation is supported by their actions and attitudes (peaceful gathering compared with stoning) and their sons, or lack of them. The former followed purely maternal interests, while the latter are, as the title indicates, "interested in politics," chanting support for the JNA and Communist Party. This political engagement is the basis for defining the latter in exclusive ethnic and gendered terms, as Serb women.

Danas also writes about the Serb Woman, using the same ethnic-political differentiation between motherhood and womanhood. In the section "A Disappointed 'Serb Mother'" (in the article "Belgrade Does Not Believe in Tears," September 3, 10) the reporter writes about one Serb woman—Ms. Kunijević, from the Mothers' Committee of Serbia. Ms. Kunijević had twin sons in the JNA during the Slovenian war, and in July 1991 was among the parents interrupting a session of the Serbian parliament, demanding their return. However, in late August she refused to join the Wall of Love convoy when it reached Belgrade, and talked about it on the Belgrade TV. The journalist has some critical comments to make of Ms. Kunijević's dismissal of the women in the convoy as "only Croats and Muslims, not a single Serb woman from Bosnia."

> She tried "to be objective," but she had to say "that the emotions of the guests are polluted with politics and I am not at all sure whether these are really mothers." Thus, these so-called mothers "did not come either for peace or for children," and Ms. Kunijević is "very disappointed," and has a "bitter taste" after meeting [the convoy]. Before she left to wash out the bitterness, she had just enough strength to tell Serb and Belgrade mothers: "I am proud of you. We were the only ones who did not allow politics to mix with our motherhood." It may be worth reminding her of her own words, which she uttered less than two months ago, demanding that her sons be "immediately" returned from Slovenia. "I do not know," she was saying then, "why and against whom my children are fighting in Slovenia, but I do know that I do

> not want them to die for anybody's borders." Something has changed meanwhile, obviously. Someone else's children are dying and the war is not in Slovenia any longer. But Ms. Kunijević did comply very well with her task—to prevent, at any cost, the antiwar protest in front of the Guard Hall. . . . And the task was successfully completed. Who contributed more to that success: Serbian police or military police, Ms. Kunijević, or provocateurs . . . is less important. (*Danas*, September 3, 9)

What is interesting in this excerpt is that the journalist uses the same Mother/Woman distinction and turns it against Ms. Kunijević: while she expressed her doubs that the Croatian women were actually mothers, the reporter questions her own motherhood, by placing the word between the inverted commas. Equally, while she accuses others of being politically motivated, her own acts are characterized as political, which puts her in peculiar company: among the police, military men, and provocateurs.

It seems, however, that the military also found themselves in unexpected company in the Croatian weekly. The subtitle of the same article in *Danas* mocks the generals with whom the women had requested a meeting but who did not come, sending a lower-ranking officer in their place: "The Top Yugoslav Officers Were Scared of Women" (ibid.). In the cultural-patriarchal context of the Balkans, this statement is a potent way of mocking manhood and consequently stripping the generals of their masculinity. That this conflation of military men and the women was not just an aside but a very specific move in the representation can be further confirmed by cartoons appearing in *Vjesnik*.

On September 1, 1991, a cartoon followed a *Vjesnik* story about a military press conference regarding the Wall of Love (6). The cartoonist, Srećko Pintarić, depicts a group of women carrying banners, shouting, and marching, with their fists raised and their mouths wide open. They do not look at the reader, and there is nothing written on the banners they carry. Among them, however, there is a figure that does look at the reader: a man in military uniform but only from the waist up; below we see a skirt and hairy legs, and he carries a handbag on his arm. He too carries a blank banner. The caption to the cartoon reads: "Fifth-columnist among women." Following upon the articles in *Danas*, this cartoon clearly implies that the military—the JNA generals, to be precise—are not only afraid of women, they *are* women. Their manhood is not only mocked, it is erased. The Balkans

"Fifth-columnist among women," *Vjesnik* (Croatia), September 1, 1991, 6.

are not Scotland. A man in a skirt is not considered a man. And a general in a skirt is definitely not considered a general.

But the cartoon does not speak about military only. For, while mocking generals, it also mocks women. Not the Serb Woman, this time—the stone-throwing and treacherous nonmothers—for there are no ethnic references in this cartoon. In an interesting shift, this cartoon refutes the clear-cut ethnic-political distinction between the Serb Woman and the Croat/ian Mothers established in the earlier representations. It obviously reacts to the mothers' demonstrations, but still, there is not a single clear reference to motherhood in the drawing (compared to the photos, for example, in which women are either with children on their shoulders, or holding banners claiming their children).

It might be possible to assume that these are, then, Serb women, demonstrating together with generals against the mothers. Nevertheless, another caricature by the same artist, published the same day, counters this reading. There, women stand in a group, all looking alike, funnily ugly

The reversed lettering on the small banner reads: "Stalin fucks you." The large banner carries the mocking plea "Sirs, Generals! Let love enter your icy unitarist hearts, poisoned by ideological deceptions from the communist-centralist darkness." *Vjesnik* (Croatia), September 1, 1991, 15.

as they can only be in a caricature, their breasts hanging low, their fists raised high (the images are the same as in the first cartoon), and all looking at the viewer. One carries a banner reading: "Sirs, Generals! Let love enter your icy unitarist hearts, poisoned by ideological deceptions from the communist-centralist darkness" (ibid., 15). Another woman, standing, like the banner holder, in front of the group, looks across at the banner; she wears an apron and headscarf and carries another, smaller banner. On it, in letters reversed as if reflected in a mirror, the following words are written: "Stalin fucks you." Whether the message is addressed to the generals mentioned in the other banner, or to the other women standing around is not clear. The banner addressing the generals, however, makes it indisputable that these women are participants in the Wall of Love.

If the female figures in the cartoon carry neither ethnic nor maternal references, if they are neither the Serb women nor the Mothers of Croatia, who are they, then? They are—the Women. They mark female political subjectivity as a field of nationalist discomfort and, at the same time, indicate the ambiguity of the maternal metaphor. For in this cartoon the female political subjectivity *as such* is mocked. The language on the banners—or the absence of it—clearly shows it. The slogan from the first banner (to the generals) belongs to the often mocked socialist terminology, pompous and void. Polite address ("Sirs") and the mention of love in connection with the generals is supposed to show the naïveté of the women, if not their total lack of grasp of political reality (already described in the Croatian press as characterized by cruelty, barbarity, and aggression). The second banner has the word "fuck" in it—a word never used in the quality press. The woman using it wears an apron and a bandanna, as if caught in the middle of dusting her apartment. These are two different languages that belong to two different realities: the official socialist rhetoric and the language of the streets. In the dominant gendered division of domains, both of these realities—politics and the streets—belong to the male domain and are thus rendered unfit for women. As if to prove the point, the banners on the first cartoon are blank, constructing politically active women as mute. Displaced from their domestic place and space and stripped of symbols of motherhood, these women have nothing to connect them to Croatia, because Croatia is already defined exclusively through the maternal body. However, they also have nothing to link them to the Serb Woman. Instead, they are linked to the enemy man—to the JNA generals.

There are ambiguities and contradictions in these associations. On the one hand, they render women's political subjectivity per se not only as inimical to the nation but also as nonfeminine. Thus, one could argue that even maternal politics are a potential threat to the nation. After all, it was on this ground that many feminists in Croatia and Serbia embraced the Wall of Love. On the other hand, these cartoons indicate that it is not really a particular women's political agency but the *possibility of its appropriation* for a particular political project that makes it or breaks it. This cautions against feminist optimism. For the representations of the Wall of Love in the Croatian press show that the possibilities of discursive appropriations of the maternal body for the production of ethnicity are many. An analysis of the Serbian press further supports this argument.

The Serbian Press

In their representation of the Wall of Love, the Serbian daily *Politika* and the weekly *NIN* also relied on the maternal body to produce the ethnic

Self, and used politics as a point of distinction between motherhood and womanhood. But where the Croatian press presented stories about the birth of the new country, the Serbian press told about destruction of the old. This framed the way the stories were told. Womanhood, motherhood, sexuality, and ethnicity were all important there too, but the stories were not as much about maternal powers and vulnerabilities as they were about manipulation, truthfulness, and falsehood. The Woman appeared here too, not mocked as a potential enemy, but explicitly sexualized.

On August 27, 1991, mothers broke into the Bosnian parliament demanding the return of their sons from military duty in the JNA. In *Politika*, this action and numerous similar actions in Bosnia and Croatia were not associated with the Wall of Love, although many of them were organized and inspired by the Wall of Love. *Politika* presented them separately, preserving the name Wall of Love only for the bus convoy to Belgrade. Furthermore, the word "parent" was used for actions in Bosnia, and the word "mother" for the convoy. That way, in one move *Politika* diminished the scope of the women's actions, increased the scope of the threat to Yugoslavia, the JNA, and the Serbs as an ethnic group, and created two different groups of ethnic enemies: Muslims in Bosnia, and Croats in Croatia.

MANIPULATED PARENTS AND FALSE MOTHERS

In an article titled "Parents' Storming of Parliament Orchestrated" (*Politika*, August 28, 1991) a Serb member of parliament was quoted stating that the march of the parents on the Bosnian parliament was "organized and preconceived." He stressed that the Serb members of the Bosnian parliament did "understand the worries of the parents for their sons who are soldiers," but that they called upon all parents in Bosnia not to fall prey to "manipulations of parental concern."

This piece is typical of *Politika*'s articles about the demonstrations that summer. It also illustrates the style: unlike the Croatian daily *Vjesnik*, which had fewer, but much longer, articles, the Serbian daily had many short pieces, some only a couple of sentences in length. The majority of the pieces in *Politika* focus on the "genuine concern" of parents for their children, adding always a "but": for example, the unscrupulous manipulation of "humane and parental emotions" by "Croat nationalists" or "antiarmy elements" (both August 29, 15). Manipulated mothers are added into the picture, here and there, particularly after the Wall of Love was first mentioned, on August 30 (12), but parents remain the main carriers of honesty and concern, as well as the main target of manipulation and misuse according to all the *Politika* reports. *Politika* makes it also clear that the honest, concerned parents and tearful mothers are Muslims and Croats, used by their own leaders: "There are no Serb parents among those manipulated by HDZ and SDA" (the main Croatian and Bosnian-Muslim political parties) (August 29, 15). This is so because Serbs in Bosnia and Croatia could "see through" these "shamefully orchestrated protests and the unskillfully designed plot against the JNA" (August 30, 12). Depicting the parents, as confused, helpless, and tearful, and continually referring to the ease with which they were manipulated, *Politika* indicates that they are not a grave threat to public security.

The real danger is posed by the women from the Wall of Love. *Politika*'s picture of politically naive and emotionally driven manipulated parents serves as a backdrop against which another enemy is produced: the False Mother and "trained groups of fascistic instigators"[8] (August 29, 15).

The "fascistic instigators" are introduced through the already mentioned article "Parents' Storming of Parliament Orchestrated" (August 28, 10). The piece tells about a "violent entry into [the building] of a group (mainly women) that presented itself as the parents of the children currently in military service." The bracketed words "mainly women," together with the words "presented itself" tell it all: just as Serb parents saw through the manipulative politics of Muslim and Croat leaders, *Politika* has seen through these pretenders. This is the first article in which the parents' truthfulness is questioned, and interestingly enough, the only one in which the word "parents" is used when related to falsehood. After this, the word "parents" will be associated exclusively with genuine, albeit manipulated, feelings. The lying will have another association, established in the first sentence of another article, "Protest of Women Who Do Not Have Sons in the JNA":

> A group of "mothers" from Banja Luka,[9] whose sons serve in the military in Croatia, killing their brothers there, organized a protest in front of the military barracks. Colonel Stanimir Pešić came to speak before the more than 150 women, mainly Muslim and Croat. He succeeded in calming down these "mothers," who, filled with hatred, shouted insults to the JNA and individual officers. . . . These women and false mothers from this "peacemaking" meeting against the JNA were shamed [by the colonel] and left the gathering with their heads down. . . . One of the "mothers" admitted that she "intervenes" on

> behalf of her neighbor's son, because the neighbor could not come herself. (August 29, 15)

The falsehood of these mothers is established in *Politika* along the same lines used in the Croatian press to deny motherhood to Serb women: they do not have sons in the military, their motives are political and not maternal, and they are ethnically specific groups, in this case, Muslims and Croats.

Politika is also consistent in stressing the difference between the women from the convoy who came to protests against the JNA, and Serb women. The motherhood of the former is always denied, appearing between quotation marks, while the motherhood of Serb women is upheld as the true one. Another article, "Yet Another Attack on JNA," shows clearly that there are "mothers" and mothers:

> Regarding yesterday's announced protest by "mothers of soldiers" from Zagreb and Sarajevo in Belgrade, the Socialist Party of Serbia [SPS] issued a statement saying that this protest was yet another organized attack against the JNA, at the time when the army is protecting the Serb population from being obliterated by the paramilitaries lead by the Croatian government. . . . For these reasons, SPS calls upon the citizens of Belgrade and Serbia, and all patriots, not to join the gathering of these "mothers of soldiers." . . . The Socialist Party of Serbia understands and comprehends the concern of mothers for the life of their soldier-sons. (August 30, 8)

Thus, in *Politika*, there are the Serb mothers and women who support the JNA and, there are the Croat and Muslim "mothers." Unlike the manipulated parents who have no political will of their own, the false mothers, although organized and paid by the Croatian and Bosnian leaders, act on their own hatred against the JNA. An article titled "False Mothers and True Mesić"[10] makes the same distinction, and names the enemies not only in ethnic but also in religious terms:

> The invasion of the JNA Guard Hall, organized by Stjepan Mesić, Franjo Tudjman, and Irfan Ajanović [Croatian and Bosnian politicians] ended Friday with messages of fierce hatred from the "Wall of Love." With mothers and fathers of soldiers it was possible to talk, but they were the minority there. . . . The [convoys were] organized by priests in Zagreb and imams in Sarajevo; those [who were] paid to make noise

[at the protest] and who have nothing to do with parenthood showed the lowest level of "civilized manners." (September 1, 9)

On the same day another title claimed "There Were No Mothers in the 'Wall of Love'" (ibid., 11). The piece goes on to state that the "gathering of quasi-mothers was the best example of the dirty attacks" on the JNA.

As if to remind the readers of what it was all about, one week later *Politika* published a letter to the editor, titled "Misuse of Mothers" (September 6, 17). In the letter, the manipulated parents stand beside the "hypocritical forum of the 'sorrowful mothers.'" Besides using the expression "sorrowful mothers" in the inverted commas twice, the letter writer implies the falseness of the mothers in the Wall of Love through use of language.

With the rise of nationalism, language became a contested site of ethnic identity. In that context, repeated attempts have been made to classify the languages spoken in Serbia and Croatia as different. The names "Serbo-Croat" (in Serbia) and "Croato-Serb" (in Croatia) for the two versions of what is basically the same language were suddenly considered inadequate, and every effort was made to define two separate languages.[11] Nationalists claimed that languages spoken in Serbia and Croatia are not only different, but are also directly linked to different ethnic groups. This would suggest that only Croats speak Croatian, and only Serbs Serbian, while nothing could be further from reality. In both Serbia and Croatia (as in Bosnia) the same dialect is spoken by different ethnic groups, depending on the territorial locality in which they live. Thus, when the Serbian daily uses the language now considered Croat/ian—as in the case of the letter to the editor—it is, unmistakably, a political statement. And in that letter the word "children" is used in two different versions: Croatian and Serbian. Furthermore, the Croatian version of the word is marked by the quotation marks, while the Serbian version is not:

> The two-day gathering of the forum of parents for the return of "children" from the JNA, which started in Sarajevo and continued in Belgrade, will be remembered as a huge farce and hypocrisy. . . . Why did the mothers not ask that the "children" from western Herzegovina and elsewhere from Bosnia abandon Tudjman's guards and the illegal terrorist military formations? . . . Did the parents in the forum not have problems with their consciences, knowing that this guard expelled thousands of frail children into the mountains?" (September 6, 17).

By using the Croatian version of the word "children" (*dijeca*) in reference to the children of parents who protested, the letter writer in *Politika* defined these children ethnically, as Croats and Muslims. By putting the word in the quotation marks, it also defined them as not being children at all, but as being Tudjman's paramilitary terrorists. Real children are defined, too: without quotation marks, and using the Serbian word (*deca*); they are defined as Serbs. Thus, while the first sentence of the letter names the perpetrators, the last sentence names the victim. In both cases, they are defined ethnically, through the use of language.

The difference between "the children" and the children established in this letter has one more consequence: the establishment of the difference between "the mothers" and the mothers. For false mothers have "children," while real mothers have children. Through these representational strategies the Serbian daily *Politika* produces for its readers the true enemy: not the pitiful, emotionally broken parent but the forceful woman full of hatred, who only pretends to be a mother. Claiming maternity only proves the viciousness of the false mothers. Nevertheless, by reading these texts, one can easily infer that there is a True Mother, somewhere, between the lines. But the Serbian daily *Politika* did not tell us where and what she is. That was done by the Serbian weekly *NIN*.

THE TRUE MOTHER

A short piece in the regular column "The Word of the Week" (mentioned in chapter 1) and an illustration were all the space given to the Wall of Love in the Serbian weekly *NIN* during the events. On September 6, 1991, the word of the week was "mothers." Besides explaining that the word has Indo-European roots, and that it is quite similar in many languages, Jovan Ćirilov, the author of the column, notes that in Latin the word "mamma" means breast. Commenting on the Wall of Love, he emphasized the dilemma of "mothers facing the fact of sending their sons to the war." As a crystallization of that dilemma, Ćirilov added to his piece an excerpt from a poem by a famous Yugoslav poet, Branko V. Radičević, "When the Mother Sends [Her Son] to the Army":

> One day, when you are grown up your mother sends you to army.
> And you never think that on the other side of the border
> is all the same: decorated train stations.
> There, too, a soldier's mother sends her son to an army.

While the gun swings on your right shoulder,
your mother marches invisible, behind you.
But look, there, on the opposite side,
behind the enemy soldier and son his mother steps. . . .
And you may wonder, but you will never know:
what hindered your hand in that moment of horror
and instead of sowing death your hand turned golden?
Night. Somewhere the wolves are terribly howling.
But someone else's mother, like a shadow, approaches you.
While she whispers her gratitude, her tears pour on your rough palm
and she kisses your hand.

In this poem there is inevitability in the act of the mother sending her son to the army, and—clearly—to the war. Mothers from both sides of the border are repeating the same somber rituals, giving up their sons, and sending their own souls after them. No alternative is presented in *NIN* to such a reality of motherhood, only submission to this inevitability. Consequently, it is the mothering-of-sons-for-war that is upheld as the True Motherhood in the Serbian weekly.

Interestingly, the alternative is presented, but it is given to the son, not to the mother. The proximity of death brings it. Nancy Huston (1982) stressed that in the war narrative, the soldiers go to the battle to become heroes. For that, they have to kill the enemy and/or to be killed. But in the poem in *NIN* something else happens. Is it mercy, or pity? It is not clear: the soldier himself does not know why he did not shoot and kill the enemy. In any case, this brings him gratitude of the survivor's mother, expressed in an age-old act of hand kissing.

The representation of this soldier is also diametrically different from the soldier images in the Croatian press. In the Croatian papers, soldiering is split into two incompatible pictures: on the one hand, the brutal and merciless JNA burning everything before it; on the other hand, innocent soldier-sons claimed by their mothers, as if these two had nothing to do with each other.[12] The impossibility of any overlap was sustained through ethnicity: the JNA generals and soldiers were defined as Serbs, the soldier-sons as Croats and Muslims. This representational strategy corresponded with the need of the newly formed country to build its own army, while fighting against another. In the Serbian papers, however, the image of the soldier grew out of a different need: the need to counter accusations linking barbarity, the JNA, Serbhood,[13] and war atrocities, as well as the need to draft new soldiers for the war. The absence of the ethnic reference to the soldier, in combination with the image of a gentle soldier who does not kill the enemy thus reconciles these two contradictory needs: the need to deny the killings of which the JNA and Serb (para-)militaries are accused, and the need to man the army.

The image of the crying mother in the poem resembles the picture of the crying mothers presented in the Croatian press, although the maternal tears that appear in the former are those of gratitude. But in both cases mothers are powerless to change the fate that befalls their sons. There is also a resemblance between the image of the True Mother in the poem and the image of the praying woman in the Croatian daily. They belong to the iconography of submission, with the kneeling in prayer symbolizing submission to God, and the hand kissing symbolizing submission to authority, as well as respect from a subordinate.[14] This means that in both images women submit themselves to the sons—the God Son, and the Soldier Son, one's own, as well as that of another woman.

The difference is that—unlike the mothers in the Croatian daily and weekly, and the false mothers in the Serbian daily—the True Mother in the Serbian weekly is not defined ethnically. One could suggest that ethnic reference is not necessarily excluded, because ethnic coordinates are already set: in the Serbian press the JNA is the army to which the mothers should submit their sons, and, as the Serbian press explicitly names Muslim and Croat "mothers" as those intent in taking their sons out of the JNA, the True Mother may also be read as the Serb mother. But one could also read the absence of ethnicity in a different way: as a (frightening) essentialism of maternal war sacrifice. Being a True Mother here means only one thing—giving your son away to soldiering and war. This essentialism is softened with the hope that the son will not kill. But the reality of the ethnic war disproved the poetry.

THE WOMAN OF BREASTS

Accompanying the column "The Word of the Week" there is an illustration by the famous Yugoslav cartoonist Jugoslav Vlahović.[15] The illustration shows the shadow image of the former Yugoslavia, with its original borders: Yugoslavia before the disintegration, with Slovenia and Croatia as integral parts of the federal state.

Whoever has learned geography and history in school will recognize the

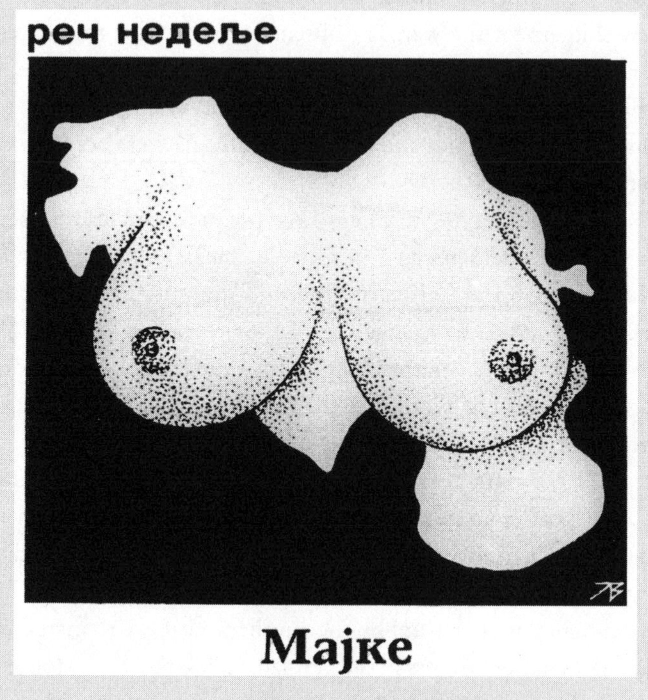

Illustration for the article "Mothers," *NIN* (Serbia), September 6, 1991, 4.

map of their country, even if the map is only a curved outline or a vague shape. That shape belongs to our intimate knowledge of the world as we learn it. Together with the range of other symbols by which we live, national symbols appeal to our emotional experience, not necessarily our cognitive selves. We do not have to think: we see and we know. Whatever emotions these symbols stir up—rage, devotion, sadness, or indifference—they belong to our intimate knowledge of the world (Billig 1995) and thus have a special power. The recognizable undulating outline of the Yugoslav borders published in the Serbian weekly *NIN*, however, had an addition: a pair of women's breasts bursting out of it.

While the text in *NIN* (September 6, 4) has a title that says "Mother" and that links the root of the word to the breasts, milk, and feeding, the illustration is not necessarily motherly. These are simply woman's breasts, as large as the country, exposed to the viewer. It is the female body, much more than the maternal body that is represented. Still, with the title in-

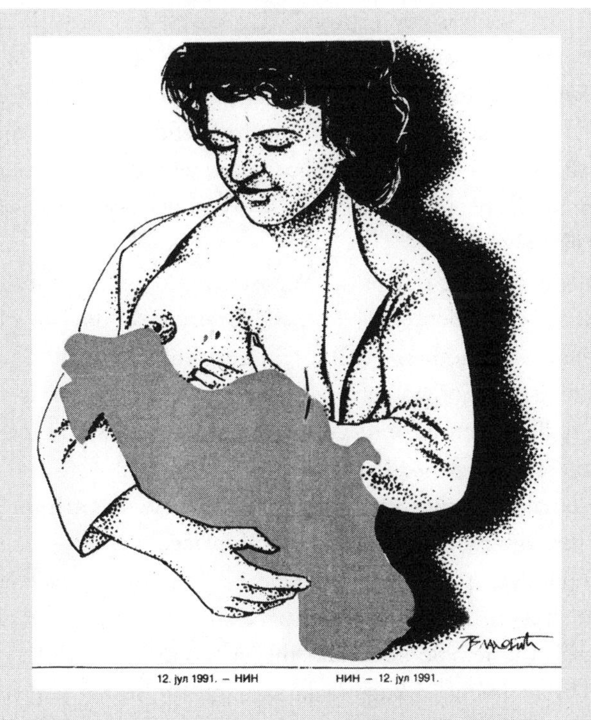

Illustration for an article on ethnic relations in Yugoslavia, "Fatal Optimism," *NIN* (Serbia), July 12, 1991, 32–33.

voking maternity, could the viewer be convinced to look at these breasts as nurturing, nursing, mothers' breasts? Another illustration by the same cartoonist that brings together the same elements—the map of Yugoslavia and the breasts—published in *NIN* a few months earlier gives a clear answer: no. The earlier illustration accompanied a piece in which the Serbs are asserted to be the only ethnic group genuinely concerned for the well-being of Yugoslavia and the fate of its different nationalities (July 12, 32–33). The July article argues that the Serbs are not interested in forcing Yugoslavia to stay as it is, one state, but that they are interested in finding a peaceful solution, if possible. Especially, a concern is expressed for the Serbs living in territories outside Serbia. The journalist urged Serbian and other political leaders to find a peaceful solution to the Yugoslav conflict. The illustration shows Yugoslavia as a baby in the hands of a nursing mother.

In every detail of this illustration—the gentleness, protectiveness, posture—the status of the motherhood is clearly confirmed. The breasts are truly maternal—only shyly exposed, half covered. The baby-Yugoslavia that covers these breasts desexualizes the female body in the illustration and makes it into maternal body, into the True Mother. Furthermore, the ethnicity of this maternal body is implicitly defined through the text, as it defines the Serbs as the only ones truly concerned for the well-being of Yugoslavia and its peoples. The others work to destroy Yugoslavia, not to nurture it like a baby.

The breasts bursting out of the Yugoslav map, on the other hand, are stripped of maternal elements—first and foremost, of the baby. If there is no baby, there is no mother. If there is no Mother, there are no Serbs either. All that is left is a pair of women's breasts, with neither maternal nor ethnic reference, spilling over the borders of a disintegrating state, pointing to one clear and present danger—the Woman.

While female sexuality was only implied in the Croatian press in the cartoons, through the representation of displaced women usurping male social and physical space (politics and streets) and using male languages, the Serbian press makes direct and explicit connection between the sexual geography of the female body and the geopolitics of the disintegrating country. The mapping of Yugoslavia through the sexual female body in the Serbian press may be different from the mapping of Croatia through the maternal body in the Croatian press. And the faceless female breasts in the September 4, 1991, issue of the Serbian weekly *NIN* may be different from the muted bodies of the politically active women in the cartoons in the Croatian daily *Vjesnik*. One thing is the same, nevertheless: the radical distinction between the maternal body, as the only one that can remap and rename the motherland, and the body of the Woman, unclaimed and unclaimable by a nation and thus potentially very dangerous.

3

TROUBLES WITH MOTHERHOOD

As Nira Yuval-Davis (1989) pointed out long ago, women are actual and symbolic reproducers of the nation. Woman's own subject position within a nation is secured (if at all) by mothering the children—or better, the sons—of or for the nation.[1] But the nation itself is produced through its multiple and diverse claiming of the maternal body and its actual as well as representational capacities; its citizenry is often secured through selective demographic policies,[2] and its territory often feminized and equated with maternal fecundity.[3] What makes motherhood, and the maternal body, so important for nationalism are, at the end, the ambiguities of the maternal body, and all the multiple roles of the real and imagined Mother in the production of the national(ist) subject that these ambiguities create.

In dramatic times of violent conflicts and wars, when the nation is perceived as threatened and its existence put to test, the maternal body as well as maternal-filial relationships acquire additional meanings. At such times, feminization of the nation and its territory may go hand in hand with naturalization and territorialization of the maternal body. In other words, the maternal body is not only the symbol of national territory through the gendered images of fertility or gentle landscapes: the maternal body is the marker, as well as the maker, of national territory. As new, maternal cartographies of the nation are delivered, motherhood ceases to be merely a metaphor, and becomes a site of discursive struggle as well as identity politics.

In the intersections of symbolic-geographical spaces and places, on the one hand, and identity politics, on the other, motherhood seems to be hijacked and the maternal body appropriated by nationalism; the maternal-filial relationship is either victimized and put in the service of othering, or militarized and put in service of (justification of) violence (Enloe 2000). This continuum and merger of victimization and militancy within specific places and spaces, and the constant repositioning of motherhood within them, produces a wide range of images of the maternal body within nationalism.

But this production is not without problems. In her study of metaphors of motherhood in India, Sandhya Shetty (1995, 56–57) uses the terms "multiple valences" and "slippage in meaning" to indicate that because of their complexity and ambiguity, feminine metaphors—and the metaphor of the Mother in particular—need to be negotiated by nationalist discourse all the time. Shetty (ibid., 56) further points out that the metaphor of motherhood "must be viewed as a representation constructed in interactive relations with several internal and external pressures." Her points proved to be true for the representation of motherhood in the Croatian and Serbian press in the period between 1987 and 1994, where complex exclusions and inclusions of ethical and ethnic attributes defined different maternal and sexualized bodies, with all their inconsistencies, contradictions, and slippages in meanings. Because of the ambiguities of feminine metaphors, nationalists do have to work hard in order to sustain clarity and transparency in their representations. And they have worked hard in the Croatian and Serbian press. It is not only the familiar notions of femininity, sexuality, and ethnicity, and their associations with power and vulnerability, that made maternal body recognizable and transparent in the images of the Whore, or the Fierce Mother, or the Woman of Breasts. It is also the submerging of these images into the gendered practices of daily lives as well as historical narratives. The symbolic capacity of the maternal body to acquire different meanings and represent different realities without any apparent contradiction may be carefully guarded through different representational strategies. But its success makes me rather skeptical toward Shetty's expectation that "textual volatility of the signifier 'mother' . . . undermines nationalist allegory from within. It is the metonymic functioning of mother in the texts . . . that breaks the back of the nationalist-patriarchal allegory" (ibid., 53). My analysis shows that nationalist discourses and practices not only utilize the representational capacities of the maternal body in ways that make complex realities transparent and intimate; they also call upon maternal politics and speak to women's political subjectivity in a way that needs to be addressed by feminists anew.

It seems that media representations and the realities in which many women actually claim their motherhood vis-à-vis ethnicity are not all that different. In other words, maternal protests in former Yugoslavia appear to employ similar discursive and geopolitical strategies as do the media representations, raising the question of the relationship between maternal agency and feminist agency. In this they are similar to other maternal protests.

In her analysis of Sri Lankan Sinhalese women, who united in a "Mothers' Front" in the early 1990s to force the government to account for their "disappeared" children, Malathi de Alwis (1999) explains how places of religious worship became powerful sites of maternal fury as well as despair, and how mothers' vulnerability and victimization (evident in public tears for the lost sons) turned into a powerful weapon—the mother's curse. At the same time the women's public association with a political party rendered them vulnerable to the accusation of being manipulated, with the further accusation that their motives in their public demonstration of grief were political, not maternal. Moreover, critics suggested, had they been good mothers to begin with, their children would not have been arrested by the state (accusations almost identical to those made in the Croatian and Serbian media toward women protestors in Yugoslavia).

While maternal public manifestations usually follow the dominant gender order by inscribing femininity in general with public outburst of emotions, and motherhood in particular with the emotional responsibility of protecting offspring, de Alwis (1999, 186) argues for the "contingent usefulness" of the Sinhalese Mothers' Front at a specific point in Sri Lankan history. She also mentions, without elaboration, what the Mothers' Front did not do at the time—it did not link with women from the north and east of the country—which in Sri Lankan symbolic geography means Tamil women—who had been organized in their own mothers' fronts since the mid-1980s, also on behalf of their—in their case Tamil—sons. At that time the Sinhalese Mothers' Front also did not have links with feminist movement in Sri Lanka. Thus, while the Sinhalese mothers had entered the space of national politics, which was previously out of their reach (by openly challenging the government and its militarism), they had still done it largely within the space of their ethnic community. Only after 2000, when peace negotiations produced longer periods without fighting, did Tamil and Sinhalese mothers of "disappeared" children start joint demonstrations.[4]

From this point of departure, one could praise the Wall of Love, as feminists from the former Yugoslavia did, for the attempt to organize a multiethnic protest from the very beginning, and for bringing together in a joint action feminist and nonfeminist women. Looking back, however, some praise seem to be misplaced, the possible "contingent usefulness" of this particular movement notwithstanding. For the question remains of the relationship between maternal and feminist political subjectivity. When and how can maternal agency be recognized as political agency in its own right? Is it only when maternal politics and feminist politics coincide, or is it also when they collide?

A comparison of feminist reactions to the Wall of Love, on the one hand, and to women's demonstrations in Kosovo in 1987, on the other, may bring some insight into what troubled feminists about the self-politicized maternal body. Feminist responses to these events may be particularly relevant due to the lack of precedents. There have been hardly any other women's public protests claiming motherhood in the post–World War Two Yugoslavia comparable in magnitude to either the occupation of the streets of Kosovo in 1987, or to the public gatherings in Zagreb and other cities during the summer of 1991. Never before, or after, had women of the former Yugoslavia expressed their views on any particular political issue so publicly, in such great numbers, and with such a clear identification with motherhood.

However, these two actions drew very different responses from Yugoslav feminists. The women's protests of the summer of 1991 were addressed and analyzed almost immediately, while the demonstrations in Kosovo in 1987 received hardly any notice, even from feminists who wrote about rapes in Kosovo and toppling of Fadil Hoxha. Furthermore, feminists assessed the maternal aspect of these two public actions completely differently, although almost identical arguments were pursued. While the women demonstrating in Kosovo were condemned as politically unenlightened and patriarchal for defining themselves as mothers, the claims of motherhood by the demonstrators of 1991 were largely celebrated as an appropriation of female agency and ultimate victory over patriarchy.

From Condemned to Celebrated Motherhood

An early feminist analysis of the women's demonstrations in Kosovo came from Slavenka Drakulić, albeit within the folds of the mainstream press rather than a feminist journal. Her article "The Use of Women" was published in the Croatian weekly *Danas* (October 27, 1987, 13–14), while the demonstrations were still going on.

Drakulić begins by saying that seeing five thousand women on the streets was like witnessing again the feminist demonstrations of the mid-1970s in some of the world's major cities. A closer look, however, revealed women with scarves, dressed in black, singing the Yugoslav national anthem and carrying banners with Cyrillic letters, reading "We give away our lives but we do not give away Kosovo." That, Drakulić says, "brings other geographical and cultural coordinates in sight," within which patriarchal culture still differentiates women as mothers and whores, as ours and theirs, or good and bad, and considers them men's property (13). In a patriarchal culture sexist statements in public are not a surprise. Drakulić reminds readers that in 1984, the students' newspaper from Zagreb University freely published explicitly sexist texts. So, she continues, Fadil Hoxha may have only said out loud what the majority of men think anyway. Furthermore, men are not the only ones who are patriarchal. Women demonstrators are too. According to Drakulić, the very fact that women use motherhood as their main reference shows that their action is as patriarchal as the insult against which they acted. Drakulić insisted that Serb and Montenegrin women were not insulted so much by the sexism of the statement but "because they were divided on prostitutes and others on a 'racist' basis" (ibid.), thus not because they were called prostitutes, but because *they* were called prostitutes, while Albanian women were not (ibid.). The whole event, therefore, had less to do with sexual insult or prostitution than with patriarchy (ibid.), on one hand, and nationalist manipulation of both Hoxha's statement and the women by the Serb nationalists (14), on the other. Manipulation of women was apparent, according to Drakulić, from the fact that the women, while apparently arguing for democracy in Kosovo, called for military rule (ibid.). Toward the end of her article, Drakulić states:

> The fury of women was used for the gathering [which] was not about women (otherwise, where are the women of other nationalities? are they not insulted too?) but about the nation; that fact changes not only the character but also the objective of the demonstrations fundamentally. Women's demonstrations are an example in which it is easy to see how deep the problems are that have only an indirect relation with women as a specific group. As in many similar situations, the so called women's question is used as an argument in a political struggle, instead of being a *political* argument of its own standing and weight. The fact that on the banners and in their speeches women claimed to be "mothers, sisters and wives"—stressing, thus, their reproductive function—indicates that the context of the demonstrations is primarily po-

> litical. This distinction may appear academic, but history shows that unless women develop their own independent integrity beyond their relationship to men, they will continue being only the weapon in other people's hands, and thus *victims*. . . . If the demonstrations were really only about "women's questions" such as rapes, sexist insult, threats, and humiliation, Albanian women from Kosovo would have probably joined. There must be one among them who was raped as well; there must be one among them who was insulted by Hoxha's words, especially if—as he insists—he did not imply Serb women only. (13–14)

The issues about nation are here explicitly defined as being *beyond* "women's questions," while women's political agency is not recognized, both because women claimed the nation, and because the protest was drawn from within women's marital and familiar social relations. Identified as manipulated victims, the women demonstrating in Kosovo were denied any further analytical relevance for feminism.

Silva Mežnarić, while analyzing rapes in Kosovo, asserts that the statement of Fadil Hoxha about rapes was used by Serb nationalists for the political end of his dismissal (1993, 123), but all she said about the women's demonstrations was that the "protests of Serbian women have been made public" (ibid., 124). An earlier essay in which Mežnarić and Jelena Zlatković (1991) discuss the discourse of rapes in Kosovo also did not mention the women's demonstrations, nor any of the events associated with Fadil Hoxha. This was rather the rule than the exception: the demonstrations of women against Hoxha's statement were either ignored by feminists or mentioned only as yet another example of women being manipulated by nationalists.

The paradox of the patriarchal nationalist manipulation analytical framework is that ethnicity and femininity are not only essentialized therein, but also mutually excluded. Drakulić clearly separated demonstrations on a "national basis" and on a "women's basis" without perceiving a possibility that, for the demonstrating women, ethnic and gender identities were mutually constitutive and not mutually exclusive, and that motherhood was a relationship to both men and ethnicity, and as such, it became a powerful political agency. For, it was precisely through motherhood that gender and ethnicity met on the streets of Kosovo in 1987. Women claimed that they were mothers of the sons of Serbia, and insulted *as such*. So, while the maternal metaphors in the Serbian press constructed the narrative of collective suffering, with rape stories being central, the banners carried by the demonstrating women constructed motherhood not only through rape, insult, and victimization, but also as a multiple site of mediation, within which women claimed a position within the nation. First, in claiming that they mothered the sons of Serbia, women asserted that without them, Serbia would never have any sons to defend it. While mediating their own access to ethnicity, they also defined themselves as crucial for men's subject position within the nation.

Second, motherhood mediated the relationship between Albanian men and Serb and Montenegrin women, defining in effect, relationships between Albanian and Serb and Montenegrin men, their own relationship to Serb and Montenegrin men, as well as the difference between them and Albanian women. In classic Orientalist manner, Albanian men are defined as rapists and as sexually overactive and in need of prostitutes. As rapists they are perceived as a challenge to the Serb and Montenegrin men; as potential users of Serb or Montenegrin prostitutes they implicitly define Albanian women as sexually inactive (or sexually unattractive), or more probably—as pronatalist nationalist discourse in Serbia would have it—too busy bearing children (Drezgić 2004). Serb men, on the other hand are defined as protectors, but at the same time implicitly accused of not performing their manly duty of protection.[5] These implicit and explicit definitions of the actors in the Kosovo drama may have been uttered through the narrative of victimization in media. However, the women's actual usurpation of the streets does not attest to victimization but rather to political subjectivity. This subjectivity may have been nationalist, and may have used the space of family and filial relations to express itself, but it needs analysis, not dismissal. Failing to recognize women's subjectivity only because it cannot be defined as clear-cut politically progressive or emancipatory results in a failure to understand very concrete relationships among gender, sexuality, and ethnicity, and their meanings for the very concrete women.

Feminist theorizing on the relationship between motherhood and ethnicity proves to be the trouble in this case. Feminists assumed that motherhood claimed *through ethnicity* necessarily produces women's victimization. As the feminist attitude toward the Wall of Love shows, claiming motherhood *beyond ethnicity* was celebrated as women's agency.

From the very beginning, Yugoslav feminists recognized the Wall of Love as a significant action. Some praised it verbally, others recognized its relevance implicitly by the simple fact that they took upon themselves the task of analyzing it. Drakulić (*Danas*, September 3, 1991, 7–9) was again first to write about the Wall of Love. In this article, she asserts that the newly emerging successor countries of former Yugoslavia had "yet to see what women are capable of" and that "despite the immediate result [this action was] in the long run the most significant political phenomenon" (9). Her praise of the significance of the action, however, is followed by an ambiguous assessment: on the one hand, the enormous interest of the media and the politicians for the mothers' actions showed that women were finally being taken seriously as a political force. On the other hand, however, "women in news usually means bad news for women," simply because no action by women was ever given such a prominence if not for the possibility that it might be "politically instrumental" (7).

The tension between women as a political force and women as instruments in other political struggles is present in Drakulić's article as a tension between women's "good intentions" and the "problem of the manipulation of mothers" (ibid.). Drakulić asserts that, despite the "good intentions," the action was taken over by men because of the formulation of the aims put forward by the mothers' movement. The first demand was that the sons be released from the JNA and allowed to serve the military in their own republics. The demand for the peace was there too, but, as Drakulić points out, "it was, not accidentally, at the bottom of the list of political demands" (ibid.). Thus, if the most important demands were to bring sons back home and to restrict military drafts to the respective republics, the question remained: are these sons going to serve divided armies in the divided country? And, indeed, are Croatian boys leaving the JNA only to fight the war against it, in the new Croatian army? Commenting on the way women defined their priorities, Drakulić states: "In such a situation the common denominator should have been only the greatest one: the peace" (9).

Searching for the answer to why mothers defined their priorities in such a way, Drakulić states that "in such a situation there are no naive people, only manipulated ones" (ibid.). The relationship between the naive and the manipulated, however, is not so clear-cut. Some years later, writing again about the Wall of Love, Drakulić (1993b, 130) actually asserts that the mothers were manipulated because they believed that their actions would avoid political manipulation and because they were politically inexperienced: "Women fell victim not only to their nationalism, but to their spontaneity, and to their lack of organization and political vision, itself a product of their alienation from politics over the past forty years" (ibid., 130).

While apparently recognizing the women's own nationalism, the emphasis is on their inexperience, which was due to exclusion from political life during socialism and its consequences for women's political agency. The same point is made by Daša Duhaček (1993). Noting how, on one occasion, women from the Wall of Love were welcomed by Franjo Tudjman and chanted slogans in his support, Duhaček concluded that "women's inclusion in political life—in historical, linear time—seem to lead to only one, closely controlled, result: . . . a woman . . . fighting like a man (!) for her nation" (ibid., 134).

The tension between something that should be a specifically women's way of doing politics, and the male, nationalist style of participation in politics, present in both Drakulić and Duhaček, is apparent in yet another analysis of the Wall of Love. Remembering her own participation in the demonstrations, Lepa Mladjenović, a radical feminist from Belgrade, spoke about the excitement felt when women from the convoy entered the military headquarters in Belgrade: "Never before in this male space had there been such a scene. In front of the auditorium, on the podium, were the 'fathers'—the army officers. In the auditorium there were women, sitting everywhere, talking and eating. . . . Women were able to subvert the traditional role of mothers and use it for fighting against authority and for saving men. . . . However, some women acted with the support of men, whose goal was their own nationalism and interest" (Hughes et al. 1995, 515–516).

The usurpation of the military headquarters—an ultimate male space—by women, produced enormous enthusiasm and hope for the success of the action on the part of feminist participants in the Wall of Love. They praised women for rejecting a "deep-rooted patriarchal model of the proud mother of the soldier son" (Nikolić-Ristanović 1996, 359). However, this feminist praise of women's subversive capacity rested on the assumption that nationalism is an exclusively male ideology, to which some women eventually succumb due to their inexperience. But, as I discuss later, in chapter 11, nationalism was soon to become a force not only *around* but *within* Yugoslav feminism. The signs that things were changing were already present.

Talking about a failed feminist conference in March 1991, Duhaček stated that feminists from Slovenia refused to form any kind of movement, even an umbrella organization, if it was "under a 'YU' sign," that feminists from Croatia were divided among themselves about the issue, and that feminist from Serbia, while critical of nationalism within their own movement, refused to react to nationalism in other feminist groups: "Ultimately, feminist groups, by yielding to the calls of their respective nations, became just a part of the mainstream course of events. Women, with some exceptions, thus recognized and respected their national interests over women's issues" (Duhaček 1993, 136).

Feminists of the former Yugoslavia would eventually recognize nationalism as part of the political subjectivity of feminists but not of women. Thus eventually, one would talk about feminist nationalists as a political position, but nationalist women would still be seen as manipulated. But, as South Asian feminists came to realize, analyzing the participation of Hindu women in the radical nationalist Hindutva politics, women's interests do not necessarily exclude nationalist interests; they are not formulated and fought for beyond nationalism, nor do they necessarily have to be formulated within the agenda of women's emancipation. The old feminist assumption that women cannot be active in right-wing political movements in any other way but as "manipulated and separated from each other in the service of a male-defined project" (Seidel 1988, 6) is increasingly seen as outdated among South Asian feminists. Anita Roy even suggests that this assumption tells more about feminism of the North—"willfully and perversely blind to the specificities of different women's experiences"—than about women on the right (1997, 261). Thus, issues concerning ethnicity, religion, nation, and nationalism *are* women's issues, and issues upon which women's political subjectivities are formed. Women from the former Yugoslavia not only took to the streets but would also take up arms between 1991 and 1995 to defend those interests as their own and would join radical right-wing political parties.

There is another point to consider here. Analyzing the Wall of Love, Andjelka Milić (1993) situated its failure within the specific and different political contexts of various Yugoslav republics. She emphasized that the authorities of the former Yugoslav republics used twofold tactics to undermine the mothers' action: a suppression of women's resistance to war, on one hand, and a transformation of the action to suit their own needs, on the other. In short, women's demonstrations were used in different republics for different political purposes: "in one for pro-Yugoslav Army propaganda and the army's protective role toward the Serbian population in Croatia; in another . . . for propagating abroad the sovereign striving of the Croatian nation; in others still . . . [to] stress the right to one's own sovereignty (as in Macedonia and Bosnia). Thus, this spontaneous protest by mothers was not only suppressed; it began to have an entirely different, unplanned effect on the troubled political scene" (119).

This brings us to militarization in relation to motherhood, as another issue that has troubled feminists in maternal politics. It also provides another clue as to why Yugoslav feminists did not recognize maternal agency in 1987, yet celebrated it in 1991.

Writing about the Wall of Love during the action, Drakulić mentions the demonstrations by women in Kosovo in 1987. She does so to stress a difference between the two women's actions: "Some years ago, women in Kosovo toppled Fadil Hoxha, or, to put it more correctly, Hoxha was toppled with the help of women (the famous case, using his statement that "all Serb women are whores"). Then, women asked to be protected by the JNA and called for military rule" (*Danas*, September 3, 1991, 7).

Women in the 1991 Wall of Love movement apparently did the opposite—they raised their voice against the JNA. The difference between the mothers of 1987 and these of 1991 seems to be that the former were manipulated and militant, while the latter, although also manipulated, were pacificist and nonmilitant. This apparent difference allowed for an outright condemnation of the former and an optimistic if cautious welcoming of the latter. But this difference is illusory, as it came about only because the anti-JNA sentiment of the mothers demonstrating during the summer of 1991 was seen by feminists as against militarism in general. However, being anti-JNA was not the same as being antimilitary in general. For the mothers of the Wall of Love did not demand that their sons demobilize. They only demanded that they be allowed to withdraw from the JNA and fulfil their military service in their own republics. The fact that this actually meant serving newly emerging national armies of the newly emerging states did not appear as a concern, maybe also because the hope for peace was still there. But, the demand for peace, as Drakulić noted, was, not accidentally, listed last in the appeal issued by the Wall of Love. The immediate concern of the mothers was to get their children safely back home. The fact that these homes were not safe any longer did not enter the equation.

Motherhood, Ethnicity, Subjectivity

The relationship between maternal politics and ethnicity stands central to the feminist recognition of women's political subjectivity in 1987 and 1991. When associated with ethnicity, motherhood was defined as patriarchal and manipulated, thus lacking in agency; women's demonstrations were defined as being based on "national issues" and dismissed. When dissociated from ethnicity motherhood was seen as a powerful, positive, feminine force with transformative potentials; women's demonstrations were defined as being based on "women's issues" and thus celebrated.

The trouble with maternity as well as ethnicity, from the feminist point of view, has to do with another factor: in the mid- and late 1980s, a majority of Yugoslav feminists considered Serbian nationalism the arch enemy, with Kosovo as its most prominent and most persistent reference. As already noted in chapter 1, Yugoslav state interventions in Kosovo against the Albanian population had been marked by police crackdowns throughout the 1980s. Solidarity with the Albanian population in most of Yugoslavia had often cast the plight of Serbs, Montenegrins, and other nationalities in Kosovo as only part of a Serbian nationalist plot, that is, as imaginary and untrue. Consequently, the analysis of how ethnicity merged with motherhood in the women's demonstrations in Kosovo, and how maternal agency was formed thereby, was precluded by the need of feminists to distance themselves from Serbian nationalism. The feminist conceptualization of nationalism at the time also contributed to such assumptions. Nationalism, like war, had been, for a long time, perceived within feminism as a male game in which women were incidental and temporary players. The scene described by Lepar Mladjenović (Hughes et al. 1995)—women sitting and eating in a military compound, under the watchful eyes of the "fathers" but still victorious in their resistance—confirms this assumption. It invokes the atmosphere of the late 1960s, the warmth of sisterhood and the hopes of unity on a "women's basis." The problem is that, for some women, that basis *includes* ethnicity. Instead of analyzing it, instead of searching for the ways that ethnicity, motherhood, and political subjectivity constituted one another, feminists decided that female subjectivity makes its presence felt only in opposition to ethnicity and, especially, nationalism.

Thus, feminist theorizing on female subjectivity in the late 1980s and early 1990s had its role too. No matter how different some streams of feminist conceptualization of agency, subjectivity, or autonomy may have been, it seems that some social and cultural roles and some positions of women are seen simply as devoid of subjectivity.[6] Seen as cultural or social dupes, some women appear only to contribute endlessly to their own subordination. In the words of a feminist who wrote about women's self-sacrifice and victimization in Serbia: "It is a well-known fact that the repression is most efficient if the victim *cooperates*" (Blagojević 1994, 475).

The question remains, however, is female agency only progressive? Or is it insignificant whether patriarchal relations are reproduced or not, and whether such reproduction (or lack of it) is done by women themselves? I would agree with Sarah Radcliffe (1993, 104) that the political meanings of gender-specific movements are not easily categorized as "progressive" or "feminist": the politics around gender as a mobilizing center for identities depends on the histories of gender relations and wider sociopolitical power relations, which vary widely from one place to another. Furthermore, I would add, gender does not operate in a vacuum, but is produced through, and implicated in other relations of power, within these wider sociopolitical relations. In the former Yugoslavia, ethnicity became a crucial mode of being and thus a privileged social relation. Excluding it from the analysis of women's lives and maternal politics only because the politics was nationalist, hardly makes sense.

Radcliffe's own analysis of the probably most famous mothers in politics—the Argentinean Madres de la Plaza de Majo—is an example of an inquiry that avoids categorization and gives instead a multilayered analysis of the different, sometimes even contradictory, discourses through which mothers demanded to have their "disappeared" children returned. The actions of the Madres de la Plaza de Majo questioned the legitimacy of the military regime and authoritarian state and redefined relationships between public and private spaces and identities, but they also brought about a tension with Argentinean feminists. Radcliffe showed that the activities of the Madres both reflected the values of Catholic cultural history and family relations, and refuted the role of the silent and suffering mother. She showed how the claims of motherhood were both contingent on the dominant definitions of femininity and innovative, producing different forms of political resistance.

Radcliffe's analysis is relevant also because she reveals the different social relations against which the Argentinian women positioned their claim of motherhood. In South Asia, faced with women's increased participation in militant Hindu nationalist movements, feminists have also started to research different contexts wherein women define their social roles, including motherhood, *within* communal identities, and not against them. Thus the image of the manipulated woman with "false" consciousness (Sarkar 1995,

210) falls too short of explaining "limited but real empowerment" (211) of these women within their communities.

Thus, if motherhood and ethnicity are to gain theoretical and political relevance for feminism, then obviously, feminists cannot afford to ignore the thousands of women on the streets, only because these women are nationalist. For nationalism speaks a language that many women not only recognize but also adopt and develop as their own. It is particularly telling that the Serbian and Croatian press used similar mechanisms of representation in linking maternity and ethnicity, while similar assumptions about maternal agency resonate in both feminist texts and in the press. These similarities, in my view, speak more loudly to the power of nationalism than to its "broken back."

PART II.

THE VICTIMIZED BODY

4

THE BODY OF ALL SERBS

This chapter and the next look closely into the different context of the media war and the ethnic war in Serbia and Croatia and analyze the narrative of collective victimhood and the significance of the victimized female body therein.

For feminism, the focus on the victimized female body is not surprising. Feminism could hardly explain its presence as political movement, were there not for the claim—and the fact—that women are victimized, not only by men but also by gendered social and cultural systems. More specifically, male physical violence against women, in war or in peace, and sexual violence in particular, have been a major field of feminist theoretical and political engagements. From Griffin (1977) to Brownmiller (1986), from Ruddick (1989) to Smith (1990) and Kelly (1996 and 2000), feminists have invested intellectual passion and emotional energy to understand and prevent the victimization of women. For nationalism, the victimized female body is equally significant. Its vulnerability, its powerlessness, and its need for protection have inspired and justified many a nationalist project.

The previous chapters have shown that the ambiguities of the female body, and the representational capacities that grow out of these ambiguities, produce numerous possibilities for nationalism to claim and appropriate the female body. Nevertheless, the story about the victimized female body is hardly ever straightforward. It is dependent on specific political strategies as much as on particular patterns of representations. Differences and similarities in the Serbian and Croatian media show this clearly: although gendered assumptions form the basis for definitions of the victim in both media, there is still considerable representational work to be done, in order to produce specific narratives of victimhood that make sense in the context of the media war as much as in the context of the ethnic war. Thus the victim in the Serbian media and the victim in the Croatian media—while using similar representational strategies—are never the same. This is particularly so when the victim stands for the ethnic Self. While ultimately represented through the female body, the victimized Self in Serbian and Croatian media are very different. In the Serbian media, it is the Serbs—the ethnic group. In the Croatian media, it is not the Croats, the ethnic group, but Croatia—the nation-state. This difference is due to the specific—and different—contexts of the media war and the ethnic war operating in Croatia and Serbia.

In Serbia, the media war functioned in the context of the denial of any responsibility for the ethnic war. This denial was sustained through the narrative of Serb victimization—a narrative rather paradoxical and difficult to understand from the outside. Many families from Serbia have kin among the different ethnic groups in Bosnia and Croatia. Many Serbian citizens had also been housing refugees from Bosnia and Croatia, sharing with them their ever more meager portions of food. Thus, one would assume that facts about atrocities committed by, and committed against, the Serb population in Bosnia and Croatia would be equally familiar to the Serbs. However, while the suffering of Muslim and Croat refugees housed in Serbia would be acknowledged on individual level (if for no other reason than to show how charitable the Serbs in Serbia are), on the collective level the Serbian press would invariably focus on the Serbs as the ultimate victims of the war.

There are at least two reasons why this narrative was rather easy to produce and rather difficult to resist. First, it had already been a common feature of Serbian nationalist and cultural politics regarding Kosovo since the mid-1980s. The fact that political elites and media in other Yugoslav republics largely ignored the plight of Serb population in Kosovo through the 1980s was seen replicated in the fact that international political elites and media largely ignored the plight of Serb population in Bosnia and Croatia in the early 1990s, sustaining a "whole world against us" discourse. Second, and probably more important, the war was not fought on Serbian soil, but its effects were nevertheless felt in Serbia, and this fact made it easier for the press to ignore violence committed by the JNA and the paramilitaries (from Serbia as well as from Bosnia and Croatia), and focus on the victimization of the Serb population in Serbia as well as in Bosnia and Croatia. Within Serbia, the large majority of the population had fallen victim to the economic and social effects of the wars in Bosnia and Croatia. Overwhelming economic deprivation was widespread in the early 1990s, hitting hardest in the winter months of 1993–1994. That was the time when industrial production all but stopped, unemployment exploded, hyperinflation reached a four-digit peak, with prices of goods changing hourly, and monthly salaries worth only two kilos of bread and a pack of cigarettes. A huge proportion of the Serbian population lived below the poverty line.[1] Enormous energy was necessary just to survive from day to day, with constant reorganizing and redefining of daily life and continuous renegotiation of its meaning.

It was the combination of the decade-long media war and this political isolation and economic and social breakdown that created conditions within which the narrative of victimization made sense to many people within Serbia, regardless of whether they actually supported the Serbian politics of war, or then president Slobodan Milosević. There was, of course, a segment of the population that rejected and actively resisted the discourse of victimization. Feminist groups and political opposition parties were most prominent among them. In Belgrade, Women in Black specifically pointed to the war crimes committed by the Serb forces in their weekly vigils in the city center.[2] There were massive demonstrations against Milosević and his politics of war in March 1991 in Belgrade (before the war broke out), which were violently suppressed. There were also mass demonstrations in Belgrade against shelling of Sarajevo in 1992, with slogans such as "Slobo, Sadame," equating Milosević to Saddam Hussein.[3] These demonstrators obviously acknowledged and condemned Serbian involvement in the wars. However, in the mainstream media—both in the serious press and in the tabloids—Serb victimhood continued to be a prominent theme throughout the 1990s.

Tabloids had a rather specific take on Serb victimhood, compared to the serious press. Unlike the serious press—the Serbian daily *Politika* and the weekly *NIN*, for example, which were analyzed in the previous chapters—tabloids in general highlight the topic of sex, in stories about money, family dramas, celebrity lives, or crime. This is their daily bread in any time. Necessarily, the female body stands central to these stories. As this chapter will show, with the war, these stories do not disappear—they only get a different edge, as stories about war are told as stories about sex.

In February 1994 one such story appeared in issue 520 of the Serbian weekly tabloid *Duga* (Rainbow), which at the time styled itself "the vanguard of Serbian democracy" (February 5–18, 1). *Duga* often engaged in glorifying Serb nationalist myths using explicitly sexist, and often vulgar, language. In many columns, male and female sexuality was taken as the dividing line in defining the Self and the Other ethnically, with Serbs, Muslims and Croats being attributed different sexual practices, capacities, and performances. And if in time of peace male and female bodies were little more than sexual objects in *Duga*, in wartime these bodies were not only objectified but also ethnicized, with the bodies of Serb women, or women who could be claimed to be Serbs, appearing as victimized and exploited sexually by the ethnic others. Thus, if the sexualization of war denied war violence, the ethnicization and objectification of the sexual female body produced again Serb victimhood. So, while the war became something else—no longer a frightening, consuming violence that destroys towns and villages, maims and kills people, and forces them to flee, but something familiar, something one can relate to intimately—it is precisely this familiarity and intimacy that helped create Serb victimhood.

Voices and Frames of the Two Wars

The article in *Duga* had an intriguing title: "Little Eagles for 'Those Things.'"[4] It refers to a nickname for the German currency—the deutsche mark coin, which features an eagle—and an everyday expression for sex, "those things" (*one stvari*).

The story fills four pages of *Duga*: one with photos, another three with text. A panoramic photo of Sarajevo covers one whole page, with two smaller inserted photos of wrecked cars. The text has three parts: a short introduction, an even shorter conclusion, and the five-column main section. This main section of the article is, according to the article's author, an authentic transcript of a talk show on a Sarajevo local radio station, Radio Zid (Radio Wall), established in a Muslim-controlled part of Sarajevo during the war. The talk show transcribed in *Duga* had a theme—"those things"—and a special guest, a young woman from Sarajevo who was a student before the war, but who had started working as a prostitute when war broke out. Her pseudonym was Vanja—an interesting name that can be both male and female, and it is associated with both Serbs and Croats, but not with Muslims.

Listeners called to ask Vanja various questions about "those things." In the conversation the issues of prostitution, money, and sexual morality were discussed in relation to the fighting and fighters, problems of everyday life in besieged Sarajevo, and hopes and worries about the future. The conversation was at times grim, at times playful. One recurrent topic was whether Vanja supported the Bosnian government troops, either with money or services. Another was whether the listeners could profit from Vanja's profession. They offered themselves as customers, pimps, or colleagues.

On first reading, the article appears to be just another tabloid story about sex and war, basically in bad taste, sexist, and patronizing, as usual. Still, when I read it, I found it somehow both compelling and puzzling. There was something in there that, somehow, did not "fit." I was puzzled that the panorama of Sarajevo, covering the facing page, was a peacetime photo. As I reread the article, I started wondering what a transcript of a talk show in Sarajevo was doing in an article in a Belgrade-based tabloid. I could not know whether the transcript was original, or whether the talk show had ever existed, but the structure and the dynamics of the conversation appeared highly probable and true to life. Nevertheless, the text appeared as a strange puzzle of places and perspectives that created both the distance and proximity of the war and the ethnically defined protagonists.

To resolve the puzzle, I first had to analyze separately the talk show transcript and the pieces of text (the introduction and conclusion) that frame it. Only after approaching the two as different but related frames, did I bring them back together and look at how they produced the reality of war in Bosnia for the readers in Serbia. The concept of framing, as it was originally used in photography, means that something is present in the photo while something else is excluded, and that the camera has a particular angle. As it entered anthropology, literary studies, and the arts, the concept is used to unpack mechanisms of normalization and foreclosing, in "political, social, historic, economic, aesthetic" and other "fields that traffic in transparency and truth" (Spyer 2001, 182).[5] The concept is useful in the analysis of normalizing representational modes, because the framed view is presented as an equivalent of reality (Taylor 1991) and the frame serves to mark the boundaries of inclusions and exclusions; in the *Duga* article, for example, many—apparently convergent—realities seemed framed together: Sarajevo and Belgrade, war and peace, sex and survival.

The First Frame: The Talk Show and the Voices from Sarajevo

The talk show focuses on Vanja, who works as a prostitute in Sarajevo because she "simply needed money." Concerned about the morality of the job, she keeps it secret from her family and friends, and she and a female friend with whom she works make it more acceptable by being selective about their customers: "We thought that it is not so terrible if it is done under certain conditions, with certain customers. We try to keep it that way, to work only with selected men." Worries about the morality of her job are so dominant that she is thinking of leaving Sarajevo: "Something tells me that I should go away from here, that it will make me feel much safer morally. . . . What I do has not been discovered up to now, but it will be tomorrow. This is a small city. And how can I face people then?"

Vanja feels uncomfortable with her profession, and she insists on making a sharp difference between what she does and who she is. She struggles to defend her own definition of herself, against the listeners and the program's host. But throughout the conversation both listeners and the host consistently disregard her attempts to distance herself from her profession. Many callers make jokes about her, and the transcript has the phrase "laughter in studio," several times. There are two striking instances in which Vanja is drawn back into "being a prostitute." First, during her conversation with the host, Vanja explains that she will try to leave Sarajevo before the end of the war to finish her engineering course and find a job: "I want to use the knowledge I have gained so far, except, of course, what I am doing now. That is never, ever to be considered again." The host's reply is: "Is there any work these days?" While she struggles to explain that prostitution is only an episode in her life as a student, he repositions her as a prostitute. Just after this exchange, one of the male listeners calls in and a similar repositioning occurs:

Caller: Milan [non-Muslim male name] calling. Vanja knows me. I respect what she is doing and I wish to ask her, would she accept my offer to be her pimp when she leaves the city?

Vanja: No, not yours nor anybody's, because, as I said already, I do not intend to do this once I am out, nor ever again.

Caller: Do you really think that this—what you are doing now—is your life?

Vanja: No, I do not think that this is my life. Far from it.

Unlike Vanja, who maintains consistently that her job is morally bad, whatever the circumstances, most of the callers take a different perspective. When identifying her as a prostitute, many expressed the opinion that hers was a normal job, like any other. Others were not concerned so much with the morality of prostitution, but with the women who did it. But their concept of morality was linked to the war, and not to the sex for money:

Caller: Good evening, Munib [Muslim male name] speaking. I am a butcher from Hrasnica. I would like to ask Vanja what does she think of the colleagues in her profession who left us in these difficult times and went to the aggressor.

Vanja: Nothing.

Caller: Aren't they really disgusting? Should they be allowed to come back here at all after the war?

Vanja: Why not? It's all the same.

Caller: Let me ask you, I could come through the tunnel [under the Sarajevo airport] if we can agree. I see that you are the right person for me.

Vanja: How do you see it?

Caller: Simple, I have been dealing with your kind before and I see that for you it is really only a job that comes out of need, and that you are a woman of character. But those others who went over to aggressor's side, well. . . .

Vanja: All right, if you think so. . . .

Caller: What? Imagine, they slept with Ljuban [non-Muslim male name], and then to come here, and I have not had electricity for two years. No way!

So, although this caller excludes Vanja from the questionable morality of the others "of her kind," he defines the moral perspective from which she will be judged—her attitudes toward the parties involved in the war. Other callers take a step further. They question Vanja directly about her own attitudes and, unlike Munib, judge her negatively:

Caller: I would like to ask whether there is any reduction in price for members of the Bosnian Army? [*Everybody in the studio laughs*]

Host: You are appealing to her patriotism.

Vanja: No, no, there isn't really any reduction.

Caller: But there should be, even if just a little bit, for people who defend this city, this country.

Vanja: And why do you think I am doing this?

Caller: I know why do you do it, but still you should find some time to give it with reduction.[6]

While this caller only asked for reduction in price, others requested a financial contribution:

Caller 1: I would like to ask the lady if she is paying a contribution to the Bosnian armed forces.

Vanja: [*laughing*] No, this lady is not paying anything.

Caller 1: How come you don't? When I see how much you charge, well, this is a value of one gun, of a "zolja" [nickname for a type of gun] for me. You should help a bit. Considering how much you work, we could all be getting good ammunition. So not everything is against us, poor Muslims. It would even things out.

Caller 2: Think of paying some financial contribution to the armed forces.

The advice is not always as polite, and aggression is sometimes expressed openly, as in the following dialogue:

Caller: I have some advice for our Vanja. I think that she shouldn't give her hen[7] to UNPROFOR[8] men, let their balls dry, they should fuck their mother. Give it to our poor men, for coupons,[9] too.

Vanja: It is not possible for coupons.

Caller: There are no German marks now, fuck it. Give a bit to the fighters, and they'll be sharper, too.

The frustration at how Vanja practices her profession has financial motives: she asks for foreign currency, she offers no reductions, and she only takes cash, in a situation when few people have any cash, let alone foreign currency. But the real source of aggression is patriotic: she does not help "the cause." For there are those who do. One woman caller states this explicitly:

Caller: Due to the force of circumstances, I have also started doing this job, now, in this war. But I help the soldiers, and everybody, and I will be able to look in everybody's eyes tomorrow with a clear conscience.

Host: Oh, you are colleagues!

Thus, Vanja is judged morally bad by listeners not because she is a prostitute but because she does not help the soldiers, whose fighting eagerness ("sharpness," as one caller named it) is presumed to be linked to their sexual satisfaction. So, while soldiering and virility are clearly linked, and the success of the "us" against "them" is conditioned by this link, Vanja appears not to even acknowledge the difference between "us" and "them." For her "it's all the same."

Nevertheless, she is there, in the studio, and many callers hope to profit from this. Milan was only the first who attempted to profit as a pimp. Other men also called in with offers to be pimps, or clients, or to ask Vanja again to consider financial or other contributions to the armed forces. The only caller who did not ask anything from Vanja was another woman, who talked about the slim prospects for jobs in Western Europe, where Vanja wanted to go, and chatted with the host about her own life. At one point, the host asks her whether she is happy:

> *Caller*: I am, as much as one can be in Sarajevo.
>
> *Host*: Vanja told me, before this official part, that she was very unhappy in love, that she has had a lot of disappointments. She doesn't believe she could fall in love again.
>
> *Caller*: Listen, I do not believe that this could have been a reason to start doing this job. After her job, if it is discovered, I do not believe she will ever be happy in love, at least not in Sarajevo, or Bosnia.
>
> *Host*: Well, she doesn't see any prospects here, anyway. . . .
>
> *Caller*: This pessimism is really not what we need tonight in this city.

There are male callers who share this desire to be less pessimistic. One calls in with the following question:

> *Caller*: May I ask if there is going to be a quiz, so that one who wins can . . .

The implication is clear, Vanja will be the prize. The host explains that Vanja would not allow such a quiz, but adds that it would cost money and, anyway, he would win because he would know the answer to the quiz question. Throughout the transcript, the issue of a quiz is repeated by callers, each time with a bit more enthusiasm. Callers offer to collect money or look for a sponsor. The gradual change of the tone—from a question whether there could be a quiz to the assertion that there is one—makes everything else seems irrelevant: who Vanja is or what she does, her attitude toward soldiers, her looks, described in detail earlier in the show. For men who want a prize—both the host and the male callers—the only relevant things seem to be sex and fun. Thus the connection of sex with soldiers and money turns into a connection between sex and fun.

In the transcript, the talk show speaks through different voices, representing different sexual and war moralities. Vanja's voice is strong and consistent in its view that prostitution is always morally bad, whatever the circumstances. War does not change this a bit. Her strategy is to distance herself from her profession. In doing so, Vanja also refuses to acknowledge the war, which she only ever refers to as "circumstances." She thinks nothing of "her colleagues" who went to the "aggressor's side," because she recognizes neither colleagues nor aggressors. She does not contribute to the armed forces because she recognizes only clients with hard currency. She has problems with water and electricity like everybody else, but she still "has her bath regularly," as she states at one point.

Thus apparently nothing connects Vanja with the war, despite the undeniable fact that the war made her choose prostitution as a job. And still, while the war is never there in Vanja's words, its presence is assumed in the fact that Vanja will have to leave the city in which she was born and start somewhere else, in order to provide continuity with her prewar, preprostitution life, with her true self: a twenty-four-year-old engineering student. What she learned in war (prostitution) is knowledge never to be used again. In Vanja's voice, war and prostitution belong to the same, hidden experience that appears only in traces, in her struggle to dissociate who she is from what she does, and her reasons for doing it. She still lives following the rules of the peacetime sexual morality and peacetime ethnic morality, as she refuses to divide people into friends and aggressors.

The male callers speak with a different voice. They link sexual morality and war, in that they do not question the morality of prostitution, but only Vanja's attitude to the warring parties. In defense of the people, of the city, everybody should help "the cause" of Bosnia's war, prostitutes included. For these callers, the war and prostitution are public affairs, linked within the same moral order, in need of public intervention and control, set within different coordinates of good and bad from Vanja's. These coordinates (unlike Vanja's) also define an ethnic order, asserting the ethnicity of the good (the Bosnian army and "poor Muslims"), as much as of the bad ("aggressors," UNPROFOR, Serbs represented by the caller Ljuban).

The word "war," however, does not occur in the transcript, even though there is talk about problems with water, power supply, and food, and about fighters and aggressors. Furthermore, the talk show as a whole generates humor, with a lot of laughter indicated in the studio. Thus, war is constantly pushed aside and sex, money, and fun are brought forward. The most explicit suppression of talk about the war is voiced in the caller's statement "This pessimism is really not what we need tonight in this city." The men who call for the quiz could not agree more. Their own denial of war is total: all they wanted to talk about was the female body for sex and fun.

Sex and money acquire one unexpected twist, though, through the voice of a Muslim man whose interest is different from all other callers. For he wanted to be neither a pimp nor a client. He wanted to be a prostitute himself:

> *Caller*: Greetings from Tanović Ergin [Muslim male name]. . . . This oldest profession is not very prosperous here in Bosnia, you know how it is viewed. I am interested in Vanja's opinion whether I, as a male, could do the kind of job that she is doing?
>
> *Vanja*: You could . . .
>
> *Caller*: Then let me suggest an arrangement. You are interested in powerful men, I've got them. I am interested in powerful women, but I do not mind men either. Could we, say, make a deal? I will, here, publicly leave my phone number: 440-741. So, there it is—Tanović Ergin at your service. You know what it is about, it's winter, food supplies are needed, heating, etc. . . .
>
> *Host*: That's good, that's good.
>
> *Vanja*: That's it!

Taboos about male prostitution and male homosexuality have remained very strong throughout ex-Yugoslavia. Only in Slovenia (and to a much lesser extent in Croatia) has homosexuality been a part of an alternative public scene while staying out of mainstream public debate. In Serbia, male homosexuality entered the public arena when the war started, as a label used to condemn men who refused to take part in the war. They were called "mummy's boys," "sissies," "women," and *pederi* (pederasts). Female prostitution usually appeared in police crime reports or in health scare stories stirred by AIDS. Although the topic of female prostitution seldom appeared even in tabloids, its existence was officially acknowledged. Male prostitution, on the other hand, was totally absent from the public arena throughout former Yugoslavia and its existence was simply never admitted. Thus, with the character of Tanović Ergin—a Muslim man—the *Duga* article simultaneously breaks two taboos: male homosexuality, for sale.

The Second Frame: The Text and the Voices from Serbia

The talk show transcript in *Duga* was the main body of the article, accompanied by a two-column introduction and one short concluding column. Together with the photos, these columns framed the talk show in Sarajevo for the readers in Serbia. The transcript never uses the word "war," but war is in this article's opening sentence:

> Zlaja [non-Muslim male nickname] is one of my prewar friends. . . . [A] lucky thing for Zlaja is that he was, and remains even in the war—a nonsmoker. "I always have cigarettes, I get them in my regular supplies," he said. "Otherwise, it is difficult to get them. Only for a hell lot of [German] marks. And there are so many girl smokers. The supplies are gone, the marks are gone. So we meet in a tavern, just like ordinary neighbors, for no apparent reason. I take a few boxes of cigarettes with me and 'those things' are quickly done. . . . Until the next exchange."

The war referred to in this opening paragraph of the article brings unexpected sexual advantages to some men. The war in Bosnia, according to the article, has produced relaxed attitudes to sex among the inhabitants of Sarajevo, named as a "new empire of sex." International media reports are quoted as saying that "sex became almost the only pleasure in the grim, wartorn, everyday life" of its inhabitants. It is asserted that "in wartime [sex is] even looser than in normal circumstances." Then the radio talk show transcript is introduced, quoting the host's assertion that "in male-female relations in Sarajevo there are, on average, 23 (!) members of the fairer sex to every man." The text continues:

> One lad quickly calls in: "So where are my 23? I haven't been able to get even one during the whole war." "There are those who can, nevertheless," the host answers him, and after a curse that comes as a reply from the caller, he is off the hook.
>
> Despite this almost unreal quantitative ratio between the fairer sex and the stronger sex in Sarajevo, the city's officials don't hide the fact that prostitution is flourishing in the city, especially among high school girls and unemployed women who took to the oldest profession while their husbands are at the front, says Smajo Karačić [Muslim male name], the head of the Criminal Prevention Office in Izetbegović's [then president of Bosnia, Muslim man] Internal Affairs Department.

At that point, a new subhead is introduced in the article and the transcript of the talk show follows. The discontinuity of the two parts of the article—the introductory columns and the transcript—seems striking. From a story about the ratio of twenty-three women to one man, the text shifts into one about the many men of one woman—Vanja. The "empire of loose sex" turns into an empire of "little eagles."

Following the talk show transcript comes a short concluding paragraph with the subhead "Drowned in Sarajevo's Swelling Stream of Destinies," in which a moving empathy is shown for Vanja:

> After night fell, heavy as lead, Vanja was at her workplace, probably until daybreak, drowned in Sarajevo's swelling stream of destinies. Or maybe . . . she met her piece of shrapnel or the bullet of death. Maybe some of the callers looked for her at the reception of her hotel. . . . Or, huddled in a corner of a UN transport plane, hiding among the tins of corned beef, she left this claustrophobic city. . . . For her, the next day means happiness if it is the same as yesterday, or five, or ten days ago.

Since the transcript ends with jokes about the quiz, the concluding column shows a distinct change of a tone, providing clues to why a transcript of a talk show in Sarajevo was published in a tabloid in Serbia. For, it brings to mind a question: whether empathy would have been displayed if the woman, instead of being called Vanja, had a Muslim name. And, indeed, whether there would have been any article at all.

Readers in Serbia do not even have to ask themselves these questions, because the ethnic names of the actors in the talk show drama create images in which certain things are simply taken for granted. It is assumed that one is ethnically recognizable and definable through one's name. Names become markers of one's ethnic belonging—such powerful markers that people who, for whatever reason, want to dissociate themselves from their assumed ethnic background deliberately take names (often foreign) that reveal no specific ethnicity. Some young parents who came as refugees to Germany and the Netherlands used this strategy.[10] Conversely, many boys born in the former Yugoslavia during the mid-1980s—a peak of nationalism of the time—bear the names of Croatian and Serbian mythical national heroes. Thus, the non-Muslim name Vanja makes sense in the text in *Duga* precisely because it implies—without any need for explication—that Vanja is not a Muslim woman. As an antiheroine whose sad fate calls for empathy among readers in Serbia, Vanja cannot be a Muslim woman. And if we look at the text in *Duga* as a production of difference between Muslims and Serbs, then clearly, Vanja can only be a Serb woman. Looking at naming of the protagonists in the article sustains this argument. The names of the participants in the talk show assert the existence of two different moralities, for two different ethnicities, both of them gendered: Muslim-named men and a non-Muslim named woman. The former accept prostitution but question the morality of a prostitute, offer themselves as homosexual prostitutes, and demand woman's services, money, or support. The latter refuses to call herself a prostitute, rejects prostitution as immoral, keeps her peacetime identity as a student alive, and struggles against a double Muslim aggression: war *and* sexual exploitation.

The juxtaposition of the ethnically named protagonists has to be placed in the context of the ethnic war in Bosnia. In early 1994, when this article was published, the knowledge that rape was a war strategy had already become public (as of summer 1992), and Serb men had been explicitly accused of systematically raping Muslim women. While I will go into issues of "ethnic cleansing" and rape as war strategy later, it is important to note here that these strategies were based on assumptions that link certain territories to certain ethnic groups. The territories were defined ethnically, as Serb, Muslim, or Croat lands, and the people defined as Serbs, Muslims, and Croats were seen as the only rightful inhabitants of these lands: Serbs in Serbia, Croats in Croatia; while Bosnia was already divided in different parts, controlled by either Serb, Muslim, or Croat forces. The expulsion of all those defined as ethnically Other from these territories went hand in hand with the silencing, marginalizing, or harassing of those who stayed. This ethnic geography, present in the ethnic names of the territories, did not always reflect the actual composition of the local population, but rather, indicated the *claim* on the given land. It is this claim that is important in the representational practice of the media. Sarajevo was divided into the Muslim-ruled and Serb-ruled zones, although Serbs, Muslims, and Croats, and many other nationalities, lived on both sides of the divide. However, because there was no Croat claim on Sarajevo—the way there was an explicit claim on it by Serb and Muslim nationalists—being a Croat in the city was inconsequential and irrelevant for the media representations. As far as *Duga* was concerned, only Serbs and Muslims lived in Sarajevo. This made Muslims the main enemies of Serbs in Bosnia. And this made Vanja a Serb woman. Her Serbhood was, furthermore, not just a local ethnic reference (for she could have had a local name then). Familiar from classical Russian novels, her name carries a broader reference that encompasses Orthodox religion as well as Slavic roots. This created a huge distance between her and the Muslim men in the talk show.

The distance can be recognized in the symbolic role played by the only male caller who had a non-Muslim name—Milan. At the first sight he is no different from others: in offering to be Vanja's pimp in the future he also does not take seriously her assertion that she is not a prostitute but only works as one. But there is one significant difference between him and all other callers: he is the only one who says that he knows Vanja personally. This claim of familiarity, in which, from among all these men, a non-Muslim woman is known personally only by a non-Muslim man, is no coincidence. It negates the idea of a common life in a shared territory and asserts the existence of ethnic seclusion. The life in which Muslims will know only Muslims and Serbs only Serbs is not only a future ideal here, but rather, it is represented as the reality in which the Serbs in Sarajevo are already living. Once this assumption is accepted, it is much easier to accept the idea that the city and its people can be split in two.

Finally, naming Sarajevo an "empire of sex" and making the sex the focus, has direct bearing on the representation of the war. The mention of "problems" with water, food, and electricity is not specific to the war. In Serbia the vast majority of people were at the time facing similar problems. They, of course, knew that there is war going on "there." But reading *Duga*, they may have wondered. The war is obscured from *Duga*'s readers, and yet made to appear tragic only from one perspective—Vanja's. There are no signs of war as destruction or as collective tragedy. The photo that accompanies the text shows Sarajevo in peacetime: white buildings, red roofs, green trees. The two small photos inserted at the bottom of the big one both show wrecked cars on the street, with people in the background. But they could be from any city in the world. By looking at these pictures we cannot possibly conclude that there is a war going on in Sarajevo.

As John Taylor (1991, 8) has said, below the horizon of the reportable war lay the never-reported-news, the news that clashes with the presented picture. In the context of the media war and ethnic war that I have been describing, the photos in *Duga* produce the reportable news because they partake in power that produces a particular reality: the reality of a nonwar in Bosnia. For both the transcript of the talk show and the article as a whole obscure the war by focusing on sex. And sex is represented as either being fun and business (or both), or being an exploitation of a Serb woman by Muslim men. The reversal of the accusations of sexual violence by Serb men against Muslim women is thus complete.

If there is no war, there cannot be any responsibility for it either. One individual Serb woman's "destiny" does not call for responsibility about the war but for the empathy with the "drowned"—this single woman, or all the other Serbs in Bosnia.

A Twice-Told Tale of War and Body Politics

The article in *Duga* mourns Serb victims, while rejecting any Serbian responsibility for the war.

For many readers in Serbia the story about this war-which-is-not-a-war, told through the life of a prostitute-who-is-not-a-prostitute has manifold, albeit ambiguous effects. To know about the effects of war, without seeing explicit evidence of it through their own windows, may be very recognizable to them. To read about a woman who finds herself in a place where she would rather not be, may feel familiar. A story of underlying moral purity untainted by the immoral job one has may reflect convictions about the readers' personal situations, as they go into the black economy in order to survive, as they find themselves buying cheap cars plundered from Bosnian towns, pretending not to know where these come from, or as they listen to their politicians telling them that every war is bloody but that Serbian lands simply have to be defended, if history is not to repeat itself.

Yet there is ambiguity in this representation that obscures the war while acknowledging its effects. For the empathetic concluding paragraph of the *Duga* article clearly names the victim. If there is a victim, there must be a war. But the only acknowledgeable war in the article is the war against the Serbs. Vanja is a metaphor of Serb victimization, her life is upheld as a reflection of the daily life in Serbia, the narrative of Serb victimization; humiliating and hopeless it may be, but it is pure, for what she does is not who she is.

This separation of doing and being as a strategy of giving sense to one's life, both individually and collectively, is also described by Ivana Maček (2001 and 2004) in her research of wartime life in Sarajevo. She describes "three utterly different moralities" (2004, 72): "civilian," "soldier" and "deserter." These are not descriptive but analytical categories, reflecting perceptions of war and ethical attitudes toward it. The first is in a sense a denial that uses opposites such as "war" and "peace" and "us" and "them" to make sense of it, and perceives the war as something far, happening to "'others' in time or 'others' in space" (Maček 2001, 199). The "soldier" mode is one of acceptance of war and the legitimization of violence as inevitable but exclusively linked to war, implying that "what one did (or does) does not make one a different person. It is understood that this mode of living shall end with the ending of war" (ibid., 204). This mode differentiates between the warring parties and their aims and methods and also sees war as a contest. The "deserter" mode accepts ambiguities of both peace and war, as well as one's own responsibilities therein (ibid., 211). All three modes can be found in personal narratives, but Maček states that unlike the other two, the "soldier" ethic of war is present in public and political narratives, from school texts and the media to official political statements.

While Maček's categorization is derived from empirical research in Sarajevo, the text in *Duga* indicates its applicability also to Serbia. In February 1994, when the article in *Duga* was published, people in Serbia had lived already for year and a half with mounting accusations that Serb forces were the principal perpetrators of ethnic cleansing and war rapes in Bosnia. At first, they had argued their innocence, dismissing the accusations; then they had justified the crimes as an inevitable part of war, or by equating the guilty parties. Doing one thing (waging war) and being something else (the ultimate victim) is thus a great discursive solution for normalizing war, and Vanja's life is thus a perfect metaphor.

The representational strategy that normalized war and produced ethnicity through gendered and sexualized images of the victim in *Duga* drew directly on the body politics. Vanja always has a name and ethnicity: her body is not only female but also a body of a Serb woman. Female and ethnic at the same time—this body is a site upon which the normalizing and victimizing practices of the media war are as fierce as the violent practices of the ethnic war. Both symbolic and utterly physical, these practices rely on representational capacity of the female body to integrate individual experience with larger social meanings. In nationalist discourses in Serbia, it is an experience of the Serb victimization and the meaning of it. Vanja can embody these meanings for yet another reason: her name carries yet another symbolic significance. It is not a gender-specific name, but is both male and female. With her female body and a potentially male name, Vanja is the name and the body of all Serbs.

5

ALL THE BODIES OF CROATIA

While in the Serbian media the female body supported production of the Serbs as a collective victim of the war, in the Croatian media, the female body was crucial in producing Croatia as the ultimate victimized Self. The reasons for this striking difference lie in the different contexts within which the media war and the ethnic war operated in Serbia and Croatia.

The media war in Serbia had to seek its legitimacy in the people, not in the state, because the state of socialist Yugoslavia, which Serbia supported, had disintegrated and was consequently delegitimized, both from within (by its constitutive units, which demanded secession) and from outside (by the international community, which condemned the military force used by that state to preserve its unity). The newly named Federal Republic of Yugoslavia (consisting of Serbia and Montenegro) initially had no international recognition and lacked legitimacy. At the same time, the media war in Serbia had already focused on the people and their suffering in Kosovo, through the discourses of the "history of ethnic hatred"[1] against the Serbs in many previous conflicts and wars. These historical references, together with the actual political situation of disintegration of Yugoslavia, defined parameters within which the collective Victim could be produced and could claim its legitimacy. With the state(s) delegitimized, the only source of legitimacy for the media war was the people.

In Croatia, the political situation was quite different. The media war and the ethnic war there made the establishment of an independent state their objective. Few were the speeches of the first president of independent Croatia, Franjo Tudjman, in which the "centuries-old dreams of Croatian statehood" were not mentioned. Thus, in its media war, the ethnic war was largely defined not as a war against Croats, but as a war against Croatia. In 1992 Croatian statehood was recognized internationally, providing legitimacy not only for the defense of the borders of this state, but also for claiming its symbolic victimhood. But this symbolic victimhood of the state came about long before it was officially recognized internationally.

The existing borders of the former Yugoslav Republic were seen as more or less the borders of the new state by the media, and the state itself was seen, and referred to, as a woman. As such, Croatia had many different embodiments, each produced to symbolize a particular aspect of the ethnic war.

The Abandoned Body: The World and the Victim

On August 11, 1991 (1), *Vjesnik* published a cartoon by its regular cartoonist, Oto Reisinger. It was the summer of fierce fighting between JNA and Croatian forces in eastern Slavonia and Krajina. Croatian cities and villages were being destroyed, while mothers started organizing in the Wall of Love, protesting against the military draft of their sons into the war. On the international level, negotiations went on and on, with an endless stream of European Union and United Nations envoys being sent for talks with the political leadership of the countries in the war. The cartoon in *Vjesnik* mocks one of these efforts (by three representatives of the E.U., nicknamed the "troika") by pointing out the uneven power relations of the warring parties. The cartoon shows a firing squad: a squatting Chetnik[2] (recognizable by the beard and black fur cap with insignia), next to him Serbian president Milošević holding the ammunition box, and next to him a JNA officer. They are firing at a woman tied to a pillar, on which the letters JNA are inscribed. Standing next to her, one of the "troika" negotiators, De Michelis, is telling: "My advice is still the same—do not give up peaceful democratic negotiations."

The woman on the cartoon stands doomed, receiving the bullets. One presumes that her body is a symbol of all those Croats who had been killed by the aggressor, who died or fled their villages seeking safety elsewhere; in short, she could symbolize the collective suffering of Croats affected by the war in Croatia. But unlike the other figures on the illustration who are not named but rather drawn in such a way as to be recognizable, the woman's skirt bears the word *Hrvatska*—Croatia. Thus she does not represent the people, but the newly founded *state* that is sovereign yet threatened, struggling to secure its future yet tied to its past.

This image, personified and feminized, represents all that Croatia is, and should be—or is not. Her frail, female, skin-and-bones body is clearly different from the fat-bellied and double-chinned bodies of her attackers. The "troika" negotiator is not different from the aggressors—their male physiques all bear the same signs of abundance. The words of De Michelis

JNA
HRVATSKA
De Michelis: Moj je savjet još uvijek – ne odustati od mirnih demokratskih pregovora
Oto Reisinger

The pillar is inscribed with letters *JNA*, for Yugoslav National Army. The caption reads: "De Michelis: My advice is still the same—do not give up peaceful democratic negotiations." *Vjesnik* (Croatia), August 11, 1991, 1.

further indicate that the woman tied to the pillar stands not only as a victim of aggression but also as a victim of abandonment by the world.

Another image of the aggressor and the world was published in *Vjesnik* two weeks later (September 2, 1991, 7). The aggressor—represented by the image of Milošević as a bullfighter—is the same, and so are his intentions, inscribed on his cloth: "War for Bolshevik Serboslavia." But, this time the world is represented through a female image. This change has a significant effect. For the second cartoon establishes the presence of an element that is absent from the first cartoon: explicit sexuality. It shows a woman sitting on the bull and wearing a hat with one word on it: *Europa*. Her finger is pointed at Milošević, telling him: "I warn you that he [the bull] also has horns."

Two questions come to mind. How does Europa as a woman differ from Europe represented by De Michelis? And, how different is the woman Europa from the woman Croatia? The answer to the first question is ambiguous. On the one hand, there is no difference at all, for there, again, the figure of Milošević is in control. He is the bullfighter, and we know all too well the fate of bulls fighting with men. On the other hand, there is a difference. In the first cartoon—with its discourse on democracy versus bullets—Europe could have been simply naive, or stupid, or uncon-

Milošević carries a cloth on which is written "War for Bolshevik Serboslavia," while Europa says, "I warn you that he also has horns." *Vjesnik* (Croatia), September 2, 1991, 7.

cerned. The second cartoon suggests, however, a lack of power. For, while the Europa riding the bull could imply that the rider has control, the myth of the rape of Europa by Zeus disguised as a bull suggests otherwise. The strange construction of the sentence further stresses the power of the bull. I wondered initially why the word "also" was put in the sentence "I warn you that he also has horns" ("Upozoravam vas da ima i rogove"). In the original sentence construction, it is clear that "also" refers to the listing of all the things that the bull has, implying that he had something else to threaten with, beside the horns. Otherwise, the sentence could have been simply "I warn you that he has horns." Going back to the myth of the rape of Europa, it is clear that this particular bull has, first and foremost, a penis. The penis marks Europa's lack of power with respect to the bull. But the horns seem to mark the bull's lack of power with respect to Milošević. For this cartoon not only mocks the helplessness of Europe. It also suggests the impotence of Europe's threat to Milošević. Maybe the bull was able to overpower Europa, but before Milošević he stands no chance.

The powerlessness of Europe with respect to Milošević is not all that this cartoon conveys. The exposed breast of Europa sends a signal of sexuality. This indecency questions the nature of Europe's rape, suggesting, if not compliance, then at least her part in responsibility. The bare breast defines the body of Europa as a sexual body, making it very different from the body of Croatia on the previous cartoon. For we know that the latter is a woman by her skirt, not by her bare breasts. Her body is of a different kind—an asexual body marked by physical suffering and starvation, standing before the fat bellies and bare breasts of all her enemies.

That Croatia—and not Croats—is the principal victim in the Croatian media war is also obvious from many articles published in *Vjesnik* and *Danas*. But in no other piece from the Croatian media—through the whole period between 1986 and 1994 that I have examined—is the image of feminized and personified Croatia drawn so clearly and so explicitly as in four articles about Bosnian refugees published between April and June 1992. In these texts, the feminine yet asexual vulnerability of Croatia is developed even further. The betrayal by a complacent world has, however, lost its sexual connotations, and the Serb aggressor has become less prominent. Instead, an unlikely and unexpected element is added: the new cause of Croatia's suffering are the Muslim refugees from Bosnia.

The Exhausted Body: A Beauty and Her Burden

In April 1992, while the fighting in Croatia was slowing down, war broke out in Bosnia. Refugees started fleeing, some using boats to cross rivers along the border between Bosnia and Croatia. In one of the first articles about Bosnian refugees in *Vjesnik*, they were named "boat people,"[3] and—identified with the waters they crossed—described as a threatening flood that was devastating Croatia. The article covers the whole page, with a photograph of a woman with child in her hands in the middle, under the huge headline "Croatian S.O.S. Due to Refugees" with a subhead "Crushing Refugee Load." Below, a boldface quotation from the text reads: "Our Beautiful cannot refuse to help, but it remains a question whether she is able to attend to the refugee explosion in her territory, and for how long" (*Vjesnik*, April 23, 1992, 5). The expression "Our Beautiful"—*Lijepa naša*—is a familiar reference to the Croatian national anthem, which begins:

> Our beautiful homeland
> Oh, you heroic beloved country
> The ancestral land of old glory
> Be happy for eternity.[4]

In nationalist parlance the expression "Our Beautiful" was often used to refer to Republic of Croatia within socialist Yugoslavia, and later, for independent Croatia. With the creation of the new state the anthem was more present in public, on state occasions, small-scale celebrations, TV, and radio. The main TV Croatian evening news starts with the anthem. In the media war the words "Our Beautiful" came to mean our beautiful, new, independent, and sovereign state Croatia, attacked and ruined by the JNA. In the text about refugees from Bosnia, Our Beautiful is threatened by a new enemy—the "boat people."

The argument in the texts expresses a dilemma. The S.O.S. is sent to the world: Croatia asks for help because it cannot cope with the refugees. Her good will to help is not in question. It is her moral duty to help the helpless. Nevertheless, the high cost of that help is emphasized, and so are Croatia's diverse responsibilities toward refugees from Bosnia and refugees from Croatia:

> Having no right, or wish, to stop the arrival of the desperate, Croatia is, together with thousands of newly arriving refugees, sentenced to starvation. With so many homeless people, she cannot guarantee anything more but mere physical security. . . . Croatia is helping, since she cannot refuse to help, but it remains a question whether she is able to attend to the refugee explosion in her territory, and for how long. Her position is not like that of Slovenia . . . which chooses to simply close the border before the panicking flood. Her position is also different from that of European countries, . . . which approach the problem as a natural calamity . . . Being a neighbor with Bosnia means [for Croatia] a prolonged fear of her own war problems and adding to the burden of her own refugees. . . . Croatia is drowned by a million of dispossessed people. . . . *Boat people* are nothing but helpless victims of Yugo Army–Serbian aggression. If the world and Europe are trying to stop the hundred-headed beast of Milosević's Chetniks, then they cannot remain deaf before its victims. (Ibid.)

Thus the refugees are named as victims, and the world is called upon to help them. But the S.O.S. is sent by Croatia. She carries the "crushing refugee load," She is "sentenced to starvation," She is "drowned." The text further emphasizes that Croatian resources are already limited, not only by the destruction caused by war but also by the need to care for "her own refugees." That this differentiation between one's "own" refugees and those from Bosnia is an ethnic differentiation is expressed in the following words: "And, let's make that clear, it is not only Croats who fled Bosnia" (ibid.). Meaning: there were Muslims, too. And they are not "her own."

Articles in *Vjesnik* and *Danas* seldom used the expression "Muslim refugees." Most often the wording is "Bosnian refugees." Thus, it may appear that all the refugees from Bosnia—both Croats and Muslims[5]—are equally threatening to Croatia. This is the implication, for instance, of a lengthy article, "Croatia under the Refugees," from *Danas*:

> Every hotel, every sports hall, every mattress in Croatia is occupied. The West must understand that refugees are their problem too, otherwise a dangerous spillover could occur. . . . The latest wave of Bosnian refugees, rising from hour to hour, threatens to exhaust completely the already drained Croatia. . . . The number of refugees raises from moment to moment. . . . Croatia must appeal to other countries to understand that refugees are their problem too. . . . Croatia cannot manage without the help of international community. . . . The question is, how long can Croatia endure?" (*Danas*, April 28, 1992, 7–10)

The terrifying answer to the last question is given in a short passage appearing in a box within this main article. With the title "There Is No More Food" (ibid., 8), the passage starts by listing the numbers of refugees in various municipalities in Croatia, as well as the tonnage of food aid. It asserts that the situation is worse in the regions that Bosnian refugees occupy, because, while Croatian refugees have been taken care of, the "endless lines of Bosnian refugees were not expected."

However, the fact that the "occupiers" of Croatia are actually Muslim refugees, although called "Bosnian," becomes clear on the next page—again, not by saying it explicitly, but by revealing the rationale that establishes a difference between Muslim refugees from Bosnia, and Croat refugees from both Bosnia and Croatia.[6] Writing about a need to provide aid to the refugees, the author points out that aid is not the core concern with regard to refugees. Rather, "it is expected that the refugees will go back as soon as possible and 'humanize' [*humaniziraju*] the captured territories, because without people, these territories will never be Croatian again" (ibid., 9).

"Humanization" of a territory is a cynical term, even within quotation marks, for the practice of sending refugees back to unsafe areas, as well as the practice of forced resettlements. Compared to the practice of forcing a population out of a territory—referred to by the no less cynical expression "ethnic cleansing"—it has received far less attention. But it was often used nevertheless.

In 1994 I interviewed Marija—a Croat woman[7] from central Bosnia. When in spring 1993 the Vance-Owen peace plan drew demarcation lines through the map of Bosnia, the town of Rudnik in which Marija lived, until then controlled by Croat forces, became Muslim territory. I met her in Germany, where she was visiting her daughters who had fled Bosnia earlier. She told me how Rudnik was evacuated during a single night at the beginning of November 1993. All the Croats were taken together to another little town, Polje, some one hundred kilometers away, in territory controlled by Bosnian Croats. Guarded by Bosnian Croat forces, Marija and her fellow citizens from Rudnik—all Croats—were not allowed to resettle anywhere else, because then, they were told, Polje would be lost as Croat territory. Many people from Rudnik had relatives in Croatia or Serbia, or abroad, and wanted to leave. Nevertheless, they were held captive in Polje and allowed movement only with officially issued travel documents. They were given houses and jobs and told that this was where they would live from now on. Marija said:

> Of course, that rule applied only to those who had no money. Those with money paid their way out. Then it was not important which territory belonged to whom! Crooks! They are all crooks. But they will not see my money. [*Raises her voice*] I told myself, I will not pay them even if I die here! I was so furious. I went to the City Hall and burst into the office of the military commander of the city. I told him off, oh, how I barked.[8] [*Makes a gesture as if still surprised by her own behavior*] He had that big cross on the chain around his neck. I told him, "Take this cross off your chain, you are a disgrace to faith." On the way back I saw our car. When we arrived in Polje they had "appropriated" our car. They just stole it from us! So I wrote on the window, it was all dusty: "Return it to the rightful owner, thief." Was I crazy! [*Laughs out loud*][9]

Marija was in Polje with her husband, and they were never allowed to travel together. Nevertheless, she obtained permission to go to Croatia to visit her daughter in Zagreb. Once in Croatia, she decided not to return to Bosnia, except to help her husband out of Polje. In Zagreb her daughter persuaded her to pay a bribe and obtain Croatian documents, which she did in the end. When I met her in Germany, her husband was still in Polje, and she was just about to get new documents for him too. On our second meeting, in 1995, I learned that they were both living in Croatia, with Croatian citizenship.

In the Croatian media, the difference between Muslim and Croat refugees from Bosnia is that the Muslim refugees were not invited to "humanize" Croatian territories. On the contrary, they are presented as the burden that drains resources for that "humanization." They belong to a different sovereign state, and they are expected to return there. That is not to say that Croat refugees from Bosnia were all warmly welcomed in Croatia. As Marija's story shows, they were expected to go back to Bosnia, too, to the territories controlled by Bosnian Croats. Nevertheless, a number of Croat refugees from Bosnia became Croatian citizens without major problems, something that Muslim refugees had very little chance of doing.[10]

Thus, although the Croatian press did not explicitly name Muslim refugees as the threatening flood and the occupiers of Croatia, it provided many subtle and not so subtle indicators. These include an article, "Croatia Cannot [Manage] Alone Any Longer," in *Vjesnik* about an international meeting organized in Zagreb at which aid was sought for "Bosnian refugees." The president of the Croatian government is quoted as saying that "the plans for income from tourism will not be realized this year because hotels on the Adriatic coast are occupied by the refugees" (June 10, 1992, 6). The photo accompanying the text shows the participants of the meeting: foreign leaders whose turbans clearly define them as Muslims. The fact that many Muslim countries sent aid for Muslim refugees was well known; thus it can be inferred that the "Bosnian refugees" occupying the Croatian coastal areas were Muslims.[11]

In the article "On the Back of Exhausted Croatia" (*Danas*, May 26, 1992, 41–43), the exodus of Bosnian refugees is referred to as being of "epic dimensions" and "biblical proportions," while Zagreb is named a "biblical refugee center" (41). Both the main text and the accompanying box with the title "Stay Where You Are" discuss in a sarcastic way the attitude of several European countries toward refugees in Croatia. But a warning to the West is issued in the text: the refugee problem could "spill over the edge" (43) and pose the same threat to Europe, if Europe does not help exhausted Croatia. "Thousands upon thousands of Bosnian refugees on the train station in Zagreb will soon show that the 'bullet from Belgrade' is fired into Europe" (42), *Danas* writes, adding that Croatia was spending 2 million

German marks on refugees daily (ibid.). It goes on to assert, "It is unjust that a country burdened with its own refugees has to take care of refugees from the neighboring sovereign state" (ibid.). At the end of the article, after discussing how Slovenia, Italy, Austria, and Germany had avoided accepting more refugees, it asserts that, despite everything, Croatia will not abandon those in need. Nevertheless, readers are reminded of the high price of this generosity: "Croatia will carry alone the heaviest burden of the refugee wave from Bosnia. It will do so as its moral duty, when all the others, despite conventions and obligations, do not feel concerned. . . . There should be no doubt that Croatia will give considerable humanitarian and financial aid, but there should be no hope, then, that Croatian hotels and sports halls will soon be empty" (ibid.).

In these articles Croatia is what it was in the first of the cartoons: starved, exhausted, and abandoned by the world. And she is also drowned by floods of Muslim refugees, people who are not "her own" and will never be.

The Generous and Forgiving Body: A Divine Mother

How clearly Muslims are seen as alien to Croatia is further apparent through media definitions of those who do belong. The four texts analyzed above were published between April and June 1992. In August 1992 *Vjesnik* published another article on Croatia. This time, the text was not about those who threaten the country (Muslims), but about those in whom it rests its hope (Croats). The article headline already shows the difference of atmosphere: mellow gentleness instead of the righteous gloom: "Sweet Blisters for Croatia" (*Vjesnik*, August 14, 28). This is an article about labor of love: young Croat expatriates from North America and Europe who had come to Croatia to spend their summer working in a youth camp, rebuilding the ruined country:

> It was their wish to do something worthwhile and useful for their suffering homeland. There they earned the first blisters in their life. The name of the action is just that: "Blisters for Croatia." . . . One of the participants said: "I do not feel like a Canadian. A true and real Croat lives in me." . . . Two girls from the U.S.A. said that every time they leave Croatia it is more and more difficult. . . . We ask them, had they fallen in love? "Maybe," Ana says enigmatically. "But if so, then we fell in love with everything here. We are in love with people, new

> friends. . . . In America what is yours is yours, you do not share. And here, we share everything." . . . Reluctantly, we leave the camp teeming with youth, friendship, and love of a generation that need not search for its identity. For this is their Croatia. They are in their own home, to which they will come back for ever, one day. The future awaiting them here is much closer to them than that in the foreign lands. . . . We look at the ruins of these homes. These houses have no roofs now. Their common roof is the sky above them. . . . And we, together with them, will build new roofs and embrace their homes. Because Croatia can do it. And she has to.

Obviously, the hope and future of Croatia is bright when she is in the safe if blistered hands of young Croats, wherever they may come from. Unlike the Muslims from the neighboring state (and for that matter, unlike the Serbs from Croatia), Croats from all over the world will find their home with Croatia. Because the "foreign land"—*tudjina*, from *tudj*, meaning both alien and not one's own—is not theirs and they do not belong there. That foreign land is, after all, the same cold world that abandoned Croatia to the bullets of the aggressors and to starvation under the refugees. These young Croats belong to the new Croatia. Her frail body might still be marked by war, she may still be exhausted and starved, but her spirit is not drowned any longer. She has a future.

Changed, she can be forgiving to those who tried to drown her, and she can show benevolence by accepting their gratitude. So, toward the end of 1992 *Vjesnik* printed two stories on Muslim gratitude to Croatia. Both texts appeared in a regular column entitled "A Day of Reporting"—the same column that had produced "Sweet Blisters for Croatia" three months earlier. In these stories, reporters talk with Muslim refugees from Bosnia. Both take quotes from the refugees as their titles. The first is "Croatia Is Our Mother" (November 10, 28), accompanied by a photo of women and children. The article describes the sorry conditions in which 250 refugees from Bosnia live on a small island off the Croatian coast. As there was no money to repair the derelict buildings on the island, the refugees had no water or electricity and endured cold winds and rain leaking into the tents they live in: "'It's good when it doesn't rain. You should have seen us during those rainy days! You can't stay inside when the tents start leaking,' we are told by Muslim refugees to whom the management of the island has provided a prayer room. They also have a doctor" (ibid.).

The reporter is trying to be both true to the facts and full of empathy, adding that, on this otherwise uninhabited island, for refugees there is nothing to do but think of their loved ones. They are mostly old men and women, a few younger invalids, and about forty children. They do not really complain, even when they express their discomfort in being surrounded "by water": "'If I could only cross this water'—Aziza says, and then asks for help. 'I have family in Split [one of Croatia's bigger coastal cities]. If I could only move this tent to the continent. I *can't* live near this huge water.'" (The word *can't*, italicized in the original, is in the Bosnian dialect, clearly different from Croatian.)

After describing conditions normally considered appalling, the reporter writes that the Muslim refugees are grateful. An old Muslim man, after worrying that the cold and humidity of the island are bad for the children's health, adds: "Thanks to Croatia for accepting us, caring for us. What would we do without Croatia?" (ibid.). And yet another old Muslim man says: "I will tell everybody that Croatia is our mother. Were it not for Croatia, there would be no Muslims left in Bosnia" (ibid.).

This last sentence appears odd, as that particular old Muslim man was not in Bosnia, but in a refugee camp on a little island off the Croatian coast. But given the definition of Muslim refugees in the Croatian media—as not belonging to the Croatian state but to another sovereign state—this sentence makes perfect sense. It does not say that, were it not for Croatia, there would be no Muslims left. It says, rather, that those who are left are preserved by Croatia, for Bosnia. It not only expresses the gratitude of Muslims to Croatia, it denies them a right to stay where they are.

One month later *Vjesnik* published another piece, whose title is a quote from another grateful Muslim refugee: "Thank God and Croatia" (December 8, 1992, 32). The refugee camp is brand new, built by the Belgian military. A neat and orderly place is described, with an amiable atmosphere, "safe and warm." Reporters knock at the door of one of the little houses. A Muslim woman lets them in. She tells them about her son, a Bosnian government soldier, whom she last heard from six months ago. Then she says: "Croats accepted us nicely here. Thank God and Croatia, were it not for them, I do not know what would become of us." No thanks are given to the Belgians who actually built the village. All the gratitude is due to God and Croatia. Previously personified, Croatia is finally deified. For there she is, next to God.

The Body of the Newborn: Ethnicity and the State

In her analysis of colonial and nationalist representations of Africa and Ireland, Catherine Innes (1994) discussed cartoons and illustrations published in newspapers. Both Africa and Ireland were represented through the female body—from seductive nudes and heroic militants to savage witches and pale, frightened girls. She makes the important point in her analysis that these images have been changing, following changes in colonial and nationalist projects and politics. The symbolic bodies of Africa and Ireland, as well as that of Britannia, were fitted into daily political and social needs as much as they reflected historic aspects of each particular power relation. For example, caricatures and illustrations of Ireland in Irish newspapers used more asexual and spiritual images of the female body than those in British newspapers. Furthermore, in British press, the symbolic embodiment of Ireland changed from a fair-haired, virginal, and frail woman protected by the matron Britannia holding a sword of the late nineteenth century to a dark-haired and robust mother of unruly children in the 1920s (ibid., 6 and 9).

The change is also apparent in the images of Croatia, even though it may come in an unexpected way. The body in the cartoon—attacked by Chetnik, JNA, and Milošević figures and abandoned by the world—also belongs to the starved and exhausted Croatia, drowned by floods of Muslim refugees. But Croatia built by "sweet blisters" and the motherly divine Croatia of Muslim gratitude is quite a different one. And precisely that moment when the change occurs points to the productive role of these female images in defining ethnicity. The first two images are merged in one starved, victimized body in order to define not only Croatia but also its Other(s). In this representation, the symbolic body of Croatia is—ironically—victimized not only by the Serb aggressors and the unconcerned world but also by those who have experienced bullets and starvation, that is, the refugees. While the appropriation of refugee experiences constructs the suffering body of Croatia, Muslim refugees in the Croatian media are symbolically equated with Serb aggressors through constant association with "occupation." Even when these refugees are named as victims, the effects of their very existence on Croatia are the same—ruinous. These are quite unlike the effects of those who build and love Croatia, those whose blisters will bring her to life.

In the texts about Muslim gratitude, the image of Croatia is that of a protective, divine Mother. By contrast, the image of Croatia cherished by Croats from the diaspora almost resembles a child—a baby born in pain and blood. The symbolic birth of the new, independent state is reenacted in this image. This symbolism links the new state with the definition of ethnicity through purity of origin. Croatia is exclusively the child of Croats, even if she can mother others. As in the representation of the Wall of Love, where the symbolic motherland Croatia apparently included Serb, Muslim, and Croat women from Croatia, here, the country seemingly accepts being the mother of Muslim refugees from Bosnia. It is as if their gratitude, which gave Her a godlike status, produced a change in their otherness, resulting in acceptance. But it did not, because the *claim* of motherhood—implied in the quotation marks—was always made only by Muslim refugees, never by Croatia. Born of Croats, she knew better—she knew the difference between them and "her own."

6

SEXUAL GEOGRAPHIES OF ETHNICITY

News about sexual violence against women surfaced in the world media in August 1992, producing immediate and widespread protests among different grassroots women's organizations, and various reactions at the international level. Toward the end of 1992, the front covers of most international weeklies featured the tear-stained faces of raped Muslim women, with almost all international broadcasters running documentaries on war rapes in Bosnia.

As Serb forces in Bosnia, and their auxiliaries from the Socialist Federal Republic of Yugoslavia and later the Federal Republic of Yugoslavia, were accused of having committed the majority of the rapes, this put the media in Serbia in quite a different position from the media in Croatia. Predictably, as the former were accused, they defended themselves, and as the latter were accusers, they sought prosecution for the perpetrators. But both the Serbian and Croatian press went far beyond familiar denials and accusations. Media representations of rapes and sexual assaults against women treated the female body as the map on which the new, sexual, geographies of ethnicity were drawn, this time in discursive terms.

The Serbian Media

Considering the worldwide publicity of the war rapes, and fierce denials by officials in (Federal) Yugoslavia and Serbia and by Bosnian Serb leaders, one would expect a broad coverage of war rapes in the Serbian press—even if only to deny them. But the Serbian daily *Politika* and the weekly *NIN* published relatively few stories on rapes.[1] Articles in the Serbian press developed two distinct themes: one about war rapes and another about forced impregnations.

WAR RAPE AND THE VIRILITY DREAM

Politika started its story on war rapes with absolute denials of the accusations that the Serb forces were ever involved in anything of this nature in Bosnia. Reports from international bodies such as the European Union, the United Nations, Amnesty International, and other NGOs were quoted in *Politika* and all condemned as politically motivated fabrications. Official denials by the Yugoslav government and the Bosnian Serb leadership were quoted. Any international organization or an individual who could be seen as doubting the veracity of the allegations against Serbs was quoted. Terms such as "alleged" and "so-called" were used to prefix these accusations and words like "rape" appeared in quotation marks.

A typical article was "Death Sentences for Herak and Damjanović," about two Bosnian Serbs captured by Bosnian government forces, tried in Sarajevo, and sentenced to death. Borisav Herak admitted multiple rapes and murders of Muslim women and murders of Muslim and Serb civilians and his trial generated international interest. The subhead in *Politika* was "Two Young Serb Soldiers Sentenced for Alleged Genocide," while the headline read, "Decision of the Court Martial in Sarajevo." The word "genocide" appeared in quotation marks throughout the article to emphasize the illegitimacy of the accusers and the innocence of the accused (March 31, 1993, 8).

Absolute denials came with counteraccusations that Croat and Muslim forces were systematically carrying out rapes of Serb women and other atrocities against Serb populations. But the rapes of Serb women by Muslim and Croat forces generally got a mention of a just a sentence or two, with no specific details. They were more part of a larger picture—that of Serb suffering under Muslims and Croats—than a story of their own—for example, a focus on pregnancies resulting from rapes of young Serb women from different parts of Bosnia.[2]

Parallel with the assertions that Serbs had not committed any of the alleged crimes went a qualification that all warring parties had committed the same crimes, of which only Serbia stood accused. Headlines featuring such terms as "all three parties," "all sides," and "the same crimes" appeared, along with the argument that this was war, and these things happen in wars. For example, *Politika* quoted a *Daily Telegraph* journalist who expressed doubts on Serb guilt over war crimes and asserted "in this terrible civil war all three ethnic groups rape women" (January 22, 1993, 5). This statement appears to admit Serb involvement in the war crimes. However, this is not exactly true. For already the next day's *Politika* offered another denial, the "all sides" argument, and a totally new line of argument, all in the space of one twenty-line column. Radovan Karadžić, then still the Bosnian Serbs' leader, was quoted as telling British TV that some rapes were committed by *individuals*, but these were incidental and without the knowledge of the high (Bosnian Serb) command (January 23, 1993, 4). The assertion about the "incidental rape by individuals" was followed by different assertions, one of which being that these individuals are actually psychopaths. A director of a mental hospital in Belgrade where raped and impregnated women were brought for post-traumatic stress disorder treatment was interviewed in *Politika*. In "They Keep Silent from Shame" (February 10, 1993, 22), the director stated that about 3 to 5 percent of people in every society are psychopaths, and that these are the people committing crimes like rape. He offered a formula, based on this percentage, for determining the true extent of rapes in Bosnia. Significantly, nowhere in *Politika* were these "individuals," "psychopaths," and "sick personalities" named as Serbs. Their pathological character remained unattached ethnically, implying that psychopathic Serbs are not "real Serbs."

The story about war rapes went beyond just denials and offered an expert explanation why Serbs do not rape, by the same psychiatrist who treated the women, and in the same article: "Imagine, anyway, how would Bosnian Serbs fight the war, if they had to rape so many Muslim women every day? In different times this [accusation] would be the greatest advertisement for Serbs and their virility" (February 10, 1993, 22).

The psychiatrist makes a clear distinction between the psychopath and the Serb soldier fighting the war in Bosnia and Croatia. That distinction defines the Serbs fighting the war as true warriors: concentrated on their military task, they are not easily distracted by women—not enough, anyway, to rape them. The disproof of rapes is presented in technical terms: the number of Serb soldiers multiplied by the hours available in war divided by number of Muslim women. This simple mathematics should demonstrate to everybody the impossibility of the accusation. This argument defines rape as sex, and then takes the huge number of rapes as a compliment to Serb virility. Explicit equation of rape and sex appears in yet another article, "Those Who Speak the Truth about Rapes Denied Visas," on Belgium's refusal to issue visas to Yugoslav medical experts hoping to attend a European Parliament discussion on rapes. The same psychiatrist is quoted as saying: "Like all other crimes, the crimes of rape are also committed exclusively by psychopaths. . . . However brave the soldier might be during the fighting, he is still afraid . . . and fear and sex do not go together" (February 19, 1993, 9).

The argument that it is simply impossible for Serb soldiers to rape such a huge number of women in such a short time was repeated often in the Serbian daily and weekly, with quotes from Bosnian Serb military leaders as well as famous novelists and actors. Jokes were made about it, following the familiar pattern of old jokes about sex and virility. A piece in *NIN* (Jovan Ćirilov's regular column "The Word of the Week") links the rapes and these jokes. The largest part of the text is about the linguistic etymology of the word "rape" and classical Greek and Roman stories referring to rapes during wars. The column opens as follows: "The word 'rape' has been the theme of the day in the dirty Balkan war for weeks now. That type of violence of a man against a woman has become a part of war as much as of a media war. The dirty jokes about the sexual potency of Serb men have reached an international tragic finale" (February 26, 1993, 4).

Framing war rapes within the discourse of sexual potency and then situating them within a "media trouble" belongs to the same discourse that is apparently criticized: a discourse where rape and sex are equated.

I heard this argument, in different forms, during my fieldwork in Serbia in 1995. Once, while sitting in on a heated group discussion about the war in Bosnia, one of the men expressed a fear that the stories about war rapes may well be true. "Men are animals," he said with indignation. Another man replied: "Listen, if we were really such machos to [be able to] rape such a huge number of Muslim women, our own women wouldn't have had time to comb their hair! But, unfortunately, we are not." A couple of people laughed, but one woman burst into tears, much to the confusion of the speaker as well as the rest of the group. As the laughter faded, the crying woman got up and, saying "Idiot!" left the circle. The discussion did not continue.

Only with contempt for women, and for sex, can rape be defined as sex. But in this context, such a definition does not attest only to misogyny, and to sex as a site in which misogyny is acted out. It attests to the links between the definitions of the manhood and soldiering in the Serbian press, and obviously, among some men and women as well. It is a definition of the manhood of the soldier, and of manhood *as* soldiering—the place where the two merge. Both types of manhood are imagined in terms of the stud who dreams of an inexhaustible penis; a sex machine who could have sex whenever and wherever he wants, and with whomever he wishes. The repetition of the statement that it was not physically possible to rape so many women in so short a time sounds like the self-defense of the stud who failed. The sentence "But, unfortunately, we are not" struck me as a confession of that failure, and at the same time, as a horrific victory of the image of the Serb men produced by nationalism in Serbia. In that production, manhood is equated with soldiering *through virility*—sexual virility in the former, and a fighting and militant virility in the latter. Thus, the denial of rapes is based not only on an acknowledgment of failed sexual virility but even more so on giving precedence to fighting virility over sexual virility in the name of the nation and its needs.[3]

Strange as it may seem, it is this masculinity—failed and asserted, sexualized and militarized—that is central to the story about war rapes in the Serbian press. Raped women—Muslim and Croat women whose rapes are denied authenticity, and Serb women whose rapes are defined within the plentitude of Serb suffering—are most of the time conspicuously absent. And while the absence of the former is consistent with the denials of rapes, the absence of the latter points to a peculiar position granted to Serb women in the media production of the Serb nationhood. To them belongs another story in the Serbian papers—the story about the "crime above all crimes." And that story will bring us back, again, to the Serb man.

THE RAVAGED SERB CRADLE

Like many other dailies, *Politika* had regular columns running series of articles. In January 1993, in a series of such articles under a common rubric "The Crime above All Crimes," *Politika* had a new story to tell: "This is beyond the monstrosity of any pathology. It reminds me of stories about Turks . . . when they were making soldiers for their Ottoman Empire by Islamizing Christian children" (January 16, 23). "I haven't really ever heard that a crime like this has happened anywhere. Hitler tried something similar, but he was making his *Übermenschen* out of a pure Aryan race. . . . Here, these women are forced to be someone's mothers. No, history hasn't seen a crime like that" (January 19, 19). "The war cannot be without rape. It was always like that. In Bosnia especially. There, rape is like an appetizer with drinks. But it is not possible for one to comprehend . . . this crime, yet unrecorded in the world" (January 26, 21).

The "crime above all crimes" is not the rape of Serb women, but their forced impregnation by Muslim men from Bosnia. Already the title of the first article indicates the main theme: "Mothers of Alien [Someone Else's] Children" (*Majke tudje dece*, January 15, 21). The Serbian word *tudj* means both foreign, strange, and someone else's or not one's own. In this case—not Serb.

The *Politika* series featured the testimonies of eight women who survived rape and forced impregnation by Bosnian Muslims. At the time, they lived in Belgrade, having been released from Muslim-run camps. Some of them were in an advanced stage of pregnancy, some had given birth, and some had had abortions. Their (assumed) names show that seven of them were Serb women and one was Muslim. In contrast to the angry and indignant denials of rape in earlier articles, the tone is now emphatic, often resonating with despair. The articles are full of reminders of former happiness ruined forever, contrasted with the horrors that the women lived through. Their anxieties, fears, and despair are expressed in many different ways. Their ordeals are depicted in detail: being kept for weeks in dark cellars; being beaten, tortured, raped; pleading and crying. All this is told—mostly in the women's own words—in a language full of expressions from old Serbian folk epics and lyric poetry and songs familiar to the audience from both schoolbooks and guitar jam sessions, as this is a country where folk songs are still as big as the Beatles.[4] The structures of the articles imitates melodic folk laments:

> And then, then seemingly without any reason, the cry breaks out. Abruptly, like rain, tears are pouring, tear after tear. She wipes them away, inattentively, and wails bitterly. (January 15, 21)

> While she cries and weeps aloud, an unnatural laughter breaks through. As if she laughs and cries at the same time. "I am not crazy, am I? No, no, I am only a bit tired." (January 22, 119)

Throughout the texts these women are referred to as the "ill-fated," "the destroyed," the "wrecked creatures," and depicted as dehumanized, changed for ever:

> I did not have strength to defend myself. Everything he asked I did, not of fear any longer but just like an automaton. . . . Simply, I was not a human being any longer. (January 19, 19)

> As if all these months it was not me there, but some other woman. (January 26, 21)

Politika writes that death was always on these women's minds during captivity, and that some attempted suicide. Once they were released by their captors and came to Belgrade, the suffering and suicidal tendencies did not stop. Actually, things got much worse for them, as their pregnancies advanced. A compelling story is told of a woman who was handed a gun by her husband. He told her: "'Here it is, kill yourself. . . . Shoot in the head or in the heart, it is the safest. Death does not hurt.' . . . She thinks about that while she wanders nameless streets of Belgrade. The gun, [her husband's] war trophy, she keeps in her pocket" (January 17, 23).

It is made clear in *Politika* that it is the forced impregnation, not the horrors of rape, that will make "the days to come . . . much worse than the days in captivity" (January 23, 25), that convinces the women that "the worst is only coming" (January 26, 21), and accounts for the greatest despair and the ultimate loss of future, now marked by an *alien* child: "My child will be killing me, unborn, now, and in the future, slowly and silently. And that will be for the whole of my life" (January 16, 23).

Thus, in *Politika*, the children conceived in rape—born or unborn—remain the source of ultimate torment for the impregnated women. The "mental murder" of forced pregnancies would assure that the "dismembering of [women's] souls will never end" (January 25, 23). Women would remain prisoners of these children forever, regardless whether they chose to abort or give birth. One woman, uncertain whether she aborted a child conceived from her husband or from the rapist, half-mad, screams at her own image in the mirror: "Baby-killer" (January 26, 21). Another one loves her child, despite everything: "You know . . . this is also my child" (January 17, 23). And yet another, already too far along in pregnancy for an abortion, could not decide what to do: "I will kill my child. If I don't do that, I will commit suicide, and thus kill my son too. That is how I think one day. And the next morning I am awakened by the child moving in my belly. I love him. I cannot kill him" (January 16, 23).

There are two directions in which these representations of forcefully impregnated, not just raped, women point. Both are concerned with defining Serbhood, but one of them defines the Serbhood of the women, and the other, the Serbhood of the men. Importantly, both of these directions speak about shifts at the intersections of gender and ethnicity. The practice of rape defines women as both the female and the ethnic Other at the same time—with gender and ethnicity appearing equally relevant. But the practice of forced impregnation, wherein the child's ethnicity is defined through the father, tells us about a gendered hierarchy of ethnicity—it tells us about the primacy of gendered difference in the midst of the ethnic war. This indicates that gender and ethnicity, while mutually productive, do not have fixed relationship, and produce each other in competing and conflicting ways. For here the discourse of ethnic purity, which assumes that the child's ethnicity is produced by both the man and the woman, is apparently brushed aside to assert the exclusive right of the man to determine ethnicity of the child. And this is what points away from the impregnated Serb women, toward the Serb man, making him the ultimate victim of these impregnations: "wronged" by seeing his ethnic stock polluted and his ethnic lineage disrupted by Muslim men, *he* is the embodiment of the Serbhood.

That the Serb man is actually seen as the principal victim of forced impregnation of Serb women is confirmed—albeit in an unexpected way—by the Serbian weekly *NIN*, in the lengthy article "Exorcists—Rape—Propaganda" (February 19, 26–28). The text starts as follows: "The world is outraged. It is said that Serbs have raped at least 20,000 Muslim women in former Yugoslavia. The result—thousands of unwanted children of the devil. . . . This is the story about the devilish Serb children" (ibid., 26).

The text comments on international media coverage of the rapes in Bosnia. It denies them, qualifies them as "alleged," and uses the "all sides," "same crimes" argument. In between runs the story about "little victims in a terrible war" (26). The media and international organizations concerned with the children born out of forced pregnancies are the "exorcists" of the title, who hate those "heretics, the red Serbian nationalists" (26). The text is extremely interesting because it is very ambiguous. It plays with the demonization of Serbs, using it in an ironic way to argue that the overall hatred toward Serbs is resulting in hatred toward Serb children. But the "devilish children" with whom the text sympathizes, and whom the world supposedly hates, are explicitly defined as produced through forced impregnations of Muslim women by Serb men. The paradox is that the sympathy with victimized Serbhood—symbolized in the "little victims" and the "devilish children"—is conflated with the love for one's own, Serb offspring; thus the children are acknowledged, even if that meant actually admitting what was fiercely refuted, that the Serb soldiers did rape and forcefully impregnate Muslim women.

In the story about war rapes, the failed sexual virility of the Serb men and the militarized virility of true soldiering provided a defense from the accusations of rape. But it seems that nationalist imagery could not deny the male body both sexual virility and potency; thus male Serbs' potency betrayed the efforts to refute allegations that Serb men forcibly impregnated Muslim women. A child, as the only remaining proof of Serb men's sexual performance, had to be recognized, no matter how it was conceived.

THE OTHER WOMAN

A story about forced impregnation has yet another aspect. Told as a story about the ordeal of Serb women, it is, at the same time, the strongest possible definition of who a Serb woman *is*. Despair, madness, and death are represented as the only reaction to rape and forced impregnation that a Serb woman could possibly have. Femininity, defined as sexual violability, is a core definition of a Serb woman's ethnicity. In other words, *Politika* implies that a woman who survives all these torments without going mad is worth neither her womanhood nor her Serbhood. At the same time, these representations, while offering to readers a compelling call for empathy, could almost be read as an epitaph for the Serb women, marked forever as "mothers of aliens." There is a warning here too, with madness, death, and rejection as an ultimate punishment for those Serb women who wronged the Serb men by giving birth to, and—potentially, against all odds, even against their own better judgment—loving their non-Serb offspring, and seeking a future life for themselves as well as the child. For, as such, they come dangerously close to being the Other Woman. She too was present in the Serbian press.

In *Politika*'s series, beside the stories of the Serb women, there was the story of a Muslim woman, Suada, also violated and impregnated by Muslims after her Serb husband joined the Bosnian Serb forces. Her story too is told in the first person singular, also with many details of the past. Her ordeal is described in detail too, as is her life after it. But her story is told in a different language, literally: in Bosnian dialect. In *Politika*, only Suada uses that language, although the readers are told that all the interviewed women—seven of them Serb and this one Muslim—come from the same Bosnian town. This should mean that the women actually spoke the same, Bosnian dialect, but while the stories of the Serb women are told in Serbian dialect, the Muslim woman's story is in a version spoken in Bosnia.

The different language is employed to tell a very different story: a story where rebellion, challenge, and survival instincts replace madness, despair, and suffering. Suada tells how she chose her Serb boyfriend, later husband, against her father's wishes: "I was in the third grade of gymnasium. Went into heat[5] over [him]. . . . Went all around, but at the end, he was at my place. My old man was telling me not to marry a Vlaj [pejorative expression for a Serb]. I told him: 'Fuck off, old man. Yours is over. This does not count any more. Who asks you for religion? He is mine, so cut the crap'" (January 23, 25).

They married, had two children, lived happily. The war started in Croatia, and then in Bosnia. Suada was arrested twice. First by Muslims. They demanded that she condemns Chetniks, and she did, without a second thought. Then Serbs arrested her, asking her to condemn Muslim fundamentalism: "'What's that?' I ask. 'That is, Suada, a state in which there would be no place for your husband Danko,' they say. 'For my Danko? Then fuck such a state.' I signed it cool. Then the real trouble started. They took Danko away, to defend Bosnia from other Bosnians. What a crazy country, I thought'" (January 23, 25). . . . "My neighbors and friends told me to keep my mouth shut. But how? If there was ever time to bark, then it is now" (January 24, 21).

Only when she was arrested the second time, by Muslims, and locked in the cellar, did she understand the gravity of her situation. But she did not surrender. "The same evening the first *kabadahija* [macho] arrived. It was clear to Suada what is awaiting her. So I barked on him, in the darkness: 'Come on hero, show off yourself. Let's see what you have between your legs.' He ran away, and I was still shouting after him" (January 24, 21). She relates how various other men are sent packing when she shouts at them, before a drunken soldier rapes her.

In these representations Suada is a different kind of woman. She expressed openly her sexual desires, and uses sexual curses. She disrespected her father, and does not acknowledge the city authorities. She is as vividly untamed as the Serb women are defeated. Not even rape breaks her down. Her reaction to impregnation is also different: "What else could I tell you. . . . That they called me, a Muslim woman, a Serb whore. None of that, my fellow man, humiliated me as much as the fool who told me that they will now send me to Serbia to give birth to a Muslim child. A man is a beast. So am I, it seems. After all the torment, I started laughing. . . . I told him he is an idiot and that I am a Muslim, with two children who are Muslims too, because of me. I did not see his face. He did not see my face. But he fell silent and like a beaten dog he bent his head down and went out, closing the heavy wooden door after himself" (January 24, 21).

There are two significant points to make about the excerpt above. One is Suada's definition of ethnicity of her children through herself. In the interviews I conducted with refugee women, children were often defined through their mother's ethnicity, depending on the context in which the woman found herself. One can see it in the example of a woman whom I will give pseudonym Mirjana Djuranović.[6] Born in Bosnia, from a Croat mother and Montenegrin father, married to a Muslim man, she gave birth to a boy—Jasmin—in 1990. As the war started in Bosnia her husband joined the Bosnian forces, and turned from being a secular man into an increasingly religious one. Living in the Muslim part of Sarajevo, Mirjana lost her job as a medical doctor, and was exposed to threats from the outside, as well as from her husband and his family. She fled Sarajevo with her son in secret, in 1993, and spent three days on Serb-controlled Bosnian territory before entering Serbia. Her access to Serbia was not problematic because her Montenegrin father had relatives there, and she still had her ID with her Montenegrin family name, simply because, after marriage, although she took her husband's surname, she had not bothered to change her documents. Her memories of these events both express the anguish of a mother in the ethnic war who fights to keep her child by defining him through herself and at the same time show how ambiguous and how contextual ethnic definitions are: "These three days while waiting to be transferred to Serbia, I was all paralyzed. . . . I was afraid because . . . my child's father is a Muslim. I had to hide all the documents . . . so they [Serb officials] did not find them because . . . they would let *me* into Serbia but they would not let my child. . . . I thought to myself, this name of mine . . . Mirjana Djuranović . . . it will either save me or bury me." When finally invited to an interview to obtain transfer documents (a procedure all people fleeing through Serb-controlled areas went through), the following occurred:

> He took my birth certificate and then Jasmin's . . . and then he asked me whether Jasmin was born before the war or during the war. I said before. And he started typing it. Without looking at me he commented: "Jasmin, of all the nice Serb names you gave your son the name of a *balija*[7] . . . what did I need to marry a *balija* for." He asked me what my nationality is and I said . . . "My father . . . is Montenegrin so then I am Montenegrin too," and then he asks: "And what is Jasmin, and what is your child?" he asks while taking Jasmin's documents [with stronger voice], "How did you declare him?" "Well," I said, "So far I did not have any need to declare him. Anyhow . . . [her voice drops],"

> I said, "the child is mine, the child is with me, the child is what I am." . . . So, he said: "Shall I write he is a Serb?" "Yes, you can write it." And he looks at me, he lifted his head and stared at me intensely like this [she shows it bringing her face close to mine with her eyes wide open], he says: "Can I write it without checking it up?" "You can, you can," I said, "you can check it up, and you can write it too." . . . You know . . . to check whether Jasmin is circumcised . . . to take his clothes off to see if he was circumcised or not.

Once in Serbia, Mirjana never says that she was married to a Muslim man, letting everybody believe that her husband was a Serb. She points very explicitly to a clear difference between her peacetime life in Sarajevo, and her new life in Serbia:

> In Sarajevo I never ran away from what I am, I never hid it, I am Mirjana Djuranović, period. Who likes it, likes it, who doesn't, I don't give a damn, you know. My son is who he is and my husband is who he is, whether he is still my husband or not, this does not even matter. . . . If I were a different person . . . for it is a year now that I live in Serbia. One could say, all right . . . you can reorient yourself but *I [emphasizing the word "I" with a strong voice, and bringing her left hand to her heart]* cannot reorient myself because I cannot be exclusive, I cannot say that now I am a Serb woman and I will feel great here and adopt things. . . . I cannot, I am not like that, you know. . . . There is in me . . . not that other half . . . maybe many of these . . . halves, thirds, whatever, not only through the genes of my [Croat] mother but maybe . . . maybe all these people with whom I was a friend and that other life [before the war] and also that . . . that one was never oriented so narrowly toward something. I cannot find my way in all this here, I cannot accept it like that, I mean . . . if I could say now I am this and I am here and I will adjust and think only this way, it would be different for sure, and I could then bring up my child to think that way too, and he would be a Serb and nothing else . . . but I cannot . . . and it would not be fair.

In these three excerpts we see Mirjana continuously redefining her own ethnicity through various, both ethnic and nonethnic associations, and at the same time she defines and claims her son in many different ways, both through ethnicity and through the links with her own past when ethnicity did not matter.

In many other interviews too, women claimed their children through themselves, in both ethnic and nonethnic terms. Interestingly, in the media representations, in both the Serbian and the Croatian press, children were always defined ethnically. But, while in all articles about rapes and forced impregnations children's ethnicity was always defined through the father, the articles discussed in chapter 2 attest to the relevance of the mother. For in the media representations of the Wall of Love, children were linked ethnically to their mothers: in the Croatian press by linking the soldier-sons to their Croat and Muslim mothers and differentiating them from the Serb women and JNA generals; and in the Serbian press by linking true and false mothers to true and false children, through language as a marker of ethnicity. These shifting representational strategies point to several things: to the ambiguity of the maternal metaphor, to the appropriation of women's experiences within these media representations, and to the significance of specific contexts within which both the metaphors and the experiences are produced.

In the specific context of the media narratives of rape and forced impregnations a Muslim woman who defines her children as Muslim through herself defies a gendered hierarchy of ethnicity. This makes Suada different from the Serb women in *Politika*'s series, whose "alien" children were all defined through their (Muslim) fathers.

Finally, yet another difference marks the Muslim woman, evident in Suada's words "But he fell silent and like a beaten dog, he bent his head down and went out." For there, she is shaming, instead of being ashamed. And instead of refuting her future, instead of being condemned to lose her soul and become one of the living dead, like the Serb women in the series, she makes plans: "Look, I do not understand politics. But I have my head and my barking tongue. . . . Suada is going far away. Suada and her children. She knows where she will go. Suada will go far. As far as possible from here . . . New Zealand. They say there is no further" (January 24, 21).

In this text Suada is all that Serb women are not—rebellious, untamed, and almost frightening. Instead of covering herself with tears and silence, she struggles fiercely. Her story is not one that evokes empathy—she is simply too strong and loud for that. Within the discourse that defines femininity as sexual violability, her strength, so clearly expressed through a different language, defines her as a different kind of woman. In the representational strategy, this strength shows Muslim women—the women whom Serb forces are accused of raping and impregnating—as taking it all so very differently from the Serb women. This difference produces two different ethnicities through the raped and impregnated bodies of Serb and Muslim women. The former are defined through purity, honor, and suffering, and the latter through savage resilience. Within the Serbian nationalist discourse in which the doom of extinction is defined as befalling only the truly innocent, striving for life after rape and forced impregnation marks those who cannot be wronged: Muslim men, because they are the real rapists, and Muslim women, because it doesn't affect them anyway.

The Croatian Media

Croatian newspapers developed three distinctive stories about war rapes. These were the story about victims of rape, about forced impregnation, and about the rapists.[8] About half the stories were about the victims of rape, and interestingly, the majority of these were about national and international activities around the issue: United Nations or European Union resolutions, international attempts to prosecute the perpetrators or assist the victims, and actions taken within Croatia, mostly by medical experts on treating trauma. Only a handful of articles had research by Croatian journalists as their primary source. Stories on rapes and raped women in Bosnia and Croatia in *Vjesnik* came from Italian, French, German, and British newspapers, and an overwhelming majority of them were about raped Muslim women. Only a handful of the articles about rapes even mentioned that Croat women were also raped, and only one or two went into describing the circumstances of rape. An example of the articles mentioning rape of Croat women comes from the weekly *Danas*: "With regard to the severity of violence, Croat women were no better off than Muslim women, but the scope of violence against Muslim women surpasses everything ever seen in history of wars" (January 29, 1993, 65).

While the rape of Croat women was usually mentioned without further detail, the rape of Muslim women was regularly given with more concrete details. The rape of Serb women, in comparison, was hardly ever mentioned, and if so, mostly to deny it.

RAPE VICTIM(S): THE ASHAMED, THE INVISIBLE, AND THE DENIED

There were few articles on rape on Muslim women that did not mention a specific effect it had on the victim: the feeling of shame. Many of the texts were about various support activities within Croatia, about discussions and seminars on war and sexual trauma, and about medical and psychiatric clinics that organized help for raped women. In the interviews with Croatian experts involved in these activities the readers invariably learned that Muslim women were deeply ashamed of their experiences, that they "hide behind anonymity" (*Vjesnik*, November 4, 1992, 9) and "do not easily admit that they were raped" (*Vjesnik*, December 29, 1992, 8). Consequently "the (true) number of raped Muslim women will not be known because majority of women will take their secret into their grave" (*Danas*, January 8, 1993, 19). Raped Croat women were never mentioned in such contexts.

The references to trauma and shame of Muslim women notwithstanding, there was not much written about their feelings. Unlike in the Serbian press, accounts in the Croatian press were seldom conveyed in first person singular. The words of one young Muslim woman—taken from the Italian daily *Il Messaggero*—are unusual in this respect: "I felt destroyed under my skin. I was dying, my whole being was dying" (*Vjesnik*, December 15, 1992, 22a). These few exceptions, when presented, conveyed the same image of the broken and ashamed victim, as given by the experts. In a box added to a larger piece of text, under the title "They Must Not Be Rejected," one raped Muslim woman pleads for the understanding and help, saying: "The number of raped women will never be known because these women are terribly degraded and humiliated. Most of them will keep their disgrace to themselves and I do not believe that they will admit that they are raped or pregnant. . . . The Muslim woman is raised as pure and chaste, she is her husband's woman, society watches her and the more she is secluded the more desirable she is" (*Vjesnik*, December 9, 1992, 32).

So, while this Muslim woman herself spoke to the journalist, she maintained—like everybody else—that no others would. There was only one voice different from others in *Vjesnik*, which contextualized the silence or demand for anonymity in a completely different way. It was in the very first *Vjesnik* report on rapes: "They only asked that their names were not revealed to the public for the time being, because each of them still had some family member in Chetnik camps" (*Vjesnik*, September 21, 1992, 7a).

After this article, the argument in *Vjesnik* changed, and the sole cause of the raped Muslim women's feelings of shame and attitude of hiding was related to their traditional and religious upbringing. Such representation, however, stands in sharp contrast to the fact that raped Muslim women were, at the same time, rendered highly visible. The fact that Croat women were so seldom mentioned made Muslim women stand out prominently, positioning them at the center of the narrative of rapes in the Croatian media. The fact that so many international and national institutions, organizations, and media also engaged in aiding them positioned them in the center of public attention.

Thus, the representational strategy of the Croatian press was quite different from that of the Serbian press. Experts were speaking of, and for, Muslim women. The Serbian newspapers also used the words of experts and reported about various committees and institutions, but they also wrote the most compelling stories, quoted the women's own words, described every move of their hands and eyes, and expressed deepest empathy for the women. Croatian papers could have done the same—they could have constructed their own tragic epic, told through the mouth of the raped Croat women. But they did not. Instead, they filled their pages with experts' speeches and activities on behalf of the Muslim women, exposing them while rendering them invisible, making them public while describing them hidden, naming them anonymously.

In the Serbian media representations of rape, ethnicity is defined through norms of *ethnic purity*, and the representation is focused on a presumed threat to that purity posed by Muslim men raping and impregnating Serb women. In the Croatian media representations of sexual violence, however, ethnicity is defined through the norms of *sexual purity*, guiding the focus away from those Croat women who are defined as sexually impure—raped and impregnated. It is the inconsequentiality of Muslim women for the media production of Croatian nationhood and statehood that is crucial in producing the narrative of war rape with Muslim women in its center.

In this narrative, the raped Muslim woman is not only a victim, but also a problem that needs sorting out. While some of the raped women were actually themselves engaged in self-help groups, in assisting other victims, and in collecting testimonies about rapes, and while the majority of them, especially at the beginning, were aided by feminist NGOs and other civil groups and not by the state, in *Vjesnik* they were turned into a kind of "Croatian burden." Regularly described as Bosnian refugees, they were clearly named as belonging to another state, and thus not as a legitimate part of Croatian statehood. Their nonbelonging to the Croatian state was confirmed through different means. One is by direct association of women with their presumably rightful state: for example, "Rape affects equally the raped woman and the raped country. Thus, I do not allow talk of raped

Croat and Muslim women without talking about raped Croatia and Bosnia" (*Vjesnik*, January 1993, 15).[9]

Another is through differentiation between a raped Croat woman and a raped Muslim woman. For example, one of only two articles that go into some detail about the rape of Croat women is taken from the French newspaper *Liberation*, commenting on a French TV program (*Vjesnik*, November 4, 1992, 9) in which a Croat woman relates her capture, rape, and escape. *Vjesnik* notes that the woman stated her full name and surname for French television. Apparently, unlike the numerous Muslim women who seem to prefer to remain anonymous, she was not ashamed to tell her name (though it is not reported in *Vjesnik*). While it is a normal practice that the names of the victims of crimes, including sexual crimes, are not reported in media, the point here is that *Vjesnik* mentions that the woman told her name, making her in this very fact, different from all the Muslim women, who were consistently represented as seeking anonymity.

Thus, the spotlight remained on the mute and humiliated Muslim women, and on the Croat experts who provided aid. It was, actually, among experts that the Croat woman took a visible and proud place: among doctors, nurses, psychiatrists, psychotherapists, religious activists, help-line activists, and politicians aiding the raped Muslim women.

The different representations of rapes of Croat and Muslim women in the Croatian press established the difference between all Croats and Muslims. The visibility of the Muslim woman only as the rape victim produces her as having nothing in common with a Croat, man or woman. For, according to the Croatian press, Muslims and Croats belong to different levels of civilization, which simply do not touch each other. One expert said as much: "All the people cannot achieve humanity and pacifism at the same time. Actually, rape is, for both the victim and the perpetrator, a sign of an insufficient humanity" (*Danas*, February 22, 1993, 64–65).

Rape, as a question of "humanity," would mean that the raped Croat woman, if visible, would be a link to those dehumanized Others—both the Serb rapist and the raped Muslim woman. And this needs to be prevented in order to preserve the humanity of the ethnic Self.

Dehumanization that equates the victim with the perpetrator is crucial for the representation of Serb women in the Croatian press. The rape of Serb women is mostly mentioned as a denial: that Serb women were not raped at all, or that rape was not on a mass scale, or—using indirect statement—that Muslim and (particularly) Croat forces did not commit any rapes, or had committed only incidental rapes. An article explicitly denying the rape of Serb women was published in *Vjesnik*, taken from a German TV documentary on rapes in Bosnia: "Serb organizations contacted German TV demanding that the other side of the strory be examined, because, allegedly, Serb women were raped just as much. So it was done. . . . Reporters went to hospitals in Belgrade and talked with Serbian officials without finding one serious trace of mass rape of Serb women. All the information [that Serbs had] was secondhand . . . without witnesses except for one single case [of rape] found in a military hospital in Belgrade. In the end, even Serbs were stunned, asking themselves how come that there is no information [about the rape of Serb women]" (*Vjesnik*, November 17, 1992, 3a).

Another article explains that there is a difference between rapes committed by Muslim and Croat forces and those committed by Serbs; quoting the statement of a member of the Bosnian government's War Crimes Commission, it says: "Rapes committed by soldiers of the B&H army [are] isolated cases, 'marginal consequences of war,' which will be punished if found out. These crimes cannot be compared with those committed by Serbs, because the latter were systematic, with the aim . . . to 'humiliate and destroy the whole nation.' . . . [There have not been] any rumors that members of Croat forces have committed such atrocities" (*Vjesnik*, February 4, 1993, 15).

Croatian newspapers also sometimes used the "all sides" argument, but always pointing to the minimal involvement of the Croat forces. One article states that the "rapists are all men participating in this cruel war, but Serb irregular forces committed the crime as a planned genocide" (*Vjesnik*, February 1, 1993, 22). While these statements often correspond with the findings of the United Nations Commission of Experts enquiry (Bassiouni and McCormick 1996), they are regularly followed by denials, which, according to the U.N. Commission of Experts Final Report, are clearly not true.[10]

Where Serb women are mentioned in the press as rape victims, the descriptions of Croat soldiers, the rapes, and official reactions to the rapes make the crime very different from that committed by Serb rapists: "[In Croatia] there was no organized violence of that kind, and there was especially no tolerance by the authorities. . . . Rapes occurred immediately after military operations, without women being in captivity for long and without continuous violence against them. The victims protested to the highest levels of Croatian government, and each captured perpetrator of such a crime faced justice. Raped Serb women received at least a moral vindication. . . . Not enough, certainly, but from the other side [i.e., Serbia] there are not even signs of such a moral and political concern" (*Danas*, January 29, 1993, 65).

In articles about rapes, an important strategy in writing about Serb women was to cast them as perpetrators of violence. *Vjesnik* carried a report from the German newspaper *Die Tageszeitung* about a preliminary gathering (held in Germany) of women's groups engaged in organizing an international congress on sexual violence in Zagreb. Under the headline "Serb Women Mocked the Victims," the article in *Vjesnik* states that "several women of Serb nationality protested loudly that their interests were not taken into account" and that *Die Tageszeitung* printed the statement by one of the organizers, in which she says: "Serb women tried deliberately to change the function of our gathering, to mock the victims and shift the concern to the futile discussion about the place where the congress should be held. 'Our men do not do such things!' they shouted. A day later they performed the same political theater in Strasbourg. . . . But we will not allow them to deceive us" (February 1, 1993, 22).

While Serb women are here presented as indirect perpetrators of violence, through their solidarity with rapists, in other articles they are named as directly involved in committing, or actively supporting, war crimes. In one article, a wounded Croat soldier told of his experience in a hospital in a Serbian town, which included a Serb woman regularly coming to beat him in his hospital bed (*Vjesnik*, April 27, 1992, 1). In another report, taken from an Austrian TV documentary on the Serb-run Omarska camp, where Muslim and Croat civilians were held, three women ex-prisoners named a woman, a former English professor, as the "assistant to the male chief of the camp" (*Vjesnik*, February 25, 1993, 30). In an article on the Serb soldier Borisav Herak, accused of genocide by the Bosnian government, another woman is named as a "chief of the Café Kod Sonje," where Muslim women were raped and killed (*Vjesnik*, December 17, 1993, 11).[11]

Vjesnik carried one very different story about the perpetrators of rapes and their victims: an article on the Center for Rape Victims in Zenica, Bosnia, sourced from the German *Frankfurter Rundschau*. Published in late 1993, when media interest in rapes had waned, it acknowledged that the patients in the center were "victims of rape of all nationalities," and it stated that rapists too were not limited to one nationality. It is exceptional in making the only concrete reference to rapes committed by Croat forces that I have found anywhere in the Croatian press. Muslim women patients at the center were described as falling into two categories—women from Serb-occupied regions raped a couple of months previously by Chetniks, and women from the Croat-occupied region: "We received women raped 24 hours ago, and two days ago. They come from villages in which the HVO [Croatian forces] killed or took away their husbands, and tortured women before the eyes of their children. Meanwhile, a great number of women in the occupied villages are kept in private houses, marked by a big letter 'B,' suggesting a brothel" (November 10, 1993, 16). In all other articles published in the Croatian newspapers I studied, the male perpetrator of war rape is a Serb man.

THE FACE OF SODOMY

Croatian papers invested much space to depicting the Serb rapists as "beasts," "monsters," "Chetnik bandits," and "Balkan butchers" led by "monstrous fanaticism" and accused of committing "crimes incomprehensible to human reason." Just as the Serbian *Politika* (January 18, 1993, 25) described as her former boyfriend a Muslim man who raped a Serb woman, Serb rapists were described in *Vjesnik* as former neighbors (November 29, 1992, 8), whose attitude had turned 180 degrees, and whose cruelty and treachery had suddenly become apparent.

Thus, the story about Serb rapists in the Croatian press used much the same language as the story about the Muslim rapist in the Serbian press, where the Muslim rapist was defined as treacherous, primitive, and bestial and relegated to the darker periods of human history. Reports of the forced impregnation of Serb women introduced Orientalist discourse, defining Muslim men and their acts as a remnant of a terrifying past through which the Serbs had once already lived. However, while in the Serbian newspapers Muslim rapists were regularly featured in stories about rapes and forced impregnations of Serb women, there was no distinctive, separate story about them. No single text was dedicated to a Muslim rapist. The Croatian press, however, besides mentioning the rapists in its articles about the victims, also had a number of specific articles about the rapists. Most of these dealt with one man—Serb soldier Borisav Herak—his trial in Sarajevo for war crimes against the Bosnian population, and his death sentence. For example, a two-part interview with Herak with a total of nine large photos appeared over two weeks in *Danas* (April 16 and 23, 1993; four and five pages long respectively). The interview—interwoven with extracts from the judge's summing up, shows no disbelief or disgust toward the accused, and makes no fierce accusations. The photos show an almost shy and confused man, head bowed, arms folded. Toward the end of the article we read: "Asked by a judge if he had anything to say as the judgment was passed, Borisav Herak (22) said: 'I ask for the death sentence for myself, and if possible that my father comes and brings some cigarettes, because I do not have any'" (ibid., April 23, 31).

Similarly grim is the *Vjesnik* piece, which reprints "What Are Monsters For?" by Slavenka Drakulić, from the German newspaper *Die Woche*. The article deals with the fear of the evil in each and every human being, of ordinary people turning into war criminals, and the need to "name the evil, so that it could be removed, killed, or shut away in a ghetto. For, as long as there are the guilty parties, there are the innocent as well." Drakulić ends with: "Worse than identifying a killer is identifying his ordinariness, a fact that it could have been any of us—we were just not in the same situation. That is what the monsters are for too: so we can wash our own bloody hands" (July 3, 1993, 24).

In both these texts Herak is strangely remote from the horrific reality of his crimes. His detailed and detached description of his crimes, his dispassionate explanation, and his acceptance of the sentence position him in a larger picture of the meaning of regional history that repeats itself in massacre after massacre. Drakulić frames him in a philosophical quest—the meaning of life, humanity, and sanity. Herak himself disappears in the inevitability of her statement that "it could have been any of us." These texts, which are in stark contrast to other *Vjesnik* pieces on Herak, show that there was discursive space for a representation that is not engaged in Othering.

Most of the articles about Herak place him firmly in the concreteness of his crimes and connect him with the Bosnian Serb military and political leadership, with Serbia, and finally, with the Serbs in general. "A Criminal with a Childlike Face" quotes a psychologist giving a portrait of Herak, noting that he was "brainwashed" and "manipulated," and that in a "normal situation" he would not have become a criminal: "He was exposed to huge pressure, a terrible disinformation. The really guilty parties are those who pushed him and used him" (*Vjesnik*, December 17, 1992, 11).

"I did not enjoy it," quotes the journalist in Sarajevo, David Crary, who reports Herak as saying not only that he did not enjoy his crimes but that he was forced to perform them, under the threat of death: "soldiers had orders to do these things" (*Vjesnik*, March 17, 1992, 32). While the previous articles had portrayed Herak as a pawn of history or a hostage of human nature, this one depicts him as a pawn of his criminal political masters from Serbia. In both cases, however, were it not for these powers beyond him, he himself would remain almost insignificant.

Herak's photograph appeared over and over again, until his face was no longer a face of a "young man from the neighborhood" (Drakulić in *Vjesnik*, July 3, 1993, 24) but the face of a half-witted rapist (*Vjesnik*, December 17, 1992, 11), for whom the rape was his "first sexual experience" (*Danas*, April 16, 1993, 23). But this face was also a Serb face, as many headlines indicated. The *Vjesnik* headline above the story reads "I, the Serb Rapist," March 16, 1993, 10).

In *Vjesnik* the only rapists are the Serbs, so Herak's face is the face of them all. With this face attached to all Serb rapists, "the Serb" becomes a general term for rapist. This production of ethnicity tied to violence continues in the long article "Europe Is Raped Again" by Professor Muradif Kulenović, with the long subhead "Compared to Current Pre-Planned Rapes and Forced Pregnancies, the Practice of Sodomy in the Past Represents a More Humane Level of Serbian History" (*Danas*, February 22, 1993, 64–65). The text starts by stating: "The act of rape is an act of power, revenge, and humiliation. All the evil in the human genome." The author continues by elaborating the definition of rape, asserting that rape is an issue of power and male domination over women, explicitly crediting feminism for this analysis. Eldridge Cleaver is quoted as describing rapes as a "dialogue between races" as well as a form of male communication through women, the "rebellion" of a black man against the white master by "desecration of his woman." Freud and Levi Strauss are quoted on the production of myth: the subconscious and savage turned into the emotional and intellectual. Then the author quotes the leader of Bosnian Serbs, Radovan Karadžić, saying that "God is a Serb" and that a "Serb is God," and explains that national myths created by Karadžić and the supporters of Greater Serbia are responsible for the development of rape as a war strategy. All these intellectual contributions, however, fulfill one objective—to define the Serbs, and their place in humanity as well as in history:

> There is a well-known Serbian proverb, "King Marko f-- a foal, not because he wants c-- but because he wants revenge."[12] Everything is clear here. Sodomy represents a more humane level of Serbian history, and today's regressiveness seems deeper. The power of sup-

> pressed hatred in the past was enormous, for how else can we explain rapes that seek power and spill aggression, humiliating the humanity of the nation. Most homosexual rapes are not openly of sexual nature. Research shows that rapes in prisons are not motivated by sexual need. On the contrary, autoerotic masturbation brings relief much faster, and it is a far more normal way . . . [T]he rape of men by men is not rare. . . . I heard prisoners released from Serb camps talk about horrific rapes and evil against men, but other truly perverse pseudosexual acts were committed too; such as forcing men to perform oral sex, pushing a baton into the anus, and other extreme perversities. (*Danas*, February 22, 1993, 64–65)

The article ends with the statement that rape dehumanizes both the rapist and the victim. The dehumanized rapist becomes, in this article, a collective definition of the Serbs, with the faces of Herak and Karadžić merged, to give one face to all the Serbs. In such representations as these, the Croatian papers developed a distinctive story about the Serb rapist as a monster, centered on an unnatural and abnormal sexuality, which defined all Serbs as perverts. Rape was only one of their perversions, alongside homosexuality and sodomy. It is on that basis that all Serbs were denied humanity, as well as civilizational progress in history.

ETHICS OF ETHNICITY

Like the Serbian press, the Croatian press also developed a story about forced impregnations. But this was a very different story. The victims and the perpetrators in these stories were different—Muslim women impregnated by Serb men—and so were the representational strategies of the press. The Serbian press focused mostly on the ethnic Self, passing through the female bodies to reach the male. The Croatian press focused almost exclusively on the ethnic Other, continuously shifting between the female and the male body. The Serbian story on forced pregnancies was about the endangered ethnic survival of the Serbs and represented the Serb men as its true victims, with the impregnated Serb women as a secondary casualty. In the Croatian version, there was no story of ethnic survival, only a story about morality, in which the mothers' responsibility, abortion, and rejection of a newborn child, on the one hand, and civilizational moral standards, on the other hand, stand central.

Between December 1992 and April 1993 several articles appeared in the

Croatian press on forced pregnancies resulting from rapes. With "Heaven's Children," the issue is defined explicitly in moral terms: "The data about concentration camps, the data about rapes of women—girls, women, and old women—had lain for a long time in the relevant drawers and files of Western democracies before they became a media hit. Postponing the publication of these facts, and the suspension of the starry sky and moral laws, put Western democracies on the same level as Serb rapists. There is no astonishment at this delay. There is no timing for moral categories" (*Vjesnik*, January 1, 1993, 15).

It is this accusation of Western complicity that prompts the journalist to conclude: "From the rich Western democracies we already hear about those who wish to adopt children conceived by crime. . . . [T]hey do have paternal right to these children."[13] But the ethical point is then taken to a much more fundamental level, a level that establishes a new ground upon which the Serbs are defined:

> A qualitative change occurs when the issue of rape, and raped women, is concentrated on forced pregnancies. The problem of rape belongs, even if it is denied, to the human society that we know through our experience. The problem of forced pregnancies goes beyond it. The Croatian language helps in understanding the difference. One says to "give life" and to "cause death." In the case of forced pregnancies the life is not given but is caused, like death. . . . I have always hesitated to name a nation as a culprit, knowing that all prejudices, genetic and otherwise, return to those who express them. But the fact of forced pregnancies does not compel me so much to condemn the Serb nation as to date it. Namely, this is an absolutely pre-Judeo-Christian act. It is notable that the crime of forced pregnancies is not prohibited by any of the Ten Commandments. . . . If it is possible that one nation commits crimes for which the time and space in which they occur have no measure, then that nation is not from that time and space. It belongs, thus, to the remote past of the barbarian world, a definitely different and other world, marking it by this unforgettable mark. (*Vjesnik*, January 1, 1993, 15)

This passionate plea for defining the Serbs as collective outcasts from European Judeo-Christian history and civilization is quite dissimilar in style to the other texts about forced pregnancies in the Croatian press. It stands along the texts that define the Serbs through the image of the rapist. But it is similar through the connections it makes between religion and ethics. In most of the texts about forced pregnancies of Muslim women—and all the texts are about Muslim women—the focus is not on the perpetrator but on the victim. Thus the ethical issue is no longer the crime, but its consequences: termination of pregnancy or not, and the fate of the children born from rape.

As in their story about rapes and rapists, the Croatian papers' story on forced pregnancies came in the form of either reports from the foreign press or expert opinions of religious leaders, doctors, and aid workers about the matter. For example, one of the first of the articles about pregnancy to be published in *Vjesnik*, entitled "Raped Woman Does Not Have to Give Birth," presents the issue as one of religious beliefs and ethics. It is an interview with the leader of the Muslim religious community in Croatia, who is also the imam of Zagreb. The article has six sections: on women, rape, rapists, the case of one particular raped woman, abortion, and a woman's relation to the conceived child—in Serbian and Croatian, her *plod*.[14] The imam discusses Muslim religious laws and attitudes to each of these issues. At the end he states: "The Muslim standpoint about abortion is similar to the Christian one, and the life of a child in the mother's belly must not be questioned in any way; but Islam presumes that the *plod*, until it becomes alive, may be aborted under certain conditions. It is certain that a woman cannot accept carrying in her belly the *plod* of violence, let alone give birth to it and raise it. Her psychic and mental state must be respected. It is her sovereign right to decide about the fate of that *plod*; because it was she who was violated it is her decision, for her mental health, and it is not up to anyone else. . . . To work on awakening motherly love in these women means to touch their psyche" (*Vjesnik*, December 9, 1992, 10 and 23).

These two questions—about abortion and (the possibility of awakening) mother's love—are present in many other texts. Under the title "Raped and Conscience" the same article is reprinted in *Danas* a month later, with additional statements from Catholic and Orthodox officials. These are, interestingly, presented not as official positions of the churches, but as opinions of the interviewed individuals. A professor from the Catholic Faculty of Theology at the University of Zagreb says, under the subhead "Multiple Sin": "Abortion is unacceptable . . . [T]he better solution is for the women to give birth . . . because one trauma—rape—cannot be healed by another—abortion. But what if they cannot find strength to give birth? In these difficult times we will respect their conscience, because the conscience is the final subjective ethical arbiter" (*Danas*, January 8, 1993, 18). It is worth noting here that official position of the Catholic Church was a prohibition of abortion, so this opinion obviously differs. An official of the Serbian Orthodox Church presents the most conservative view, stating that for him, abortion is "a murder, a destruction of human life. The exception is possible only if the life of the mother is endangered. Those who kill cannot be reckoned as true Christians" (ibid., 19).

The highest religious authority of the Catholic Church—the pope—was also mentioned in different occasions. *Vjesnik*'s correspondent from Rome, for example, commented on the reaction of Italian press and public—especially the negative reaction of Italian women—on the pope's advice to the raped women in Bosnia to "turn the act of violence into an act of love" and give birth to the children conceived in rape. Readers were reminded that only a few days before, the pope had urged Catholic women not to marry Muslims. The correspondent concluded that pope's message expressed "too much tolerance toward the violator and the intended objective of his violence" and that "in case of rapes in Bosnia, the literal following of [evangelistic] ethics would mock the faith itself" (*Vjesnik*, March 1, 1993). A week later another controversy from the Italian press is discussed: two nuns from a Catholic monastery in Bosnia, raped and impregnated by Serb paramilitaries asked the pope to approve abortion in their cases. But the Italian daily *La Repubblica* stated that the Vatican officials rejected any possibility for abortions, and advised the nuns to either leave the cloister and raise the children or give them for adoption (*Vjesnik*, March 8, 1993, 30).

Doctors were also interviewed on the question of abortion, and their concerns, as quoted in *Vjesnik*, were similar to the Vatican's. While one doctor recommended that "an ethics committee should be formed to make a common decision with regard to the termination of pregnancy" (January 10, 1993, 4) others explicitly opposed abortion. The Croatian Association of Catholic Doctors invoked the innocence of the conceived while stating that they did not approve of terminating pregnancies resulting from rape, and promised that the Croatian Catholic Church and Caritas (a Catholic humanitarian organization) would help the mothers and the newborns (January 21, 1993, 11). In the article "A Child Is Born to Live," the director of Caritas, a woman, pointed out that in their shelter "there are about 20 women and children, and only one of them has abandoned her newborn," concluding that "it is a misconception that a child not born of love cannot be loved" (*Vjesnik*, April 1, 1993, 6).

These articles reveal the prominence of the question of abortion for the Croatian national(ist) project. Croatian feminists have struggled hard since the early 1990s to redress some of the consequences of the pronatalist stance of the church and the government.[15] They have had to counteract the aggressive campaigns of right-wing organizations and a well-organized and well-funded Catholic Church. At one time, the streets of Zagreb and other Croatian cities were plastered with posters of a fetus in a womb with the huge words "Mother, why are you killing me?" Forced impregnation reawakened the debate, with new Croatian legislation on abortion allowing doctors and hospitals to exercise "conscientious objection"—to refuse to perform abortions based on their religious or ethical objections. Some forcibly impregnated women were denied abortion, even when it was still medically and legally possible.[16]

Within nationalist discourses in the Balkans the question of abortion was never confined to ethics or religious beliefs. It was always a question of how many Serbs or Croats would be born, compared to other ethnic groups, especially those perceived as archenemies. The so-called white plague—the nationalists' nightmare of their ethnic stock declining while the others multiplied—meant that abortion remained a significant question in various nationalist projects in Serbia as well as Croatia.[17] Representations of forced pregnancies in the Serbian press, however, touched the issue of abortion only in passing, without going into its ethical and religious ramifications, and ultimately dealt with the issue of national survival. The Croatian press, on the other hand, focused on the ethical and religious issues, and never saw abortion in terms of the survival of the ethnic group. This difference is not surprising, because the focus of the representation in the Croatian press was on Muslim women and their impregnation by Serb men, and thus had no implications for the survival of Croats. Abortion is perceived as a threat to national survival only when Croat women have them, thus when it is about unborn Croats. As raped and impregnated Croat women remained hidden, this allowed the issue of forced pregnancies to be *ethnically* inconsequential, while *ethically* relevant. Only when the Serb perpetrator is in the picture, do ethical issues meet ethnicity in the Croatian press, to create the highest moral order, which names humanity and dates history after itself.

7

ON VICTIMS AND VILLAINS

When reports came out of mass rapes in Bosnia, feminists throughout the world reacted promptly. Numerous women's groups and organizations, both national and international, mobilized to support raped women and to force violence against women onto the international agenda. Their efforts also had a theoretical dimension, with feminists analyzing the international law and human rights aspects of prosecuting rapists and investigating war rapes in former Yugoslavia. But the most outstanding analyses addressed the rapes in former Yugoslavia as a specific, gendered war strategy.[1] These persistent and well-organized feminist efforts contributed to the establishment of the International War Crime Tribunal and the international acknowledgment of women's human rights, although the credit is more often given to media images of starved male bodies and stories about raped women.

Writing about war rapes in the former Yugoslavia, Cynthya Enloe (1993) asserts that the timing of the war rapes in Bosnia made all the difference to public perception of the issue, and how the raped women were treated by feminists. After describing the characteristics of contemporary feminism—feminist theoretical and activist work on rape, feminist internationalism strengthened by electronic networking, and feminist involvement in redefining some of the oldest mainstream political ideas, such as the meaning of Europe or of human rights—she asserts that feminists involved in supporting raped women from Bosnia did so "not to instrumentalize women as victims . . . but to explain anew how warmongers rely on peculiar ideas about masculinity and rethink the very meaning of both sovereignty and national identity" (220). She further notes:

> [Women] who have suffered wartime rapes in Bosnia are being spoken about by feminists in many countries in ways unheard of only a generation ago: these women are *not just rape victims*; they are being portrayed by feminists as simultaneously women with particular sort

> of positions within their evolving communities' political systems; they are women who have voices that are expected to be heard—or to be silenced; they are women with self-perceptions of their own and sexuality shaped by cultural norms and commercial exchanges. If this feminist understanding is widely accepted, Bosnian women who have been raped will hereafter have to be treated—and listened to—not as conveniently one-dimensional cartoons but as actors in their own complexly gendered political communities (ibid., 223–224; emphasis added).

In many cases, Bosnian women were in fact treated as actors by feminists, but there were many examples of just the opposite. Enloe's essay appeared in *Mass Rape: The War against Women in Bosnia-Herzegovina*, edited by Alexandra Stiglmayer (1993a), the single most often quoted book by feminist academics dealing with rapes in Bosnia. This book, however, contains quite different accounts of attitudes alongside the one offered by Enloe. Susan Brownmiller's contribution in the book, for example, gives a dire and prophetic warning in summing up the attitude of many journalists, academics, and feminists to war rapes and the raped women. She asserts that in this war Balkan women *are* perceived as being just the rape victims, that this is their new identity (Brownmiller 1993, 180). This warning finds many a reflection in the writings on war rapes in Bosnia, within which further victimization was part and parcel of the politics of writing, and within which textual practices of inclusion and exclusion paralleled those seen in the representational practices of the media war.

Victims Included

In the foreword of Stiglmayer's book, Roy Gutman, a journalist who helped bring to light the war rapes in Bosnia, states: "A great many of the women were raped while held captive, unprotected and vulnerable, their husbands and fathers having been taken away. . . . In the conservative society in which the Muslims of rural Bosnia grew up, women traditionally remain chaste until marriage. Rape is a trauma with far-reaching consequences for these victims, who have well-founded fears of rejection and ostracism and of lives without marriage and children" (Gutman 1993, x).

This production of Muslim Bosnia—through the images of conservatism, traditionalism, and remote villages—is a moral map against which an image of a Muslim woman is drawn. The word "chaste," powerfully invoking images of the innocence and vulnerability of girls awaiting marriage and childbearing, frames the presumption that this situation is particular to Muslim communities and Muslim women of Bosnia, and that because of that, rape has far-reaching consequences for them.

Gutman is not the only author in Stiglmayer's book who produces that imagery. Azra Zalihić-Kaurin (1993, 170) praises the Muslim society and men of Bosnia for the courtesy, respect, and honor they show to women. She gives an idyllic picture of Muslim traditions before communism, condemns socialism for marginalizing Islam, and welcomes the return to the Islamic traditions in postcommunist Bosnia—traditions defined through the Muslim women's virginity: "Young Muslim women today may wear miniskirts and have boyfriends, may study and work, but they still respect the commandment of virginity. Marriage is as self-evident as is a mother's responsibility for the education of her children. In remote villages Muslim traditions are even more alive. There is still the custom that after the wedding night a mother-in-law hangs out the sheet on which a young couple has slept so that everyone could see that the bride was a virgin" (172–173).

The contribution ends with a glorification of a young Muslim woman—a heroine from a Second World War story—who demanded to be killed rather than raped by Chetniks. This image of a Muslim woman, who prefers death to dishonor, framed into the discourse of Muslim traditions of male protection of women, reduces Muslim woman once again to the blind follower of the cultural norms, and at the same time asserts her difference from the other women in the region, even if this difference here is evaluated in positive terms.

Writing about her work with raped women from Bosnia and Croatia, Vera Folnegović-Šmalc notes that because of the social and cultural pressures, raped women "even now respond only rarely to offers of . . . psychiatric help and seldom ask for help on their own initiative. If they do come forward they try to remain anonymous" (1993, 177). Similar imagery is produced by Seada Vranić, a journalist from Bosnia, in her book *Breaking the Wall of Silence*: "The silence of the victims during my investigation was also my adversary. Very often I felt as if I were standing in front of a wall, yet it was human beings, not bricks that were in front of me. Human beings who were unhappy, shamed, humiliated and lost" (1996, 29). At the same time, Vranić states—without noticing the contradiction—that her book is the result of over two hundred interviews with raped women, men, and girls who did not stay silent.

Nevertheless, the same imagery of silent and ashamed Muslim women is repeated in many other academic texts, even those informed by feminism, and then used as an argument to bring justice to victims of rape. Caroline Krass (1994, 321), for instance, states that the stigma attached to victims of rape "proves especially severe in Muslim communities, where the religion emphasizes virginity and chastity before marriage." Using the adjective "Bosnian" and "Muslim" interchangeably, Elizabeth Kohn (1994, 204) states, "Because of their culture, many Bosnian women, especially those in small villages, are ashamed to come forward and testify publicly." Michael Jordan (1995, 20) quotes a Western diplomat claiming "the greater-than-usual degree of shame felt by the primary victims, the Bosnian Muslims, as a result of their religious beliefs." Underpinning these statements is the ethnicization of the images of shame and religious traditionalism, with Muslim women from Bosnia as their exclusive embodiment.

For those familiar with life in Bosnia the equation of the former Yugoslav republic with the traditional Muslim countryside ruled by religious customs strikes a false note. Since the 1970s the Muslim population of Bosnia has been predominantly urban, with educated, urbanized, modern Muslim women being no different from educated, urbanized, modern Croat, Serb, Yugoslav, or any other women living in Bosnia.[2] But even if not, one cannot but ask: how different are Muslim women who cherish the importance of virginity, from Croat and Serb women who think the same? Are non-Muslim women less "chaste," and does rape hold fewer consequences for them, because of that? Is rape a lesser trauma for those women who do not think of marriage and children as their only future, or for those already married? Further, how different is the experience of rape for a religious Muslim woman from that of an equally religious Catholic or Orthodox woman? Does rape have less traumatic consequences for women who are not religious? What is the usual degree of shame appropriate for the rape victim? Censuses in Bosnia have always showed a high rate of people who declared themselves in nonethnic terms; so how many of the raped women would actually define themselves exclusively as "Muslim," "Croat," or "Serb"?[3] And why is the Bosnian Muslim community singled out as the one that stigmatizes and ostracizes raped women?

These images produced by experts and journalists and used further by feminist academics define the Muslim woman from Bosnia as the ultimate rape victim, powerless and ashamed, and consequently, as Brownmiller (1993) asserts, produce a rape victim identity as an exclusive preserve of the Muslim women. That identity would come as a direct insult to the raped women from Bosnia and Croatia, because many of them refused to be silent and ashamed. They not only spoke out and demanded justice, but also worked for it, in the midst of war. Their swift denunciation brought two of their few gains—aid for raped women (however inadequate compared with the needs) and the establishment of the International War Tribunal, where rapes of women have been tried officially.[4] Women from Bosnia and Croatia did not have to wait fifty years, like the women forced into the Japanese military system of sexual slavery system from World War Two,[5] to see at least some justice, at least some accountability for the crimes against them. They showed courage and determination in naming the rape and the rapist, relived the trauma, and gave it shape in a testimony. This was acknowledged by the United Nations Commission of Experts.[6] The Commission's main sources were 700 interviews with refugees from former Yugoslavia, commissioned by the Austrian, German, and Swedish governments, and 223 interviews with refugees in Bosnia, Croatia, and Slovenia, as part of its own fieldwork (Bassiouni et al. 1996, 9). Several of the men and women interviewed were assessed by the United Nations as "key witnesses, because they [had] not only seen or experienced a great deal, but also [had] the emotional strength and clarity of presentation to play a pivotal role in a prosecution case" (United Nations 1994c, 5).

There would have been no prosecution were it not for these witnesses who testified, refusing to stay silent or ashamed. Many others spoke to journalists; their faces appeared in photos in almost every newspaper and magazine around the world. They obviously did not hide, and they deserve credit for this. Those who spoke out but requested anonymity, or who spoke only to their doctors, also deserve recognition. As do all those raped women who, besides speaking, also engaged in activities of numerous women's and feminist groups—from giving and collecting testimonies, to forming self-help groups and organizing antiwar and antinationalist actions nationally and internationally.[7] It was this courage that furnished feminist engagements with regard to violence against women in wars, and women's human rights, throughout the 1990s. But in the process of politicizing the plight of all women, the raped Muslim women from Bosnia and Croatia were delegitimized politically, and the rape victim identity was produced to represent them.

Why was it so easy to make the Muslim women the ultimate victims? An indication could be found in Tone Bringa's (1995) analysis of ethnographic research on Bosnia. She pointed out that Orientalism affects the capacity of European ethnographers to deal with the Europeanness of Muslims in Bosnia, noting that, in European ethnographic literature, Bosnian Muslims were defined either as not really European, or as European but not really Muslim (7). The production of "greater-than-standard shame" of the raped Muslim women is a recreation of an Orientalist myth of a conservative Muslim community that is cruel to its women, even with evidence to the contrary. Cheryl Benard (1994, 43 n. 19) wrote that while working with raped Muslim women she "found no evidence to support the idea that Bosnian victims of rape or families reacted differently from any other European victims and families" and found most Bosnian "families have been highly supportive."

Orientalism is still a powerful force in Western politics and culture, and feminist production succumbs to it, too, as Willy Jansen's (1996) analysis of the representations of Arab Muslim women shows. Colonial, missionary and native literature and paintings from the eighteenth to the twentieth century, as well as today's social science scholarship is still focused on "women's illiteracy, political muteness and victimization" (ibid., 248), alongside the "presentation of female sexuality" (239) in Orientalist paintings of scenes from Turkish baths. Jansen establishes a link between the two representations stating that "muteness" can be combined with the exposed sexual bodies, for it is easy to depict Arab Muslim women as sexual objects when they are denied intellectual autonomy and political subjectivity.[8]

Rachel Bloul (1997) has analyzed how French feminists engaged in the debate about headscarves for Muslim schoolgirls often used arguments and vocabulary similar to those used by the right-wing politicians, while Helma Lutz (1991, 1997) points out in her research on the representation of Muslim migrant women in Europe that Orientalism has shaped both mainstream and feminist representations. Both authors emphasize that Muslim women are regularly represented as blind followers or victims of traditional norms, and thus denied any personal autonomy or political subjectivity of their own. Thomas Spijkerboer (1994), in his analysis of the position of refugee women in Europe, also finds similarity between feminist and nonfeminist arguments. He emphasizes that the supposed powerlessness of nonwhite women reproduces the depoliticization of refugee women's situation, even when they act as political subjects.

Victims Excluded

One particular consequence of the rape victim identity produced for Muslim women was the delegitimization of Serb women who were raped. They were delegitimized in different ways, by simply being omitted when rape victims are mentioned, in numerous feminist and nonfeminist academic texts on rape victims in Bosnia and Croatia, or by the specific way in which perpetrators were talked about. The ethnic logic of rape was here followed by the ethnic logic of talking about them: mentioning only the "Bosnian Serb forces," the "Serb forces," or "the Serbs" as rapists meant that the victims were non-Serb women. Sometimes, Croat and Bosnian forces were explicitly defended. Seada Vranić (1996, 29) asserted that "not one neutral and official investigative team identified the Army of Bosnia-Herzegovina as perpetrators of rape. Rapes which were committed by some of its members or by civilians were qualified as 'individual cases' and were 'infrequent incidents.'" Vranić does not source any of these documents, but they cannot be from the U.N. Commission's report, because it lists by name and location the camps run by Muslim forces where rapes were systematic.

That denial of the rape of Serb women was clearest in two essays in Stiglmayer's book by the American feminist Catharine MacKinnon, who led an antipornography campaign in the United States, using rapes in Bosnia as her weapon. One of these essays was reprinted from the American magazine *Ms.* The fallacy of MacKinnon's arguments has been exposed by several authors, but her international fame made her essays among those most often quoted by other feminists writing on the war rapes, thus spreading the victimization of Muslim women and demonization of Serbs and rendering raped Serb women invisible.

MacKinnon believes Serb men are rapists because Yugoslavia was saturated with pornography—a conclusion based on an assertion of Serb men's love for pornographic magazines, on detailed descriptions of horrific atrocities, and on an unproved statement that the rapes were systematically filmed. But, as Erica Munk (1994) rightly pointed out, the problem with MacKinnon's thesis is that pornography in socialist Yugoslavia was anything but widespread. It was mostly confined to large urban centers and tourist areas, while hardcore porn was underground and unavailable—as in some Western countries—over the counter at newsstands.[9] The magazine *Start*, which featured naked models in the 1980s in socialist Yugoslavia on its center spread (so that the pages could be used as a poster) also featured one of the first regular feminist columns by Slavenka Drakulić, and was published in Zagreb, in Croatia.[10] Thus, the pornography-entails-rape link does not explain why only the Serbs, in all of ex-Yugoslavia, turned out as rapists.

MacKinnon also argued that the rapes were regularly filmed for use in pornography for sale or as war propaganda (MacKinnon 1993, 75–76). The U.N. Commission's Final Report contains only one reference to a filmed rape—of two women imprisoned in the Serb-held camp Bučje (United Nations 1994b, 58). Every recorded incident of rape and sexual assault in the Final Report is sourced; for the statement about the filmed rape, the source given is MacKinnon's *Ms.* article (United Nations 1994b, 111 n. 686). In the gruesomeness of the Balkan wars, every horror is imaginable, including the filming of rapes. But had this practice been more prominent, let alone widespread or systematic, it would have been mentioned in the conclusion of the U.N. report, the way others have. It was not mentioned. However, MacKinnon's entire argument of the genocidal nature of war rapes by "the Serbs" is based on war rapes being systematically used as pornography. However problematic or unsubstantiated her argument was, it was frequently quoted in international feminist meetings and in academic articles on rapes in Bosnia, as well as in the world media, with criticism or doubts usually confined to footnotes.[11] At the same time, in Croatia, the nationalist press widely used MacKinnon's attack on Croatian feminists (for mentioning that Croat forces also committed rapes) to substantiate their own antifeminist campaign. Vesna Kesić,[12] a feminist from Zagreb's Women's Lobby and the Center for Women War Victims asserted that MacKinnon's argument has become "part of the war propaganda used to stir ethnic hatred and promote revenge." Demonized Serb rapists from MacKinnon's essays automatically delegitimized raped Serb women as victims.

It is interesting that Stiglmayer's own contribution to the book she edited (1993a) addressed the absence of Serb women in the reports of rapes in Bosnia: "They are wives, sisters, and daughters of the aggressors. There is hardly a journalist who feels motivated to seek them out, to check up on what has happened to them and thus offer propaganda material to the Serbian side—that is, the 'bad' side, the side 'responsible for the war'" (Stiglmayer 1993a, 137–138). So one would expect Stiglmayer not to make the same mistake. And she does mention several cases of rapes of Serb women. However, in doing so, her language betrays her own perspective as the same as one that she apparently criticizes. After describing at length the "suffering of Muslim and Croatian women" (137), Stiglmayer describes "recurrent instances of misconduct toward Serbs" (137). The U.N. Commission documented not "instances of misconduct" but rather "patterns of conduct . . . , regardless of the ethnicity of the perpetrators or the victim," noting that "it is clear that some level of organization and group activity is required to carry out many of the alleged rapes and sexual assaults" (1994b, 13). Their report also names numerous camps as sites of systematic rapes and sexual assaults against men and women, including "the Serb-run Ušara High School camp in Doboj, Muslim-run Čelebići camp in Konjic and Croatian-run Dretelj camp in Čapljina" (ibid., 10).

The absence of Serb women as visible victims of rape in international media and scholarly work may be due to one objective factor. As seen in the U.N. Final Report (1995c, 5), few Serbs gave testimony, as most of them had fled not to Croatia or Slovenia (where the data were collected), but to Serbia. Among the 223 refugees interviewed by the U.N. Commission, 146 were from Bosnia (100 Muslims, 43 Croats, and 1 Serb). Of the 77 interviewed refugees from Croatia, 26 were women and all were Croats (ibid.).

The Yugoslav government was collecting testimonies of atrocities against Serbs, but first, it did not allow independent international observers or direct access to witnesses, and second, both the Yugoslav government and Bosnian Serb leaders refused for a long time to cooperate with the International War Tribunal, leaving many testimonies of Serb victims unheard.[13]

However, the definition of the Serb women within the discourse of the perpetrators is a much more likely reason, as a comparison of the writings about rapes in Bosnia and rapes in Kosovo shows. The Independent Committee investigating the accusation of rapes of Serb women by Albanian men in Kosovo published its report in 1990 (Popović and Petovar 1990). Police records of prosecuted and convicted rapists were used as an indication of the numbers of rapes inspired by political motives (i.e., Albanian separatism). Fewer alleged rapists were convicted than were prosecuted, which indicates some acquittals. But in general, the number of cases of rape of Serb women by Albanian men was very low, and steadily decreased from 1982 to 1989. In the last three years of investigation no cases were reported in police records at all (41).

However, the data in the committee's report show that Serb and Montenegrin women were overrepresented among the victims of rape by Albanian men. In all rapes of Serb and Montenegrin women, 57 percent were by Albanian men, and 38 percent by Serb men. As a comparison, 95 percent of raped Albanian women were raped by Albanian men and only 5 percent by men of other nationalities (43). Thus, while Albanian women were generally raped by Albanian men, Serb women were still more likely to be raped by Albanian men than by Serb men.

The committee pointed out that, given the patriarchal culture in Kosovo, "rough estimates" are assumed to be high, especially among Albanian women. Finally, the committee concluded that given the tense ethnic relations, the projected theoretical incidents of rape—projections that rested on general statistics on rapes—are higher than those actually encountered on the ground, meaning that Kosovo had in fact a much lower rate of rapes than other regions of Yugoslavia. According to the committee, this is an indication that the ethnic conflict actually had a reverse effect—instead of increasing violence, it separated ethnic groups, and thus reduced incidents of rape (46). The fact that Albanian men raped predominantly Albanian women was used as grounds for dismissing the argument that rapes of Serb women were "politically" inspired (47). The higher social mobility of Serb women was given as an explanation for their overrepresentation among victims of rape in general (compared to their numbers in Kosovo population), and by Albanian men specifically (43), although this argument contradicts the argument of high level separation between the two communities.

Silva Mežnarić, a feminist from ex-Yugoslavia who compared rapes in Kosovo with the rapes in Bosnia, interpreted the report in an interesting way. She asserted that "from 1987 to 1989 there was not one case of rape of a Serb by an Albanian" (1993, 124), while, in fact, the report had noted only that in that period there were no *reported* cases of rape in police record (Popovic and Petovar 1990, 41). In an article published a year later, Mežnarić went a step further: "According to some sources, a few girls, after losing their virginity, would invent stories of rape and, to prove it, would injure themselves. Such cases seemed to be equally distributed among the Albanian and Serbian population" (1994, 83).

As I show in chapter 1, the issue of rapes *was* used by Serbian nationalism in the 1980s, in order to produce the victimized ethnic Self and the demonized Albanian Other. There is no dispute there. My dispute is with how facts and figures have been interpreted by Mežnarić, and what the consequences of such interpretations are. In Kosovo, police records have been taken as exact numbers in relation to Serb women, while in Bosnia grey figures and estimates—ranging from sixty thousand to a hundred thousand—have been taken as exact numbers in relation to Muslim women.[14] Mežnarić (1993 and 1994) argues that in both cases, the rapes were a result of Serbian nationalism: those in Kosovo belonging to nationalist fantasy, those in Bosnia and Croatia belonging to nationalist reality. Such interpretations not only produced a Serb woman who cannot be (considered) raped, but in effect, strengthened the argument that the crimes of the Serb forces in Bosnia were fundamentally different from those committed by the other forces. The distinction between "ethnic cleansing" and "opportunistic" rapes certainly points to a fundamental difference. However, rapes in detention were not opportunistic, and the distinction between ethnic cleansing and systematic rapes in detention as documented by the U.N. Commission is "an extremely negative measure of innocence," as Munk points out (1994, 50).

It seems, however, that for many authors, admitting to the crimes of Croat and Muslim forces would diminish the crimes committed by Serb forces, and naming Serb women as raped would diminish the suffering of Muslim and Croat women. In contexts in which naming is such an important political strategy, not naming is a political act as well. This is particularly important when acknowledging that, in Serbia, one of the strategies of denying crimes committed by Serb forces was precisely a continual emphasis on the suffering of Serb population and the crimes committed against them, as well as a consistent refusal to name the rapists among Serb forces and their allies as Serbs. And the Croatian media, while highlighting the shame and the silence of the raped Muslim women, not only denied that the Serb women were raped, but also named them as perpetrators.

In all the media representations of the raped women, the raped female body is always ethnic. Only as such—as simultaneously female and ethnic—is it vested with meanings within different narratives of victimization. Furthermore, in media representations specific female bodies are always linked to specific territories. In both the Croatian and Serbian press, Muslim women are excluded not only from sharing the prerogatives of femininity ascribed to Croat and Serb women, but also from belonging to the specific territories to which Croat and Serb women presumably belong. This persistent linkage of the raped female bodies with specific ethnicity and territory is one of the main representational strategies of the media war. The raped ethnic-female body always belongs to one specific ethnic territory, symbolically expelled or separated from all the others. Its representational function is to establish a particular ethnic geography.

Those same strategies are imbedded in the practice of rape within the ethnic war. Julie Mostov (1995) pointed out that one of the main purposes of war rapes in the former Yugoslavia was in marking ethnic boundaries and distinguishing ethnic groups. But rape as an instrument of ethnic war defined the female body not only as an ethnic boundary but also as the ethnic territory. As Robert Hayden has indicated (1996), for new ethnic boundaries to be established in Bosnia and Croatia, old territories had to be renamed, repopulated, reclaimed in ethnically exclusive, and exclusively ethnic terms. Only Serbs could live in Serb territory, and only Croats on Croat land. "Ethnically mixed" territories and "ethnically mixed" marriages—once a pride of "brotherhood and unity"—were unimaginable, as much as the "ethnically mixed" children of forced pregnancies became an impossibility and were ascribed clear ethnic belonging. Remapping the old territories meant renaming and reclaiming them ethnically. And this process rested on the possibility that the bodies attached to land can also be separated and expelled from it with violence, once their belonging is denied symbolically.

It is this link of ethnicity and territory through raped female bodies that in effect, makes both the victims and the perpetrators imaginable only through their ethnicity. It is the ultimate victory of the ethnic war and the media war that raped women and rapists were so consistently counted, included, and excluded, exclusively through their ethnicity, and because of it, that the analysis of rape repeated—instead of subverting—the ethnicization of both the victim and the perpetrator.

8

THE BODY OF THE OTHER MAN

It may seem strange to talk about men as victims of sexual violence while discussing a war that was infamous for making rape of women one of its weapons. But the United Nations Commission of Experts Final Report and other reports list numerous incidences of sexual violence against men. They were beaten across the genitals, forced to strip, raped and assaulted with foreign objects, and castrated. Sometimes prisoners were forced to perpetrate these acts of violence on each other; at other times the prison guards performed them.

The U.N. Commission's finding that sexual assaults conducted in the wars in Bosnia and Croatia were systematic and executed with a clear political purpose (United Nations 1994a, E3; 1994c, 5) was received by the public, already familiar with the large-scale sexual violence against women, as referring to women only. The report's conclusion actually does not specify that the patterns of rape and sexual violence also affected men. What the U.N. Report does show is that testimony about sexual violence against men came mainly from witnesses and not from victims themselves. The expert witnesses in front of the Tribunal also pointed out that they had close to no firsthand encounters with male victims of sexual violence (ITCY 1995, 19).

Had I not read the United Nations report in full, I would never have learned that men were also subjected to systematic and widespread sexual violence. There was little academic attention to the issue at the time. Adam Jones (1994) was the first to assert that the war in former Yugoslavia produced gender-specific violence against men. Catherine Niarchos recognized, in a note, that the "situation of male victims [of sexual assault] raises different issues" (1995, 653 n. 13), but she did not pursue it. Seada Vranić (1996) included the testimony of a raped man in her book but did not analyze it. The medical doctors Mladen Lončar and Petra Brečić (1995), who treated male victims in Croatia provided a rare, detailed account of characteristics of sexual abuse of men that they encountered in their practice.

The international media—so fervent in reporting rapes of women—shied away from the topic of sexually assaulted men. In coverage that relied heavily on images of starving Muslim men behind barbed wire and on the tear-stained photos of raped women, no one saw a photo of a raped man.

Intrigued by the fact that sexual violence against men, while present in the U.N. report, was absence from public debates, I decided to pay more attention to it and reviewed the Croatian and Serbian press once again. I found a handful of articles dating from November 1991 to December 1993 on sexual assaults of men in the Croatian daily and weekly, compared to over one hundred about other forms of torture experienced by the Croat population in Serb-held camps and over sixty referring specifically to rapes of women. In the Serbian daily and weekly I did not find a single article about sexual assault on men, despite both extensive writing about the torture and killing of Serbs in camps held by Croat and Muslim forces and frequent denials of accusations of atrocities committed by Serb forces. Unlike the rapes of women, sexual assaults on men seemed to be absent from the public domain in both Serbia and Croatia.

Why was sexual violence against men so invisible? Were men even more reluctant than women to report that they were victims of sexual assault, or were the number of assaulted men so much smaller than that of assaulted women? Did the men's ordeals leave fewer survivors to tell their story, or were the media simply not interested in them? In the earlier chapters I have already shown that the male ethnic Other is represented in the media as being significantly different from the male ethnic Self. The male Other was feminized by being dressed in a skirt, demonized as an aggressive rapist, and sodomized through representation of his sexual desires and inclinations. These elements of othering are even more pronounced in media representations of male sexual violence against men. While the number of men who endured sexual assaults will probably never be established, their invisibility has to do with the role of the male body in the production of ethnicity, and with notions of masculinity and norms of (hetero)sexuality therein.

The Visible: Ethnic Victim, Ethnic Perpetrator

The first two articles, out of a handful, about male victims of sexual violence in the wars in former Yugoslavia, appeared in *Vjesnik* in early 1992—almost six months before sexual violence against women became an issue in the war.

In February 1992, a short *Vjesnik* article conveyed the disbelief of the journalist writing it—or his editor—with both a question mark and an exclamation mark at the end of the headline "Chetniks Raped Lorry Drivers?!" In the text, which is dry and much more neutral, a Muslim refugee hiding in a ruined house described how four trucks of a Bosnian aid organization—under protective escort by the JNA—were stopped by Serb paramilitaries: "With their guns pointed they forced the military patrol to abandon the drivers of the lorries. Then they started the maltreatment of the drivers, who were Muslims, and at the end they raped them. Chetniks tortured the men and plucked a fingernail for every attempt of the naive drivers—who believed that the JNA would ensure their security on the roads—to refuse cooperation" (February 16, 1992, 7).

In March 1992 another story, from the Croatian news agency and with no author name given, filled the bottom quarter of a page with the testimony of a Catholic priest about his ordeal in two Serb prisons. He described how he was taken to a police building in a nearby town. There he was first beaten inside the building, and then taken outside, in front of about forty Serb civilians: "I was covered in blood. They took off all my clothes and poured cold water on me. They were suffocating me with water, mocking my nakedness and continuing to beat me with whatever they had around." (March 5, 1992, 7). The torture lasted about half an hour. Then a new group of civilians arrived, demanding that the torture be repeated; their demand was fulfilled. The next day he was interrogated and beaten again: "When they all beat me I had to take off my clothes and one [Serb paramilitary] carved on my chest the Serb coat-of-arms with a knife, laughing like a madman, caressing my shoulders while telling me: 'You are a Serb now.'" Torture continued the next day. After twenty-three days in that prison the priest survived a mock execution and went again to jail, this time sharing a room with about ten Serb soldiers who were imprisoned "because they refused to kill Croats." Sent to yet another jail in Serbia (near Belgrade), he was eventually released. The article ends with: "Catholic priest Josip Bogović is ready to testify before the international commission as well as to submit his medical documentation."

There are several differences in these two stories. While the former is told by a witness, a survivor tells the latter. The former is very short and, except for the headline, not very emotional. The latter uses dramatic language to describe events. The victims in the former are Muslim men, and in the latter a Croat priest. A closer look shows that the representations of the crimes described—those against Muslim men and those against a Croat priest—are also different.

The first story lists the facts, but also expresses disbelief that a man can rape a man. That disbelief frames the event into a story about sex, and not about war crime or torture, as the exclamation and question marks remind the reader of the taboo of male sexual contact. The association of Muslim men with homosexuality belongs to the ready-made imagery in both European and local production of the Orient. As true children of Europe, Slovenian, Croatian, and Serbian nationalists have systematically Orientalized their southern and eastern neighbors, including subsequently both the "Eastern Christianity" of the Orthodox Serb (in Slovenia and Croatia) and Islam. The association of the Chetniks with the raping of men was a new element that would become important in representations of the Serb men in general.

In the second story, the cruelty of the Serb offenders is more prominent, both in the detail (the destruction of a village, the murder of the villagers, and torture of the village priest) and the emotional language through which perverse bestiality and madness are depicted, as in the laughter of a man who, while carving on the chest of a naked priest, caresses his shoulders. Furthermore, the "civilians" here are not innocent bystanders but Serbs who demand the priest be tortured.

While the perpetrators are represented very similarly in the two texts, the representations of the events and victims differ significantly. *Vjesnik* explicitly calls the experience of the priest "hideous torture," but not the rape of Muslim men. The second article repeats the descriptions of the priest's torments three times, highlighting his ordeal. The repetition acts as representational strategy that, besides highlighting the nature of the Serb offenders, also underscores the nature of the offence: it makes sure the readers understand that nothing else happened to the priest, except what is depicted. He may have been stripped naked, but, unlike the Muslim men, he was not raped.

Once the rape of women and rape camps became publicly known, sexual violence against men appeared only sporadically in the Croatian press. It was mentioned only a few times, and in quite different kinds of texts. Most of these texts were imported, one way or another. Furthermore, save for the article in *Danas* that I discussed in chapter 6, where rapes of women, forced impregnations, and rapes of men were discussed together by a psychiatrist (*Danas*, February 22, 1993, 64–65), there were no further articles about the sexual assault of men, only sentences imbedded in longer texts.

On October 24 and 25, 1992, *Vjesnik* (now renamed *Novi Vjesnik*) published, verbatim, an extract from an official United States report on human rights abuses in the war in Bosnia, along with testimonies collected by journalist Roy Gutman and international organizations such as Amnesty International. With the title "No Survivors in Omarska Camp—New American Documents about Crimes in B&H" (October 24, 10A–19A), the text covers two pages and includes a photo of faces behind the wire (a detail from a well-known image showing withered bodies of Muslim men in the Serb-run camp Omarska). The report lists war crimes by date and gives a brief description, including the ethnicity of the victims and the perpetrators in most cases. Listing the crimes committed by Serb forces against Muslim civilians, a former Muslim prisoner of the Serb-held Camp Luka[1] describes that "he saw once about 15 corpses of young men, age 18 to 30, all naked, with their genitals cut off. The guard threatened him [saying] that the same would be done to him" (ibid., 19A).

These two sentences are all the article says about sexual violence against men. The article does not mention the ethnicity of the victims, but it is apparent from the ethnicity of the witness, a Muslim man. The next day *Vjesnik* continued with "The Latest Report from Amnesty International" (October 25, 7A), listing the crimes in order of date—a Muslim imam killed by Serbs, Serb civilians killed and mutilated by Muslim forces, and Serbs raping Muslim women, destroying religious sites, and emptying villages. Then there's a mention of the sexual assault of Muslim prisoners by Serb guards in Omarska camp. A Muslim man "witnessed public beatings and sexual assaults in the camp. He said that the camp guards forced a few prisoners to have intercourse, and that . . . the guards cut off their hands and penises, as a punishment, and as a means of frightening other men" (Ibid.).

In a December 1992 article, "There Are Other Camps," sexual assaults on men are mentioned again in a short column. The article was written by *Vjesnik*'s Paris correspondent. It states that Medecins Sans Frontiers presented evidence, at a press conference in Paris about the existence of these other camps and listed their locations. Refugees living in France who had survived torture told Medecins Sans Frontiers of the killings by Serbs that they witnessed in the Kozarac camp.[2] "Women and children were raped and tortured" and "many men were tortured, and some of them had their genitals severed" (December 10, 9A). The ethnicity of the victims is not given.

The article "In the Death Camp in Vjesnik" of February 25, 1993, (30) was taken from the Austrian newspaper agency ORF and carries the long subhead "Mehmedalija Sarajlć Did Not Want to Rape a Girl. He Was Castrated, His Eyes Gouged Out, His Throat Slit. Three Women Recognized Some of the Perpetrators." Accompanying the article is a photo of prisoners entering a camp, their hands tied behind their backs, which bears the caption "Omarska, Manjača . . . they say it is the same in other camps." The subhead is repeated almost verbatim in the body of the article.

The only exception to these short articles is a lengthy article in *Danas* from February 1993 (mentioned also in chapter 6, in relation to the representation of the Serb rapist). It gives expert, scientific authority to the definition of the Serb perpetrator. In this article, the rape of men functions as the final proof of the Serbs' bestial, perverse, sodomist nature: "[T]he rape of men by men is not rare. . . . I heard prisoners released from Serb camps talk about horrific rapes and evil against men, but other truly perverse pseudo-sexual acts were committed too; such as forcing men to perform oral sex, pushing a baton into the anus, and other extreme perversities" (64–65).

Not surprisingly, in all of these texts the only victims of sexual assaults whose ethnicity is explicitly stated are Muslim men, and the only violators named are Serb men. Thus they are men who, by the logic of the ethnic war were neither a part of the Croat self nor a part of the emerging Croatian national territory.

Masculinity, Heterosexuality, Victimization

In their analysis of the legal aspects of prosecution and conviction of perpetrators of rape and other types of sexual assault in former Yugoslavia, Dutch legal experts Tineke Cleiren and Melanie Tijsen,[3] (1996) state:

> From the legal point of view . . . rape and other types of sexual violence should not be regarded as specifically gender-based offenses but as crimes of violence of a sexual nature, although gender should not be disregarded when such crimes are committed against women. If violence is considered to be the determining element, then there is no

> ground to distinguish between male and female victims, or between adult and child victim. Until now, however, international law has not paid much attention to sexual assaults on men. This is hardly surprising since homosexuality is a topic not freely talked about in many cultures. But sexual assault on men, both of a homosexual nature and a non-homosexual nature (such as mutilation of genitals), has been reported in the war in former Yugoslavia. In general, it can be said that customary international humanitarian law does not discriminate on the ground of sex and that, therefore, the law relevant to sexual assault on women should apply with equal force to men. (111)

In this statement there are obvious misconceptions of gender and sexuality, as well as of meanings of sexual violence. The misconception of gender is clearest in the assumption that gender matters for violence against women, but not men, and that by excluding gender and focusing on "violence of a sexual nature" instead, victims would be given equal footing in the eyes of international law. The misconception about violence is evident in the assumption that sexual violence has the same meaning regardless of the victim and that it is experienced in the same way by everybody—men and women, adults and children. Furthermore, Clieren and Tijsen also define sexual mutilation of a man as violence of a nonhomosexual nature, implying that rape of a man by a man is a homosexual act.

There are a few things to distinguish here. First, neither the fact of sexual violence of a man against another man, nor any particular act of violence is in itself of either homosexual or heterosexual nature. Which of these acts will be *represented* as homosexual is a matter of dominant notions of masculinity and the norms of heterosexuality in a particular cultural and political context. The acts of violence are informed by the same set of discourses and practices—produced through intersections of gender, sexuality, and ethnicity—that informs the representation of these acts. In other words, the cultural meanings of violence predefine the violent act as well as their representations, while political context—in this case the context of the ethnic war—makes some victims visible, while obscuring the others.

It is the intersection of gender and sexuality with ethnicity that makes a difference here. Within the Western academic construction, masculinity has been mainly researched in relation to femininity and homosexuality, both of which are defined as the Other of the dominant forms of masculinity, be it a dominated social Other (women, gay men) of the masculine institutionalized power, or an "enemy within" of the masculine sexuality (femininity, homosexuality).[4] Many of these studies were inspired by theoretical frameworks developed by psychoanalysis, focusing on heterosexuality as the main site in which masculinity is constructed.[5] The privileged position of sexuality as difference in these studies impacted on perceptions of male violence against women and gay men. While the former was seen as an issue of power, the latter was viewed as a manifestation of men's subconscious desires for another man. The argument goes that men would be frightened of such a desire and, in order to dispel it they direct their aggression toward gay men (Easthope 1986). In this context, it is taken for granted that only women would be assaulted *sexually*.

Studies that include other social and cultural domains or power relationships are still relatively few in number. But they bring into masculinity studies much needed insight into the concrete workings of masculinity in different social contexts and specific cultural relations.[6] While some of these studies show that the production of masculinities in different societies may be quite different, other cross-cultural studies point out certain similarities: the need to negotiate certain roles and positions, the struggle to maintain continuity or introduce change, the frailty of established boundaries and differences.[7] The most significant contribution of these studies is in showing that different, often competing forms of masculinities exist within the same culture, that every society has a plurality of socially unequal masculinities, and that only some of these—associated with the most powerful social groups—will assume the position of dominance or hegemony, while the others will be marginalized or subjugated. Hegemonic masculinities are supported by powerful social institutions and ideologies, the authority of which rests on violence as well as on identities internalized through culture (Connell 1987, 1995).

It is however through black studies and (post-)colonial histories that the issues of race and ethnicity get their rightful place in the studies of masculinity and violence. The significant contribution of these studies is the assertion that the production of different masculinities occurs in a particular sociopolitical and historical context.[8] Mrinalini Sinha (1995), for example, analyzes the colonial constructions of the "manly Englishman" and the "effeminate Bengali" against changes within English colonial politics in India. She asserts that the colonial constructions of different masculinities was an element of "specific practices of ruling," in which a straightforward defense of racial exclusivity was substituted by a "supposedly more 'natural' gender hierarchy between 'manly' and 'unmanly' men" (5). Such studies have opened new theoretical perspectives, showing that the Other of masculinity is not only the feminine and homosexual Other, but also the racialized, colonized, ethicized Other; and that it is the body of the male Other that becomes the site of violence.[9]

In his analysis of representation of manhood in popular culture Antony Easthope asserts that the "most important meanings that can be attached to the idea of the masculine body are unity and permanence" (1992, 53). Echoing this assertion, Joanna Bourke writes about the social discomfort with amputee soldiers in Britain, pointing further to another aspect of the absent body parts of men: they had not only special, if ambiguous, public appeal, but also a "special patriotic power" (1996, 244). The British state acknowledged the patriotic power of missing limbs by providing artificial limbs, as well as state pensions, according to estimates of the value of each particular limb. Each part of a man's body was allocated a moral weight and was measured by the degree to which it "incapacitated a man from 'being' a man" (ibid., 243). However, there was a limb—the "member"—not mentioned on the carefully assembled list that Bourke provided at the end of her text, nor does she mention it herself. The silence in her book makes the silence of the men who lost their genitals—and were thus incapacitated from being men—hardly surprising.

The analysis of the representation of European men and women in an Indian anticolonial uprising by Jenny Sharpe (1991) points to yet another layer in the relevance of the unified male body. Unlike bodies of colonial (European) women, the bodies of colonial (European) men were never depicted as mutilated. The absence of mutilated bodies of Englishmen from the colonial narrative represented the "absence of narratives that objectify English men" (ibid., 34). The white colonial master is *one who objectifies* both the natives and the white women, and thus cannot be in the position of an object himself.

But if Bourke's and Sharpe's arguments are brought together, one could conclude that it is the obscured, the made-invisible, the rejected, mutilated body of the hegemonic male that stands as the metanarrative of European histories of colonialism and racism and informs all other narratives, including the narratives on the male Other, thus providing justification for the violence against him. As Cynthia Enloe (1989, 44) says about nationalism, it is masculinized memory, masculinized humiliation, and masculinized hope that lie in its beginnings. When linked to race and ethnicity, masculinization here actually appears as the process of producing the hegemonic body as intact and powerful, and objectifying the body of the Other.

As scholars in black studies have noted, the male body as an object—mutilated and hated—was a part of black history, the history of slavery and lynching. Jonathan Rutherford (1988) points out that castration often preceded the lynching of black men, and that it was executed by heterosexual men who often held central positions in the white community. Rutherford's analysis of lynching defined the sexually mutilated black male body as a site of the white men's power. James Messerschmidt (1998, 147) adds explicitly that lynching was about sexual power, because race and sexuality *together* defined what it meant to be a white man. To preserve this definition, the sexuality of the racial Other had to be redefined (demonized through the imagery of the black rapist) as well as destroyed (through castration).

These analyses of the intersections of masculinity and heterosexuality with other relations of power and other identities in the context of male-to-male sexual violence, together with research on sexual violence in prisons and the sexual torture of political prisoners, show that the tortured and violated male body is the site of multiple power relations, and that sexual violence against men is a manifestation of a struggle for social dominance, rather than subconscious homosexual desires.[10]

However, within the dominant cultures of the contemporary North and West, there is still an assumption that heterosexual men do not assault other men *sexually*. This assumption homosexualizes sexual assault against men by other men. The position of subordination, passivity, and violability, assigned to women in gendered hierarchy, further feminizes the victim of the assault, be it a woman or a man. If the act of violence both feminizes and homosexualizes the male victim, its result is demasculinization. In other words, it means stripping a man of all the prerogatives of proper masculinity defined by the dominant discourse. This makes it impossible for such a man either to make the violence against him visible or to claim retribution without admitting to the loss publicly. When his manhood also symbolizes ethnic identity, the loss is not only individual but also applies to the entire ethnically defined community.

Julie Peteet (2000) indicated something similar in her analysis of the role of violence in the imprisonment of the young Palestinian boys and men in Israeli prisons. Surviving Israeli prison and being exposed to torture is experienced by the survivors, as well as by their community, as contributing to young men's sense of heroic masculinity, adding to their social prestige.

Thus, the Israeli system of imprisonment, which is meant to bring humiliation to Palestinian men, is actually turned into the very base of the heroic masculinity in the narrative of collective Palestinian resistance.[11] Having learned this, Israeli jailers seem to be changing tactics: some interrogations now seem to include sexual assault, with photos being taken of prisoners fondling other prisoners. Peteet (2000, 121) rightly asserts that sexual torture serves to deprive imprisoned men "of claims to manhood and masculinity" and consequently of their symbolic and actual position of leadership within Palestinian community.

It is this symbolic and actual position of men within their racialized, ethnicized communities that both informs sexual violence against men and makes the crime hidden. For the same reason, only some of the victims are, exceptionally and selectively, made visible. To follow Sharpe (1991) it is the position of the "master of the narrative" that makes a difference. In other words, the act of violence is directed against the ethnicized/racialized Other whose power needs to be denied, destroyed, or appropriated. But the visibility of the victim will depend on whether the victim is the "master of the narrative" or its Other; the former being spared the visibility, the latter being exposed.[12]

The Body of the Other Man

Dominant notions of masculinity in the Balkans, as in most phallocentric, Western societies, are inseparable from norms of heterosexuality and notions of power. The embodiment of that dominance is the penis, and its symbolic equivalent is the phallus. In that light, castration and the cutting off of a man's penis are acts of physical as much as symbolic emasculation, because the lack of a penis symbolizes the lack of phallic power. The phallic power however is not linked only to possession of the organ. In many cultures, having a penis and also being penetrated by it both feminizes and homosexualizes the penetrated man, and him only. As some research shows, it is the gendered role of passivity, submission, and subordination in the dominant gender hierarchy that feminizes the penetrated men.[13] Thus, while castration and rape as acts of violence are not per se an expression of homosexuality but of the struggle for power, they nevertheless feminize and homosexualize the man who is subjected to the violence.

In the Balkan context, however, there is a difference between these two acts of violence. While castration is the symbolic appropriation of the male

Other's phallic power, rape is not. In Balkan norms of sexuality, both men involved in the sexual act are homosexualized. Thus the drastic difference in the acts of sexual violence performed by the camp guards and the prisoners themselves, as well as in their media representations. It seems that prison guards have mutilated and assaulted male prisoners with foreign objects in public, but have not not raped them in public. Evidence provided by Lončar and Brecić (1995) seems to indicate that when the prison guards engaged in raping male prisoners, they did not want witnesses. This may mean that men raped by prison guards may have had much less chance to survive. For only the death of the raped—as an erasure of the evidence—could spare the heterosexual masculinity of the rapist.

Contrary to this, when prisoners were forced to assault each other, this was done in public. As the U.N. report indicates, the prisoners were forced to assault each other in many different ways, including placing them in positions that mock sexual intercourse and forcing them to commit rape. The Croatian daily *Vjesnik* mentions the fact, but uses a euphemism: prisoners were forced "to have intercourse" (October 25, 1992. 7A). The difference in wording is significant, as it frames the assault as sex. Thus in the Croatian daily Muslim men were feminized and homosexualized as victims, while the Serb men were homosexualized and demonized as perpetrators.

The practice of sexual mutilation of men in former Yugoslavia, together with the practice of its media representation, confirms the significance of the intact male body for the nation, indicating that the unity of *some* male bodies—those belonging to the Self— is always most important. In *Vjesnik*, the bestialized bodies of the Serb men and the mutilated bodies of Muslim men produced the Croat men as the masters of the national narrative. The Croat man's unquestionable heterosexuality and unchallenged masculine power are symbolized in his absence from the narrative of rape and castration. That absence is what renders Croat nationhood potent and the Croat state powerful; the masculine power of the emerging nation state is thus preserved in the unity and permanence of the manly bodies of Croat men.

A similar dynamic of violence and its representation seem to have been in play in the sexual assault of prisoners in the Abu Ghraib Prison in Baghdad. The 2004 report of the Article 15-6 Investigation of the 800th Military Police Brigade (the so-called Taguba Report)[14] also indicates numerous acts of abuse, very similar to those in the Bosnian and Croatian camps, including stripping and leaving detainees naked for days, forcibly arranging them in sexually explicit positions, forcing male detainees to wear female underwear, forcing them to masturbate, attaching wires to their penises, and forcing them to pile up on one another naked; and in most of these situations detainees were photographed or videotaped (Taguba 2004, 16 and 17).[15] The obvious homosexualization and feminization of the detainees functioned as a producer of difference between the prison guards and the prisoners, defining the guards as both powerful and heterosexual. The participation of the female guards in these atrocities, which seem to have stirred the (feminist) public additionally, has a function within this framework. While it was supposed to increase humiliation and emasculation of the prisoners (for being both physically and sexually overpowered and controlled by women), it also served the symbolic function of preserving the heterosexual masculinity of the American guards. It is worth noting here that this participation is neither incidental nor unwitting. While partaking in preserving heterosexual masculine order, the female prison guards simultaneously took part in preserving Western and American racialized order, *as their own*. Within these orders, the tortured and abused men were defined as the multiple Other—through race, religion, and culture as much as through masculinity and sexuality.

The othering of the Iraqi prisoners did not stop at the act of violence, however. It continued in media representations, where their naked bodies were openly displayed in the press, on TV, and on Web sites. Initially this display seemed to have been concerned only with the sexual sensitivities of the viewer, with the images blurring the prisoners' private parts. Only after a while were the faces of the prisoners also blurred, to protect their identities. Their bodies, however, have been on display in the media ever since the first reports appeared. In some of the photos, however—such as in the photo of the pyramid of naked bodies, or on photos where the frame captures only the mid-section of the body—it is the body parts that are prominently in view.

What these media representations show is a complex interplay of gender, sexuality, race, and religion, within which the *other man* is the one who is continuously homosexualized, feminized, and dehumanized.[16] This interplay has a particular political, not only cultural, context: the "war against terror" wherein the face of the Arab Muslim man is the face of the terrorist. The outrage with which American authorities reacted when the media showed the dead bodies of American soldiers being dragged through the streets of Mogadishu, Somalia, some years earlier, the sensitivity with which the burned bodies of the American civilian contractors hanged by the Iraqis were blurred, and the constant concern of the American government to keep even the coffins of dead American soldiers out of public view, proves all too well that the visibility of the violated Iraqi prisoners in American, as well as in European, media is conditioned by their otherness. This further tells us that the media partake in social power, both by adhering to the dominant discourses of othering (merging old colonial imagery with the ideology of the "war against terrorism") and by reproducing them further in their own practice of representation.[17]

Othering as the clue in the visibility of the male victim of sexual violence in the Croatian press is confirmed by the attitude of the Serbian press, which made no mention of men involved in sexual assaults on other men. As already noted in previous chapters, the homosexualization of the enemy was a common practice in Serbian press. Men from Serbia who opposed the wars in Bosnia and Croatia were regularly labeled *pederi* (pederasts) and denounced as "not real Serbs." Articles in Serb tabloids explicitly called Muslim men homosexuals and used historically and culturally constructed arguments to "prove" that homosexuality is a natural state of Muslim men. Thus, producing difference in ethnicity through different masculinities and sexualities has been used for a long time in the Serbian press. So, if we follow the logic of the Croatian press, and assume that the Serb victim and perpetrator will be hidden, why didn't the Serbian media mention sexual assaults on/of Muslim or Croat men?

The answer seems to be that the representational strategies of Serbian press differed from those in the Croatian press when it comes to sexual violence against women and men. The Croatian press relied much more on producing the ethnic Other, while the Serbian press was much more focused on producing the ethnic Self. In the Croatian media representations, Muslim women and men as the victims of sexual violence, and the Serb rapists, were the most significant figures. In the Serbian press, the ultimate victim of rapes of the Serb women, through their forced impregnation, was the male Self—the Serb man. In the Serbian media the Serb man was represented through the notions of virility and fertility—all prerogatives of unshakable heterosexual masculinity and power. At the same time, the Serb soldier was represented as a larger-than-life hero, a knightly protector of the weak, and the master of the narrative. This narrative was of suffering and victimization, but the suffering was ethnicized, not sexualized. Consequently, the focus on the ethnic Self left no discursive space within which a narrative of male rape or castration could be developed, as such a narrative requires the ethnic Other.

Representations of sexual assaults against men in the Croatian media, and their absence in the Serbian media, further indicates that homosexuality and heterosexuality are not defined simply as opposition, but as an essentialized and ethnicized difference. Homosexuality is produced as a natural characteristic of men of certain ethnic groups—Muslims in the Serbian press, Muslims and Serbs in the Croatian press. Furthermore, in the Croatian press the homosexuality of Muslim men and the homosexuality of Serb men are defined as very different: the former are feminized through victimization, the latter demonized and pathologized through their perpetration of violence. It is the strategy of representation to define different masculinities and sexualities as determined by different ethnicities, precisely because these different masculinities and sexualities are used to produce ethnic differences, and to produce those differences as essential. Finally, in all these examples, it is clear that there is a definite choice of masculinities and sexualities from which media can produce the ethnic Self and the Other. Dominant notions of masculinity seem to carry very specific representational limitations, precisely because they are so intricately linked to power and heterosexuality. This is why there was so little written about sexual violence against men even in the Croatian press, compared to hundreds of texts about all the other atrocities. Ethnic communities in the former Yugoslavia were never as segregated as some racial or colonial communities might have been. Many of the cultural practices—and especially notions of gender and norms of sexuality—were generally shared, and the differences were often much stronger between rural and urban areas than between ethnic or religious communities.[18] Thus, while the Other was central in the representation of the sexual violence against men, the commonly shared cultural code that "masculinity equals heterosexuality equals power" still posed restrictions on exposing too many mutilated male bodies, albeit of the other man.

9

TROUBLES WITH THE VICTIM

In her analysis of rapes of women in Bosnia and Croatia, Rhonda Copelon points out that "rape takes many forms, occurs in many contexts, and has different repercussions for different victims" (1993, 213). She asserts that each instance of rape has its own dimension that must not be taken for granted, pointing out that specificity does not mean uniqueness, or exclusivity: "The rape of women in the former Yugoslavia challenges the world to refuse impunity to atrocity as well as to resist the powerful forces that would make the mass rape of Muslim women in Bosnia exceptional and thereby restrict its meaning for women raped in different contexts. It thus demands recognition of situational differences without losing sight of the commonalities. To fail to make distinctions flattens reality; and to rank the egregious demeans it" (ibid., 214).

After the rapes in Bosnia and Croatia were ranked by many as unique and exceptional, the worst in human history, it is time to place them alongside others, without losing sight of either differences or commonalities. There are at least three good reasons for doing this. One is the centrality of sexual violence against women, and men, in political violence and armed conflicts around the globe since World War Two.[1] Another is the centrality of sexual violence directed against women for their feminist theorizing as well as their activism, in peace and war alike. The last reason rests in centrality of the victim and her/his visibility in both the violence and the feminist theoretical and political strategies concerning it.

Analyzing Sexual Violence and Its Visibility in Armed Conflicts

When it comes to sexual violence in the context of violent conflict, the intersection of gender and sexuality with other social relations of power is impossible to overstate. Histories of slavery and racism show this all too clearly. Racist discourses have dehumanized black women's sexuality and effectively relegated the rape of black women to nonexistence. This dehumanization and the consequent assumption of *unrapability* still figure among the defining elements of black femininity in European sexual politics.[2] Besides protecting white rapists, the racist discourses on rape pose significant difficulties in addressing the rape of black women by black men, as accusations of that kind verge on disloyalty to "one's own race" while at the same time threaten other affiliations—feminist being among them.[3] Finally, the racist discourses produce black men as the ultimate rapists while at the same time obscuring (sexual) violence against them.[4]

Analyzing these issues, Valerie Smith (1991) asserts that slavery, the lynching of black men, and the rape of black women have informed the construction of racial and gender identities in America. Consequently, rape as a crime defines women in more than one way. It does not represent only a violation of a woman's body: "Rather, in terms of interlocking issues of race, class and gender, these crimes suggest that certain women's bodies are more valuable than others" (278). This differential value of female bodies was also obvious in the war rapes in Bosnia and Croatia, as well as in the representational strategies used by the Serbian and Croatian press.

Black and (post-)colonial studies have found that rape functions within a (time and space) specific political contexts. In her analysis of rape in colonial India, Jenny Sharpe (1991, 36–37) points out that colonialism was a "signifying system" within which the meanings of rape were produced. My own analysis shows not only that the two wars (media and ethnic) framed the main political context that produced meanings of rapes in the Balkans, but also that specific local politics—such as shifting alliances between the warring parties—played a role in this production. Susan Pedersen (1991, 662) makes a similar observation when describing the concerns of colonial administrators in Kenya, that their interfering with "native issues" regarding Kenyan women could endanger the (sexual) safety of white women.

The centrality of sexual violence against women in producing collective identities within specific political contexts is also well known in South Asia. So is the differential place of violated femininity as a cradle of collective—in this case communal—values, identities, histories, and traditions. Kumari Jayawardena and Malathi de Alwis (1996, xv) show, on the one hand, that violence "'facilitates' the formation of particular identities and the dissemination of specific ideologies" in postcolonial societies of South Asia. They also find that the more marginalized a woman and the group to which she presumably belongs are, the more exposed she is to the sexual violence, and the less access she has to protection. This analysis is supported by the war strategies in the Balkans.

In their sophisticated analyses of sexual violence during the Partition of India in 1947, Urvashi Butalia, Ritu Menon, and Kamla Bhashin[5] convincingly show that the female body became one of the primary sites of communal violence.[6] The accounts of "rapes, of women being stripped naked and paraded down streets, of their breasts being cut off, of their bodies being carved with religious symbols of the other community" (Butalia 1993, 14) indicate that the violence functioned in the production of collective identities. Menon and Bhasin (1998, 43) assert that the divisions between India and Pakistan were "engraved . . . on the women . . . in a way that they *became* the respective countries, indelibly imprinted by the Other." This symbolic geography of the sexually violated female body and its role in the construction of collective identities was, according to Menon and Bhasin a significant similarity between the violence against women during Partition and that during the wars in Bosnia and Croatia. According to Chiseche Mibenge (forthcoming) similar acts of violence against women were also seen in Rwanda, even against dead women, indicating further the symbolic value of the violated female body in the production of collective identities.

As I argue in chapter 8, sexual violence against men follows a similar logic when the individual male bodies carry attributes of specific collective identities and function as symbols of ethnic, racial, or religious communities. But, this is where the similarities between meanings of the rape of women and the rape of men in nationalist and communal violence stop, and parallels between victimized masculinities and femininities disappear. In chapter 8 I show that the constitutive nature of the relationship between power, heterosexuality, and dominant masculinity is broken by rape. Disempowered, homosexualized, and feminized, the raped man loses all the prerogatives of dominant masculinity and consequently ceases to be a man. For women, the consequences of rape are somewhat different. First, the issue of homosexuality is totally absent here, because the rape of a woman by a man remains completely within the dominant norms of heterosexuality. Second, modern forms of femininity, especially in the North and West, are not produced through power but through vulnerability in general, and sexual vulnerability in particular. In other words, woman is already defined—socially and culturally—as rapable. Thus, while in many places around the globe the raped woman would become an outcast, the rape of a woman does not destroy her femininity in the way the rape of a man destroys his masculinity. In a darkly ironic way, it actually confirms it. This means that the relationship between power, heterosexuality, and masculinity does not have its female counterpart or parallel, because female homosexuality and female vulnerability do not carry the same ontological relevance as male homosexuality and vulnerability.

When intersected with collective identities, these differences become a crucial rationale of sexual violence. But they also indicate why the (discursive and actual) visibility of the violated male and female bodies does not follow in the footprints of the acts of violence, but has its own logic. We have seen already in the case of the media representations of war rapes of both women and men in the Croatian and Serbian media, that some violated fe/male bodies remain hidden, while others are exposed, depending upon their positioning within the particular media narratives.

When it comes to the visibility of the violated female body, South Asia again offers examples, and South Asian feminists offer analyses that are relevant far beyond the region. Butalia (1993) notes that within Hindu and Sikh communities, those remembered in ritual commemorations of Partition today are not the raped women, but rather the so-called martyred women—those killed by the members of their own families and communities in order not to be raped by the "enemy." They are remembered by their communities, often by individual name and place of residence, precisely because they were *not* raped. The lives of those who were actually raped, or those who would rather risk being raped than die were not written about in the popular booklets celebrating "martyrdom," sold currently to schoolchildren on the street corners (ibid., 24).[7]

Selectivity and the differential visibility of the rape victim seems to have relevance in the Sri Lankan conflict, too. The Tamil Tiger militant women raped by government forces are awarded a public space—and with it all the glory of the martyr—within the Tamil community only if and when the women are already dead or killed. The same women were systematically silenced when they tried to talk about their experience of sexual violence while they were still alive (De Mel 2001). Furthermore, the symbol of the sexually violated woman is regularly used for propaganda and other purposes by both the Sri Lankan government and the Tamil separatist movement, and so is the practice of sexual violence.[8]

ANALYZING SEXUAL VIOLENCE AND ITS VISIBILITY IN FEMINISM

The analyses of sexual violence against women in violent conflicts, as well as the selective visibility of the victims, show that the rapes of women in violent conflicts do not have a fixed or single meaning. Sexual violence against women in general, and rape in particular, gain meanings through intersections of the dominant (or hegemonic) notions of gender and norms of sexuality (which position women within a symbolic hierarchical, culturally specific, system of gender relations); relations of race, ethnicity and religion, or other social relations and identities (within which the woman, and her respective/presumed group are positioned); and through a very specific political context or political project, be it colonialism, communalism, or nationalism, in a particular time, at a particular place.

Furthermore, all these elements inform both the particular acts of violence and the visibility of the female and male victim, indicating that both the violence and its representations are produced through the same discursive practices, in which gender, sexuality, and ethnicity (or any other collective identity) are mutually constructive. This further means that dominant notions of femininity and masculinity, and norms of sexuality and definitions of ethnicity, are necessarily shared by the victims and perpetrators: in order for the act of violence or its representation to be effective, both the victim and the perpetrator have to decode the cultural and social reality that frames the violence in the same way. This does not mean that there is only one way of decoding violence, for the dominant social norms are always contested: there are always ambiguities and contradictions attached to meanings produced through dominance. Rather, it means that, "in constructing their experience, women who have been raped draw on the same resources, same cultural vocabularies, as do the men who rape. And while women and men may use these resources somewhat differently, they do so for similar purposes—accounting for action and constructing identities" (Wood and Rennie 1994, 146). While Linda Wood and Heather Rennie deal with peacetime rapes, Robert Hayden (2000) and Veena Das (1987) have come to the same conclusions analyzing rapes during Partition and rapes during the Yugoslav disintegration. When Das (1987, 12) observes that violence operates not only on an instrumental level but also on a ritual level, a level that "resonates with the culture," she points to the significance of the shared cultural norms.

These norms affect the visibility of the victim by providing (or withdrawing) the discursive space within which the victim can speak, or be spoken about. Diana Taylor (1993) and Biljana Kašić (2000), for example, both point out the links between the violated female bodies and the voicelessness of the women victims in Argentina and Bosnia respectively, asserting that the muteness of the female victim went hand in hand with the appropriation of her pain and her voice for political purposes (dictatorship, nationalism). My research on the male victim of violence shows that the lack of discursive space within which men could be seen as violated and still remain heterosexual and masculine renders them either invisible or visible in otherness.

Jolanda Withuis (1995) also links discursive space and visibility in her research on three groups of Dutch women who were raped during World War Two: Dutch Jewish women raped by Dutch men in whose houses they were hiding from Nazis; Dutch communist women detained in concentration camps in Germany, raped by Russian soldiers when the camps were liberated; and Dutch colonial women living in Indonesia, raped and imprisoned in a system of sexual slavery by the Japanese military in South East Asia. Next to many biographical, intimate choices these women made in speaking out, they also had to find a language, a vocabulary, and a discursive space within which to tell their own narratives of rapes. The Jewish women had to overcome, among other things, the discourse of (self-)gratification used by the protectors (which also served as a cover for the Dutch refusal to accept responsibility when Jews were expelled from the Netherlands).[9] The communist women had to overcome ideological barriers (their own, their party leaders', and those embedded in postwar anticommunism in the Netherlands). And colonial women had to overcome colonial and racist discourses of sexual and racial purity in Dutch postwar society.

Interestingly, Withuis attributes the visibility of these rapes in the Netherlands in the 1980s to changes in the social discourses on rape, brought about by the feminist movement. In the decades after World War II rape was still defined within the discourse of moral decency and respectability, while in the 1980s the feminist movement redefined rape as an issue of power and patriarchy, woman's bodily integrity, and the right of a woman to her own sexuality. That feminism had this impact is also supported by the fact that it was in the late 1980s and the beginning of the 1990s that another story about rapes committed during World War Two became public: those committed by the Japanese military within a system of sexual slavery.[10] Cynthia Enloe (1993, 220) pursues a similar argument, when she says that rapes in Bosnia became visible thanks to feminism. Research on sexual violence during Partition also started in the later 1980s, lending further support to the argument that feminism played a crucial role in increasing the visibility of rape.

Feminism thus became both a discursive space and a political platform from within which the rape of women gained visibility, voice, and meaning. The feminist theoretical and political strategies concerning rape, developed mostly through analyses and strategies of the peacetime rapes, ended up impacting also the public perception of war rapes and thus contributed to the visibility of the female victim. But is it all good news? There are two instances where the links between the analyses and strategies of peacetime and wartime rapes become potentially problematic. One is the assumption of woman's rapability; the other is the reliance on legal remedy.

Probably the most significant feminist work for understanding peacetime sexual violence is Susan Brownmiller's book *Against Our Will: Men, Women and Rape*, first published in 1975. In it, she analyzes rape as the most powerful means of male control over women, and the core source of women's need for male protection. In her words, through rape "*all men* keep *all women* in a state of fear" (Brownmiller 1976, 51). Susan Griffin (1977) contributed to the same perspective by asserting the reality of women's constant fear of rape and defining the social condition of that fear as the "rape culture."

For many feminists these analyses remained unshakable truths twenty years after Brownmiller published her book, although she herself criticized the "rape victim identity" concept in 1993, when writing about rapes in Bosnia (Brownmiller 1993). Catherine Niarchos (1995, 650), however, states, referring to Bosnia: "All women know a great deal about rape, whether or not we have been its direct victims. Rape haunts the lives of women on a daily basis."

The inevitability of female rapability inscribed in this paradigm has consequences: if women are already defined as rapable, then rape defines femininity as violability, and becomes a female mode of being, at the same time that raping women becomes an essential male capacity. These definitions, paradoxically, reinforce the greatest of all gender distinctions, assuming, once again, the omnipotence of men and the absolute powerlessness of women. The context of war further underscores the inevitability of female violability and powerlessness, when the man is also the soldier.

This female powerlessness before rape, however, has consequence for women's agency. Wood and Rennie (1994) pointed out in their research on peacetime rapes that the victim's lack of power, of blame, and of responsibility—as asserted in legal narratives—also means a lack of control, and a lack of control means a lack of agency. Consequently, the raped woman becomes *only* and *always* the victim. Wood and Rennie (1994) also show that some raped women construct narratives in which they present themselves as agents, albeit by speaking of actions that they haven't taken, or knowledge that they haven't used. These women do not see themselves as absolutely powerless, nor do they accept the victim status without ambivalence. Some have difficulty defining their experience as rape precisely because they could not perceive of themselves as powerless victims.

The fatal linkage between femininity, sexual violence, and victimization appears in many places, even in those where raped women exercise agency. Julie Mertus (2004) shows how victimization also comes into play at the International Criminal Tribunal for the former Yugoslavia. The testimonies of witnesses—raped women—are turned into legal narratives that benefit either the prosecution or defense, but hardly the women themselves. As both the defense and the prosecution focus on the acts of violence, within which a description of (the victim's and perpetrator's) body parts and the actions of the perpetrator figure prominently, the victim's testimony takes the form of a staccato exchange of questions and answers, and the testifying woman is reduced to a dismembered and passive victim. Thus the very act of agency—the public testifying—is turned into an act that reproduces the woman's victimization, if not becoming itself an act of victimization. Showing instances of women's defiance to such victimizing legal practice, Mertus (2004, 112) is wary of the enthusiasm of "the (mainly western) champions of 'universal justice'" who have not yet learned the lesson of the limits of legal response to rape.[11] She concludes that legal processes such as tribunals hardly bring a possibility for a closure for the witness, and that the visibility of the victim is not necessarily followed by the recognition and respect. Thus she argues for alternative (legal and nonlegal) modes of justice (truth commissions, memory projects, and "people's tribunals") in which the narrative of violence would be controlled by the witness. However, Antje Krog (2001) and Chiseche Mibenge (forthcoming) show that there is no easy access to justice for women who experienced sexual violence in South Africa and Rwanda, respectively. In both places, public witnessing and prosecution had to be replaced by special, closed hearings in order to protect the women from the intimidation, violence, and contempt that accompanied testifying in public. Thus victimization seems to accompany both the violence and its legal remedies, as much as it accompanies its media representations and its collective narratives.

All the limitations of international and national justice for war rapes notwithstanding, few feminists would actually want the legal remedies abolished. But the ubiquity and diversity of victimizing practices against women who have already been raped, and the overwhelming visibility and presence of women as rape victims in public discourses, suggest that caution is needed, for—as already shown—the victimized female body is one of the most powerful metaphors in the violent production of collective identities. The ubiquity and visibility of these practices continue to produce women as victims only, and as the only victims, denying women both subjectivity and agency and denying men their vulnerability, and ultimately grant sexual violence the power to produce dominant notions of both femininity and masculinity, producing the former through violence endured, and the latter through violence perpetrated. If there are no alternatives to this productive power of violence, then there are no alternatives to the dominant notions of femininity and masculinity, nor to the dominant practices that sustain them.

Beyond Victimized Femininity and Omnipotent Masculinity

During the 1990s feminists started to reevaluate perspectives on rape and offer radical alternatives to the discourse of female rapability and male omnipotence. They challenged the privilege of masculine representations of rape that silence women (Seifert 1993) and resisted the construction of rape as the ultimate or "unspeakable" crime, which "obliterates the victim" or brings about an irrevocable destruction of woman's "inner self." The constant association of rape with silence and shame in the representations of Muslim women in Bosnia, and the assumption that raped women are expelled from their communities, are masculine representations that privilege the definitions of raped women as property, and the exclusive sexual territory of their husbands while linking them symbolically to the nation.

Furthermore, such exclusive access to sexual bodies of the women defines both the femininity of women and the masculinity of their husbands. In her study of rapes committed by Pakistani forces in Bangladesh in 1971, Nayanika Mookherjee (2004) shows that, once this exclusivity is destroyed through rape and made public, a complex struggle unfolds between the spouses, as well as between each of them individually and the different communities within which they participate. Verbal insults are used by a local community to remind the husbands of raped women (who went public with the information and demanded legal remedy) that they are not "proper men" any longer, as they have lost both exclusive sexual access to and control over their wives. The husbands react with silence in public, and with abandonment, insult, and violence at home. Mookherjee insists that *power* is at the center of the complex strategies employed by each party, and that raped women are not without power precisely because they are the key of their husbands' demasculinization. Her study also shows the high price—in poverty, domestic violence, and social and intimate losses—that such power struggles brings about.

Mookherjee's study shows that a woman's experience of rape cannot be abstracted from her experience of the world in which she learns what it means to be raped, and furthermore, that this world is neither unambiguous nor transparent. Agency and victimization do not only stand side by side, but actually constitute each other. Language, silencing, and visibility all play a role here. While showing that women and men use the same vocabulary to describe rape, Wood and Rennie (1994) also show that women's experiences of rape go beyond the available vocabulary about victims and villains. Women use different rhetorical strategies in order to find a language that will suit their own accounts of events, accounts that differ from the dominant versions of absolute victimization.

This is precisely what Sharon Marcus (1992) points out in her groundbreaking criticism of feminist politics on rape. Indicating the significance of language for the interpretation of rape, she writes that feminism has to invent a language about rape within which we have to "imagine women neither as already raped nor inherently rapable" (387).

It is worth noting that the discourse of female vulnerability has never been the only discourse in feminist dealings with rape, nor has it been the only discourse in feminist dealings with war. As Pamela Haag (1996) has indicated, numerous counterdiscourses can be traced back, which claim women's power to both prevent and resist rape. One of them has been, and must in the future be, changing the assumption of female (sexual) vulnerability and social practices that produce both these assumptions and the vulnerability. The feminist critique of traditional research on rape promotes results that show that women who try to defend themselves from rape often do succeed. This is particularly significant given the old advice that a woman should not "anger the rapist" by trying to defend herself. Marcus is particularly sharp in criticizing that advice: "In a culture which relentlessly urges women to make up for our lacks by accessorizing, we are told that we cannot manage bodily accessories if we manipulate them for the purpose of self-defence, and that we will best be served by consenting to be accessories to our own violation. We are taught the following fallacy—that we can best avoid getting hurt by letting someone hurt us. We absorb the following paradox—that rape is death, but that in a rape the only way to avoid death is to accept it. Consenting to the death of rape forms our only possibility of fighting for our lives, but these lives will have been destroyed by rape" (Marcus 1992, 395).

These studies call for several strategic interventions. One is to dissociate femininity from sexual vulnerability—not by making men sexually vulnerable (by inverting the dominant practice of violence), nor simply by making such vulnerability visible, but rather, by exposing and subverting practices through which the meanings of power and violability become productive of specific masculinities and femininities. The word "practice" does not refer here only to the practice of violence, but equally to representational practices, the politics of writing, and identity politics within feminism.

Another intervention is to rethink the strategy that makes the visibility of the victim its central point. According to Renée Heberle (1996), this is precisely where early feminist strategies of "speaking out" from the 1980s have failed. Underpinning those strategies was an assumption that, once men and society realized how devastating the consequences of rape were to women, they would do everything to stop it. So women "spoke out" about their devastation publicly, and feminist writers published detailed descriptions of rapes and their effects on women.[12] According to some feminists, however, in Western societies at least, where the voyeuristic alienation of sex through pornography objectifies the female body, this was a dangerous strategy.[13] Aware of that danger, Heberle asked:

> What if in emphasizing the strategy of piecing together our reality as a rape culture through speakouts and detailed descriptions of experience, we participate in setting up the event of sexual violence as a defining moment of women's possibilities for being in the world? What if, in our emphatic responses to women's suffering and insistence that "it could happen to any of us" we participate in conferring a monolithic reality onto an otherwise phantasmagoric, illegitimate, and therefore fragile edifice of masculinist dominance rent with contra-

> diction and internal conflict? What if there is an immanent fragility to masculinist dominance that has been obscured by the construction of a *political* strategy grounded upon the exposure of women's suffering? Simply put, what if this strategy furthers the reification of masculinist dominance? (Ibid., 65)

These questions are significant because of the intersection of gender with other forms of collective identities—some women will always be more vulnerable than others, and some women will always be *perceived* as more vulnerable than others. In other words, women's vulnerability and the visibility of that vulnerability are conditioned on the multiple positioning of the women within societies in which they are violated, as well as within the discourses that give meaning to the violation. In her article for *Ms.* Magazine, Catharine MacKinnon (1993b) shows this clearly: in her account, raped Muslim women had no existence beyond their fractured bodies. Turned into objects through which a Serb murderous and pornographic pathology was constructed, their bodies existed only in relation to the rape and the rapist. Reacting to MacKinnon's description of the rape and torture in *Ms.*, and its possible consequences, Robin Schott (1996) asks: "How should these horrors be described? Is any description a form of complicity and voyeurism? Or is the greatest form of the complicity silence? Are there some people who can speak 'truly' or 'authentically' about these events?" (23).

Diana Taylor (1993) offers a possible answer to these questions in her analysis of a theatrical production about Argentina's "Dirty War." She concludes that, instead of condemning political terror, a play actually produces a spectacle that "replicates and affirms the fascination with eroticized violence." Taylor situates this paradox in a lack of a "critical distancing" between the play and its topic. She warned that representation that "does not create or even permit the critical distancing between itself and the topic" fails to "encourage the spectator to reflect on the structure and significance of this sexualized, militant violence" (26).

But the most significant element of Taylor's criticism of the representation of violence regards the relationship between social constructions of masculinity and femininity. The play, she asserts, "does nothing to demystify the fatal linkage between male identity, male violence, and male pleasure. The female body . . . is simply the inert mass on which that violence and pleasure takes place" (31).

In my view, there is nothing more important for feminist theorizing of sexual violence against both women and men, as well as for feminist theorizing on war, than deconstructing these "fatal linkages." For they have power to produce very specific, ethnicized identities of victims and villains, by using universalized gendered and sexualized identities. Violent bodyscaping of female and male sexual territories is both universal and specific: informed by the dominant gendered interpretation of an experience of being that of a woman or a man, which is then applied selectively to a particular group of women and men. If an experience of being a raped woman is lived as shame, despair, and degradation, then the production of that particular experience is already constructed into the practice of raping. And, as my analysis of the Serbian and Croatian media shows, the representation of difference between women will center precisely around this particular experience.

Following upon Heberle, thus, I would argue that displaying shame, despair, and degradation as the ultimate female experiences of war rapes will only further affix dominant notions of female violability, and continue to produce difference and division between ethnically or racially defined groups of women. So, instead of feeding our reality with more muted and dismembered female bodies, dressed in shame and silences, feminist representation itself has to deobjectify the female body and invite, if not force, others, to do the same. As Pamela Haag (1996, 62) states, feminists have to reinvent their approach to rape and to define a new political strategy that would entail "not the elaboration of the individual victim's pain or civil rights, but the reunification of the [female] body with the will through learning to use it effectively and the elaboration of physical assault as a reiteration of antecedent violence and social conditions that need not totally destroy its victim."

Instead of defining rape as "unspeakable" and then demanding of women to speak out, and in public, Heberle suggests a political strategy on rape that will redefine the way rape is spoken about. At its core lies a deconstructive narrative of rape, which exposes the naturalized social truth about gender and victimization (Heberle 1996, 70). Marcus suggests the redefinition of rape as "one of culture's many modes" of "imprinting gender identity," asserting that masculine power and feminine powerlessness "neither simply precede nor cause rape" (1992, 391). Rhonda Copelon adds another significant element to our understanding of war rape: "Women are targets [of rape] not simply because they 'belong to' the enemy, but precisely . . .

because they too *are* enemy; because of their power as well as vulnerability as women, including their sexual and reproductive power" (1993, 207).

Instead of either idealizing or forgetting about that power, we should utilize it, making it a core of feminist approaches to rape, breaking the naturalized link between femininity and victimization, searching for the gap "between the threat and the rape—the gap in which women can try to intervene" (Marcus 1992, 389), focusing on the prevention of rape as much as on aiding the rape victims.

Beyond Sisterhood in Rape

Could these feminist theories and strategies on rape, developed in peacetime, be relevant for the theories and strategies on war rapes? Could the theorizing on peacetime rape learn something from the theorizing on war rape? It is clear that both peacetime and wartime rape theorizing would benefit from the deconstruction of the naturalized link between femininity and victimization, as the deconstruction of male power and female powerlessness allows for envisioning different relations between men and women. But, then recognizing and reconstructing different experiences and meanings of rape would also allow for envisioning different relationships among women. This would require leaving behind the assumption that rape as a crime unifies all women, creating a global sisterhood in rape. Feminist sensitivity to differences among women's experiences has to be extended to the experiences of rape.

In spring 1994 I participated in a closed session with a small group of women, where a woman survivor of detention in one of the Serb-held caps in Bosnia, who has been collecting testimonies about sexual violence, talked about her work (it was agreed that she would not talk about her experience from the camp). The woman—whom I will give a pseudonym Slavica—introduced herself as a Bosnian Croat. A feminist psychotherapist was moderating the session. During a session, following a question from a member of the audience, an exchange occurred that raises several significant issues for feminist theorizing of and strategies against sexual violence against women in war, and in general:

> *Audience member*: Some anthropologists show that the rape of women is actually an attack on her man; that woman is considered male property and as such she is attacked. Was this the case in Bosnia?

Slavica: In Bosnia woman is not man's property. She is man's honor. If you touch her, you touch his honour.

Audience member: Were men hurt by the fact that they were powerless to protect their women?

Slavica: Yes. There were husbands of raped women together with them in the camp. Can you imagine how powerless a man feels? That was the greatest punishment for a Bosnian man. He is brought up with the idea that a woman is sacred, that she has to be honored and protected. And he found himself in the situation of being completely powerless.

Audience member: Are the rapes still going on?

Slavica: At the beginning of 1993 we were optimistic, but it is still going on, unfortunately.

[*The psychotherapist intervenes*]

Therapist: In the camp, the rapists belong to one ethnic community, and the raped to another. But that is not the whole picture. These same rapists, after raping prisoners in the camps, get heavily drunk, go home and beat up and rape their own wives.

Slavica: But this is not systematic violence. This is a question of morals.

Therapist: [*annoyed*] But violence grows systematically throughout former Yugoslavia! All these soldiers go home and rape their own wives!

Slavica: [*also annoyed*] Oh, they are not that virile! And besides, I am not sorry for Serb women. Bosnian and Croat mothers were crying when they had to send their sons into war, and Serb mothers were singing. These Serb soldiers were going into Serb villages, not their own but other villages in Bosnia, and raped Serb women there. It was easier for them than to go home. Alcohol, drugs, and savagery together. There was violence everywhere. But this cannot be compared with violence against another nation.

Slavica's statement indicates clearly that raped women do not necessarily condemn rape as such, even when they do condemn the rapists. In other words, for the raped women, not every rape has the same meaning. Slavica distinguishes between Serb soldiers raping Serb women and Serb soldiers raping women from another ethnicity. The former, in her eyes, is a matter of morality and common savagery, within which she assumes that rape is a replacement for sex; the latter is an attack on a nation—and here, not incidentally, she does not say violence against "women of another nation," but against "another nation." This indicates vividly that meanings attached to individual experiences, media representations of violence, and the acts of violence are all produced through the same discursive practices wherein gender, sexuality, and ethnicity are mutually constructive. Slavica's definitions of rape function within the preexistent definition of the Serb as the ethnic enemy. Both Serb men and Serb women are defined as enemies, and essentially violent: men through rape, women through their support of war. At the same time, rape as a "violence against the nation" is given meaning through the erasure of women from the nation and the simultaneous appropriation of women's experience of rape for the nation.

The therapist uses strikingly different definitions. Evident in her intervention, there lies an assumption that raped women, everywhere, would and should automatically have understanding for each other and feel solidarity. For Slavica that was obviously not so; she not only explicitly refused solidarity with raped Serb women but assumed that rape was an appropriate punishment for them. For a feminist therapist, however, a need for a "sisterhood in rape" deleted the differences in meanings between rape in detention and rape in the domestic context, and erased the intersections with ethnicity and gender in both of them. In privileging gender hierarchy above all others, this intervention ascribes the same meaning to all rapes and assumes that all raped women have only one real enemy—the rapists.

Thus, the questions that come out of this exchange are about the experiences and meanings of sexual violence against women in violent conflicts, both for the raped women and for feminists as well as about the possibilities for feminist interventions against such violence. These are inevitably linked. The experiences and the meanings of rape can be seen as potentially unifying among women across ethnic divides and even be used as a starting point in the reconciliation process. But the work of Elissa Helms (2003) and Cynthia Cockburn (1998), clearly points out that this is not automatically so; to the contrary, these issues have a high potential to divide women's groups. As I argue in chapter 11, these issues actually caused a split within the feminist movement in Croatia, and raised heated debates within feminism in Serbia.

Through my contacts with refugee lawyers, I heard about Lena (pseudonym), who fled to the Netherlands seeking refugee status. She was from Mostar, a city in Bosnia divided between Muslims and Croats. Lena, although a Croat, remained on the Muslim side, for her husband was a Muslim. But their already fragile marriage fell apart soon after the war started, and her husband started beating her and raping her, using explicitly ethnic insults, with his family and friends encouraging him. Lena's family and friends had cut all contacts with her earlier, because she had married a Muslim. She fled Mostar, bribed a bus driver, and arrived in 1995 in the Netherlands. Her lawyer started legal proceedings for refugee status, but her application was rejected. The court concluded that she could not sufficiently demonstrate that the local (Muslim) authorities denied her protection, that her condition was not unbearable, and that she could and should have demonstrated other efforts in changing this condition besides fleeing her country. Had she been raped and beaten repeatedly by any other Muslim man, this would have been seen as war rape. But as this particular Muslim man was her husband, it simply had different meaning for the Dutch authorities.

We may easily condemn the hypocrisy of the Dutch authorities, who were informed by the woman's lawyer that, unlike in the Netherlands, marital rape in Bosnia was not legally defined, and that Lena, being a Croat in the midst of war, had very little, if any, chance to be protected by Muslim authorities now that Mostar was split between Croat and Muslim authorities, and fighting was still going on there. We may also use this example to demonstrate how women's suffering is easily dismissed by patriarchal institutions as "bearable." But we should never assume that Lena and Slavica will automatically understand each other, either because they define themselves as Croat women or because they were both raped by a man of different ethnicity, in the midst of an ethnic war.

Assuming that not every rape is the same would certainly relativize rape. It would make it one of many experiences that some women have. Some feminists may be afraid that such relativization may further desensitize the general public—specifically the institutions whose role is to protect women and enforce punishment on the rapist—and thus, in consequence, may jeopardize women's struggle for resources for victim support or lobbying for harsher sentences for rapists. Others may fear that this may bring into feminism the hierarchization of rapes, and the easy dismissal of some rapes, positions that obviously already exist in mainstream society. But my study attests that such hierarchization already exists in feminism, with some rapes always being seen as more devastating for women, and thus more relevant for feminism. Thus, I would argue that to accept relativization would be to take the political step of recognizing different feminist stakes in dealing with rapes, and would do more justice to both raped women and feminism and produce strategies that correspond better with the realities of women's lives (feminists included). For, taking for granted women's or feminist solidarity, based on a wrong assumption (of sisterhood in rape), can result only in wrong strategies. If feminist theorizing and strategizing on war rapes are to take seriously Copelon's call to look at both the similarities and the differences in the rapes and their meanings, they first have to accept that these differences exist, for the raped women as well as for feminism (Copelon 1993, 213).

Here, strategies of rape prevention seem crucial to me. Such strategies would have to rest on the assumption that rapes are preventable, instead of being inevitable. Without a belief that rapes are preventable, even in the midst of a war, all that feminists are left with is the devastating aftermath (wherein the devastation seems to limit feminist politics on rape to "sisterhood in rape"). Further, these strategies would have to assume that rape is not the ultimate crime against a woman. In times of war (as well as peace), there are many different losses, many different personal and collective tragedies, and their meanings are linked to many different experiences. Continuous definition of rape as the worst possible fate that can befall a woman falls into the same masculinist discourse that defines the rape of a woman as her social death. This does not mean abandoning the struggle for recognition of social consequences facing raped women, nor does it mean abandoning the struggle for changing them. It means asserting the right and the capacity of women for life after rape.

PART III.

THE ARMED BODY

10

SOLDIERS OF TRADITION

There have been few wars in the world in which women did not support the so-called war effort, or take up arms themselves. The same is true for the war through which the former Yugoslavia disintegrated. And still, feminists interested in the Yugoslav conflict have largely ignored the women who fought on the front lines or contributed to the war in other capacities.

One cannot say the same for the national media. Although, in relative terms, women soldiers did not receive overwhelming attention, every now and then newspapers from all the former Yugoslav republics would publish a piece about a woman soldier, or a photograph. In what follows I analyze a selection of articles and photographs of women who served as soldiers on the front lines, published in the Croatian and Serbian dailies and weeklies, between 1991 and 1994.

The armed female body in these representations is vested with very specific meanings: not only embodying the ethnic essence of the nation, but also symbolizing a specific national history and tradition. In the Croatian press, national history is linked to Europe, not the Balkans; the tradition is represented as liberal and democratic, not socialist; as modern and emancipated, not traditional. In the Serbian press, national history is traced back to partisan guerrilla warfare and to a history of betrayals, while national tradition is defined as the history of self-sacrifice.

The Croatian Press: Photos over the Text

We can immediately see that female soldiering is not a simple issue even for nationalism from the number of articles about women soldiers in the Croatian press. Between 1991 and 1994 the daily *Vjesnik* and weekly *Danas* published only about a dozen articles in which female soldiers and women's participation in the war were mentioned, among hundreds of reports from the front lines. Most of the texts about female soldiering were concerned with a general discussion about women in the army, elaborating on international and national practices. Different countries and conflicts were mentioned, from Israel to Lebanon, from the United States to Switzerland. One of these texts discussed the role of artists in the war, internationally and in Croatia, and within that topic female participation in wars was mentioned. Marilyn Monroe's famous visit to American soldiers in Vietnam was compared to the "unconvincing" soldiering of a few Croatian actresses and female singers who joined the Croatian army as volunteers (*Danas*, 5 November 1991, 53).

Among all the articles, however, only a handful were dedicated entirely and specifically to women working as military personnel in the Croatian army. Most of these published articles had an accompanying photograph, often several of them. In fact, in the Croatian daily and weekly there were many more photos of women in uniform than there were articles. Many different pieces—about the fighting and cease-fires, about peace negotiations in Geneva and Croatian president Tudjman's visit to a local military unit, about the seizure of Sarajevo and rapes in Bosnia—were accompanied by photos of women in military uniform, with rifles on their shoulders. Some of the photos of the armed women in *Vjesnik* had a life of their own, detached from the rest of the particular page by clear editorial interventions, such as lines, dotted borders or boxes, placed on pages that had no text about the war at all.

One of the articles and several photos were published more than once, and often exchanged between the daily and the weekly edition of *Vjesnik*. One of these photos, published in *Vjesnik* on September 19, 1991 (60), shows a woman from the waist up, in uniform, with a gun on her shoulder. The headscarf around her head hides her hair. Her right arm is on her hip. Were there not for her face, she would look like a female Rambo. But her face is not a face of an experienced, alert, and determined fighter with scars on his cheeks and an icy stare, who challenges his enemy. Rather, her face is smooth, quite beautiful, serene and thoughtful, almost sad, and her gaze is lost somewhere behind the camera.

CROAT WOMAN SOLDIER: BEAUTY, INNOCENCE, DOMESTICITY

Beauty, serenity, and sadness follow women soldiers as an important element of their representation. Their decision to become—and to remain soldiers—will often be attached to their sadness at the fate of their country, their people, or their immediate family. Their beauty will be, mostly, the frail and gentle beauty of a girl just entering womanhood. Sexualized

The caption reads: "Gardistica" (female soldier from the elite guard units). *Vjesnik* (Croatia), September 19, 1991, 60.

beauty, even when the shapes of the female bodies under uniforms are mentioned, will be far from explicit. That is not to say that their femininity is totally desexualized in the photos or in the texts. Lush blond hair and attractive body shapes were there to see and to read about. However, unlike in the photos and texts about women soldiers in the Gulf War (Forde 1995) or in the Falklands (Seidel and Gunther 1988), where pin-up images were part and parcel of the representation of war and the women soldiers, together with the images of girl-soldiers and soldier-mothers, in the examined Croatian press female sexuality was discreet, never in the foreground. The women soldiers retained only as much sexuality as it was necessary to point out that they were all marriageable and future mothers, and if married, that their beauty reflected their patriotic spirit, courage, and determination, rather than their sexual desirability.

The article "Who Are the Dalmatian Women Guards?" (*Vjesnik*, December 1, 1991, 16) expresses in a nutshell the specific kind of sexuality that links a girl, albeit a soldier-girl, with her married, procreative future, as well as with her homeland and her people. It quotes the usual reaction that women in this elite military guards unit received from old people: "Children, these guns are not for you. You should marry." Throughout the article, the tender age of the women soldiers is stressed as much as their determination to postpone the marriage until their country is freed from aggressors. If they were married mothers, like the guardswoman named Sanja, such women are said to not think of anything else but defending children—their own and all others—from the enemies.

Both the visual and the textual representations of women under arms will maintain two of the classic elements in the dominant discourses of femininity: emotions and beauty. There is a third one—domestic skills—but that will not appear in photos, only in the texts. Each article on female Croat soldiers addresses, in one way or another, the women's domestic skills. Sometimes, these skills were an antidote to their military skills, as in the aforementioned piece about the elite guardswoman. They tell how the villagers, the male soldiers, and the military command needed to be convinced that they came to fight: "There was distrust at the beginning, they looked at us with contempt, asked us where our makeup bags and coffee pots were. But we swore that we were not here to join sanitary units, make coffee and tea, or do the dishes. We came as an active combat unit of the Croatian army, with the intention to bringing freedom to Croatia, with guns in our hands" (ibid.).

The article further explains how the distrust of the male soldiers, as well as the villagers with whom the women soldiers were billeted, melted when one guardswoman cut short a moment of hesitation in a battle by jumping bravely onto an enemy tank, and when everybody was convinced that they "equal other [male] guards in every respect."

In a later article, domestic skills were used not as a contrast but as the essence of female participation in war. The title of the text is "They Replaced Australia with their Homeland" (*Vjesnik*, March 25 1993, 4). The piece is about a group of seven young Croat women, citizens of Australia, who "decided to go back to their homeland and help wounded soldiers": "They completed their paramedic's course in Australia, just before coming to Croatia. But that does not mean, they say, that they would not know how to sew and mend clothes, clean the rooms, and, if needed, cut soldiers' hair." While their tasks in this article are transformed from medical to domestic, their military status is affirmed both in the photography, where they are in uniforms, and further in the text, where they are said to have "combat medic skills."

The mixture of domestic and military skills in these texts reflects the gender heritage of representations. As I indicated in the introduction, this heritage has been the culture in which traditional and modern, oppressive and emancipatory norms and values coexisted, neither disturbing nor transforming each other. In such a culture, proper femininity was measured by domestic skills as much as by professional ones. The mention of these skills in the articles confirms women's carefully maintained femininity, and implies that their military skills are an addition to, not a replacement for, domestic skills, much as their courage is an addition to other feminine characteristics, and their beauty in uniform an addition to their beauty as potential brides.

These representational additions are recognizable in many photos in *Vjesnik* and *Danas*, where women soldiers were depicted doing "womanly" things, as well as things also done by male soldiers. In some photos women are an integral part of a military unit, participating in a specifically military performance, often a single woman among male soldiers. In other photos, female soldiers are in an all-women unit, tending their weapons or marching through the mountains. Others show a woman in uniform, photographed alone or with another woman, looking with a smile into the bright future or fixing her makeup. A few photos show women engaged with their weapons in the war: operating an artillery piece, for example, or aiming a firearm.

All these visual and textual images depict women soldiers as being both the same as, and different from, the male soldiers. Their sameness is their possession of arms, in deploying the same arsenal of patriotic claims and military attitudes: fighting for freedom of Croatia with guns in their hands, defending the children back home, having exceptional military skills, and proving courageous—in fact, even more courageous than the male soldiers. It is precisely this excellence that undermines their sameness with the male soldiers. For, in order to be accepted as the same, they have to excel. And, even when they throw away the proverbial accessories of female daily existence, their bodies are present. There—in their full heads of hair and their figure-revealing, well-fitting uniforms—all their femininity is preserved, and with it, all the difference.

This constant shift between sameness and difference would prove to be the main pattern of representation of women soldiers in the Croatian press. In some photos, the effect would be exaggerated by an inversion of classic male-female military roles. In others, it would act as confirmation that a woman is a woman, no matter what.

Two photos are especially poignant in that respect. Both are huge, taking up a quarter of a page. One is a photo of a soldier coming from the front lines, by train, with a lover waiting on the platform. The photograph captures a kiss about to happen. The soldier is a young woman, the waiting lover a young man. This reversal of a classic movie theme is underlined in the caption: "She returned from the front" (*Vjesnik*, January 2, 1992, 6).

Another photo is of a couple in the woods, both in military uniforms. She is on the swing; he is behind, giving a push, with the caption "Croatian warriors taking a break" (*Vjesnik*, June 16, 1992, 5). The iconography of this particular photo, known from romantic paintings of past centuries and romantic movies, and from the imagery of the carefree life of girlhood, shows succinctly one constant theme of both the textual and the visual representation of Croat women as soldiers in the Croatian press: their ever present femininity, imbued with girlish innocence.

EMBODYING TRADITIONS: DIFFERENCE, DIFFERENCE, DIFFERENCE

Croat women were not the only female soldiers to appear in photos published in the Croatian media that I examined. *Vjesnik* also published photos of Muslim women soldiers. One appeared on October 6, 1992 (20), showing a group of armed women in uniform, marching past bushes. The women watch their steps, unconcerned with the camera. The text below the photo reads: "The 'Blue Birds,' a unit of women aged 16 to 45, arrives at the Bosnian defensive lines." The photo is sandwiched between an article on peace negotiations in Geneva and another on the situation in Sarajevo.

Another photo of Muslim women soldiers accompanies an article about the war rapes, with the title "Rape as a Weapon," reprinted from the German *Stern* (*Vjesnik*, November 29, 1992). In the photo, several women in uniform stand in the front lines of a larger group of men and women, praying. The palms of their hands open toward the sky. The caption reads: "The fury against Serbian atrocities prompted many Bosnian women from the occupied territories to volunteer in the army, *Stern* writes." A year later, the same photo would be republished, accompanying again an article taken

"She returned from the front." *Vjesnik* (Croatia), January 2, 1992, 6.

"Croatian warriors taking a break." *Vjesnik* (Croatia), June 16, 1992, 5.

from the German press. This time, however, the text is about the rise of Muslim fundamentalism in Bosnia. It compares the prewar situation, when the Bosnian Muslims lived under "European culture," to the situation in Bosnia during the war, and asserts that fanatic mujahideen fighters have gained influence in the Bosnian government's army, as well as among civilian population of Bosnia. The caption under the photo of the praying women soldiers this time is completely different. It reads: "Before the war Muslim women dressed and made themselves up in Western style. Because

Na bosanske linije obrane stižu »Plave ptice«, jedinica žena u dobi od 16 do 45 godina
Telefoto FaH-Reuters

"The 'Bluebirds,' a unit of women aged 16 to 45 arrives at the Bosnian defense lines." *Vjesnik* (Croatia), October 6, 1992, 20.

of the war some of them put on uniforms. What was it all for, if today they cover their faces?" (*Vjesnik*, November 22, 1993, 17). None of the women on the photo does, but the question is there, nevertheless.

The year that elapsed between these two photos saw strained relationships between the Croatian and Bosnian governments as well as their military forces. The change of tone in the captions under the photos is an indication of these political strains, going from a "moving story" and "the fury against Serbian atrocities" to religious fanatics and veiled women. The note that Muslims of Bosnia were, before the war, culturally European, clearly indicates that they are not Europeans any longer, that they are different from Croats. The photo of Muslim women soldiers in prayer is the only image of praying female soldiers. No Croat woman soldier is photographed in prayer. The absence of religion in the stories of Croat women soldiers is yet another element in representation of modern, this time secular Croatia. Furthermore, the texts accompanying the photo of Muslim women fighters are not about them, but about other matters of war. Thus, we do not know anything about these women besides what we are told by the photos. No military or domestic skills are mentioned, nor are they praised

Prije rata muslimanke su se odjevale i šminkale u zapadnjačkom stilu. Zbog rata neke su odjenule uniforme. Zar zato da bi danas pokrivale lice?

"Before the war Muslim women dressed and made themselves up in Western style. Because of the war some of them put on uniforms. What was it all for, if today they cover their faces?" *Vjesnik* (Croatia), November 22, 1993, 17.

for their beauty, bravery, or determination. All we know is what we see. And we see them praying, the way Muslims do.

When the photo of praying Muslim women soldiers was published the second time, the readership in Croatia could read almost every day about clashes between Croat and Muslim forces, as well as about camps in which "the Muslims" tortured "the Croats." Thus photos of the Muslim women soldiers were not there to tell us about them, but to tell about the danger that all Muslims pose to all Croats, and to establish the difference between them. The bodies of the women soldiers bear the signs of their different belongings. They are the symbolic embodiments of the ethnic-religious communities and their respective cultures and tradition.

This is also true of the absence of articles about partisan women, who would be a logical point of reference, considering the tradition of female soldiering in the region. Their absence has a function of creating discontinuity with the socialist Yugoslav past, to disclaim common history and traditions shared with other Yugoslav nations and thus create space for the new, European tradition and identity. Croatia was becoming a new state, claiming new identities, associations, and traditions, and disclaiming the old ones. The insistence of so many Croatian politicians that Croatia belongs geographically and culturally to Central Europe, and not to the Balkans, is a clear indication of this struggle for achieving new identity and throwing away the old one. It is not only a matter of reinterpreting history in ethnic terms; it is a matter or inventing a new political geography, in which Marilyn Monroe visiting soldiers in the Vietnam War is closer to Zagreb than any partisan woman fighting the socialist revolution in the "symbolic continent of the Balkans,"[1] half a century earlier.

THE FINAL DISTINCTION: SOLDIERING OF THE OTHER

On October 19, 1991, a short column and a photo almost twice that size were joined in *Vjesnik* under the title "Women in the First Line of Defense." The photo shows a woman in uniform, sitting in a van. In her right hand is a gun. With her left hand she holds a cigarette to her mouth to inhale. She has a band around her forehead and a ponytail.

The first paragraph of this short article is about a particular front line, between eastern Slavonia and Vukovar, after a cease-fire had been signed between Croatian forces and the JNA. The text starts with praise for the "heroic and determined people" and a denunciation of "uninterested

S vinkovačkog ratišta

Žene na prvoj liniji obrane

Ni u kakve garancije vojske ne vjerujem, rekla je Biljana, nakon što je vojska, unatoč potpisanom primirju, raketirala položaj na kojem se ona nalazila

Vukovar, Vinkovci, Osijek... Ne tako davno ravna i plodna Slavonija i njeni gradovi, sada već mjesecim ne silaze s naših usana. U našim su mislima na udarnim stranicama novina, u prvim televizijskim izvještajima. I koliko još smrtonosnih bombi i projektila treba pasti na te herojske i odlučne ljude, da bi Europa i nezainteresirani svijet iz svojih udobnih naslonjača pokrenuli kotačiće svojih silnih mehanizama i pružili nam zaštitu i pomoć?

Biljanu smo zatekli u Nuštru, na prvoj liniji obrane Vinkovaca. Njena je jedinica držala položaje u tom selu u vrijeme kada se konvoj pomoći Vukovaru nekoliko puta preko Nuštra pokušavao probiti kroz susjedne Marince u Vukovar. Nakon raketiranja konvoja, promatrači EZ su dobili uvjeravanja da se put može nastaviti u Vukovar. Konvoj je krenuo, a znamo i dokle je i kako stigao. Pitali smo Biljanu što misli da li će konvoj stići na odredište. Gorko se nasmijala, kazavši nam da ona u nikakve garancije vojske ne vjeruje, jer, iako je primirje, položaj na kojem je ona prošlu noć i jutro cijelo su vrijeme raketirali. Kaže da se do Vukovara treba probiti samo oružjem. Sumnjamo da će ova informacija stići do javnosti u Srbiji, ali važno je spomenuti da je Biljana Srpkinja iz Vojvodine zaručena za Hrvata iz Vinkovaca, koju, kako kaže, nitko nije i ne treba uvjeravati koja je strana u ovom ratu u pravu. (Ž. Peratović)

ŽELJKO PERATOVIĆ

"Women in the First Line of Defense." The dateline above the headline reads: "From the battlefields of Vinkovci." *Vjesnik* (Croatia), October 19, 1991, 11.

Europe" and continues with a conversation with Biljana—a woman soldier. She expresses her bitterness and distrust of the JNA and a belief that JNA's front line can only be broken by armed force. The article ends with the following sentence: "It is important to note that Biljana is a Serb from Vojvodina [a northern Serbian Province], the fiancée of a Croat from Vinkovci [city in Croatia]. She, as she herself says, does not need anybody to tell her which party in this war is the right one" (October 19, 1991, 11).

Compared to the pieces about the Croat women soldiers, this text negotiates difference and sameness in a peculiar way. Biljana's sameness with the Croat women soldiers is through arms, as they fight on the same side. The important difference is ethnicity, as the text insists. It could be argued that an article about a Serb woman in the Croatian army could be a sign of openness in the Croatian media discourses, that ethnicity is less significant than a political perspective expressed as a readiness to take part in the defense of Croatia. However, *Vjesnik* did not write about a Serb woman in order to establish an ethnically inclusive political platform, nor to make ethnicity less significant in its representation of female soldiering. Throughout the media war and ethnic war, at different moments, different ethnic groups would be more or less acceptable in different parts of former Yugoslavia. In Croatia, at all times, Serbs would have the least chance of being included, while the inclusion of Muslims, as seen above, depended on the political situation of the moment, and on the territory in question. Muslims were much more acceptable in the Croatian media if they were in Bosnia, than if they were in Croatia.

All the articles about women soldiers are about the war in Croatia. In that war, the Croatian press produced the Serbs as the chief enemy. The Serb woman soldier fighting on the Croat side thus offers additional legitimization of the just cause—implying that even the women of the chief enemy know that the Croats are fighting a just war.

However, Biljana's difference is not only in ethnicity. It is in femininity too. For, unlike the Croat soldier women, this Serb woman is at no point associated with the symbols of femininity used to describe the others. No "gentle voice," no "lush hair," no "figure-hugging uniform." The text has no reference to domestic skills either. We will never know if she could cut her male comrades' hair. Instead, we are offered a photo of a woman with a classic symbol of masculinity in this region: a cigarette in her mouth. Biljana is the only female soldier, in over thirty photos in *Vjesnik* and *Danas* who is depicted with a cigarette. Although many women in former Yugoslavia smoke, and do it in public, smoking is still perceived as unfitting for women. The argument against it is not about (women's) health, but about women's manners. It is seen as something men do, so women who smoke are often accused of being masculine-like (*muškobanjasta*). Consequently, Biljana is different from the Croat women soldiers both through her ethnicity and her femininity. Her only sameness with them is through arms.

In other words, the place of the armed female body is defined through both femininity and ethnicity in the Croatian press. Articles and images negotiate the differences and similarities between male and female soldiers, on the one hand, and Croat and non-Croat soldiers, on the other. A woman could be both a Croat and a soldier, as long as all the symbols of her femininity were preserved—the gentle voice, the shape of her body, and her domestic skills. Without them, she could be a soldier, but not a Croat. In other words, the acceptability of the armed female body within the definition of ethnicity is limited by very specific attributes: physical beauty, gentleness, and frailty must stand side by side with boldness and determination. Only this mixture of female delicacy and soldierly resilience guaranteed the armed female body a place within the Croat nation. It was the same mixture that characterized the newly established nation-state: delicate but brave, beautiful and resilient. The armed female body defined who belonged to it and who did not, and what the conditions were of belonging. The armed female body made an incision in geography as much as in the history of the region, and separated the Self from the rest.

The Serbian Media: Language over the Text

If you can imagine a Greek daily writing about divided Cyprus using the language of Homer's *Iliad*, or a British weekly writing about Northern Ireland using the language of Shakespeare, then you have a pretty good idea of the language used in the Serbian press to write about women soldiers: archaic, poetic, and epic at the same time. Reading articles in the Serbian daily *Politika* and weekly *NIN* sometimes felt like reading the same grand, tragic myth, which integrated, in a rather spectacular manner, several traditions: folk and lyric poetry about love and maidens; epic Serbian poetry about medieval battles, heroes, and betrayals; and partisan traditions from World War Two.

What makes language such a powerful mechanism in bridging these traditions is the fact that they are all gendered in a special way. In Serbian oral and written folk poetry, gendering does not appear only in grammar, or through the different, gendered roles given to men and women. It appears already in the foundation of that poetry, divided into "female," or lyric, and "male" or epic. The difference between the two is both thematic and linguistic. Love poetry is "female," even when it speaks about the feelings of a man. Epic poetry is "male," even when the main character is a maiden. Similar patterns of gendering appear in many of the partisan songs and stories that replicated folk poetry.

Given all this, one would assume that the verbal representation of female soldiering in the Serbian press would tell a completely different story from the one told in the Croatian press through photos, that a medieval, poetic story would be radically dissimilar to the modern, European story. But that is not the case. Actually, however different the images of the female soldiers in these two media might be, they have precisely the same function: to embody the nation and its identity, as well as its history and tradition.

SISTERS AND LOVERS: LINKING TRADITIONS

Between 1991 and 1994 the Serbian dailies published dozens of articles about women soldiers, a similar number to the Croatian press. But the Serbian press published only a handful of photos. Furthermore, unlike the Croatian press, the Serbian papers published a few articles about partisan women guerrillas from World War Two.

In January 1991 two very short articles about women in World War Two appeared in *Politika* in the space of a week. Both were accompanied with the same photo by a famous French photographer, George Skrigin—"Partisan woman with a gun," showing a beautiful woman in profile, in uniform, her dark hair brushed by the wind, and a gun over her shoulder. In the first article, "Moving Testimonies" (*Politika*, January 6, 1991, 16), the woman in this "world-famous" photo is said to be a Yugoslav woman who was decorated with the National Hero Medal.[2] The article is about a new documentary series on French TV about women during World War Two, and the place of Yugoslav partisan women in the series. The director of the Yugoslav segment of the TV program tells us about quality and serenity with which the whole project is pursued: "Without any ideological intentions, this saga about overwhelming human anguish comprises a microcosm of the female world and offers an astonishing insight into human suffering as well as the unbelievable bravery and commitment of the fairer sex" (ibid.).

The article ends with the journalist expressing the wish that the Yugoslav audience be given a chance to see this exceptional TV documentary, not only because of its unquestionable quality "but also as a reminder to all those who devalue and deny the significance of all our mothers, sisters, and kin who fought in the war, for the Yugoslav revolution, with courage and dignity and who deserve our eternal empathy."

Similar language, full of pathos, and similar narrative, full of empathy, are used in the articles about Serb women soldiering in the 1990s. It is interesting that, unlike representations in the Croatian press, where betrayal is defined as coming from outside (from Europe), representations in the Serbian press define betrayal as coming from within: from the contemptible Serb leaders, corrupted by power and totally unconcerned for their own people. Not surprisingly, the grand narrative of suffering also evident in other representations in Serbian press, serves as a background against which Serb history and tradition are constructed, and betrayal by one's own leaders makes it all the more powerful.

"An Unusual Artillery Story: Sister Targets, Brother Assists" is rather short, but together with its accompanying photo it takes up a quarter of the page in the December 30, 1991, issue of *Politika*. The photo shows a woman and a man behind an artillery gun. He looks at the camera, she looks at the gun. The text starts as follows: "The brother went to war. To defend the hearth of his fellow nationals. Maybe also to bury the pain caused by a personal tragedy, to revenge. Boundless love and concern led the sister to the war too, to watch over her brother. Heroism and love do not go one without another. This is the core of many epic and romantic stories from our past. Unfortunately, we came across one such a story today, in the trenches of Slavonia" (11).

The man, Slobodan, decided to go to war after his brother-in-law, a Croat, killed his pregnant sister. Another sister, Jadranka, followed him: "With a childish stubbornness she repeats that she will go wherever Slobodan goes." There was no mistrust in accepting her into the unit, nor any regrets: "'Jadranka is not different in any respect from other warriors; she fulfils all the military duties. Tonight she was at the night watch,' her commander asserts. 'She perfected her handling of the artillery piece. Slobodan is her assistant. How could we fail when Jadranka is with us! The other warriors always try to do better when she is around'" (ibid.). Still, Jadranka's military skills seem to be only secondary to her sisterly role, for she says, "My place is next to my brother." And in the concluding paragraph the journalist agrees: "'All I wish is to be on the front line,' Slobodan says. 'I wish the same,' Jadranka whispers quietly. Although both of them refused to explain, we understood their anguish. Jadranka is on the front lines to watch over her brother'" (ibid.).

The love of a sister for her brother is a familiar trope in Serbian folk poetry. However, in Serbian folk poetry there is no example of a sister following a brother to war. Instead, she dutifully awaits the brother's return, or, more often, for the message that the brother is dead. In that case, the sister's way of mourning is a measure of her love for the brother. The folk poem "The Greatest Sorrow Is for a Brother" expresses that very clearly. A young woman welcomes the warriors returning from a battle. Among them, she awaits her husband, her brother-in-law, and her brother. But these three do not return. In her mourning, she expresses her sorrow for each of them:

> For her husband she cut her hair,
> For her brother-in-law she scratched her face,

> For her brother she gouged her eyes out.
> The hair she cuts, it grows back again.
> The face she hurts, it heals again.
> But the eyes do not grow back,
> Nor can the heart bleeding for her brother ever heal.[3]

To be sure, the poem does not describe a practice (gouging out one's own eyes) but, rather, establishes a symbolic value of the relationship, based on past practices of a different kind: the brother used to introduce the sister to the world, to marry her off, and to protect her throughout life. The married woman in the past could have always gone back to her brother, if her marriage failed. The brother used to be, empirically and symbolically, a guarantor of sister's safety as well as her link to the world. That used to make him, in comparison to all other men in a woman's life, the most important figure. Thus her devotion and love, as well as subordination to his wishes—and the need to watch over him, protect him, keep him alive.

In the text above, the sister's military role and commanding position is completely subordinated to her role as a sister. While this is a role of protection, she does not appear strong and powerful, but rather soft, as a shadow that follows in his steps. Love and devotion define this woman soldier more than anything else, and the explicit reference of the journalist to the epic and romantic stories from the past places her firmly within the medieval tradition, even when acknowledging her very contemporary skills.

Another text about love and devotion, published in *Politika* in February 1993, uses the same mixture of medieval and contemporary elements and at the same time presents a most striking example of how epic narrative and romantic story can merge. "We Know Our Place" is the longest of the articles about female soldiers in *Politika*. It starts with a description of the photo accompanying the text, in which two young, handsome people—a woman and a man—in uniforms, look at the camera. His hand is on her shoulder.

They met only a month ago, on the front line, and fell in love, the text informs us, describing them in highly lyrical terms: "Their human faces, so rare here, today, and their eyes, these mirrors of their souls, most beautiful, full of goodness." Their story is told in language rhythmic and symbolic, full of pathos, like a long and tragic epic:

> [The two people on the photo] are perfect in everything except in one thing, one terrible thing. Their clothes: the uniforms that they wear,

> so unfitting. They say they feel uncomfortable dressed like that. Until only yesterday he was proud of his uniform. But now, with pain in his soul, he feels it almost repulsive. Because of those who betrayed that uniform, who betrayed the people. And why? Because of the throne! He wears it, nevertheless, because of the most unhappy, the most terribly hurt people, there, across the Drina river [i.e., across the Serbian border, Serbs in Bosnia and Croatia]. People who cry in despair, to the sky, to God, the Only and the True. The lonesome people. In their grave misery, they rest their hopes only in this uniform. God, how beautiful Mirjana would look in a pink wedding dress, with black hair. Or in a white dancing dress made of soft silk. Somewhere, with the scent of sea around her, the sounds of waves and a gentle tango. Oh, how fitting it would be for him to bow to such a beauty, and he, he alone, in a fashionable suit befitting his youth, to ask her for a dance with well-chosen words. But . . . Life, or was it something else, threw them into this wild game, the bloody wheel, driven by devils. (Ibid., 16)

The text goes on in the same manner right to the end, quoting lyric poetry and calling upon God, assigning shame and grace, cursing fate and lamenting the youth of two lovers as well as the betrayed and the corrupt politicians. The structure and the rhythm of Serbian epic poetry echoes throughout, transforming the love story into a heroic and tragic national narrative. The vividly portrayed youthful yet self-sacrificing bodies of the man and the woman are turned from the living flesh-and-blood bodies of soldiers into innocent, noble, and virtuous souls. Their story is the reminder of all what they could have become, were it not for the terrible tragedy that fell upon them and their people. Classic movie scenes of the romantic dance on a beach and a pink wedding dress are there to show a paradise lost. The language of epics and poetry is there to point out the guilty, as well as the innocent.

MANLY GIRL-SOLDIER

There are other texts in *Politika* about female soldiers where similar mixtures of innocence and betrayal, empathy and love appear: the story about Mara, for instance, a young peasant woman turned soldier. Two articles written by the same journalist were published about her, one in 1991 and another a year later. The first article introduces a young peasant, age nineteen, who with a handful of other villagers has defended her village from an attack by Croatian forces and become famous as the bravest among the defenders. "Nobody Should Remember Me for My Gun" (*Politika*, August 7, 1991, 10), is about the battle, Mara's participation in it, her motivation to be the first in the village to fight, and the reluctance with which she deals with her soldiering, indicated in statement that she does not like to be remembered for her gun. The second article, "From a Heroine to a Tiller" (*Politika*, July 28, 1992, 11) is about the aftermath: a fallen heroine.

In the first article, admiration and sympathy for young Mara alternate with descriptions of the suffering of Serbs in Krajina, Croatia. With her "tiny posture" and her "maiden soul, toughened by the war," Mara is "neither a woman, nor a child." Her "childish embarrassment" is described when she uses the word *Ustashe*, "the real name of the Croatian army." She speaks about her readiness to die, to defend her village, "homes and honor, freedom and faith." She says: "If my five brothers are to die, that will be only after me." At one point Mara recalls the concentration camp Jasenovac from World War Two, established by the puppet Croatian state under a fascist government, in which Jews, Serbs, and antifascist and communist Croats were executed. The partisan tradition is recalled in yet another remark: "Croatian TV calls Chetniks the partisans of today." That means that the "partisan war is now officially declared as being antagonist to Croatia." But it is certainly not antagonist to the story about young peasant woman who is at one point called "partisan Mara" (*partizanka Mara*).

Throughout the text Mara draws attention away from herself, to all the other brave and determined defenders of the village, and to the collective suffering of the Serbs: "Maybe we Serbs in Croatia were born to suffer." Regretting her fame, she says she would have preferred to remain an unknown peasant girl, tilling rented land.

That is precisely what we see happen in the next article, a year later. The village celebrates the first anniversary of the battle, but Mara is not among the celebrities, although the village officials have given her a seat in a front row. Instead, she sits in the café "with men, with a cigarette in one hand and the beer bottle in another, without a glass." Her glory is long gone. She was forced to leave the police—a job she got while still a hero—and, having no other work, she tills rented land. The journalist recalls his worry about the "remnants of her childhood and her maiden soul" from his first meeting with her, a year before. She hides whatever is left of it now, leaning on the bar "in a way men do." But she is too short for that, journalist states.

She "tries to hide her tears" while telling how she was accused of being "too trigger-happy." All her gestures are continuously described as an unsuccessful imitation of male attitude: "she puts her hand on the journalist's shoulder, giving the gesture a bit of male charm, proving that she is cool, without emotions." She repeats several times that she still has her hoe: "nobody fights about that . . . nobody will want to take that away" the way they took away her gun. Despite her male posture, she is on the edge of tears while telling about corruption in the police station, about the complicity of the officials, about her determination to do the "male job" properly, about stepping on some toes on the way. All the time "she imitates, as a routine, the male charm."

If the first story about Mara is about the heroism of a partisan maiden ready to die for her people, the second story is, again, about courage and betrayal. This time, however, the betrayed are not only the Serbs in Croatia. Mara is betrayed, too. The journalist makes clear that her status of a heroine and the due reward are denied by those unworthy of her—the officials in power who, among other things, stole packets of chocolates sent as aid to the village children. This act of ultimate corruption separates them from Mara, a woman with a "maiden soul," whose love for her people made her refuse to partake in corruption. But, while both texts tell a story about love and empathy, courage and anguish, the partisan references present in the text from 1991 have disappeared from the text published in 1992. What remained were the people, and a maiden betrayed and innocent.

In the Serbian daily, the presence of the specific texts about partisan women, and the references to World War Two in the articles about soldier women, function as a bridge that links different traditions and establishes the continuity of the history of Serb suffering and sacrifice, from medieval times, through revolution and partisan war, all the way to the war in which socialist Yugoslavia disintegrated. The uninterrupted continuity of that history is reinforced by language, where epic and lyric poetry narrates one long myth, as the myth of the past and the myth of the present, for the future.

In that myth, femininity has a special place. Bravery, military skills, beauty, motivation, they are all there. But, in *Politika*, the Serbian daily, they are all less significant. Beyond them lie the boundless love and self-sacrifice of the Serb maiden soldiers. They do not sit in castles awaiting sad messages any longer. They carry arms, command military units, and operate artillery; they become trigger-happy and know their place. But their maiden souls watch, all the same, over their brothers and their people. As they are true children of their tragic nation, their true powers are not in guns, but in love; not in what they are now, but in what they once were, or will never be. So few of them are depicted with guns—in text or in photography—because they do not fight with guns, but with love and self-sacrifice, with spiritual beauty of their own, as well as of their people, unacknowledged and betrayed.

These images of medieval heroines could hardly be more different in the images of the modern, European women soldiers in the Croatian press. But they have the same function: to embody the nation and its tradition. What makes them different is the fact that the Croatian and Serbian media seek to establish completely different traditions and used different means to accomplish the goal: photography in the Croatian daily, language in the Serbian daily. The former placed the Croat women soldiers, and Croatia, on the map of a new symbolic geography—as part of Europe. The latter reinforced the narrative of continuous suffering and history of self-sacrifice.

Just as in the Croatian press, in the Serbian press too, femininity and ethnicity are defined through the same attributes: self-sacrifice, love, and devotion. They are placed in the same history of internal betrayal and external animosity and situated within the same tradition of a higher moral order—one defined by love. This is also a reason why in the Serbian daily *Politika* there are only Serb female soldiers, only the representation of the Self. In a discourse that defines both ethnicity and femininity through self-sacrifice, there is simply no space for the Other, because in the Serbian daily, the self-sacrifice is not constructed as a political choice, but as an essence of both femininity and ethnicity, as well as of the (continuously) tragic Serb history.

In these representations, the Serbian papers faced the same problem that Croatian papers did: how to reconcile femininity and soldiering. The surprising thing is that—although the images of the female soldiers in the two media are completely different—the basic presumption is the same: men are natural soldiers, while women are there only conditionally. And even though the conditions differ significantly between the two media, in both the Serbian and the Croatian press, soldiering and militancy are still defined as inherently alien to women.

11

TROUBLES WITH ARMS

While the Serbian and Croatian (and occasionally, international) press was interested in the women fighting the wars between 1991 and 1995 with weapons in their hands, feminists—both in the former Yugoslav territories and internationally—largely ignored them. At the first sight, this may seem surprising: first, because Yugoslav partisan women in World War Two had been the subject of study both nationally and internationally, and second, because women's contributions to the "war efforts" during World Wars One and Two, their participation in nationalist, anticolonial armed struggles of the Third World, their presence in insurgencies and separatist movements (especially of South Asia and Latin America), and their entry into national militaries have all been studied internationally.

However, a closer look at feminist discourses about the Yugoslav disintegration reveals that, during the wars and immediately afterward, the focus of feminist analysis as well as activism, nationally and internationally, was firmly on women's victimization. Consequently, there was no discursive space within which women's active participation in nationalist projects and in war violence could have been addressed.

With the numbers of the women soldiers participating in the Yugoslav disintegration unknown but argued as rather insignificant, and with the emergence of evidence that sexual violence and rape against women occurred on a mass scale, the fact that feminist academics and activists largely focused on the battered and raped female body may be seen as corresponding to the situation on the ground. Nevertheless, among women refugees many have become (feminist) activists in their new places of residence. Among women who survived rape camps some have become extremely active in collecting and giving testimonies for the International Criminal Tribunal for the former Yugoslavia. Furthermore, much of the feminist activist documentation calls for the assertion of women's resilience and strength. Thus, seeing women only as victims is not a simple matter of reflecting the empirical situation. Feminist theory has produced the concepts of agency and subjectivity, not only that of victimization, precisely because in the gravest of times women have had the stamina to act. Still, the victimized female body seems to have been not only the most visible of all the bodies in Yugoslav wars but also the most visible body within feminist discourses—activist, as well as academic.

Thus the invisibility and absence of the armed female body in regional feminist debates has to be traced back to the ways Yugoslav feminism of the time theorized agency, in relation to gender, ethnicity, and war or violence. The invisibility of women soldiers from the Balkans in international feminist discussions, on the other hand, may be seen as indicative of two things: first, certain shifts within recent feminist analyses of militarization and war in the Western scholarship, and second, Eurocentrism, and separateness of this scholarship from the body of knowledge on women participating in violent conflict elsewhere.

Yugoslav Feminism: Feminist Agency, Female Victimization?

It is worth noting that ethnicity became a feminist issue in socialist Yugoslavia only in the late 1980s, with the rise of nationalism, and with women becoming the focus of many nationalist debates.[1] Thus, from the start, ethnicity was defined by feminists as collective identity and as part and parcel of nationalism. Among the most significant public debates that feminists engaged in were those on differences in the demographic growth of various ethnic groups, and on changes in abortion and rape legislation.[2]

Feminist grassroots activism in the 1980s was in its very beginnings, mostly concentrated on the issue of violence against women.[3] However, as nationalism rose, feminist activism included public protests such as street demonstrations, as well as lobbying and issuing press statements. In the late 1980s, for example, new proposals for changes in legislation on rape, abortion, and child benefits, drafted by nationalists, brought feminists onto the streets as well as into the republican and federal parliaments.

In these public actions Yugoslav feminists from different republics were acting not only in solidarity but as a front. This is especially true for feminist activists from Zagreb and Belgrade. Differences in viewpoints that existed among them never followed republican or ethnic lines, nor were they seen as such. Indeed, at the very beginning, nationalism, and especially Serb nationalism, was seen as a common enemy. Furthermore, ethnicity was seen as incompatible with women's agency, let alone with feminist agency.

This stance was already apparent in feminist reactions to the women's demonstrations in Kosovo in 1987, when women who defined themselves as Serb were denied agency even at the time when they very clearly demonstrated their political positions.

Once the war started this incompatibility of ethnicity and women's and feminist agency became even more prominent. As feminists throughout the region initially defined themselves as antinationalist feminists, and as they perceived ethnicity only as a collective identity, and only within nationalism, they vehemently rejected all ethnic identifications. One feminist from Croatia expressed a thought shared at the very beginning of the war by many feminists: "It is impossible to merge nation and gender—they are different understandings of human nature and human essence. It is therefore impossible to be equally of one's nation and of one's gender" (Cullen 1992, 414).

For many feminists from Serbia and Croatia who operated within the heated nationalist discourses and realities, which were increasingly reduced to ethnicity, the denial of national and ethnic identities created a powerful starting point in communication and a common political agenda. Their refusal of their own ethnic identities came to symbolize their refusal of nationalism. For them, feminism equaled antinationalism.

However, in 1992 and 1993, when mass rape and sexual violence against women as a gendered war strategy became public, and raped women started appearing among the refugees fleeing war zones in Bosnia and Croatia, the feminist antinationalist bloc started to crumble. For some feminists, ethnicity gained new relevance. As others have already pointed out, the interpretation of the war rapes, and especially definitions of the victims and the perpetrators, became a contested issue that finally split Croatian feminists into nationalist and antinationalist groups and led to heated debates between academic feminists and a group of radical feminists activists from Belgrade.[4]

Nationalist feminists from Croatia insisted that only Croat and Muslim women were victims and only Serb men the perpetrators of the war rapes. For them, the woman became a metaphor of the nation-state. They talked about the "rape of Bosnia and Croatia" as much as about the "rape of Muslim and Croat women" (Boric 1997, 39). Furthermore, they claimed their own ethnicity and nationhood as inseparable from their feminism, and defined themselves as patriotic feminists.[5] Their work merged different aspects of the feminist agenda with the agenda of supporting the emerging nation-state and claims of national and ethnic identities: they worked on recovering (Croat) women in Croatian national history and addressed the issue of domestic violence by fiercely accusing Croat men of oppressing Croat women; they published feminist journals and lobbied the parliament for legislation to protect women's rights. Some of them, like the women of O-ZONA: Assistance to Women in Crisis, for example, openly defined themselves as a radical feminist group.[6]

Antinationalist feminist activists in Zagreb and Belgrade, on the other hand, argued that women of all ethnic backgrounds had been raped in the war, and that men of all (para)militaries were the perpetrators, though they accepted that Bosnian Serb forces and their allies had committed most of the crimes. They also argued that women were the main victims of the wars in Bosnia and Croatia. However, the notion of a woman as the main victim did not always have the same meaning among antinationalist feminists, because of the very different contexts of war and nationalism within their states, as well as very different personal, professional, and feminist histories that predated nationalism and war. In Belgrade, a small but very active group of radical feminists, led by Lepa Mladjenović from the Autonomous Women's Center initially refused, when talking about war rapes, to acknowledge that ethnicity or nation were in any way relevant, and defined rape as "male violence against women."[7] They asserted that "rape is not a nationalist but a gender issue" and that nation, state, armies, patriotism, and wars are all products of patriarchy, conceived in, and sustained through, male violence against women, and male hatred of everything female and feminine (Mladjenović and Litričin 1993, 113). This assumption that all women are victims of all men defines woman as an ultimate metaphor of victimhood and, paradoxically, adopts the dominant patriarchal notions of gender—with aggressive masculinity and violable femininity—even when wanting to subvert it. At the same time, this definition extracts both masculinity and femininity from power relations defined by ethnicity and heterosexuality.

One consequence of such a standpoint is that, for antinationalist feminists, all women are seen primarily through the prism of victimization. Even women who, by every possible criterion, could have been defined through agency—nationalist feminists—are regularly described as "manipulated" and "trapped" (Borić 1997, 41), or the word "activism" is placed in quotation marks when referring to them (Korać 1993, 109). Thus, their own agency is discounted as riding on the wave of a borrowed, nationalist agency.

Such a conceptualization, on the one hand, leaves nationalism and war as exclusively male enterprises. On the other hand, it separates victimization and agency, without recognizing that the two are not necessarily separate or opposite, but rather mutually constitutive, both empirically and discursively. For not only have many refugee women become feminist activists, but the victimization of women became one of the most powerful sources of women's and feminist activism as well as theorizing. Not surprisingly, these conceptualizations left no discursive space within which engagements of women voluntary soldiers could be addressed.[8]

There is yet another, subtler, level of feminist dissociation of women from agency: an assumption of women's political innocence in general, and innocence with regard to the Yugoslav wars in particular. In her analysis of women's and feminist NGOs in Bosnia, Elissa Helms (2003) points out that feminist discourses of the war as an exclusively man-made endeavor inform feminist activities and feminist writing on women and war in Bosnia, creating a gendered essentialism that invariably excuses women from political decisions leading to wars and associates them with peacemaking. Helms's concern is that such discourses places too heavy a responsibility on women's shoulders, as was evident in the attitude of donors of aid. In receiving money for "reconciliation and reconstruction" projects, women were expected to mend all the ills of the war and do what official politics with all the international assistance is obviously still not able to do—bring about reconciliation and assure a democratic future.

The backdrop of these discourses, according to which women had nothing to do with the decisions that made the war possible, is a crude annihilation of women's agency. For, one who is absolved of all political responsibility for the war cannot, at the same time, claim political agency. Claiming political agency would mean also sharing political responsibility. As Ivana Spasić (2000) pointed out, as citizens women are responsible for the social and political world in which they live, thus also for the wars. But in feminism there seems to be a paradoxical split in which women in general are the innocent, powerless victims, while antinationalist feminists are the powerful, world-transforming agents. Their activism is privileged as the only authentic expression of all the interests of all the women, and all other women appear only as victims, defined either through ignorance and manipulation (as in the case of nationalist feminists, or nationalist women in general), or through innocence (as with refugee women and raped women).

Discussing humanitarian and aid work in general, Hugo Slim (2004, 208) coined the term "innocence-based solidarity" to indicate how certain aid providers claim solidarity "with those who are somehow regarded as innocent," with the "lowest common denominator of innocence usually drawn along lines of sex and age." Spasić (2000, 352) goes a step further, asserting that raped women and other victims of war are often perceived by feminists as good *because* they are victims, allowing victimization to define the "quality of the victim." Renata Jambrešić-Kirin (2000) shows the consequences of such links in some feminist writing on women and war that has been celebrated internationally. She offers a poignant study of the seductive power of the victim status, and the slippery realm of identification and empathy with the victim in autobiographical writing (often originally written in English or German, for an international audience) of three well-known feminist writers from Croatia, Rada Iveković, Slavenka Drakulić, and Dubravka Ugresić: "skilful sliding of autobiographical discourse instances between first person singular and plural makes it possible to establish an empathic identification with the people who suffered most. . . . What anthropologists take issue with in this kind of emphatic reflection is the neglect of the fact that clearly separates the writer in temporary exile from the masses of anonymous, unfortunate people who . . . do not have the opportunity to choose" (311).[9]

The conceptualization of women through the images of victimization, innocence, and morality has multiple consequences for the feminist conceptualization of war violence, gender, and ethnicity, as well as for their relationships. By granting the ultimate victim status to the female body, Yugoslav antinationalist feminist activists largely continued to assume the omnipotence of men and the powerlessness of women. Theoretically this meant that they continued to define masculinity through power, and femininity through violability, and thus to reproduce, instead of subverting, the dominant gendered narrative of war. It also meant that they ignored the specific powers of women, including the power to perpetrate, justify, and condone violence.

Such a conceptualization of femininity is closely linked to the conceptualization of ethnicity, whereby ethnicity is both collectivized and communalized. Consequently, ethnicity and femininity were either collapsed into each other (as in nationalist feminism) or totally separated (as in antinationalist feminism). Furthermore, ethnicity was granted meaning only in the context of hatred and violence, and only as a collective identity. All the very profound personal meanings of ethnicity were lost; all the everyday manifestations of ethnic identities past and present, and the "trauma of change" brought about by the war, were erased (Dević 2000, 202).[10] This loss and erasure further meant that antinationalist feminists were ignoring the fact that nation, ethnicity, and womanhood are not mutually exclusive realms in women's lives and that women — feminists or not — do claim not only an ethnic identity but also nationalism as *their own* project.

International Feminism: Militant Agency, Female Empowerment?

Disciplinary approaches to any academic subject are necessarily linked both to a history of the discipline and its theoretical traditions and to geopolitical traditions and histories, because the histories and traditions of theoretical thinking and academic disciplining are tightly linked to the specific geopolitical projects. The study of war and violent conflict seems to be an apt example, as theorizing on violent conflicts is often inseparable from geopolitical projects such as nation-state building, colonialism, and imperialism.

Not surprisingly, in most disciplines, the feminist body of knowledge stands rather (if not entirely) separate from the mainstream theoretical production of knowledge. Furthermore, the disciplinary divisions of academic labor tell us that — while we should praise the existence of women's studies, within which the former object of a hegemonic gaze became the rightful subject of self-knowledge — these studies still remain perceived as *specific* fields of knowledge, rather inconsequential to the general production of knowledge, just as the realities they theorize remain perceived as particular realities, inconsequential to the larger sociopolitical processes.

This perception meant that feminists in any of the academic disciplines — including those doing research on war and conflict — have to counter many different hegemonies present within their discipline's theoretical and geopolitical traditions, not only hegemonies along the lines of gender. At the same time, the hegemonic position of Western academia has offered an advantage to Western feminists and feminists living in the West, prioritizing their theorizing of war and violent conflict against the knowledge produced in other parts of the world. Thus, throughout the 1980s, feminist studies of women joining armies and militaries, fighting on front lines, and participating in violent conflicts in other capacities have not only prioritized experiences of the women in the West, but also Western perspectives on the women's experiences in violent conflicts in Asia, Latin America, and Africa.

Much of this, now classic feminist scholarship on war and militarism has been informed by one of the most heated feminist discussions—equality versus difference.[11] The debate itself is a product of two fundamentally different feminist projects: liberal feminists' struggle to secure women's access to all social spheres and especially those perceived as exclusively male, and radical feminists' struggle to preserve the presumed essential difference between (nurturing) femininity and (violent) masculinity and to build society based upon the qualities of the former.

These two different feminist approaches to war, and their theoretical underpinnings are still relevant today, because they have resulted in a production of rich, complex, and diverse bodies of knowledge, applied to different geopolitical realities and different fields of research. Some of these studies have focused on the relationships between women and war (especially the two World Wars), and rallied around the idea that the dramatic social transformations caused by wars, and women's engagements in different "war efforts" (whether in war industries or in the fighting), offer a chance for expanding the scope of women's social life. The argument is that changes in gender roles—evident in many violent conflicts—potentially have a long-term effect and could bring about women's empowerment and change in gender relations. Other studies address the same relationship, using essentialized notions of feminine-maternal caring and love of peace as their starting point.[12] Yet other studies analyze women's participation in national militaries (both in the West and in the Third World) or militant (separatist and guerrilla) movements, arguing that women's presence in the militaries could bring about transformation of masculinist institutions such as militaries.[13]

While all these debates are an immensely valuable contribution to our understanding of the relationships between gender and war, the construction of militarism through notions of femininity and masculinity, and their impact on women's lives, they have often been based on Western experiences. Furthermore, emancipation and agency have emerged as the main analytical frameworks for feminist analysis of women's participation in wars and militaries as an effect of World War Two and various revolutionary and colonial struggles, when women eventually gained diverse levels of legal equality or protection in the public sphere. Thus, there is a direct linkage between the feminist conceptualization of women's agency and the conceptualization of women's participation in armies, militaries, and wars as potentially empowering and emancipatory.

However, there is a huge "but" in this conceptualization. It concerns the nature of the army, military, or conflict in which women take part. Namely, when these are seen as oppressive, hegemonic, or unjust, feminists have seldom analyzed the lives of the women who joined them. Such a feminist attitude seems to have to do with general feminist uneasiness with women's participation in the politics that can be characterized as right-wing: nationalist, racist, or religious fundamentalist movements, communal violence, or terrorist actions. It seems that the feminist discourse of male oppression of women is ill equipped for perceiving women active in right-wing political groups and militant movements.

Nevertheless, there have been studies that analyze lives of women belonging to, or associated with, movements, armies, and militaries whose definition could hardly be accurate without words such as "oppressive" or "hegemonic." The study of German women in the Nazi movement by Claudia Koontz (1986) is one of those exceptions, and it has inspired other studies too. For example, Jacklyn Cock (1992, 1994) has analyzed the lives and experiences of women in the white South African Defence Force against the backdrop of apartheid.[14] She compares the role of the women in the Defence Force in maintaining the racist and sexist social order of South Africa to that of Nazi women in Germany, who contributed to the power of the oppressive state "by preserving the illusion of love in an environment of hatred" (Cock 1994, 154). Cock also compared the position of women in the Defence Force with that of women in Umkhonto we Sizwe (The Spear of the Nation), an armed wing of the African National Congress, and came to some interesting conclusions. First, women's roles in the Defence Force extended into the male sphere but did not fundamentally change, while women in Umkhonto we Sizwe took on new roles. Furthermore, while the former "cultivated a subordinate and decorative notion of femininity," the ideology of the latter "sometimes involved a denial of femininity" (Cock 1994, 161). Whatever the differences, one conclusion that emerges from Cock's study is that combat played a fundamental role for defining women's position within the military in both the Defence Force and Umkhonto we Sizwe. Those women who participated in combat were—sometimes, and selectively—allowed to participate in the heroic myths and historic narratives of their communities; others were relegated to insignificance (ibid., 159).

Combat has been one of the most important factors in defining the position of women within Western militaries, marking an ultimate difference between military men and women.[15] As an exclusive preserve of men, combat has been the axis around which femininities and masculinities in Western militaries and wars are constructed. However, during World War Two, Russian and Yugoslav partisan women were fighting on the front lines. The same is true for Third World women in liberation movements. Therefore, the neat political, ideological, and theoretical constructions of combat as masculine crumble when the perspective is not West European. Reviewing feminist literature on women militants in Eritrea, Vietnam, Namibia, South Africa, and Nicaragua, and comparing it to literature on the United States, Sarala Emmanuel (2004) shows that the sexual division of labor in militant movements in the Third World first, did not exclude women from combat, and second, politicized highly some of the support services provided by women. Consequently, she concludes, these distinctions reflect Eurocentrism in a feminist theoretical framework based on the split between public and private, which continues to link masculinity with the public, and femininity with the private, even when the realities of women's lives defy such divisions.

These realities became ever more complex in the late 1980s and the early 1990s, as a few things happened that have impacted hugely on current feminist theorization of war and militaries. First, there were changes in feminist theoretical and political trajectories: theoretical trajectories were marked by a postmodern turn in feminism, and political trajectories were marked by the high prominence and visibility of Third World feminists within Western feminist academia. The postmodern turn has (among other things) resulted in the questioning of some classic feminist concepts conceived within modernist discourses, such as agency, emancipation, and empowerment, as well as the underlying assumption that women's agency directly and invariably leads to emancipation and enhanced agency. The rise to prominence of Third World feminists has made the feminist knowledge produced by them both more important in the West and more relevant to the Western realities. These two trajectories go hand in hand, indicating both the unsettling of Western feminist hegemony in production of feminist knowledge by the growing presence of the Third World feminists (especially those living in the West), and the growing realization within Western feminist academia and movements that new theoretical reflections and political solidarities need to be developed to suit the changing geopolitical realities.[16]

These changing realities were another significant factor for feminist theorizing on war in the late 1980s and early 1990s. Simply put, new wars opened new questions. Women soldiers participated in the Falklands and Gulf Wars, stirring up old debates and posing new challenges to classic feminist studies of war and militarism developed in the early 1980s. One of these challenges was how to analyze links between gender and other social relations of power, and especially other social identities that seem to have gained in visibility and relevance in these wars. It was obvious, for example, that the British and the American women soldiers fighting in the Falklands and the Gulf were used as multiple symbols—of nation, race, ideology, emancipation, and modernity.[17]

Wars and the strategic use of violence in Rwanda and the former Yugoslavia, on the one hand, make the links between gender and other, collectivized identities even more painfully clear, impacting largely, though unevenly, feminist conceptualization of the intersections of gender, ethnicity, and war. On the other hand, these wars exposed to a large extent the Eurocentrism of Western feminist scholarship and politics, showing that Orientalism is still alive and kicking in many feminist texts.[18] Finally, NATO's war against Serbia over Kosovo in 1999 (justified by the doctrine of the "humanitarian war") and wars in Afghanistan in 2001 and in Iraq in 2003 (justified by the doctrine of the "preemptive strike" and the discourse of the "war on terror") have been painfully exposing, each in a different way, some of the limitations in classical feminist theorizing on violent conflict, and the need for new approaches.

Consequently, throughout the 1990s, feminist conceptualizations of wars, violent conflicts, and militarization have been changing. Femininity and masculinity and their intersections with other relations of power have become much more prominent tools of analysis, after the study of women and their experiences of violent conflict and its aftermath. Furthermore, feminist studies have focused on representations of femininities and masculinities in various war narratives, on the genderedness of these narratives, as well as war practices, on links between gendered identities, violence, and military, and on the changing nature of warfare.[19]

The concepts of women's agency and empowerment through war have still preserved a lot of their theoretical appeal, becoming ever more important for feminist movement. Thanks to global feminist efforts in 2000 the United Nations adopted Resolution 1325, which requires the inclusion of women's antiwar efforts in every step of the official political and social processes that transforms a society from one at war to one at peace; the resolution also asks for due attention to women's informal ways of doing peace politics and for preserving gains that women acquire during the times of conflict. Theoretically, the analyses of women's agency in and against war continue—whether through studies of women's antiwar activism, women's individual and collective resilience and survival strategies, or women's community work and leadership.[20]

Meanwhile, however, the old optimism about the long-term impact of changes in gender roles during wartime has been losing strength. Judy El-Bushra's (2004) recent work is probably most significant in this respect. She sends two grim warnings. First, while gender roles do change in violent conflicts (sometimes dramatically), and women do take greater responsibilities within household and community, institutional support that "would provide women with decision-making power consistent with these new and more responsible roles have been slow in coming" (169). El-Bushra notes that "the ideological underpinnings of gender relations have barely been touched at all and may even have become further reinforced through conflict" (ibid.). The second issue that emerges from El-Bushra's study is that how gender becomes utilized in preserving different political and economic orders (from colonialism, to nationalism and communalism to imperialism) is only one side of a coin. The opposite has to be looked at too: how different political means, including violent conflict and war, are used to preserve gender orders. While this point has been proposed before, there are, to my knowledge, no empirical studies to prove it.[21] Through her examination of several states in Africa, she shows how violent conflict becomes a means of preserving, or rather reclaiming and consolidating, the lost prerogatives of dominant masculinity (such as property, control, and social status) as well as dominant gender hierarchies (161–168).

Studies of the militarization of women's lives—whether through direct participation in the militaries or through professional and family associations—have also continued to rely on the concept of women's agency and empowerment. But here too, the straightforward link of that agency to emancipation and empowerment has been considerably undermined. For the wars of the 1990s and of the twenty-first century have confirmed the fact that women soldiers and militants are here to stay, not only as enlightened freedom fighters in liberation movements of the Third World, nor in presumed democratic Western militaries fighting totalitarianism, but also in wars imperial, gruesome, and horrid—not only among the oppressed, but also among aggressors, on the wrong sides altogether. These women and their actions may well be contributing to the maintenance of national or international social orders based on oppression and exclusion. Their actions may well be part of male-defined ideologies and projects. But they are neither blinded, manipulated victims of patriarchal social order nor are they necessarily empowered or emancipated social agents.

Furthermore, women's presence in the militaries does not seem to either change the masculinist nature of the institution or contribute to the general advancement of women's position in the society. Quite to the contrary: Enloe (2000), for example, shows that defending the rights of women soldiers in the United States military is threatened by pursuing the rights of civilian women affected by United States militarism, and vice versa. She shows that American feminists fighting for soldier-women's rights (against harassment and sexual violence, or discrimination based on sexual preferences) are allied with the lesbian and gay movement fighting against homophobia in armies, but *not* with feminists working with prostitutes around military bases, or with military wives. Still, Enloe insists that women's soldiering may, "under certain conditions" (287), advance the cause for all women. She gives an example of exposing the cover-up of a rape of a female soldier by a male soldier. Such an exposure of a cover-up, she argues, "can tear away the legitimizing camouflage that has sustained that military as a symbol of national pride and security . . . [and] make that military appear to many citizens for the first time to be little more than a men's club. . . . [A] state official . . . may become confused. Although state confusion is not as invigorating to witness as state transformation, it can be revealing. And revelation can alter consciousness" (287). This is not only an utterly optimistic perspective, but also an utterly unrealistic one, which shows clearly the limitations posed by the equality-versus-difference and agency-emancipation frameworks and indicates that we need to look at wars and violent conflicts, as well as women's participation in them, with different theoretical eyes.

Another change in feminist theorizing of war in the 1990s can be closely traced to the wars in Yugoslavia and Rwanda, where the issue of women's victimization dominates the feminist discourse. In both these wars women were targeted by gender-specific war violence on a mass scale. In both of them there was an unprecedented growth of women's organizations, activism, and networking. And in both of them women also took part in violence. In Rwanda, women—Catholic nuns, at that—faced trials for war crimes. Still, women in the Balkan and Rwanda, as well as other African wars, continue to be studied through the prism of victimization. Interestingly, Susan McKay and Dyan Mazurana's (2004) study on girls in fighting forces in Africa indicate that large number of girls, female adolescents, and young women are both actively fighting in the African wars and being used as slave labor. But these findings seem not to have wider theoretical impact.

I would argue that the recent prominence of the woman-as-war-victim is the direct, albeit paradoxical consequence of the centrality of the concept of agency, and its relation to empowerment and emancipation in feminist theorizing. Informed by modernist discourses that split the social realities of women along the lines of what is private and what public, the feminist struggle against oppression and victimization has been a struggle for public spaces, and agency has been, for a long time, recognized only when exercised visibly, in public. Thus, women's engagement in militaries and wars with weapons in their hands was easy to conceptualize within the framework of agency and link to emancipation and empowerment. At the same time, victimhood has been the mirror image of such an understanding of agency. And, because there have always been women and regions that have been seen as more empowered and more emancipated than others, it was also easy to perceive some of them through the prism of victimization. Not surprisingly, women in the Balkan and African wars have been among the latter.

The Productive Power of Violence

As the old geopolitical and theoretical hegemonies crumble, at least two things seem to become evident: first, agency, emancipation, and empowerment are not intrinsically linked only to liberating and progressive movements; second, agency, emancipation, and empowerment may not be the best framework at all for studying women's diverse positioning within violent conflict, including women's participation in fighting.

The region in which both of these points have been taken most seriously in feminist theorizing is South Asia. There, a body of knowledge has been steadily growing on women's diverse positioning within a range of very different violent conflicts.

Hindu communalism and separatist movements such as those in Kashmir and in northeast India, the Maoist insurgency in Nepal, and the separatist militant movements in Sri Lanka are all very different violent conflicts, with different histories and trajectories. Their effects on women and women's engagements in them are also very diverse. But it seems that this diversity, as well as the overwhelming presence of women on the side of those who inflict violence, has forced feminists in the region to reexamine their old theoretical tools and search for the new ones. Women have participated in different militant and separatist movements in Sri Lanka, in Nepal, and in the militant formations of the Rashtriya Swayamsevak Sangh (National Volunteers' Union) in India. In India, women participated in riots in 1984, in the destruction of the Ayodhya Mosque in 1992, in communal violence in Bombay in 1992 and 1993, and in separatist movements in Kashmir, Assam, and Punjab. Women also took part in the communal violence in Gujarat. Anita Roy (1997, 261) remarked once that "1947 was a moment of triumph not only for anti-colonial nationalism but also for communalism." Today, one could add, communalism marks the triumph of women's will to violence.

It is not surprising then that many feminists writing on women and violence in South Asia criticize "'traditional' feminist concerns with violence, in which women are cast as victims," for their failure "to account for instances in which violence is perpetrated *by* women," and for their continuous gendering of violence as "male" (ibid., 260).[22] Darini Rajasingham-Senanayake (2001, 111) further criticizes secular feminists in South Asia who see women's political violence as a "black hole" and a part of "a male patriarchal project," and militant women as "pawns and victims in the discourse of nationalist patriarchy," while Tanika Sarkar and Urvashi Butalia (1995, 4) argue that women on the right "bring with them an informed consent and agency, a militant activism" of their own.

In their work Rajasingham-Senanayake (2001), Patricia Jeffery (2001), and Butalia (2001) suggest that feminist analysis of gender and violent conflict needs rethinking, as concepts such as agency and empowerment do not offer a satisfactory framework any longer: first, because both radical right-wing politics appropriate feminist language and offer emancipation and empowerment. This seems to be especially true for the Hindutva nationalist movement in India. Figuring prominently as followers as well as leaders of the movement, Hindutva women have defied feminist imagery of manipulated women who simply catch the leftover privileges falling from the patriarchal tables around which male leaders make all the difference. As Paola Bacchetta and Margaret Power (2002, 3) point out, "women in the right are neither dupes of right-wing men nor less powerful replicas of them"; they "consciously choose to support and help build the projects of which they are part. In so doing, right-wing women carve out a space and identity for themselves and enhance the ability of their right wings to implement their agenda." The consequence of such engagements of women in Hindutva movement is empowerment. However limited, conditional, and controversial this empowerment might be,[23] women's activism in Hindutva has a "palpable impact on women in the public sphere" (Dedhpande 1997, 197). This activism has politicized femininity and expanded the "horizons of domesticity," creating woman as a "communal subject" (Sarkar 1995, 188). In other words, within the Hindutva movement "woman has stepped out of a purely iconic status to take up an active position as a militant" (ibid.).

Second, some South Asian feminists argue that the modernist concept of agency is too reductive, as it recognizes only political and public activism, thus missing the much broader social and cultural context of women's engagement in violence outside of clearly defined political movements and public spheres.[24] The significance of this argument is in shifting the focus of theorizing from the type of women's engagement and its relation to agency or victimization, to the violence itself and its productive power. Such an approach allows for violence to be contextualized in relation to the types of political movements (nationalist, liberation, or separatist), the type of violent conflict ("ethnic wars," "communalism," "terrorism") or the forms of women's engagements (national militaries, paramilitary formations, communal violence), without being reduced to them.

My analysis of media representations of women soldiering in the Balkans, similar analyses of the Falklands and Gulf Wars, and the analysis of political discourses of right-wing women in South Asia all show that women serving in different military formations or condoning and perpetrating other forms of violence are often represented within the framework of victimization and agency by their communities. This is not accidental. Women soldiers symbolize these communities; they embody all the prerogatives of these communities. As narratives of victimization are crucial for the justification of the violence committed by these communities against its Others, victimization and sacrifice have to be present. As the right to defend or attack has to be justified, the agency is needed too, alongside the victimization. The centrality of agency and victimization for these war narratives makes them, in my view, problematic as central categories of feminist analysis. Instead of assuming the presence of either agency or victimization, I would rather ask when and how agency and victimization are prioritized in the representations as well as in the experiences, and how they are produced; what other narratives of female soldiering are there, and what norms of sexuality, notions of femininity and masculinity, or definitions of ethnicity are embodied in them? In other words, agency and victimization, far from being either the starting points or the central concepts of feminist theorizing of female soldiering, would be only two, among many other narratives of female engagement in collective violence.

This would also allow a different perspective on the experiences of the women soldiers. Victimization and agency are also present in the narratives used by the women themselves. This is to be expected: women soldiers give meanings to their own experiences in the same discursive space as the media. In my interviews with two women voluntary soldiers fighting within radical Serb paramilitary formations in Croatia and Bosnia, the victimization of the Serbs and their personal sacrifice for their people figured prominently in the narratives of their soldiering, very much as in the media narratives. Nevertheless, the women soldiers' narratives were far from being only about victimization and agency, or about empowerment and emancipation, even though they could both be described as conscious and informed agents. Throughout the narration, both women continuously repositioned themselves vis-à-vis different aspects of their soldiering: their relationships with male soldiers, relationship to the nation, relationship to the enemy, relationship to other women of their own ethnic group, and relationship to their own life and their self both before and after the war. Furthermore, none of these categories—male soldiers, nation, enemy, other women, their peacetime and postwar lives—had a fixed meaning. Both of the women have been captured and imprisoned by the Croatian forces, one of them tortured,[25] another maimed by a bomb blast and then hospitalized in Croatia. Both settled in Serbia after the war, the former continuing to be politically active, the latter withdrawing from public life altogether. The violence that they took part in and survived left many rather different marks on their narratives of soldiering, war, and nation. But it took me some time to understand their narratives, as I assumed that the beginning of the war, or at least the beginning of their own participation in it as soldiers, would mark changes in their lives. However, this was not so.

For the woman who was wounded, whom I will call Lepa, the moment of experiencing and enduring violence was a turning point.[26] Before that, Lepa's soldiering was very much like the private business she had before the war—something to be well organized and well run. Her military unit was her business, where she exercised all the professional skills learned in her prewar life. Thus this life continued into the war, with her sense of self being the same—a well-off woman who took care of her appearance and liked to see herself as a lady, who knew how to find her ways in the male world of business and who was well respected for both of these qualities, by business associates as well as war comrades. She talked with wonder about the fact that very few women joined "the men" in fighting the war, expressing contempt for their cowardice and lack of concern, underlining her own difference from them, and at the same time stressing that she was not extraordinary in any sense, but simply did what many others could and should have done.

The maiming changed it all, turning Lepa's narrative into one of suffering and sacrifice for her nation. And when she did not receive what she saw as a due recognition from Serbian government for her sacrifice—neither in political, nor moral nor financial terms—and ended up dependent on charity organizations and veteran support networks, her narrative became also a narrative of betrayal and disillusionment. Thus, it is the violence that Lepa endured that became the central point of her narrative and produced different meanings of her soldiering, her nation, and the war.

The woman who became politically active—I will call her Mirjana—on the other hand, totally excluded violence, both the perpetrated and the endured, from her narrative.[27] And, while the time of her soldiering was split into before and after her imprisonment, the soldiering itself was placed in the larger narrative where political consciousness merged with family history to provide continuity between the life before, during, and after the war. Tracing her sense of "national responsibility" to her family's belonging to Chetnik movement during World War Two, she refused to talk about violence committed by Chetniks in the past or present. For her, this was a political movement, and she was a political activist who simply endured stoically whatever her political commitment brought on her way, without ever assuming the status of the victim. It is the absence of violence in her narrative of soldiering that allowed her such positioning vis-à-vis both the war and her participation in it.

Focusing on violence, its presences and absences, and its meaning in the narratives of these two women allows for an analysis of their soldiering beyond the agent-victim dichotomies, beyond the "women-in-men's-shoes" approach, beyond the "emancipation" debate, and toward mutual production of different realities. Both women preserve a clear sense of difference from other women, as well as from the dominant notions of femininity that perceive soldiering as essentially masculine. In both narratives the violence that they or their fellow soldiers committed is absent. In Lepa's narrative, this may be partly due to the fact that she belonged to a military group formed of local residents of a small town in Croatia that stayed put in the trenches around the town, for its defense, and did not take direct part in fighting elsewhere. She was wounded when the town was overtaken by Croatian forces. But the absence of narratives of violence is striking in the case of Mirjana, who belonged to radical nationalist volunteer paramilitaries from Serbia, notorious for war crimes in Bosnia and Croatia, and especially for the war rapes, and who was personally subjected to violence. Interpreting this absence as denial of violence against the Other is too simple, as the violence was not denied, but rather unspoken. In this case, Mirjana acted totally against the mainstream nationalist discourse that engaged vigorously in discussions about war crimes committed by Serbian forces in order to deny them. Her silence about her own prison time too is not a simple hiding of one's own victimization, but may be a part of the unspeakability of violence. Here, too, the silence that covers the torture that Mirjana went through in the prison is contrary to mainstream nationalist discourse in Serbia that highlights crimes against its own population. It remained unclear whether Mirjana was raped in detention, and if so, her silence is close to the mainstream Serbian nationalist discourse that focused on rapes only in as much as they led to forced pregnancies. But altogether, this particular narrative of soldiering may also indicate that—beyond the frame of victimization—the militant far right produces few discursive spaces within which the violence experienced by women in the movement can be articulated. Their positioning within the movement, and within violence, is much more ambiguous.

Violence committed during the ethnic war in former Yugoslavia produced many different masculinities and femininities, ethnicities and sexualities. The media war treated different violent acts by, and against women and men differently, ascribing different meanings to the violence and victimization of the gendered, ethnicized, and sexualized Self and the Other. Together, these two wars acquired the power to define people, as much as villages and cities, histories and traditions, in exclusively ethnic and ethnically exclusive terms.

The task of a feminist critic is to analyze this productive power of violence, without jeopardizing the plight and the rights of those whose lives it once altered. Many feminist authors whose work guided me through this book have succeeded in this, because they situated specific acts of violence and their various representations in very concrete cultural, political, and representational contexts, without ever losing sight of the broader pictures. They analyzed violence neither as intrinsically male nor as only gendered, but as produced through the intersections of many, mutually constitutive relationships, never fixed, never neat, never simple. While many different forms of violence produce many different aspects of contemporary realities, analyzing this process of production may help a feminist critic to undo some of its machinery and deprive it of some of its components. For this to happen each of us, feminists, must see—and ask others to point out to us—not only who and what is privileged in the production of violence, but also who and what is privileged in our own analyses of it.

NOTES

Introduction

1. The Socialist Federal Republic of Yugoslavia was established after World War II as a federal state made up of six republics: from north to south, Slovenia, Croatia, Bosnia, Montenegro, Serbia, and Macedonia. Serbia had two autonomous provinces, Vojvodina in the north and Kosovo in the south (the area in between was often called Serbia proper). Each republic, except Bosnia, had one majority ethnic group (Serbs in Serbia, Croats in Croatia, and so on) but each also had a sizable number of people from other groups. These minorities were sometimes concentrated in a particular territory, especially in rural regions, and sometimes scattered and mixed with other groups, especially in larger urban, industrial centers (see Breznik 1992). According to the census of 1981, Serbs made up 11 percent of the population of Croatia; all other nationals constituted 9 percent of the population of Slovenia; and in Bosnia, Croats made up 18 percent, Serbs 32 percent, and Muslims 40 percent of the population (Petrović 1985, 27–31). It is worth noting that in 1971 (to the horror of many sociologists and political scientists), the Yugoslav census created the category "ethnically Muslim" (this was one of rare occasions when the term "ethnicity" was invoked in political terminology; see note 7 below). Ten years earlier, in 1961, the census had allowed the possibility of claiming Yugoslav identity, as a nonethnic, territorial-political reference, the objective of which was to strengthen socialist identification and transcend ethnicity (see Ramet 1990 and 1992, and Lendvai 1991). In 1981, 5.4 percent of population declared themselves Yugoslavs, most of them in Vojvodina (northern Serbian Province), Croatia, and Bosnia (Petrović 1985, 29 and 30). Thus, the Yugoslav census initially allowed many different types of self-definition. However, the early 1970s brought about a change in direction. A merger of ethnic and religious identities in the category of "ethnically Muslim" was the first step in the reduction of ethnic and religious heterogeneity. This slowly led to the assumption that a Serb could only be Orthodox and that "Croat" was synonymous with "Catholic."
2. This book is a result of research (conducted between 1994 and 1999 in the Netherlands, Germany, and Serbia) based on two types of data. One was life-story interviews with women from Bosnia, Croatia, and Serbia who lived through the war. Among them were feminists, refugees, and two volunteer soldiers from Serbia. Another type of data was collected through analysis of

textual sources (articles) and visual material (cartoons, caricatures, and press photographs) from the main daily newspapers and weekly magazines of Croatia and Serbia (*Vjesnik* and *Danas* from Croatia and *Politika* and *NIN* from Serbia) of the period from 1986 to 1994. The journalistic material was obtained from the National Library of Serbia (Belgrade), the Institute of Eastern Europe (Amsterdam), and the University Library (Amsterdam). Only a small fraction of the hundreds of newspaper articles and dozens of interviews that helped shape my arguments is mentioned here. The focus is mostly on textual material from the print media, with some exploration of the visual material and the interviews.

3. The exact beginning of the media war is also disputed by various authors. Marković (1996, 643) dates it to the beginning of 1988, Veljanovski (1996, 615) states that the media war was already long under way by 1987, and Milivojević (1996, 666) situates its start in 1986.What many analysts do agree upon, however, is that the media war started first in the press and only later spread to radio and television.
4. The eagerness of the press to accommodate itself to the political situation at this time was not all that voluntary, however. Especially after the multiparty elections in 1989—which in Croatia and Slovenia brought new political forces into power, and in Serbia confirmed the political power of the old ones—the (state-owned) media came under the direct and strict control of the political victors. The chief editors of all the major dailies and weeklies, together with directors of the main TV and radio stations were replaced with more humble figures, if not with those more eager to serve. Strict censorship was introduced. Journalists who remained in the directly controlled media had to accept the new rules of the game. Others, less likely to be obedient, lost their jobs or quit voluntarily, or after intimidation and threats and even physical violence. Some found jobs in the new, independent media, but even then they had to put up with occasional bombs exploding on their doorsteps.
5. Mark Thompson agrees with this perspective when saying that a "campaign of intense propaganda was needed to mobilize the population, to make war thinkable in Yugoslavia, let alone inevitable" (1994, 1).
6. In this, the ex-Yugoslav republics did not differ much from the rest of Eastern Europe, where discussions on abortion, sexual violence, family values, national traditions, and the like marked the period after 1989, and the transformations of socialist societies into capitalist ones. See especially Drezgić 2004, Huseby-Darvas 1996, Nechemias 1999, Oleszczuk 1998, Portuges 1992, Rukszto 1997, Watson 1993, and Zajicek and Calasanti 1998.
7. Yugoslav political terminology was rather peculiar. It recognized five nations (*narodi*: Slovenes, Croats, Serbs, Montenegrins and Macedonians, Muslims), several national groups (*narodnosti*: Albanian and Hungarian being the biggest among them), and numerous national minorities (*nacionalne manjine*: Roma, Slovaks, Romanians, Italians, Turks, and others). Yugoslav scholarship recognized the term "ethnicity" (*etnicitet*) only within folkloristic and ethnographic

study (and, as such, ethnicity had been minutely studied from the beginning of the twentieth century), not in political science. The term entered Yugoslav politics with the conflicts in Kosovo in the mid-1980s, with the accusation that Kosovo Albanians wanted an ethnically pure (*etnički čisto*) Kosovo; but the groups of people living in Yugoslavia were at that point still called nations and national minorities. All these groups, however, would usually be referred to as "ethnic groups" in international scholarly and political discourses.

8. Three out of the six Yugoslav republics opted for secession in referendums: Slovenia in 1990, Croatia in 1991, and Bosnia and Herzegovina in 1992 (Pešić 1996). After Croatia and Bosnia-Herzegovina declared secession from Yugoslavia, the Serbs who lived in a few concentrated areas in these two republics declared secession from them and formed two new political entities: Srpska Krajina within the territory of Croatia in 1991, and Republika Srpska within Bosnia-Herzegovina, also in 1991. Thus Serbs in Croatia and Bosnia did not recognize the legitimacy of the newly independent states, nor have these states recognized the right of these ethnic minorities to reject secession from Yugoslavia. On the problems that such situations posed to international law and debates on sovereignty, see Aydelott 1993, Benard 1994, Cleiren and Tijsen 1996, Kohn 1994, Krass 1994, Niarchos 1995, Philipose 1996, Pratt and Fletcher 1994, Supek 1994, and Petković et al. 1995.
9. In 1968 Albanian separatists demanded for the first time that Kosovo become a Yugoslav republic (instead of being an autonomous province of the Republic of Serbia). In 1971 Croatian separatists demanded that Croatia exercise its right to secession (which, according to some interpretations, was guaranteed by the Yugoslav constitution) and become an independent state (see Ramet 1992). In 1981, after Tito's death, Albanian demands for a separate republic were repeated in massive street demonstrations. In the mid-1980s Serbian nationalists made Kosovo their central political argument, and, with the appearance of Slobodan Milošević in 1987 and his raise to power (from the position of a mid-career party bureaucrat), they also gained institutional support (in both political and state institutions). The military and the police became major supporters of Milošević's rule over Kosovo, but there are no studies on these alliances so far. For the role of economy and economic institutions in the rise of nationalism, see especially Dinkić 1995, Djurić-Kuzmanović and Žarkov 1997 and 1998, Djurić-Kuzmanović 2002, and Group 17, 2000.
10. Orientalist and Balkanist discourses, employed amply in the studies of Yugoslav disintegration, define differences between the "symbolic continent of the Balkans" (Bakić-Hayden and Hayden 1992) and Europe. These discourses often define the nature of the war through the nature of the people, denying the Balkans and its citizens not only some of the prerogatives of civilization (read: Europeanness) but even the prerogatives of basic humanity. Instead of listing the numerous writers who have "modernized" the traditional images, created by nineteeth- and early-twentieth-century travelers and anthropologists, of the Balkans as a "powder-keg" with a savage (even if sometimes noble) male popu-

lation and subjugated womenfolk, I mention rather their critics, especially Bakić-Hayden (1995), and Bakić-Hayden and Hayden (1992) for the study of Orientalism, and Todorova (1999) for the study of Balkanism.

11. Too numerous to be mentioned here are the authors who see the main cause of Yugoslavia's collapse in the "history of ethnic hatred" and the bloody history of the Balkans—whether as "ancient enmity" (Okey 1994, 125) or as more recent product, linked to World War II and the "falseness" of Yugoslavia as a multiethnic state (Banac 1992). I have criticized their arguments elsewhere (Žarkov 1995). For similar criticism see also Gerrits 1992.
12. Some scholars (naively? or arrogantly?) perceive nationalism in Eastern Europe since 1989 as an unfortunate but inevitable phase in the postsocialist transformation of totalitarian communist systems into Western-style democracies. Their assumption is that nationalism rose out of socialist disillusionment and a shattered (but strong) need for belonging (Hobsbawm 1992).
13. Irreconcilable differences between the different parts of Yugoslavia, which fit the proverbial "clash of civilizations" model (Huntington 1993), were mentioned in many different ways. In this view, the culture, religion, and politics of the northwest of the country are pitted against the southeast. Modernity versus traditionalism, democracy versus authoritarianism, striving toward the future versus clinging to the past are some of the alleged points of differentiation offered by many. Bax 1992 and Koch 1991 are good examples of such argument.
14. A similar argument has been made by Verdery (1996) concerning socialism and nationalism in Romania during the Ceausescu era.
15. Sekelj (1990, 1991) has persistently argued this way; he draws upon earlier analyses by Rus (1971) and Stojanović (1972). A few other Yugoslav and foreign authors offer similar analysis: see, for example, Ramet (1990, 1992), Shirup (1991), Simić (1992), Gerrits (1992), Janjić (1993), Hayden (1992), and Kaldor (1999).
16. See Hayden 1996 and Ahmed 1995.
17. The United Nations Commission of Experts (Pursuant to Security Council Resolution 780, 1992) organized one of these missions. Using more than 700 interviews with refugees from former Yugoslavia commissioned from the governments of Austria, Germany, and Sweden, as well as 223 interviews with refugees in Bosnia, Croatia, and Slovenia, conducted in its own fieldwork, the U.N. Commission of Experts established a database containing allegations of rape and sexual assault. Out of "tens of thousands of allegations" (United Nations 1994b, 7) and over 4,500 reports, 1,100 cases were documented in more detail (Bassiouni et al. 1996, 10). From these data the U.N. Commission concluded that "there may be about 10,000 additional victims the reports could eventually lead to," and possibly as many as 20,000 victims (United Nations 1994b, 7). Similar results came from medical experts working for the United Nations Human Rights Commission. Inquiring into allegations of rapes, they documented 119 pregnancies resulting from rape. Citing medical studies that suggest that one in

every 100 rapes results in pregnancy, they concluded that the 119 cases of pregnancies "were likely to represent about 12,000 cases of rape" (United Nations 1993, 64). Both commissions concluded that these findings do not represent the full extent of rapes. Rather, considering multiple and repeated rapes especially, these figures may only serve as a guide to the general scale of the problem (cf. United Nations 1993, 67; United Nations 1994b, 7; and Bassiouni et al. 1996, 6).

18. Of 715 camps identified by the U.N. Commission of Experts, 237 were operated by Bosnian Serbs and the former Republic of Yugoslavia; 89 were operated by the government and army of Bosnia and Herzegovina; 77 were operated by Bosnian Croats, the government of Croatia, the Croatian army and the Croatian Defense Council; and 4 were operated jointly by the Bosnian government and Bosnian Croats. For 308 camps, it was not established with certainty who controlled them (United Nations 1994a, E1). The commission found reports of sexual assaults in 162 camps: of which 88 were reportedly run by Serbs, 35 were run by unknown forces, 17 allegedly run by Croats, 14 allegedly run by Muslim and Croat forces combined, and 8 reportedly run by Muslims (United Nations 1994b, 7).
19. Sexual crimes against men were committed by all sides, mainly in detention in camps such as the Serb-run camp Trnopolje, the Croatian-run Odžaci camp, and the Muslim-run camp in Goražde (United Nations 1994b, 100). The camps run by Serbs in Bosnia were pointed out as "the ones where the largest numbers of detainees have been held and where the cruellest and largest number of violations occurred" (United Nations 1994a, E3), although there was "significant information concerning war crimes taking place in Croatia . . . regarding rapes in detention and sexual assault of men, including castration in detention" (United Nations 1994c, 5).
20. For early works, see Ardener 1975 and 1978, Oakley 1972, Ortner and Whitehead 1981, Ortner 1984, and Caplan 1987.
21. See especially early works of de Lauretis (1987), Flax (1987), Caplan (1987), Weeks (1985), Alcoff (1988), Butler (1987, 1993), and Bordo (1993).
22. See, for instance, Wittig 1992, Rubin 1993, and hoogland 1997.
23. See also Macciocchi 1977, Gilman 1985 and 1991, Ridd and Callaway 1987, Bonner 1992, Stockle 1993, McClintock 1995, Barnes 1997, and hooks 1989.
24. Classical scholarship on ethnicity developed largely in reference to the study of the nation, nation-state, and nationalism, albeit in different disciplinary fields: while history took upon itself to theorize the nation(-state/nationalism), ethnicity has been, and still largely is, researched within anthropology and ethnography. As a consequence, ethnicity has largely been perceived as a product of culture, while nation was seen as a product of history. Nevertheless, the two fields of study have much in common, foundationalism and Eurocentrism figuring prominently (in the work of Gellner [1983], and Smith [1988 and 1991], for example).
25. Barth (1969) was first to shake some of the classical theoretical assumptions

about ethnicity, and Hobsbawm and Ranger (1983) and Anderson (1983) further undermined the foundationalist paradigm pointing out to both "inventive" and "imagined" nature of ethnicity.

26. See the pioneering work of Yuval-Davis and Anthias (1989), and Yuval-Davis (1997), as well as black and (post)colonial studies concerned with identity politics of race and ethnicity (Barrett and McIntosh 1985, Pederson 1991, Spillers 1991, Bhabha 1990 and 1996, Hall 1992 and 1996, Bhavani 1993, Brah 1993, Jackson and Penrose 1993, and Stockle 1993).
27. I appreciated very much the work of Anthias and Yuval-Davis (1992), McClintock (1995), Smith (1998), Kaplan et al. (1999), and Stoler (2002). But my conceptualization and understanding of the relationships among gender, ethnicity, and sexuality in the Yugoslav war benefited most from the work of South Asian feminists on the Partition of India, communal violence, separatist and militant movements, and identity politics in South Asia. The complexity and depth of these studies (which I mention in many of the chapters) provided continuous inspiration.
28. For heterosexism in the nation and nationalism, see especially Peterson 1999, Borneman 1998, and Alexander 1994.
29. Penrose points out the consequences of the nation-based world order for the groups that are latecomers in the bid for (inter)national recognition and sovereignty (i.e., their continuous struggle to obtain the status of nation-state) and the inevitable injustice and violence that such struggle brings to those who are perceived as not belonging to either the national place/space or the national self-definition, that is, their racial and ethnic minorities.
30. See also Papić 1992 and Kašić 2000 for the epistemological issues concerning the positioning of the female body within nationalist discourses and practices.

1. The Whore against the Mother of All Serbs

1. See Mežnarić 1993, for an analysis of links between the Serbian nationalist discourse of rapes in Kosovo in 1980s and actual war rapes in Bosnia in 1990s.
2. The Yugoslav army's offensive on Kosovo in 1998–1999, and the subsequent NATO bombing of Serbia in 1999, marked (after the wars in Slovenia, Croatia, and Bosnia) another phase in violent disintegration of the country. According to the Kumanovo Peace Agreement and U.N. Resolution 1244 (adopted by the Security Council at its 4011th meeting, on June 10, 1999) that ended the NATO war, Kosovo become a de facto U.N. protectorate (although still de jure part of the renamed Serbia). The expectation that the sizable Albanian population would gain an independent state has not yet materialized. For the time being, there is no clear signal that the international community will recognize such an independent state, nor are there any signs that Albanian politicians will be ready to give it up. Separatist Albanian parties have also remained active in the south of the Serbia proper and in northwest Macedonia.
3. In 1980, 90 percent of women were classified as dependent in Kosovo, 69 per-

cent in Bosnia-Herzegovina, 69 percent in Montenegro, 63 percent in Macedonia, 58 percent in Serbia (including Provinces), 58 percent in Vojvodina, 52 percent in Croatia, and 50 percent in Slovenia. The rates of female unemployment give a similar picture. In 1981, 1.3 percent of women in Slovenia were unemployed, in Croatia 5.2 percent, in Vojvodina 12.4 percent, in Bosnia 13.8 percent, in Serbia proper 15.8 percent, in Macedonia 21.5 percent, and in Kosovo 27.3 percent. See Žarkov, Drezgić, and Djurić-Kuzmanović 2004.

4. According to the 1981 census, the crude birth rate (number of births per 1,000 population) among Kosovo Albanians was 27.8, and in Serbia proper 11.2. The total cumulative fertility rate for the cohort of women ages 45–49 was 1.8 in Serbia proper, and 5.7 for the same cohort of Kosovo Albanian women (Drezgić 2004).
5. The census data show a steady increase of the Albanian population in Kosovo, and a decrease of the Serbian population: 67 percent Albanians compared with 24 percent Serbs in 1961; 74 percent compared with 21 percent in 1971; and 77 percent compared with 13 percent in 1981 (Breznik 1992).
6. The fast population growth among the Albanians was commonly referred to as a "population explosion," and it was contrasted to the below-replacement growth of some regions of Serbia proper. Demographers supplied material for nationalists, indicating that by the year 2050 Albanians would make up 50 percent of the total population in Serbia (Vojnović 1995).
7. The issue became so significant that, as a consequence, in October 1986 legislation on rape was changed, introducing a distinction between "rape" and "interethnic rape." A new paragraph was added to the existing Criminal Law of the Socialist Republic of Serbia. The most significant paragraph, 61b, came under the heading "Endangering the Security of a Member of Another Nation, Minority or Ethnic Group by Means of Attacking Sexual Freedom" (*Official Herald of the Socialist Republic of Serbia*, no. 39, October 18, 1994, 2740). In 1990 several groups involved in finding a democratic solution for Kosovo (the Yugoslav Forum for Human Rights, the Yugoslav Democratic Initiative, and so on) appointed an independent committee to investigate the disproportionally high migration of Serbs and Montenegrins from Kosovo. The report of the committee (Popović, Janča, and Petovar 1990) also addressed the issue of rapes in the light of interethnic conflicts, stating that the social gap between the two ethnic groups was so huge that rapes of Serbian women by Albanian men could not be considered a deliberate practice (more on this in chapter 3).
8. The presidency was composed of one representative from each constitutional unit (six republics and two provinces) and one representative from the Yugoslav National Army.
9. Again, how widespread the particular claims of motherhood were, is impossible to verify. They were mentioned in documents and written on banners, and noted by some (feminist) observers. However, for my purposes here the reach of these claims is not relevant, since my interest is not in demonstrations per se but in how they were represented.

10. For the political aspect of the women's emancipation project of the period, see especially First 1982, Despot 1984 and 1987, Drakulić 1987, Sklevicki 1987 and 1995, and Milić 1994. For contradictions between private and public in both political and professional life, see Denich 1974 and 1977, Burić 1985, Blagojević 1991, and Dević 2000.
11. Since the break up of Yugoslavia, what was known as "Serbo-Croat" in Serbia and "Croato-Serb" in Croatia are now two separate languages, called Serb and Croat; but both languages use the same words for "brothel" and "whore."
12. Her article is analyzed in chapter 3, together with other feminist reactions to the events.
13. The title "Punishment Arrives Too Late to Kosovo" (*Kasno kazna na Kosovo stize*) has a special resonance, for it is an allusion to a famous line from a Serbian epic about the battle of Kosovo, in 1389, which marked the beginning of the Ottoman rule of medieval Serbia: "Marko arrives too late to Kosovo" (*Kasno* [king] *Marko na Kosovo stize*). In nationalist discourse in Serbia the battle of Kosovo is one of the most frequently remembered, in almost mythical dimensions, and is interpreted as a source of both Serbian heroism and their tendency to see themselves as martyrs. King Marko was one of the heroes (late-arriving, as the verse indicates) of the battle.
14. In Serbo-Croatian, as in other Slavic languages, all nouns have grammatical gender: feminine, masculine, or neuter (literally "middle"). Feminine nouns often end with the letter "a" ("e" in plural). Consequently, female names also often end with "a." This rule also applies to the names of geographical units, the river Drina (separating Bosnia and Serbia), for instance, and the region Krajina (Croatian territory that had a Serb majority before the war)—to mention only two of the many that are relevant to nationalist discourses. More significant are the larger (feminine-gendered) political units: Yugoslavia, Serbia, Croatia, Bosnia.
15. Besides the main daily and weekly press, which was often heavily controlled and censored, each region had other spaces for expressing alternative opinions, such as newspapers or TV channels belonging to opposing political parties, or private interest groups. Many journalists used to find refuge there. That space, however, was not only limited but also very marginalized during the late 1980s and through the 1990s. For research of the media during this period see OIJ 1992,; Plavšić et al. 1993, Centar za Anti-Ratnu Akciju 1994, Lalić 1995, Valić Nedeljković 1997, and Čolović 1999.
16. It is interesting to note the expression "uninational gatherings" here. The other articles mentioned "gatherings on a national basis." The difference is quite significant: according to the Yugoslav Constitution, Serbs and Montenegrins are two different ethnicities. According to Serb nationalists, and some Montenegrins too, however, Montenegrins are ethnically Serbs. Thus, the expression "gatherings on a national basis" does not deny Montenegrin nationhood, while the expression "uninational" subsumes two nations into one, in this case—the Serb (like "two eyes in one head," as a Serb nationalist saying would have it).

A similar fate befalls Macedonian national sovereignty in the Serb nationalist discourse: they are called "southern Serbs."

17. Editorial interventions of this kind were extremely unusual in newspapers in socialist Yugoslavia. The texts would have been subject to editorial interventions of one kind or another (from the titles and subtitles, to the interventions in the text itself), but they were regularly invisible, and the end product in front of the reader would flow smoothly, without direct interruptions. It is difficult to know what the motivation behind this intervention was. Does it indicate that the editor wanted the text to be published as it was, but felt a need to add something that could be seen as a correction of a material error: women did shout that they want military rule, so if other slogans were quoted, this one should be mentioned too? Or did the editor want to dramatize the events even further and promote a military rule in Kosovo following the women's demands? In any case, its extraordinary nature indicates that the media war had many different levels, and editorial politics was one of them.
18. Besides the two versions quoted in Croatian daily *Vjesnik*, another version of Fadil Hoxha's words appeared in *Politika*. Noting that this is something he "apparently said," *Vjesnik* quotes: "We should be more tolerant toward some of the immoral behavior of girls who arrive from elsewhere and work as waitresses in some taverns, especially in privately owned ones, and who are prone to immoral behavior. It might be better to give tacit permission to these phenomena, for if "darkness falls on someone's eyes" it is better in such a situation to have easy access to females in these taverns than to have honorable girls and women become victims of such sexual maniacs, causing us political problems" (October 10, 1987, 15).

2. Pictures of the Wall of Love

A different version of this chapter was published in the *European Journal of Women's Studies* 4, no. 3 (1997): 305–339, under the title "Picture of the Wall of Love: Motherhood, Womanhood, and Nationhood in Croatian Media." I thank Magda Michielsens and the anonymous readers of the journal for their useful comments. My thanks are also due to Mira Oklobdzija and Dorothee Strukenboom for commenting on an earlier version of this chapter. I benefited greatly from discussions with Marga Altena about photography, and with Renee Hoogland about sexuality.

1. The JNA, save for ranking officers, was a drafted army. All able-bodied men between the age of eighteen and mid- to late twenties (depending on their studies and work) were supposed to complete between twelve and eighteen months of military service. After that they were registered as army reservists and were eligible for service until the age of sixty-five, if necessary. The majority of the JNA soldiers fighting in Slovenian war, therefore, were regularly drafted soldiers, in their late teens and early twenties. The JNA had military barracks, facilities for soldiers' training, and military personnel stationed in

all of the Yugoslav republics. Military personnel of the JNA came from various ethnic backgrounds. Drafted soldiers were usually posted to a republic other than their own—following the ideology of "spreading brotherhood and unity." Thus, when the war in Slovenia started, in June 1991, many young men of various ethnic backgrounds, serving in various Yugoslav republics, were sent to Slovenia. Some of them received no more than two months training. Some had already completed their training and were supposed to be discharged. When the war started, however, their discharge was postponed, and the communication between the soldiers and their families was either cut or restricted.

2. Tudjman was also the leader of the strongest nationalist party, *Hrvatska Democratska Zajednica* (Croatian Democratic Union).
3. Besides the Yugoslav state flag (composed of three horizontal bands of red, white, and blue stripes and a red star in the middle, on the white), each republic of the former Yugoslavia also had its own flag. The Muslim flag mentioned in the article did not exist in the former Yugoslavia as a symbol of any republic or ethnic group, although the crescent and the green color were known as Muslim religious symbols.
4. For more on the new identity claims in Croatia and Slovenia and their denunciation of "the Balkans" and its symbolic meaning, see Žarkov 1995.
5. See Nash 1993 and the concept of "remapping" in her discussion on the role of metaphors of the female body in Irish nationalism.
6. Women refused to leave before meeting high-ranking officers of the JNA, but as the officers refused to appear, and time was passing, rumors were spread that the mothers were held in the Guard Hall against their will.
7. This title obviously alludes to the title of the old movie *Moscow Does Not Believe in Tears* (1979, dir. Vladimir Menshov).
8. Interestingly enough, the Serbian daily *Politika* used for the demonstrations by Muslim and Croat parents the same noun—*bukači* (those who make noise and fuss; instigators)—that the Croatian weekly *Danas* had used for the demonstrations by Serb and Montenegrin women in Kosovo some years earlier (October 27, 1987, 8). In both cases manipulation was implied.
9. Banja Luka is a town in Bosnia, a part of the Republika Srpska.
10. Stjepan Mesić was a Croatian representative in the federal collective presidency and its president at the time.
11. The differences between the version spoken in Serbia and that spoken in Croatia are comparable to, but also fewer than, the differences between British English and American English.
12. Slavenka Drakulić maintains the same distinction between the innocence of the soldier-sons and a merciless army in her book *Balkan Express* (1993). See my criticism in Žarkov 1994.
13. The JNA was often referred to as "Serb-dominated" as well as "majority Serb" by international as well as Croatian and Slovenian media and politicians. This often implied that Serbhood was aggressive and militaristic in nature. While

the employment of the JNA for the warring and nationalist politics of Serbian leadership is under no doubt, the large number of Serbs in the army ranks, including those stationed in Slovenia, Croatia, and Bosnia, is worth thinking of in a different way: Cynthia Enloe (2002) points out that the military (like the police) often constitutes the main ladder of upward social mobility to men of marginalized racial or ethnic groups who have no access to other (social, professional, political) means of social promotion or integration.

14. The practice of hand kissing was widespread in different areas throughout former Yugoslavia not very long ago. Men used to kiss the hands of priests, of their social superiors, and their fathers; in some regions they would kiss the hand of both parents. Women used to kiss the hands of husbands, male elders, in-laws, and in some regions, even of their young sons. When I was a child, visiting my mother's (Croat) family (in Bosnia), I was expected to kiss the hands of my grandparents every evening, together with all the other grandchildren, after saying the rosary. If my grandfather was not there, we kissed the hand of my uncle, his only son, who then led the prayers. In my father's (Serb) family (from Vojvodina), my aunt would sometimes kiss the hand of my grandfather, but it was not expected of the grandchildren, nor did I ever see my father doing so. The habit of kissing the hand of a priest is still alive among many believers, women and men, Catholic and Orthodox.
15. Vlahović is the artist who contributed an illustration to the same column in 1987, for the piece about the Whore, discussed in chapter 1.

3. Troubles with Motherhood

Some of the arguments in this chapter were developed in my essay "Feminist Self/Ethnic Self. Theory and Politics of Women's Activism," published in Slapšak 2000a. I am grateful to the editor and to Rada Drezgić for commenting on different versions of this essay.

1. On maternal-filial relationships, see among others Chatterjee 1990 for India, Yuval-Davis 1987 and 1989 for Israel, Hassim 1993 for South Africa, and Innes 1994 for Ireland.
2. See Drezgić 2004 for demographic policies, practices, and discourses in Serbia in the 1990s.
3. See Nash 1993 and Innes 1994, for example.
4. Information from personal communication with feminist activists from Sri Lanka.
5. South Asian feminists show that women in the Hindu right wing position themselves very similarly vis-à-vis both (weak, but potentially powerful) Hindu men, (over-sexualized) Muslim men, and (timid and oppressed) Muslim women. See especially Butalia 1995 and Sarkar 1995.
6. For a discussion of implications of feminist theorizing on female subjectivity for the research on peasant women in Yugoslavia, see Žarkov 1991.

4. The Body of All Serbs

A different version of this essay was published in Davis 1997. I am grateful to Kathy Davis, Rada Drezgić, and Lena Inowlocki for their comments and suggestions on this earlier version.

1. It should be noted that not everybody in Serbia experienced economic hardship and disillusion. Some gained material and political advantages from the war. The social stratum of the newly rich who profited enormously from the war and from the international economic sanctions imposed on Serbia was (and remains) very visible on the streets of many cities in Serbia. Their connections to crime are privately condemned but seldom legally pursued. Furthermore, as the economy broke down, the "gray economy" (already a familiar and necessary source of income in the former Yugoslavia) expanded to include many activities that used to be considered petty crime (tobacco smuggling and drug dealing, for instance). Ideas about crime changed, as more and more people became engaged in forms of it and profited from it. Analyses of the relationship between the (war) economy and nationalism in the former Yugoslavia are still rare, however. Even rarer are examinations of the position of women in an economy affected by nationalism and war. A notable exception is Tanja Djurić-Kuzmanović (Djurić 1995, Djurić-Kuzmanović 2002, and Djurić-Kuzmanović and Žarkov 1997 and 1998), whose work links war and nationalist and economic processes in Serbia and the Federal Republic of Yugoslavia during the 1990s, and looks at the position of women within them.
2. For actions of the Women in Black, see Dević 2000.
3. After the wars in Bosnia and Croatia ended, the discourse of Serb victimhood continued to be relevant, albeit with different intensity in different times, and with somewhat changed contents—leading to the Milošević regime's being seen as the main perpetrator. Thus in the winter months of 1996–1997, there were continuous protests by hundreds of thousands of people throughout Serbia against the regime. After the 1999 NATO bombing of Serbia, the resistance against Milošević increased even further, and he was eventually ousted in October 2000. The Djindjić government offered temporary hope and enthusiasm, and opened some space for reevaluating the political responsibility of Serbian leaders and citizens for the wars in the Balkans from 1991 to 1999. But his assassination in 2003 brought back political instability and stalled the process of change.
4. G. Maljukan, "Little Eagles for 'Those Things,'" *Duga*, February 5–18, 1994, 44–47.
5. See also Nead 1992 and Meijer 1993.
6. "To give" is a slang expression used by men, referring to woman's attitude to sexual relations: "she gives easily," "she does not give."
7. Slang for female genitals, but the same word also used for a woman, especially "old hen."

8. The United Nation Protection Force that was stationed in Bosnia with the mission to aid humanitarian efforts and enforce the peace.
9. Coupons were issued by the Bosnian government and used instead of money for rations of food and gasoline, in order to provide the population with at least some basics.
10. Information from interviews with refugees in the Netherlands and Germany.

5. All the Bodies of Croatia

1. For more on the discourse of the "history of ethnic hatred" and how diversely (but consistently) it was used in different Yugoslav republics, see Žarkov 1995.
2. The Chetniks were members of a radical Serbian monarchist movement that fought against both the German occupation and the partisan movement in the Second World War and committed numerous atrocities against political opponents (communists and partisans) and other ethnic groups (especially Muslims and Croats). In 1991 their movement was revived and partly rehabilitated; it attracted many volunteers for the war in Bosnia and Croatia.
3. This expression has often been used in reference to refugees, especially in Asia. Cuban refugees in the United States are also called "boat people."
4. Original: "Lijepa naša domovono / o, junačka zemljo mila/ stare slave djedovino / da bi vazda sretna bila."
5. Needless to say, few Serbs from Bosnia fled to Croatia.
6. The English word "refugees" is translated in the Croatian and Serbian language as *izbeglice* (originally meaning those who escaped, escapees). While the Croatian population that fled its homes within Croatia should officially be called internally displaced people, the term "refugee" was often used in former Yugoslavia for all those who fled their homes. Furthermore, when the change of terminology came about in Croatia, it did not follow the rationale of the place where people escaped (from and to), but the rationale of the violence that forced them to flee. So people were called *prognanici*, that is, those expelled, rather than *izbeglice*, those who escaped.
7. Marija explicitly calls herself both a Croat and Catholic, not really presuming that the two are "the same" but that "this is what I am." Thus I refer to her as a Croat. Her name, as well as the name of the towns are made up, to protect her anonymity.
8. "To bark" is a very specific expression, used a lot in Bosnia by all ethnic groups, to indicate that someone is loud, ready to make fuss, to complain, as well as to say things one is not supposed to say, or things others are afraid to say.
9. Interview, November 1994, Germany.
10. It is worth noting that citizenship acquired in this way does not mean that a person automatically belongs to the self-image of the nation, in the way a Croat from Croatia does. This was quite evident in the way the Croatian public reacted to the attempts of the Croatian government to extradite some of the

war crimes suspects to the International War Crimes Tribunal for former Yugoslavia in The Hague. Drakulić (2004, 40–42) shows that the men who were first extradited, without public protest, were all Croats from Bosnia who acquired Croatian citizenship after 1995, and one Croatian citizen of Albanian origin. However, when in 2002 attempts were made to extradite a Croat from Croatia, war veterans (who became one of the major political instruments of the right-wing HDZ, Croatian Democratic Community), demonstrated in numbers, and were joined by the public in several Croatian cities.

11. These articles indicate the schizophrenic situation of the war in Croatia—with certain regions facing total destruction, while in others people went about their daily business and worried about the impact of war on tourism.

6. Sexual Geographies of Ethnicity

1. For the period between November 1992 and December 1993, the daily *Politika* had fewer than thirty articles focused explicitly on war rapes of women, and the weekly *NIN* had five. Most of the *Politika* articles appeared between November 1992 and March 1993, but the vast majority was actually published during a single month—January 1993, thirteen of which appeared between January 15 and 27, day after day, as a series of texts with a common title "The Crime above All Crimes." After March 1993, the rapes of women were seldom mentioned in *Politika*.
2. Only a couple of articles had rapes of Serb women figuring more prominently, again, framed in the context of larger suffering of Serb population; for example, *Politika*'s articles "A Scream the World Refuses to Hear" (December 16, 1992, 12) and "The Fate of Women Raped on War" (February 23, 1993, 6).
3. I am grateful to Rada Drezgić for discussion of this point.
4. Unlike in some countries in central and west Europe, where folk songs belong to the realm of folkloristic and ethnomusicology, the Balkans-Mediterranean everyday culture includes the singing of folk songs. In Serbia, songs from Macedonia, Dalmatia, Bosnia, and, of course, Serbia were loved and sung by young and old alike, at birthday parties, family reunions, or wedding celebrations, along with domestic and international pop and rock.
5. Needless to say, "in heat" is the expression used for period of mating of (domestic) animals. When used for men, it often has the allure of a compliment; for women, it often implies negative moral judgment of her sexual behavior.
6. Interviewed in 1994, in Serbia.
7. "Balija" is a pejorative expression for a Muslim in Bosnia, used by Serbs and Croats.
8. Compared to the Serbian press, the Croatian daily *Vjesnik* and the weekly *Danas* had twice as many articles specifically dedicated to war rape and forced impregnation—about seventy. They also started coverage of rapes earlier and ended it later. The first texts appeared in *Vjesnik* in September 1992, and con-

tinued throughout 1993. Nevertheless, the majority of the reports were published between December 1992 and March 1993.

9. While this statement links Croats to Croatia and Muslims to Bosnia, it appears to equally deny the Muslims a right to live in Croatia and the Croats a right to live in Bosnia. Considering the initial plans of Milošević and Tudjman to divide Bosnia between Serbia and Croatia, the Croats' right to live in Bosnia would lose (nationalist) relevance, as the territories of Bosnia where Croats live would become parts of Croatia.
10. As already mentioned, the U.N. Report lists the sites where Croat forces kept Serb and Muslim civilians in detention and names the camps in which the Croat military, both in Bosnia and Croatia, used rape and other forms of sexual assault systematically.
11. While the involvement of women in committing war crimes is probable, there is not much evidence of it. Except for Biljana Plavšić, one of the leaders of the Bosnian Serbs, no other woman has been indicted by the International Criminal Tribunal for former Yugoslavia. The actual presence of women among perpetrators is not the point here, however, but how these facts are represented by the media.
12. The words "fuck" and "cunt" are given only by a first letter in the original text. The King Marko mentioned is the same King Marko of the Serbian national epics mentioned in chapter 1, n. 13. The verses quoted are, certainly, not a "well known Serbian proverb," although they may be a part of a mock folk poetry production. That production includes, for instance, the so-called fratricide songs that mock the official discourse of "brotherhood and unity," as well as mock versions of the most famous partisan songs. Many of them are on various sex taboo topics such as sodomy and homosexuality.
13. This cynical remark implies that the West is responsible for the rapes anyway, thus for the children conceived in rapes too.
14. In the Serbian and Croatian language the word *plod* literally means a fruit. Its general figurative meaning is a product of work in general (as in English), and its specific meaning is the result of conception. The word is used in medical as well as in everyday language, alongside the word "fetus," but it also has poetic connotations. In the articles in *Vjesnik*, that word is used along with the word "child," "baby," and "newborn."
15. Abortion laws that were enacted by individual Yugoslav republics in the second half of the 1970s remained in place until the dissolution of the federation in 1991. In Croatia and Slovenia the Catholic Church intensified its antiabortion campaigns right after these two republics declared independence from Yugoslavia. Still, the law that applied to abortions in the first trimester of pregnancy remained in place in both republics. The Slovenian Constitutional Court declared abortion one of the basic human rights. In Croatia, even though the legislation ultimately did not change, it became more difficult to obtain abortions. As a result of the church's pro-life and pro-natalist campaign many physi-

cians declined to perform abortions in the early 1990s (see Kapor-Stanulović and David 1999). In Serbia, as long as Milošević's Socialist Party of Serbia had an unchallenged majority in the parliament, the old "socialist" abortion law remained unchallenged, but it faced restrictions with the new law in 1995. The new law keeps most of the provisions for obtaining abortion during the first trimester of gestation (ten weeks). However, it requires minors between the ages of sixteen and eighteen to obtain parental consent for having an abortion (although they have the right to work and found a family without such permission). Furthermore, it introduced several restrictions for access to abortion after the tenth week of pregnancy (see Drezgić 2004).

16. See Kesić 1995a and 1995b.
17. For a thorough analysis of the abortion debates in Serbia through the 1980s and 1990s within various political and scientific discourses (including the state, Orthodox Church, and feminism) and changing state policies, see Drezgić 2004.

7. On Victims and Villains

1. Aydelott (1993), Krass (1994), Pratt and Fletcher (1994), Niarchos (1995), and Cleiren and Tijsen (1996), for example, focus on international law aspects of prosecution, as well as possibilities and limitations facing the Yugoslav War Tribunal, while Kohn (1994) and Philipose (1996) address the human rights aspects of the war rapes in ex-Yugoslavia. Benard (1994) approaches the issue as a practice of political terror. Numerous other authors (who will be discussed in this and the following chapters) analyzed rape as gendered war strategy.
2. See, for example, Lockwood (1975) on the urban life of Muslims in Bosnia.
3. The census of 1991, although completed, was never published in full, because of the war. Separate parts of it were published in different republics and the successor states. But in the 1981 census, 38 percent of the Bosnian population refused to identify themselves ethnically (Petrović 1985, 28). Thus, the usual practice of equating "Bosnian" with "Muslim" is not only a misnomer; it is also blatant disrespect for the right of people to define themselves in nonethnic and nonreligious terms.
4. In November 1994 the International Criminal Tribunal for the former Yugoslavia—established in May 1993, with its prosecutor appointed in August 1994—produced its first indictment, against a prison guard at the Serb-held Omarska camp (case IT-94-1), including charges of rape. The Foča case (IT-96-23) was the first that clearly defined rape as torture and included the definition in the charges and in the judgment.
5. The Women's International War Crimes Tribunal on Japan's Military Sexual Slavery, known as the Tokyo Tribunal, met in Japan, December 8–12, 2000. Numerous feminist activists, groups, and organizations, as well as prosecutors and lawyers participated in it. The Tokyo Tribunal judgment was delivered December 3 and 4, 2001, in The Hague, Netherlands. The accused, Emperor Hirohito

and the government of Japan, were found guilty. See Chinkin 2001 on the Tribunal, and Sancho 1997 on the sexual slavery.

6. The United Nations Rapporteur and its various committees and expert commissions investigating war crimes in Yugoslavia all published reports. The report quoted here is from the commission established in October 1992, which worked until late April 1994, whose First Report was published in February 1993 and Final Report on May 27, 1994. The latter listed findings on detention facilities and rape (United Nations 1994a). Work on the collected data continued, in Annex IX and IX.A (United Nations 1994b and 1994c), both used here and both published in December 1994.
7. For more on women's activism in wartime and postwar Bosnia and women's organizations, see Helms 2003 and Cockburn 1998.
8. Jansen (1996) shows, in comparing the number of women professionals in higher education and in politics in the Middle East and the Netherlands, that the Netherlands comes off worse. Nevertheless, Dutch women are still seen as "emancipated" and Arab Muslim women as "traditional" (see especially 255–257).
9. Soft pornography existed before the break-up of Yugoslavia in printed media and was exposed to the popular gaze in the windows of newsstands. Naked women were to be seen on posters placed by truck drivers in the windows of their vehicles. The post-break-up period made hard-core porno films readily available even on public televisions throughout the region.
10. The first real porno magazine—*Čik*—appeared in Serbia in the 1970s. It did not have feminist columns.
11. See, for example, Allen 1996 and Schott 1996.
12. Kesić's reaction to MacKinnon's article—written as an analytical contribution to *Ms.*—was downgraded to a letter to the editor (see *Ms.* 1993). Other criticisms were ignored by *Ms.* but published elsewhere, including Munk 1994 and Korać 1994. Stiglmayer's book (1993a) contains an essay by Copelon (1993) that could be read as a direct and harsh criticism of MacKinnon, though it does not mention MacKinnon directly.
13. Bosnia's State Health Protection Office figures on war casualties are interesting in this respect. They point that 50.65 percent of all the victims of the war in Bosnia were Muslims, 35 percent were Serbs, and 10.22 percent Croats. As a percentage of the prewar population, this is 7.39 percent of the Muslims, 7.1 percent of the Serbs, and 3.76 percent of the Croats (http://www.misc.news.bosnia, item number 4076, April 2, 1996).
14. For example, Drakulić (2004, 52) notes Bosnian government estimates of sixty thousand raped women in her latest book.

8. The Body of the Other Man

A different version of this chapter was published under the title "The Body of the Other Man: Sexual Violence and the Construction of Masculinity, Sexuality and Ethnicity in Croatian Media," in Moser and Clark 2001. I am grateful to the editors, as well as to Kathy Davis, Stefan Dudink, and Helma Lutz for their comments on different versions of the text.

1. The United Nations report states that the Serb-held Luka camp imprisoned both Croat and Muslim men and women together. Muslim men were predominant among prisoners (1994b, 21).
2. According to the U.N. report, the Kozarac camp was held by Serbs and had mainly Muslim detainees. The U.N. documentations states that among the men who were sexually assaulted there, several were Croats, but the vast majority were Muslim (1994b, 39–41).
3. Tineke Cleiren was a member of a U.N. Commission of Experts collecting data on rape and sexual assaults (see United Nations 1994a, 1994b, 1994c). She also gave a testimony before the International War Crimes Tribunal (see ITCY 1995). Thus, her conceptions of gender, sexuality and sexual violence were heard by the Judges of the Tribunal.
4. See Kimmel 1987, Chapman and Rutherford 1988, Brittan 1989, Easthope 1986, Craig 1992, Garber 1992, Seidler 1994 and 1997, and Murphy 1994.
5. See Davis 1997a for criticism of this bias in masculinity studies.
6. For the rural context, see Herzfeld 1985; on urban life, see Alves 1993; on refugee experience, Camino and Krulfeld 1994; and on class, Connell 1995.
7. See Gilmore 1990, de Almeida 1996 and 1997, Cornwall and Lindisfarne 1994.
8. Mosse's (1985) work on masculinity, sexuality, and class in the formation of British nationhood (and his analysis of the symbolic functioning of the Jew's body therein) not only predates the black and postcolonial studies but also informs them.
9. See hooks 1995, Rutherford 1988, Segal 1990, Gilmore 1991, Sharpe 1991, Sinha 1995, and Savran 1996.
10. For sexual torture of men, see Lunde and Ortmann 1990, Van Tienhoven 1993, and Yuksel 1991. For a study of men as torturers, see Huggins and Haritos-Fatouros 1998. For male violence against men in prisons, see Toch 1998.
11. Of course, the question remains what the social and political consequences of such heroic masculinity and the glorification of (endurance of) violence are for women, for gender relations in the communities and for the future of Palestinian society. There are already some indications that violence against women within Palestinian communities is increasing as a consequence (Klein 1997 and 1999).
12. The history and analysis of lynching and castration are central to black studies and antiracist discourses, so one could argue that the master of antiracist narratives relies on the high visibility of the victimized Self. The same would be the case in feminist discourses on the rape of women, wherein the victimized Self is central to the discourse. However, the centrality of victimization within antiracist and feminist discourses is not, and certainly does not have to be, necessarily the same as representation of the Self (exclusively) through victimization

(even though there is a serious danger, as I discuss in the next chapters, that this happens).

13. In some cultures (e.g., Middle East and Latin America) the masculinity of the man who is active and dominant in male same-sex relations is not diminished. See Lancaster 1992 and Gutmann 1996.
14. The Taguba Report can be found on different Web sites, including the BBC's.
15. On page 17, under point 6 ("intentional abuse of detainees by military police personnel included the following acts:"), item "k," the Taguba Report lists: "A male MP guard having sex with a female detainee." Calling "sex" something that could be seen as rape with some certainty, and the general lack of knowledge about abuse of female prisoners in Iraq, is indicative of intersections of gender, heterosexuality, religion, and nation. In the West, it seems not to be known that there are female prisoners in Iraq at all, probably because women, and especially Muslim women of the Arab world, are not see as politically active or relevant. This belittling of their agency makes them invisible. At the same time, there is probably also a need to make them invisible because their presumed lack of agency may be seen as shaming their captor. Further, the women themselves and their families may want to keep the issues invisible because of the stigma of rape during imprisonment. Peteet (2000) states that for Palestinian women, for example, the very possibility of being sexually assaulted in prison forecloses access to heroic narratives of resistance.
16. The photos convey both the utter contempt for, and the denial of, the humanity of the prisoners and the utter confidence of the violators in their impunity.
17. The discourses of denial—where the violence is defined as isolated cases, with a small group of individuals accused as the only violators, and promises of swift punishment—are similar to those in the Croatian and Serbian press regarding the violence against women. What is interesting is that faces of the perpetrators are in full view in the media. Since the discourses of denial define them as outcast, their visibility may indicate their otherness. But, on a more hopeful note, it may also indicate a presence of competing and conflicting discourses of the Self in the American press, such that the discourse on the "war on terror" (that next to defining the terrorist Other also defines the wronged and just Self) is losing ground.
18. For the former Yugoslavia, see Denich 1974, Morokvašić 1981 and 1984, Kavčić 1990, and Gremaux 1994. For Bosnia, see Bringa 1995.

9. Troubles with the Victim

1. For the prevalence of sexual violence during conflicts, the different forms it takes, and the different responses by NGOs and human rights groups, see especially Sajor 1998 and Turshen and Twagiramariya 1998. For postwar violence and its consequences see Meintjes, Pillay, and Turshen 2001.
2. See Bloul 1997.

3. A detailed study of the problems encountered in dealing with intraracial rape among Aboriginal people in Australia is provided by Bell (1991).
4. The rape of white women has been made most visible precisely in cases when the rapist is not white. See, for instance, research done by Grover and Soothill (1996), who point out that the press in Britain still most often reports—in the most gruesome detail—the rape of white women by black and Asian men.
5. See Butalia 1993, 1997, and 1998; and Menon and Bhasin 1993, 1996, and 1998.
6. The estimates range from 25,000 to 29,000 Hindu and Sikh women, and 12,000 to 15,000 Muslim women, who were abducted and raped and forced into conversion and marriage (Butalia 1993 and 1997).
7. The communalization of women's bodies during and after Partition did not end in rapes, abductions, and forced conversion and marriages. As the states of India and Pakistan were established, the project of "recovery" started, among the objectives of which was bringing the abducted women back to their "rightful" religious community. The women who, after abduction, conversion, and marriage gathered their lives in the new communities were uprooted and displaced once again. This time, however, the children that came as a result of the new marriages were not allowed to go back with the mothers. Thus, for example, Hindu women from India who were abducted and married with Muslim men in Pakistan had to leave their children in Pakistan. Clearly, India, even though it praises itself as a secular state, defined the children through the religious belonging of their fathers (Butalia 1993).
8. See also Rajasingham-Senanayke 2001 and Peries 1998.
9. For a poignant analysis of discourses surrounding the Dutch prosecution of Jews during World War Two in the Netherlands, see especially de Haan 1997. On similarities between these discourses and media discourses in the Netherlands on Dutch performance within the U.N. battalion that failed to protect the town of Srebrenica from the occupation by Serb forces in July 1995, and the subsequent massacre of over seven thousand Muslim men, see Žarkov 2002.
10. At the end of the 1980s the Asian women survivors of the system of sexual slavery established by the Japanese military during World War Two started speaking out. In 1991 Korean women filed the first court case against the Japanese government (Sancho 1997, 147). Women from other regions of Asia then came forward, too, testifying both about the system of "comfort women" and about other forms of sexual violence, including rapes (Sancho 1997). In November 1996 different groups of Korean women organized into the Korean Council of Women. Its objective was not only to publicize the plight of Korean women who were enslaved by the Japanese, but also to force the Japanese government to apologize publicly, to pay war reparations, and to fulfill other obligations established by international law. In Japan itself the Council of Women has been supported by Japanese feminist groups, especially lawyers, who aided the legal case. Although the analyses of the experiences of different groups of Asian women enslaved by the Japanese military are of a recent date, some are already translated and published in Belgrade's feminist journal *Feminist Notebooks* (see

the special issue "Female Sexual Slavery," 1995), indicating the value of feminist transnationalism.

11. A lesson was learned by both the witnesses and the women's NGOs in Rwanda, where, after being unhappy with the court proceedings, witnesses and their associations refused to cooperate with the International Criminal Tribunal for Rwanda and stalled the process for more than a year. Similar resistance may be happening to the International Criminal Court (ICC) in The Hague, according to stories coming from women's NGOs from Uganda and the Democratic Republic of Congo, which have cases to be taken up by the ICC. Information from a personal contact with a member of Women's Initiative for Gender Justice (The Hague).
12. They still do it, with raped women and rapists from Bosnia being the new subject of novels that implicitly or explicitly claim documentary value (such as in Drakulić 1999 and 2004). Crime stories (such as Dona Leon's *Death and Judgment* [1995]) also use war rapes in Bosnia.
13. See especially Kelly 1996 and 2000; Kelly, Burton, and Regan 1996; and McCollum, Kelly, and Radford 1994.

10. Soldiers of Tradition

1. The expression is used by Bakić-Hayden and Hayden (1992) in arguing that the Balkans symbolize a specific history, culture, and politics from which Slovenian and Croatian politicians wanted to dissociate themselves in the 1990s.
2. A week later the same photo was published with a correction and an apology indicating that the woman on the photo is not Stana Tomašević, the woman who received the National Hero Medal, but another Yugoslav partisan, Mira Afrić, who was retired and living in Belgrade. The article carries a short conversation with her about how the photo was taken ("Partisan from Photo Is Mira Afrić," *Politika*, January 14, 1991, 12).
3. "Za Djurdjem je kosu odrezala/ Za djeverom lice izgrdila / A za bratom oči izvadila. / Kosu reže, kosa opet raste; / Lice grdi, a lice izrasta; / Ali oči ne mogu izrasti, / Niti srce za bratom rodjenim." From *Djela Vuka Karadžića, Srpske narodne pjesme* (Belgrade: Prosveta and Nolit, 1985, 305).

11. Troubles with Arms

1. The second wave of Yugoslav feminism was younger than Yugoslav nationalism. It appeared as a self-conscious movement only in the late 1970s (while open nationalist movements had already appeared in 1968 in Kosovo, and in 1971 in Croatia). At that time feminists did not look (back) at what nationalism meant for socialism, and what the place of ethnicity was in either of them, facing these questions for the first time only in the late 1980s. In their early days, Yugoslav feminists debated issues of socialist theory and practice and disputed many diverse theoretical and empirical aspects of the women's emanci-

pation project. Well-known feminists were public figures, mostly academics, excellent scholars, extremely critical and analytical, and very well versed in theoretical developments in international academic feminism, from philosophy to literature. They were based in the academia and cultural institutions of three biggest urban centers: Ljubljana, Zagreb, and Belgrade. For more on the women's movement prior to World War One in regions that after the war were included in the Kingdom of Serbs, Croats, and Slovenes, and on feminism between World Wars One and Two, see Slapšak 2000. For more on the second-wave feminism—1970s and 1980s—see especially Papić 1994.

2. See especially Ćetković 1993, Papić 1994, Zajović 1994, Kesić 1995a, Dobnikar 2000, and Drezgić 2000.
3. Like academic feminism, activism was also based in the regional capitals: Zagreb, Belgrade, and Ljubljana. The results of the grassroots feminist activism of the time were S.O.S. hotlines (special telephone lines for counseling and support of victims of family and/or sexual violence, operated by women volunteers, and organized by women's NGOs) and shelters for women and children (who wished to leave abusive and violent partners and family situations). The first S.O.S. hotline was established in 1986 in Zagreb, by the then operating feminist collective Autonomous Women's House, and in 1990 in Belgrade, by the Autonomous Women's Center against Sexual Violence. These two feminist collectives became the centers of feminist activism in their regions during the wars.
4. For more on splits within and differences between feminist groups in the region, see Benderly 1997, Duhaček 1993, Supek 1994, Milić 1993, Blagojević 1994, Korać 1996, Boric 1997, Batinić 2001, Žarkov 2002, and Obradović-Dragišić 2004. For specific women's groups, see Cockburn 1998 on several Bosnian women's NGOs, Dević 2000 on Belgrade's Women in Black, and Žarkov 2004 on the trajectories of Autonomous Women's Center (Belgrade), the Center for Women War Victims (Zagreb), and Vive Žene (Tuzla).
5. For details, see especially Batinić 2001 and Obradović-Dragišić 2004.
6. Interestingly, their radical feminism did not appear to give them a negative public image in the Croatian media, otherwise so sensitive to the word "feminism." To the contrary, their work received a positive reception in the press. Defined as patriotic by the Croatian media, they were often invited as guests on different radio programs and appeared on prime-time national television. Through these appearances, their work, as well as their perspectives received, in their own words, "an important public recognition" (Program Statement, O-ZONA: Assistance to Women in Crisis).
7. Annual Report, 1994–1995, Autonomous Women's Center (Belgrade), 1.
8. Dobnikar (2000) is one of the few feminists from the region to insist that women's engagement in aggression and armed conflict needed urgent investigation.
9. Drakulić, for example, almost invariably represents all the people of former Yugoslavia as lacking in agency. The socialist period is presented as a period

of darkness and totalitarianism, as a cancerous body on the world map, from the early *How We Survived Communism and Even Laugh* (1992) to the recent *They Would Never Hurt a Fly* (2004). The people of former Yugoslavia (especially the men) are described as brainwashed, docile, and at the same time primitive objects of totalitarian communist power, without any critical agency, without any individuality, and often without any integrity and humanity (especially when talking of men). Her writing is a blatant example of a systematic erasure of critical voices of political dissent from Yugoslav socialist history, including the most recent history—voices such as her own throughout the 1980s; voices such as those of critical intellectuals around the Praxis group that grew out of Yugoslav socialism, and openly and vigorously criticized it; or the dissenting voices of thousands of men who fled all former Yugoslav republics in order to avoid being forcefully drafted in war. At the same time, Drakulić appropriates the victim status by continually identifying herself with women victimized in the wars in Bosnia and Croatia (with refugee women in *The Balkan Express* [1993a] or a woman whose daughter is raped in *They Would Never Hurt a Fly* [2004]).

10. See, for example, the personal reflections of Hidović-Harper (1993).
11. Among the classic works on war, militarism, and masculinity, see Huston 1982, Enloe 1983 and 1989, Lloyd 1986, Segal 1987, Elshtain 1987, and Macdonald, et al. 1987.
12. For the essentialized difference between feminine-maternal-peaceloving-feminist politics and masculine-war-waging politics, see especially Ruddic 1989 and 1993 and Theweleit 1993. See also Cronberg 1997 on Russian women working in military industry.
13. Elshtain (1987) suggests that women's participation in armed struggles could subvert essentialist representation of women as peace-loving. Yuval-Davis (1997) argues that the demand for equality also demands participation in the military. For the argument that the influx of women in the peace-keeping militaries could have transforming effect, see Mazurana 2002 and Bosch and Verweij 2002.
14. See also Unterhalter 1987.
15. Besides the above-mentioned studies, see also Yuval-Davis 1985 for women in the Israeli army, and Sklevicky 1989b for partisan women in the Yugoslav army during World War Two. According to Zwerman (1994), the issue of combat roles also applies to women in clandestine armed organizations in the United States.
16. See especially Greval and Kaplan 1994 and Mohanty 2003.
17. See Seidel and Gunther 1988 for the Falklands War, and Farmanfarmaian 1992 and Forde 1995 for the Gulf War.
18. The war in Rwanda remained for a long time largely invisible in the West, although it mobilized women's and feminist NGOs across the globe. Lately, more studies of war in Rwanda have appeared in the West, although these are mostly from Western authors. See, for example, Enloe 2000 on rapes, and Gervais 2004 on Rwanda's women personal, economic, and sociopolitical security after

the conflict. See also Twagiramariya and Turshen 1998 on sexual politics, and Mibenge 2005 on the Rwandan tribunals. The Yugoslav wars, on the other hand, prompted an enormous academic production, in a wide range of disciplines, much of which is discussed throughout this book.

19. For literary and cultural representations of gender and war, see especially collections by Cooper et al. 1989 and Cooke and Woollacott 1993, and the study of World War One by Melman (1998), who redefines both the war (including the decades that led to it, and the decades after it, which were an introduction to World War Two) and Europe (including its colonial and imperial domains of power). For the changing nature of war, see, for example, Schott 1996.
20. See, for example, Turshen and Twagiramariya 1998, Afshar and Eade 2004, and Meintjes, Pillay, and Turshen 2001.
21. See especially Connell 2002.
22. For early critical work on women's violent and right-wing agency, see Sarkar and Butalia 1995 and Bacchetta 1996. For recent studies, see Rajasingham-Senanayake 2001, Basu 2001, Jeffery 2001, de Mel 2001, Butalia 2001, and Bacchetta 2002.
23. See especially Butalia 2001, Basu 2001, Jeffery 2001, and Banerjee 2001.
24. See Jeffery 2001 on political agency, and Manchanda 2001 on women's violent agency within the domestic sphere—through support of militancy and violence of their family members, especially sons.
25. She did not speak about the torture or prison time—I learned this information from other sources.
26. The interview was conducted one late afternoon, in the summer of 1995, in Serbia. After the tape-recorder was switched off, the story became more personal, and her sense of betrayal and disillusionment prevailed.
27. This was not an interview as such, because Mirjana received a party directive not to talk to me. However, she was very interested in the fact that I was looking at women's experiences of war and wanted to be part of it in some way. The first time I came to her office (at the end of 1995), after telling me she was not allowed to give me an interview, she was not in a hurry to see me off. So I stayed, observing her working and communicating with clients. Before I left later that day, I told her that I frequently came to her city, and asked if I could drop by again, to have a cup of coffee with her. She agreed. So I often went to her office and remained there for hours, sometimes engaging in conversation with her or the clients, but mostly simply listening and taking notes. This unpressured and casual framing of our encounters as "coffee-drinking visits" allowed me to have my "interview," and for Mirjana to be part of it without having to disobey the party directive.

BIBLIOGRAPHY

Accad, E. 1989. "Feminist Perspective on the War in Lebanon." *Women's Studies International Forum* 12 (1): 91–95.

———. 1990. *Sexuality and War*. New York: New York University Press.

Adams, R. C., et al. 1980. "The Effect of Framing on Selection of Photographs of Men and Women." *Journalism Quarterly* (Autumn): 463–468.

Ahmed, A. 1995. "'Ethnic Cleansing': A Metaphor for Our Time?" *Ethnic and Racial Studies* 18 (1): 1–25.

Alcoff, L. 1988, "Cultural Feminism Versus Poststructuralism. The Identity Crisis in Feminist Theory." *Signs* 3: 405–436.

Alexander, J. M. 1994. "Not Just (Any) *Body* Can Be a Citizen: The Politics of Law, Sexuality and Postcoloniality in Trinidad and Tobago and the Bahamas." *Feminist Review* 48: 5–23.

Allen, B. 1996. *Rape Warfare: The Hidden Genocide in Bosnia-Hercegovina and Croatia*. Minneapolis: University of Minnesota Press.

Alves, J. 1993. "Transgressions and Transformations: Initiation Rites among Urban Portuguese Boys." *American Anthropologist* 95 (4): 894–928.

American Journal of International Law. 1993. Special issue on international law, war, violence, and women's human rights.

Amnesty International. 1994. *Yugoslavia: Police Violence in Kosovo Province—The Victims*. EUR 70/16/94. London: Amnesty International.

Anderson, B. 1983. *Imagined Communities: Reflections on the Origin and Spread of Nationalism*. London: Verso.

Anthias, F., and N. Yuval-Davis. 1983. "Contextualizing Feminism: Gender, Ethnic and Class Divisions." *Feminist Review* 14: 62–75.

———. 1992. *Racialized Boundaries: Race, Nation, Gender, Colour and Class and the Anti-Racist Struggle*. London: Routledge.

Ardener, S., ed. 1975. *Perceiving Women*. London: J. M. Dent.

———. ed. 1978. *Defining Females*. London: Croom Helm.

Autonomni ženski centar Beograd (Autonomous Women's Center against Sexual Violence). 1995. *Izveštaj* (Report), March 1994–March 1995.

———. 1998. *Izveštaj* (Report): March 1997–March 1998.

Avramov, D. 1993. *Pojedinac, porodica i stanovništvo u raskoraku* (Individual, Family and Population in Dissonance). Belgrade: Naučna Knjiga.

Aydelott, D. 1993. "Mass Rape During War: Prosecuting Bosnian Rapists under International Law." *Emory International Law Review* 9 (7): 585–631.

Bacchetta, P. 1996. "Hindu Nationalist Women as Ideologues: The Sangh, the Samiti and Differential Concepts of the Hindu Nation." In Jayawardena and de Alwis, 126–167.

———. 2002. *The Nation and the RSS: Gendered Discourse, Gendered Action*, New Delhi: Kali for Women.

Bacchetta, P., and M. Power, eds. 2002. *Right-Wing Women: From Conservatives to Extremists around the World*. London, Routledge.

Bakić-Hayden, M. 1995. "Nesting Orientalisms: The Case of Former Yugoslavia." *Slavic Review* 54 (4): 917–931.

Bakić-Hayden, M., and R. Hayden. 1992. "Orientalist Variations on the Theme 'Balkans': Symbolic Geography in Recent Yugoslav Cultural Politics." *Slavic Review* 52 (1): 1–16.

Banac, I. 1992. "The Origins and Development of the Concept of Yugoslavia (to 1945)." In M. Van der Heuvel J. G. Siccama, J.G., eds., *The Disintegration of Yugoslavia*, Yearbook of European Studies. Amsterdam: Rodopi, 1–22.

Barnes, B. N. 1997. "Face of the Nation; Race, Nationalisms, and Identities in Jamaican Beauty Pageants." In C. L. Springfield, ed., *Daughters of Caliban, Caribbean Women in the Twentieth Century*. London: Indiana University Press, 285–306.

Barrett, Michele, and Mary McIntosh. 1985. "Ethnocentrism and Socialist-Feminist Theory." *Feminist Review* 20 (Summer): 23–47.

Barth, F. 1969. *Ethnic Groups and Boundaries: The Social Organization of Culture Difference*. Bergen: Universitets Forlaget; London: George Allen and Unwin.

Bassiouni, M. C., and M. McCormick. 1996. *Sexual Violence: An Invisible Weapon of War in the Former Yugoslavia*. International Human Rights Law Institute, Occasional Paper 1. Chicago: DePaul University.

Basu, A. 1995. "Feminism Inverted: The Gendered Imagery and Real Women of Hindu Nationalism." In Sarkar and Butalia, 158–180.

———. 2001. "Hindu Women's Activism in India and the Questions It Raises." In Jeffery and Basu, 167–184.

Batinić, J. 2001. "Feminism, Nationalism and War: The 'Yugoslav Case' in Feminist Texts." *Journal of International Women's Studies* 3 (1). www.bridgew.edu/SoAS/jiws/fall01/index.htm.

Bax, M. 1992. "The Saints of Gomila: Ritual and Violence in a Yugoslav Peasant Community." *Ethnologia Europaea* 22 (1): 17–31.

Bell, D. 1991. "Intraracial Rape Revisited: On Forging a Feminist Future beyond Factions and Frightening Politics." *Women's Studies International Forum* 14 (5): 385–412.

Benard, C. 1994. "Rape as Terror: The Case of Bosnia." *Terrorism and Political Violence* 6 (1): 29–43.

Benderly, J. 1997. "Rape, Feminism and Nationalism in the War in Yugoslav Successor States." In West, 59–72.

Bhabha, H., ed. 1990. *Nation and Narration*. New York: Routledge.

———. 1996. "Culture's In-Between." In S. Hall and P. du Gay, eds., *Questions of Cultural Identity*. London: Sage, 53–61.

Bhavani, K. 1993. "Towards a Multicultural Europe?: 'Race,' Nation and Identity in 1992 and Beyond." *Feminist Review* 45: 31–45.

Billig, M. 1995. "Socio-Psychological Aspects of Nationalism: Imagining Ingroups, Others and the World of Nations." In F. Benda-Beckmann and M. Verkuyten, eds., *Nationalism, Ethnicity and Cultural Identity in Europe*. Utrecht: ERCMER.

Blagojević, M. 1991. *Žene Izvan Kruga, Profesija i Porodica* (Women Outside the Circle. Profession and Family). Belgrade: Institut za sociološka istraživanja Filozofskog fakulteta.

———. 1994. "War and Everyday Life: Deconstruction of Self/Sacrifice." *Sociology* 36 (4): 469–493.

Bloul, R. 1997. "Victims or Offenders? 'Other' Women in French Sexual Politics." In K. Davis, ed., *Embodied Practices: Feminist Perspectives on the Body*. London: Sage, 93–110.

Bonner, F., et al., eds. 1992. *Imagining Women: Cultural Representation and Gender*. Cambridge: Polity Press in association with the Open University.

Bordo, S. 1993. *Unbearable Weight: Feminism, Western Culture, and the Body*. Berkeley: University of California Press.

Borić, R. 1997. "Against the War: Women Organizing across the National Divide in the Countries of the Former Yugoslavia." In R. Lentin, ed., *Gender and Catastrophe*. London: Zed Books, 36–49.

Borneman, J. 1998. "Towards a Theory of Ethnic Cleansing: Territorial Sovereignty, Heterosexuality, and Europe." In *Subversions of International Order: Studies in the Political Anthropology of Culture*. Albany: State University of New York Press, 273–310.

Bosch, J., and D. Verweij. 2002. "Enduring Ambivalence: The Dutch Armed Forces and Their Women Recruits." In Cockburn and Žarkov, 122–145.

Bourdieu, P. 1989. "An Interview with Pierre Bourdieu: For a Socio-Analysis of Intellectuals—On Homo Academicus." *Berkeley Journal of Sociology: A Critical Review* 34: 1–29.

———. 1991. "Epilogue: On the Possibility of a Field of World Sociology." In P. Bourdieu and J. S. Coleman, eds., *Social Theory for a Changing Society*. New York: Westview Press, 373–389.

Bourke, J. 1996. "Fragmentation, Fetishization and Men's Bodies in Britain, 1890–1939." *Women: A Cultural Review* 7 (3): 240–250.

Bowker, L. H., ed. 1998. *Masculinities and Violence*. Research on Men and Masculinities Series 10. Thousand Oaks, Calif.: Sage.

Brah, A. 1993. "Re-Framing Europe: En-gendered Racisms, Ethnicities and Nationalisms in Contemporary Western Europe." *Feminist Review* 45: 9–30.

Breznik, D., ed. 1992. *Fertility and Family Planning in Yugoslavia*. Belgrade: Institute for Social Sciences, Demographic Research Center.

Bringa, T. 1995. *Being Muslim the Bosnian Way: Identity and Community in a Central Bosnian Village*. Princeton: Princeton University Press.

Brittan, A. 1989. *Masculinity and Power*. Oxford: Basil Blackwell.

Brownmiller, S. 1986. *Against Our Will: Men, Women and Rape*. New York: Bantam Books.

———. 1993. "Making Women's Bodies Battlefields." In Stiglmayer 1993a, 180–183.

Bugarski, R. 1995. *Jezik od mira do rata* (Language from Peace to War). Belgrade: Biblioteka XX Vek.

Burić, O. 1985. "Yugoslavia." In J. Farley, ed., *Women Workers in Fifteen Countries*. New York: ILR Press.

Butalia, U. 1993. "Community, State and Gender: On Women's Agency during Partition." *Economic and Political Weekly* (New Delhi), April 24, 12–24.

———. 1995. "Muslims and Hindus, Men and Women: Communal Stereotypes and the Partition of India." In T. Sarkar and U. Butalia, eds., *Women and Right-Wing Movements: Indian Experiences*. London: Zed Books, 58–81.

———. 1997. "A Question of Silence: Partition, Women and the State." In R. Lentin, ed., *Gender and Catastrophe*. London: Zed Books, 92–110.

———. 1998. *The Other Side of Silence: Voices from the Partition of India*. London: Penguin.

———. 2001. "Women and Communal Conflict: New Challenges for the Women's Movement in India." In Moser and Clark, 99–113.

Butler, J. 1987. "Variations on Sex and Gender: Beauvoir, Wittig and Foucault." In S. Benhabib and D. Cornell, eds., *Feminism as Critique: Essays on the Politics of Gender in Late-Capitalist Societies*. Feminist Perspectives. London: Polity Press, 128–143.

———. 1993. *Bodies that Matter: On the Discursive Limits of "Sex."* New York: Routledge.

Camino, L. A., and R. M. Krulfeld, eds. 1994. *Reconstructing Lives, Recapturing Meaning: Refugee Identity, Gender, and Culture Change*. Washington, D.C.: Gordon and Breach Publishers.

Caplan, P., ed. 1987. *The Cultural Construction of Sexuality*. London: Tavistoc Publication.

Card, C. 1996. "Rape as a Weapon of War." *Hypathia* 11 (4): 5–18.

Centar za Anti-Ratnu Akciju (Center for Antiwar Action). 1994. *Govor Mržnje* (Hate Speech). Belgrade: Centar za Anti-Ratnu Akciju.

Centar za Žene Žrtve Rata (Center for Women War Victims). 1994. *Zbornik* (Proceedings). Zagreb: Centar za Žene Žrtve Rata.

Ćetković, N. 1993. "Achtung! Achtung! Attention! Upozorenje." In S. Zajović, ed., *Women for Peace: Anthology*. Belgrade: Women in Black.

Chapman, R., and J. Rutherford. 1988. *Male Order: Unwrapping Masculinity*. London: Lawrence and Wishart.

Chatterjee, P. 1990. "The Nationalist Resolution of the Women's Question." In K. Sangari and S. Vaid, eds., *Recasting Women: Essays in Indian Colonial History*. New Brunswick, N.J.: Rutgers University Press, 233–253.

Chinkin, C. 2001. "Women's International Tribunal on Japanese Military Sexual Slavery." *American Journal of International Law* 95 (2): 335–341.

Cleiren, T., and M. Tijsen. 1996. "Rape and Other Forms of Sexual Assault in the Armed Conflict in the Former Yugoslavia." *Nemesis Essays* 3: 111–131.

Cock, J. 1992. *Women and War in South Africa*. London: Open Letters.

———. 1994. "Women and the Military: Implications for Demilitarization in the 1990s in South Africa." *Gender and Society* 8 (2): 152–169.

Cockburn, C. 1991. "A Women's Political Party for Yugoslavia: Introduction to the Serbian Feminist Manifesto." *Feminist Review* 39: 155–160.

———. 1998. *The Space between Us: Negotiating Gender and National Identities in Conflict*. London: Zed Books.

———. 2000. *Gender and Democracy in the Aftermath of War*. Utrecht: Universiteit voor Humanistiek.

———. 2001. "The Gendered Dynamics of Armed Conflict and Political Violence." In Moser and Clark, 13–29.

Cockburn, C., and D. Žarkov, eds. 2002. *The Postwar Moment: Militaries, Masculinities and International Peacekeeping*. London: Lawrence and Wishart, 33–40.

Čolović, I. 1994. *Bordel ratnika* (Brothel of the Warriors). XX Century Book 78. Belgrade: Slovograf/XX Century Books.

———. 1999. *Kad Kažem Novine* (When I Say Newspapers). Belgrade: Samizdat-FreeB92.

Connell, R. W. 1985. "Masculinity, Violence, War." In P. Patton and R. Poole, 4–10.

———. 1987. *Gender and Power: Society, the Person and Sexual Politics*. Cambridge: Polity Press.

———. 1995. *Masculinities*. Berkeley: University of California Press.

———. 2002. "Masculinities, the Reduction of Violence and the Pursuit of Peace." In Cockburn and Žarkov, 33–40.

Cooke, M., and A. Woollacott. 1993. *Gendering War Talk*. Princeton: Princeton University Press.

Cooper, H., A. Auslender Munich, and S. M. Squier, eds. 1989. *Arms and the Woman: War, Gender and Literary Representation*. Chapel Hill: University of North Carolina Press.

Copelon, R. 1993. "Surfacing Gender: Reconceptualizing Crimes against Women in Time of War." In Stiglmayer 1993a, 197–218.

Cornwall, A., and N. Lindisfarne. 1994. *Dislocating Masculinity: Comparative Ethnographies*. London: Routledge.

Craig, S. 1992. *Men, Masculinity and the Media*. London: Sage.

Cronberg, T. 1997. "The Feeling of Home: Russian Women in the Defence Industry and the Transformation of their Identities." *European Journal of Women's Studies* 4 (3): 263–282.

Cullen, H. 1992. "Feminism and Nationalism." *Journal of Gender Studies* 1 (3): 408–417.

Das, V. 1987. "Anthropology of Violence and the Speech of Victims." *Anthropology Today* 3 (4): 106–109.

Davis, K. 1995. *Reshaping the Female Body: The Dilemma of Cosmetic Surgery*. London: Routledge.

———. 1997a. "Was Will Der Mann? Some Reflections on Theorizing Masculinity." *Theory and Psychology* 7 (4): 555–564.

———. 1997b. "Embody-ing Theory: Beyond Modernist and Postmodernist Reading of the Body." In K. Davis, ed., *Embodied Practices: Feminist Perspectives on the Body*. London: Sage, 1–23.

de Almeida, M. V. 1996. *The Hegemonic Male: Masculinity in a Portuguese Town.* Oxford: Berghahn Books.

———. 1997. "Gender, Masculinity and Power in Southern Portugal." *Social Anthropology* 5 (2): 141–158.

de Alwis, M. 1999. "Motherhood as a Space of Protest: Women's Political Participation in Contemporary Sri Lanka." In Jeffery and Basu, 185–201.

de Haan, I. 1997. *Na de ondergang: De herinering van de Jodenvervolging in Nederland 1945–1995* (After the Downfall: The Memories of the Prosecution of Jews in the Netherlands 1945-1995). The Hague: Sdu Uitgevers.

de Lauretis, Teresa. 1987. *Technologies of Gender: Essays on Theory, Film, and Fiction.* Bloomington: Indiana University Press.

de Mel, N. 2001. "Agent or Victim? The Sri Lankan Woman Militant in the Interregnum." In *Women and the Nation's Narrative: Gender and Nationalism in Twentieth-Century Sri Lanka*. New Delhi: Social Scientists' Association, 203–232.

Denich, B. 1974. "Sex and Power in the Balkans." In M. Z. Rosaldo and L. Lampherte, eds., *Women, Culture and Society*. Stanford: Stanford University Press, 243–263.

———. 1977. "Women, Work and Power in Modern Yugoslavia." In Schlegel, 215–245.

Deshpande, S. 1997. Book review. *Thamyris. Mythmaking from Past to Present* 4 (1): 195–199.

Despot, B. 1984. "Marks i Emancipacija Žena" (Marx and Emancipation of Women). *Gledišta* 1 (2): 51–61.

———. 1987. "Žensko pitanje u socijalističkom samoupravljanju" (Women's Question in Socialist Self-Management). In Sklevicky 1987b, 39–49.

Dević, A. 2000. "Women's Activism between Private and Public Spaces: The Case of Women in Black in Serbia." In Slapšak 2000a, 195–210.

Dijkstra, A. G. 1997. "Women in Central and Eastern Europe: A Labour Market in Transition." In A. G. Dijkstra and J. Plantenga, eds., *Gender and Economics: A European Perspective*. London: Routledge, 118–138.

Dinkić, M. 1995. *Ekonomija destrukcije* (Economy of Destruction). Belgrade: Video Nedeljnik.

Djurić, T. 1995. "From National Economies to Nationalist Hysteria—Consequences for Women." In Lutz et al., eds., *Crossfires: Nationalism, Racism and Gender in Europe*. London: Pluto Press, 121–141.

Djurić-Kuzmanović, T. 2001. "From State Directed Non-Development and Organized Gender Violence to Transition in Vojvodina and Serbia." In R. Stryker and J. Patico, eds., *The Paradoxes of Progress: Globalization and Postsocialist Cultures*. Kroeber Anthropological Society Papers 86. Berkeley, Calif.: Kroeber Anthropological Society, 27–35.

———. 2002. *Rodnost i Razvoj u Srbiji. Od Dirigovanog Nerazvoja do Tranzicije* (Gender and Development in Serbia. From Directed Non-Development to Transition). Novi Sad: Budućnost, Ženske Studije, Istraživanja.

Djurić-Kuzmanović, T., and D. Žarkov. 1997. "Ekonomija razvoja i rodnost u tranziciji 'Drugog Sveta'" (Economy and Gender in the Transition of the "Second World"), in T. Djurić-Kuzmanović, ed., *Dirigovani Nerazvoj: (Post)socijalističko iskustvo i feministička alternativa* (Directed Non-Development: (Post)Socialist experience and feminist alternative). Novi Sad: EXPO Press, 131–146.

———. 1998. "Poverty, Social Stratification and Directed Undevelopment in Serbia." *Journal of Area Studies* 13: 184–201.

———. 1999. "Poverty and Directed Non-development in Serbia." In "Reassessing Peripheries in Post-Communist Studies," special issue, *Anthropology of East Europe Review: Central Europe, Eastern Europe and Euroasia* 17 (2): 31–38.

Dobnikar, M. 2000. "War, Discourse, Women—What about Us?" In Slapšak 2000a, 359–368.

Drakulić, S. 1987. "Smrtni grijesi feminizma/Dečki se zatrčavaju" (Mortal Sins of Feminism/ Lads are Warming Up). In Sklevicky 1987b, 173–181.

———. 1992. *How We Survived Communism and Even Laughed*. London: Vintage.

———. 1993a. *Balkan Express: Fragments from the Other Side of War*. London: Hutchins.

———. 1993b. "Women and New Democracy in the Former Yugoslavia." In N. Funk and M. Mueller, eds., *Gender Politics and Post-Communism*. London: Routledge, 123–130.

———. 2004. *They Would Never Hurt a Fly*. London: Abacus.

Drezgić, R. 2000. "Demographic Nationalism in the Gender Perspective." In Slapšak 2000a, 211–234.

———. 2004. "(Re)producing the Nation: The Politics of Reproduction in Post-Socialist Serbia: 1980s and 1990s." Ph.D. dissertation, University of Pittsburgh.

Duhaček, D. 1993. "Women's Time in the Former Yugoslavia." In Funk and Mueller, 131–137.

Easthope, A. 1986. *What a Man's Gotta Do: The Masculine Myth in Popular Culture*. London: Routledge.

Einhorn, B. 1993. *Cinderella Goes to Market: Citizenship, Gender and the Women's Movement in East Central Europe*. London: Verso.

El-Bushra, J. 2004. "Fused in Combat: Gender Relations and Armed Conflict." In H. Afshar and D. Eade, eds., *Development, Women, and War: Feminist Perspectives*. A Development in Practice Reader. London: Oxfam, 152–171.

Elshtain, J. B. 1987. *Women and War*. New York: Basic Books.

Enloe, C. 1983. *Does Khaki Become You? The Militarization of Women's Lives*. London: South End Press.

———. 1989. *Bananas, Beaches, Bases: Making Feminist Sense of International Politics*. London: Pandora.

———. 1993. *The Morning After: Sexual Politics at the End of the Cold War*. Berkeley: University of California Press.

———. 2000. *Maneuvers: The International Politics of Militarizing Women's Lives*. Berkeley: University of California Press.

———. 2002. "Demilitarization—or More of the Same? Feminist Questions to Ask in the Postwar Moment." In Cockburn and Žarkov, 22–32.

Epstein, E. K., ed. 1978. *Women and the News*, New York: Hasting House.

Epstein, F., and L. Coser, eds. 1981. *Access to Power: Cross-National Studies of Women and Elites*. London: George Allen and Unwin.

Farmanfarmaian, A. 1992. "Sexuality in the Gulf War: Did You Measure Up?" *Genders* 13 (Spring): 1–29.

First, R. 1982. "The National Liberation Struggle and Women in Yugoslavia." In M. Mies and R. Reddock, eds., *National Liberation and Women's Liberation*. The Hague: Institute of Social Studies, 53–64.

Flax, J. 1987. "Postmodernism and Gender Relations in Feminist Theory." *Signs* 4: 621–643.

Folnegović-Šmalc, V. 1993. "Psychiatric Aspects of the Rapes in the War against the Republic of Croatia and Bosnia-Hercegovina." In Stiglmayer 1993a, 174–180.

Forde, C. 1995. "Women Warriors": Representation of Women Soldiers in British Daily Newspaper Photographs of the Gulf War (January to March 1991). In M. Maynard and J. Purvis, eds., *(Hetero)sexual Politics*. Bristol: Taylor and Francis, 108–123.

Funk, N., and M. Mueller, eds. 1993. *Gender Politics and Post-Communism*. New York: Routledge.

Fuss, D. 1989. *Essentially Speaking. Feminism, Nature & Difference*. London: Routledge.

Garber, M. 1992. *Vested Interests: Cross-Dressing and Cultural Anxiety*. New York: Routledge.

Gellner, E. 1983. *Nations and Nationalism*, London: Basil Blackwell.

Gerrits, A. W. M. 1992. "Some Comments on the Civil War in Yugoslavia." *Helsinki Monitor* 3 (1): 54–56.

Gilman, S. 1985. "Black Bodies, White Bodies: Toward an Iconography of Female Sexuality in Late Nineteenth-Century Art, Medicine and Literature." In H. L. Gates, ed., *Race, Writing and Difference*. Chicago: University of Chicago Press.

———. 1991. *The Jew's Body*. New York: Routledge.

Gilmore, D. 1990. *Manhood in the Making: Cultural Concepts of Masculinity*. New Haven: Yale University Press.

Glenny, M. 1992. *The Fall of Yugoslavia: The Third Balkan War*. Harmondsworth: Penguin Books.

Gremaux, R. 1994. "Woman Becomes Man in the Balkans." In G. Herdt, ed., *Third Sex, Third Gender: Beyond Sexual Dimorphism in Culture and History*. New York: Zone Books, 241–285.

Greval, I., and C. Kaplan, eds. 1994. *Scattered Hegemonies: Postmodernity and Transnational Feminist Practices*. Minneapolis: University of Minnesota Press.

Griffin, S. 1977. "Rape: The All-American Crime." In D. Chappell et al., eds., *Forcible*

Rape: The Crime, the Victim, and the Offender. New York: Columbia University Press.

Group 17. 2000. *Bela knjiga Miloševićeve vladavine* (The White Book of Milosević's Rulership). At http: //www.g17.org.yu/ (10.09.2000).

Grover, C., and K. Soothill. 1996. "Ethnicity: The Search for Rapists and the Press." *Ethnic and Racial Studies* 19 (3): 567–584.

Gutman, R. 1993. Foreword to Stiglmayer 1993a, ix–xv.

———. 1996. *The Meanings of Machismo: Being a Man in Mexico City*. Berkeley: University of California Press.

Haag, P. 1996. "'Putting Your Body in the Line': The Question of Violence, Victims, and the Legacies of Second-Wave Feminism." *Differences: A Journal of Feminist Cultural Studies* 8 (2): 23–67.

Hall, S. 1992. "New Ethnicities." In J. Donald and A. Rattansi, eds., *"Race," Culture and Difference*. London: Sage.

———. 1996. "Who Needs 'Identity?'" In S. Hall and P. du Gay, eds., *Questions of Cultural Identity*. London: Sage.

Hassim, S. 1993. "Family, Motherhood and Zulu Nationalism: The Politics of the Inkatha Women's Brigade." *Feminist Review* 43: 1–25.

Hayden, R. 1992. "Constitutional Nationalism in the Formerly Yugoslav Republics." *Slavic Review* 51 (4): 654–673.

———. 1996. "Imagined Communities and Real Victims: Self-Determination and Ethnic Cleansing in Yugoslavia." *American Ethnologist* 23 (4): 1–19.

———. 2000. "Rape and Rape Avoidance in Ethno-National Conflicts: Sexual Violence in Liminalized States." *American Anthropologist* 102 (1): 27–41.

Heberle, R. 2000. "Deconstructive Strategies and the Movement against Sexual Violence." *Hypatia* 11 (4): 63–74.

Helms, E. 2003. "Women as Agents of Ethnic Reconciliation? Women's NGOs and International Intervention in Postwar Bosnia-Herzegovina." *Women's Studies International Forum* 26 (1): 15–33.

Herzfeld, M. 1985. *The Poetics of Manhood: Contest and Identity in a Cretan Mountain Village*. Princeton: Princeton University Press.

Hidović-Harper, I. 1993. "Personal Reactions of a Bosnian Woman to the War in Bosnia." *Feminist Review* 45: 102–197.

Higonnet, M. 1989. "Civil Wars and Sexual Territories." In Cooper et al., 80–96.

Hobsbawm, E. 1992. "Ethnicity and Nationalisn in Europe Today." *Anthropology Today* 8 (2): 3–8.

Hobsbawm, E., and T. Ranger, eds. 1983. *The Invention of Tradition*. Cambridge: Cambridge University Press.

hoogland, r. 1997. *Lesbian Configurations*. Cambridge: Polity Press.

hooks, b. 1989. *Talking Back: Thinking Feminist, Thinking Black*. Boston, Mass.: South End Press.

———. 1990, *Yearning: Race, Gender, and Cultural Politics*. Boston: South End Press.

———. 1995. "Reconstructing Black Masculinity." In A. Perchuk and H. Posner, eds., *The Masculine Masquerade: Masculinity and Representation*. Cambridge, Mass.: MIT Press, 69–88.

Huggins, M. K., and Haritos-Fatouros, M. 1998. "Bureaucratizing Masculinities Among Brazilian Torturers and Murderers." In Bowker, 29–54.

Hughes, K. 1997. "Women and War: The Greek Cypriot Experience." *Women: A Cultural Review* 8 (1): 81–88.

Hughes, M. D., L. Mladjenović, and Z. Mršević. 1995. "Feminist Resistance in Serbia." *European Journal of Women's Studies* 2 (4): 509–532.

Huseby-Darvis, E. 1996. "Feminism, the Murder of Mothers: The Rise and Fall of Neo-nationalist Reconstruction of Gender in Hungary." In B. F. Williams, ed., *Women out of Place: The Gender of Agency and the Race of Nationality*. New York: Rutledge, 161–185.

Huntington, S. 1993. "The Clash of Civilizations?" *Foreign Affairs* 72 (3): 22–50.

Huston, N. 1982. "Tales of War and Tears of Women." *Women's Studies International Forum* 5 (3–4): 271–282.

Innes, C. L. 1994. "Virgin Territories and Motherlands: Colonial and National Representations of Africa and Ireland." *Feminist Review* 47: 1–14.

ITCY. 1995. Transcript of the Court Hearing, Case no. IT-95-18-R61, International Tribunal for War Crimes in Former Yugoslavia, July 2.

Iveković, R. 1993. "Women, Nationalism and War: 'Make Love Not War.'" *Hypatia* 8 (4): 113–126.

Jackson, P., and J. Penrose, eds. 1993. *Constructions of Race, Place and Nation*, London: University College London Press.

Jambrešić-Kirin, R. 2000. "Personal Narratives on War: A Challenge to Women's Essays and Ethnography in Croatia." In Slapšak 2000a, 285–322.

Jambrešić-Kirin, R., and M. Povrzanović. 1996. "Negotiating Identities? The Voices of Refugees between Experiences and Representation." In R. Jambrešić-Kirin and M. Povrzanović, eds., *War Exile: Everyday Life. Cultural Perspectives*. Zagreb: Institute of Ethnology and Folklore Research, 3–19.

Janjić, D. 1993. "Socialism, Federalism and Nationalism in (the Former) Yugoslavia: Lessons to be Learned." In "Antagonism and Identity in Former Yugoslavia," special issue, *Journal of Area Studies* 3: 102–119.

Jansen, W. 1996. "Dumb and Dull: The Disregard for the Intellectual Life of Middle Eastern Women." *Thamyris* 3 (2): 237–261.

Jayawardena, K., and M. de Alwis, eds. 1996. *Embodied Violence: Communalizing Women's Sexuality in South Asia*. New Delhi: Kali for Women.

Jeffery, P. 2001. "Agency, Activism and Agendas." In Jeffery and Basu, 221–243.

Jeffery, P., and A. Basu, eds. 2001. *Resisting the Sacred and the Secular: Women's Activism and Politicized Religion in South Asia*. New Delhi: Kali for Women.

Jones, A. 1994. "Gender and Ethnic Conflict in Ex-Yugoslavia." *Ethnic and Racial Studies* 17 (1): 115–134.

———. 2001. "Genocide and Humanitarian Intervention: Incorporating Gender Violence." At *www.cide.mx/archivo-eventos/DTGHumanitarian-Documento.PDT*.

Jordan, M. 1995. "Rape as Warfare." *Transition* 1 (20): 20–22.

Joseph, S. 1993. "Women, War and History: Debates in Middle Eastern Women's Studies." *Journal of History of Sexuality* 4 (1): 129–136.

Kaldor, M. 1999. *New and Old Wars: Organized Violence in a Global Era*. Cambridge: Polity Press.

Kannabrian, K. 1996. "Rape and the Construction of Communal Identity." In Jayawardena and de Alwis, 32–42.

Kapor-Stanulović N., and H. P. David. 1999. "Former Yugoslavia and Successor States." In H. P. David, ed., *From Abortion to Contraception: A Resource to Public Policies and Reproductive Behaviour in Central and Eastern Europe from 1917 to the Present*. Westport, Conn.: Greenwood Press, 279–296.

Kašić, B. 2000. "The Aesthetic of the Victim within the Discourse of War." In Slapšak 2000a, 271–283.

Katić, V. 1988. "Žene i rituali u živitnom ciklusu" (Women and Rituals in Life Cycles). Unpublished paper (author's collection).

Katunarić, V. 1987. "Strukturalne i ideološke varijable ženskog pitanja u Jugoslaviji" (Structural and Ideological Variables of Women's Question in Yugoslavia). In Sklevicki 1987b, 113–125.

Kavčić, B. 1990. "Women and Power Structure: The Yugoslav Case." *Sociologija*. Suppl. no. 32: 156–172.

Keith, M., and S. Pile. 1993. *Place and the Politics of Identity*. London: Routledge.

Kelly, L. 1996. "When Does the Speaking Profit Us?: Reflections on the Challenges of Developing Feminist Perspectives on Abuse and Violence by Women." In M. Hesler, L. Kelly, and J. Radford, eds., *Women, Violence and Male Power*. Buckingham: Open University Press, 34–49.

———. 2000. "War against Women: Sexual Violence, Sexual Politics and Militarized State." In S. Jacobs, R. Jacobson, and J. Marchbank, eds., *States of Conflict: Gender, Violence and Resistance*. London: Zed Books, 45–65.

Kelly, L., S. Burton, and L. Regan. 1996. "Beyond Victim or Survivor: Sexual Violence, Identity and Feminist Theory and Practice." In L. Adkins and V. Merchant, eds., *Sexualizing the Social: Power and the Organization of Sexuality*. London: Macmillan, 77–101.

Kesić, V. 1993. "Witch Hunt, Croatian Style." *Women's Review of Books* 10 (10–11): 16.

———. 1995a. "Abortus nije Aushwitz" (Abortion is not Aushwitz). *Feminističke sveske* (Belgrade: Autonomni Zenski Centar), nos. 3–4, 47–49.

———. 1995b. "From Respect to Rape." *Warreport*, no. 36, 36–38.

Kimmel, M., ed. 1987. *Changing Men: New Directions in Research on Men and Masculinity*. Newbury Park: Sage.

King, R. 1973. *Minorities under Communism*. Cambridge, Mass.: Harvard University Press.

Klein, U. 1997. "The Gendering of National Discourses and the Israeli-Palestinian Conflict." *European Journal of Women's Studies* 4 (3): 341–352.

———. 1999. "'Our Best Boys': The Gendered Nature of Civil-Military Relations in Israel." *Men and Masculinities* 2 (1): 47–65.

Koch, K. 1991. "Back to Sarajevo or beyond Trianon." *Netherlands Journal for Social Science* 27 (1): 29–42.

Kohn, E. 1994. "Rape as a Weapon of War: Women's Human Rights During the Dissolution of Yugoslavia." *Golden Gate University Law Review* 24: 199–221.

Koontz, C. 1986. *Mothers of the Fatherland: Women, the Family and Nazi Politics*. London: Cape.

Korać, M. 1993. "Serbian Nationalism: Nationalism of My Own People." *Feminist Review* 45: 108–112.

———. 1994. "Representation of Mass Rape in Ethnic Conflicts in What Was Yugoslavia: Discussion of C. MacKinnon's Concept of 'Genocidal' Rape in This Conflict." *Sociologija* (Belgrade) 6 (4): 495–514 (in Serbo-Croat).

———. 1996. "Understanding Ethnic-National Identity and Its Meaning: Questions from a Woman's Experience." *Women's Studies International Forum* 19 (1–2): 133–145.

Krass, C. 1994. "Bringing the Perpetrators of Rape in the Balkans to Justice: Time for an International Criminal Court." *Denver Journal of International Law and Policy* 22 (2–3): 317–374.

Krog, A. 2001. "Locked into Loss and Silence: Testimonies of Gender and Violence at South Africa Truth Commission." In Moser and Clark, 203–216.

Lalić, L. 1995. *Tri TV Godine u Srbiji* (Three TV Years in Serbia). Belgrade: Nezavisni Sindikat Medija (Independent Media Trade Union).

Lancaster, R. 1992. *Life is Hard: Machismo, Danger and the Intimacy of Power in Nicaragua*. Berkeley: University of California Press.

Lazaro, J. 1990. "Women and Political Violence in Contemporary Peru." *Dialectical Anthropology* 15: 233–247.

Lendvai, I. 1991. "Yugoslavia without Yugoslavs: The Roots of the Crisis." *International Affairs* 67 (2): 251–263.

Lloyd, G. 1986. "Selfhood, War and Masculinity." In C. Pateman and E. Gross, eds., *Feminist Challenges: Social and Political Theory*. Sydney: Allen and Unwin, 63–76.

Lockwood, W. G. 1975. *European Muslims: Economy and Ethnicity in Western Bosnia*. New York: Academic Press.

Lončar, M., and P. Brečić. 1995. "Characteristics of Sexual Violence against Men During the War in Croatia and Bosnia-Hercegovina." Paper presented at the conference "Engendering Violence: Terror, Domination, Recovery," Zagreb, Croatia, October 27–28.

Lunde, I., and J. Ortmann. 1990. "Prevalence and Sequel of Sexual Torture." *Lancet* 336 (8710): 289–291.

Lutz, H. 1991. "Migrant Women of 'Islamic Background': Images and Self-Images." Occasional Paper 11. Amsterdam: Middle East Research Associates.

———. 1997. "Borders of European Identity," *Feminist Review* 57 (1): 93–112.

Macciocchi, M. A. 1977. *Vrouwen en Fascisme* (Women and Fascism). Amsterdam: Sara.

Macdonald, S. 1987. "Drawing the Lines: Gender, Peace and War. An Introduction." In Macdonald, Holden, and Ardener, 1–26.

Macdonald, S., P. Holden, and S. Ardener, eds. 1987. *Images of Women in Peace and War*. London: Macmillan and Oxford University Women's Studies Committee.

Maček, I. 2001. "Predicament of War: Sarajevo Experiences and Ethics of War." In B. E. Schmid and I. W. Schroder, eds., *Anthropology of Violence and Conflict*. London: Routledge, 197–222.

———. 2004. "Sarajevo Soldier Story: Perceptions of War and Morality in Bosnia." In P. Richards, ed., *No Peace, No War: An Anthropology of Contemporary Armed Conflicts*. Athens: Ohio University Press and James Currey, 57–76.

MacKinnon, C. 1993a. "Rape, Genocide, and Women's Human Rights." In A. Stiglmayer, ed., *Mass Rape: The War Against Women in Bosnia-Herzegovina*. Lincoln: University of Nebraska Press, 183–196.

———. 1993b. "Turning Rape into Pornography: Postmodern Genocide." *Ms.* (July–August): 24–30.

Makdisi, J. 1997. "Powerlessness and Power: Women and the War in Lebanon." *Women: A Cultural Review* 8 (1): 89–91.

Manchanda, R., ed. 2001. *Women, War, and Peace in South Asia: Beyond Victimhood to Agency*. In J. Butler and J. W. Scott, eds., *Feminists Theorize the Political*. New York: Routledge, 385–403.

Marković, Z. 1996. "Nacija—žrtva i osveta" (Nation, Victim and Revenge). In Popov, 637–662.

Markowitz, F. 1995. "Rape, Torture, Warfare . . . and Refugees." *Anthropology of East Europe Review* 13 (1): 44–50.

Massey, D. 1994. *Space, Place and Gender*. London: Polity Press.

Mayer, T. 1994. "Heightened Palestinian Nationalism: Military Occupation, Repression, Difference and Gender." In T. Mayer, ed., *Women and the Israeli Occupation*. London: Routledge, 62–87.

Mazurana, D. 2002. "International Peacekeeping Operations: To Neglect Gender is to Risk Peacekeeping Failure." In Cockburn and Žarkov, 41–50.

McClintock, A. 1991: "'No Longer in a Future Heaven': Women and Nationalism in South Africa." *Transition* 51: 104–123.

———. 1995. *Imperial Leather: Race, Gender and Sexuality in the Colonial Contest*. London: Routledge.

McCollum, H., L. Kelly, and J. Radford. 1994. "Wars against Women." *Trouble and Strife* 28: 12–18.

McKay, S., and D. Mazurana. 2004. *Where Are the Girls? Girls in Fighting Forces in Northern Uganda, Sierra Leone, and Mozambique: Their Lives During and after War*. Montreal: Rights and Democracy.

McKechnie, R. 1987. "Living with Images of a Fighting Elite: Women and the Foreign Legion." In Macdonald, Holden, and Ardener, 122–147.

Medica Zenica. 1995. *Research Report on Dominant Gynaecological and Psychological Consequences of Rape*. Document 01–386/95. Zenica: Medica Zenica.

Medica Bulletin. 1996. "Surviving the Violence: War and Violence against Women Are Inseparable." Inaugural issue, *Medica Bulletin* (Zenica: Medica Zenica and Medica Mondiale).

Meijer, M. 1993. "Countering Textual Violence: On the Critique of Representation and the Importance of Teaching Its Methods." *Women's Studies International Forum* 16 (4): 367–378.

Meintjes, S., A. Pillay, and M. Turshen, eds. 2001. *The Aftermath: Women in Post-Conflict Transformation*. London: Zed Books.

Melman, B. 1998. *Borderlines: Genders and Identities in War and Peace (1870–1930)*. London: Routledge.

Menon, R., and K. Bhasin. 1993. "Recovery, Rupture, Resistance: The Indian State and Abduction of Women During Partition." *Economic and Political Weekly* (New Delhi), April 24, 2–11.

———. 1996. "Abducted Women, the State and Questions of Honour: Three Perspectives on the Recovery Operation in Post-Partition India." In Jayawardena and de Alwis, 1–32.

———. 1998. *Borders and Boundaries: Women in India's Partition*. New Delhi: Kali for Women.

Mertus, J. 1999. *Kosovo: How Myths and Truths Started a War*. Berkeley: University of California Press.

———. 2004. "Shouting from the Bottom of the Well: The Impact of International Trials for Wartime Rape on Women's Agency." *International Feminist Journal of Politics* 6 (1): 110–128.

Messerschmidt, J. 1998. "Men Victimizing Men: The Case of Lynching, 1865–1900." In Bowker, 125–151.

Mežnarić, S. 1985. "Theory and Reality: The Status of Employed Women in Yugoslavia." In S. Wolchik and A. Meyer, eds., *Women, State and Party in Eastern Europe*. Durham: Duke University Press, 214–221.

———. 1993. "The Rapists' Progress: Ethnicity, Gender and Violence." *Revija za sociologiju* 24 (3–4): 119–129.

———. 1994. "Gender as an Ethno-Marker: Rape, War and Identity Politics in the Former Yugoslavia." In V. Moghadam, ed., *Identity Politics and Women: Cultural Reassertions and Feminisms in International Perspective*. San Francisco: Westview Press, 76–97.

Mežnarić S., and J. Zlatković. 1991. "Gender and Ethnic Violence: The Case of Kosovo." *International Review of Sociology* 2: 113–120.

Mibenge, C. Forthcoming. "The Right to Access to Remedy for Victims of Wartime Sexual Violence: A Case Study of Rwanda (1994–2004)." In D. Žarkov, ed., *Gender, Violent Conflict, Development: Challenges of Practice*. New Delhi: Zubaan.

Milić, A. 1993. "Women and Nationalism in Former Yugoslavia." In Funk and Mueller, 109–122.

———. 1994. *Žene, Politika, Porodica* (Women, Politics, Family). Belgrade: Institut za političke studije.

———. 2002. *Ženski pokret na raskršću milenijuma*. Izveštaj o empirijskom istraživanju u Srbiji I Crnoj Gori (Women's Movement on the Millenium Crossroad. Report of Empirical Research in Serbia and Montenegro). Belgrade: Institut za Sociološka Istraživanja.

Milivojević, S. 1996. "Nacionalizacija svakidašnjice" (Ethnicization of Everyday life). In Popov, 662–686.

Mladjenović, L. 2001. "Caring at the Same Time: On Feminist Politics During the NATO Bombing of the Federal Republic of Yugoslavia and the Ethnic Cleansing of Albanians in Kosovo, 1999." In Meintjes, Pillay, and Turshen, 172–188.

Mladjenović, L., and V. Litricin. 1993. "Belgrade Feminists 1992: Separation, Guilt and Identity Crisis." *Feminist Review* 45: 113–119.

Mohanty, C. T. 2003. "'Under Western Eyes' Revisited: Feminist Solidarity Through Anticapitalist Struggle." *Signs* 28 (2): 499–535.

Mookherjee, N. 2004. "'My Man (Honour) Is Lost but I Still Have My Iman (Principle)': Sexual Violence and Articulation of Masculinity." In R. Chopra, C. Osella, and F. Osella, eds., *South Asian Masculinities: Context of Change, Sites of Continuity*. New Delhi: Women Unlimited, 160–174.

Morokvašić, M. 1981. "Sexuality and Control of Procreation." In K. Young, et al., eds., *Of Marriage and the Market: Women's Subordination in International Perspective*. London: CSE Books, 127–144.

———. 1984. "Being a Woman in Yugoslavia: Past, Present and Institutional Equality." In M. Gadant, ed., *Women of the Mediterranean*, trans. A. M. Berrett. London: Zed Books, 120–139.

Moser, C. 2001. "The Gendered Continuum of Violence and Conflict: An Operational Framework." In Moser and Clark, 30–51.

Moser, C., and F. Clark, eds. 2001. *Victims, Perpetrators or Actors? Gender, Armed Conflict and Political Violence*. London: Zed Books.

Mosse, G. L. 1985. *Nationalism and Sexuality: Middle-Class Morality and Sexual Norms in Modern Europe*. Madison: University of Wisconsin Press.

Mostov, J. 1995. "'Our Women'/'Their Women'—Symbolic Boundaries, Territorial Markers and Violence in the Balkans." *Peace and Change* 20 (4): 515–529.

Ms. 1993. Letters by V. Kesić, E. Jong, et al. to the editors in response to MacKinnon 1993b. Ms. (July–August): 8.

Mršević, Z. 2000. "War Makes Us Feminists." In Slapšak 2000a, 323–342.

Munk, E. 1994. "What's Wrong with This Picture." *Women's Review of Books* 11 (6): 5–6.

Murphy, P. F. 1994. *Fictions of Masculinity: Crossing Cultures, Crossing Sexualities*. New York: New York University Press.

Nash, C. 1993. "Remapping and Renaming: New Cartographies of Identity, Gender and Landscape in Ireland." *Feminist Review* 44: 39–57.

Nead, L. 1992. "Framing and Freeing: Utopias of the Female Body." *Radical Philosophy* 60: 12–15.

Nechemias, C. 1999. "The Russian Women's Movement: Facing the Issues of Reproductive Rights." Paper presented at the World Bank Conference, Washington, D.C., July.

Nenadović, A. 1996. "'Politika' u nacionalističkoj oluji" ("Politika" in the Nationalist Storm). In Popov, 583–609.

Niarchos, C. 1995. "Women, War and Rape: Challenges Facing the International Tribunal for the Former Yugoslavia." *Human Rights Quarterly* 17 (4): 649–690.

Nikolić-Ristanović, V. 1996. "War, Nationalism and Mothers." *Peace Review* 8 (3): 359–364.

———. 1998. "The Protection of War Rape Victims before The International Criminal Tribunal for Former Yugoslvia." *Temida* 1 (2): 13–21.

———. 2000. "From Sisterhood to Non-Recognition: Instrumentalization of Women's Suffering in the War in the Former Yugoslavia." In Slapšak 2000a, 147–194.

Nikolić-Ristanović, V., et al. 1995. *Žene, Nasilje i Rat* (Women, Violence and War). Belgrade: Soros Fond.

Oakley, A. 1972. *Sex, Gender and Society*. Melbourne: Sun Books.

Obradović-Dragišić, G. 2004. *War, Feminist Activism and Identity in Croatia (1990–1995): Case Study of Four Feminist NGOs*. Master's thesis, Institute of Social Studies, The Hague, Netherlands.

OIJ. 1992. *Reporters and Media in ex-Yugoslavia*. Les Cahiers de l'Organisation Internationale des Journalistes 2. Paris: Organisation Internationale des Journalistes.

Oleszczuk, T. 1998. "Women of Trust: The Press and Lobby Campaign in Poland." In *La Strada Program: Prevention of Trafficking in Women in Central and Eastern Europe*, Year Report, 1 January 1997–31 May 1998, 18–21.

Olujić, M. 1995. "Women, Rape and War: The Continued Trauma of Refugees and Displaced Persons in Croatia." *Anthropology of East Europe Review* 13 (1): 40–43.

Ortner, S. 1984. "Theory in Anthropology since the Sixties." *Comparative Studies in History and Society* 26 (1): 126–166.

Ortner, S., and H. Whitehead, eds. 1981. *Sexual Meanings, the Cultural Construction of Gender and Sexuality*. Cambridge: Cambridge University Press.

Pandey, G. 1997. "Community and Violence: Recalling Partition." *Economic and Political Weekly*, August 9, 2037–2045.

Papić, Ž. 1992. "Telo kao 'proces u toku'" (The Body as a Continuous Process). *Sociologija* (Belgrade) 34 (3): 259–275.

———. 1994. *The Women's Movement in Former Yugoslavia: 1970s and 1980s*. Belgrade: Center for Women's Studies, Research and Communication.

———. 1995. "How to Become a 'Real' Serbian Woman?" *Warreport*, no. 36: 40–43.

Parker, A., et al., eds. 1992. *Nationalisms and Sexualities*. New York: Routledge.

Patton, P., and R. Poole, eds. 1985. *WAR/Masculinity*. Sydney: Interventions.

Pedersen, S. 1991. "National Bodies, Unspeakable Acts: The Sexual Politics of Colonial Policy-Making." *Journal of Modern History*, 63: 647–680.

Penrose, J. 1993. "Reification in the Name of Change," in P. Jackson and J. Penrose, eds., *Constructions of Race, Place and Nation*. London: University College London Press.

Peries, S. 1998. "Metamorphosis of the Tamil Woman in the Nationalist War for Elam." Paper presented at the Women in Conflict Zones Network Conference, York University, Toronto, December.

Pešić, V. 1996. "Problemi konstituisanja država na prostoru bivše Jugoslavije: etnički redukcionizam u srpskoj nacionalnoj politici" (Problems of State-Constitution on the Territories of Former Yugoslavia: Ethnic Reductionism in Serbian National Politics). *Filozofija i društvo* 9 (10): 265–274.

———. 1993. "Nationalism, War and Disintegration of Communist Federations: The Yugoslav Case." In S. Biserko, ed. *Yugoslavia: Collapse, War, Crimes*. Belgrade: Centre for Anti-War Action and Belgrade Circle.

Peteet, J. 2000. "Male Gender and Rituals of Resistance in the Palestinian Intifada: A Cultural Politics of Violence." In M. Ghoussoub and E. Sinclair-Webb, eds., *Imagined Masculinities: Male Identity and Culture in the Modern Middle East*. London: Saqi Books, 103–126.

Peterson, S. V. 1999. "Sexing Political Identities/Nationalism as Heterosexism." *International Feminist Journal of Politics* 1 (1): 34–65.

Petković, R., et al. 1995. *Internationl Law and the Changed Yugoslavia*. Belgrade: Institute of International Politics and Economics.

Petrović, R. 1985. *Etnički mešoviti brakovi u Jugoslaviji*. Belgrade: Institut za sociološka istraživanja.

Philipose, L. 1996. "The Laws of War and Women's Human Rights." *Hypatia* 11 (4): 46–62.

Phoenix, A. 1997. "Youth and Gender: New Issues, New Agenda." *Youth, Nordic Journal of Youth Research* 5 (3): 2–19.

Pierson, R. R. 1987. "'Did Your Mother Wear Army Boots?' Feminist Theory and Women's Relation to War, Peace and Revolution." In Macdonald, Holden, and Ardener, 205–227.

Pillay, A. 2001. "Violence against Women in the Aftermath." In Meintjes, Pillay, and Turshen, 35–45.

Plavšić, P., et al. 1993. *Toward Democratic Broadcasting*. Belgrade: Soros Foundation.

Popov, N., ed. 1996. *Srpska strana rata* (The Serbian Side of the War). Belgrade: BIGZ/Republika.

Popović, S., D. Janča, and T. Petovar. 1990. *Kosovski Čvor: Drešiti ili seći? Izveštaj Nezavisne Komisije za Kosovo* (The Knot of Kosovo: To Disentangle or to Cut? Report of the Independent Committee for Kosovo). Belgrade: Chronos.

Portuges, C. 1992. "Lovers and Workers: Screening the Body in Post-Communist Hungarian Cinema." In A. Parker et al., eds., *Nationalisms and Sexualities*. New York: Routledge, 285–295.

Pratt, K., and L. Fletcher, eds. 1994. "Time for Justice: The Case for International Prosecutions of Rape and Gender-Based Violence in the Former Yugoslavia." *Berkeley Women's Law Journal* 9: 77–102.

Radcliffe, S. 1993. "Women's Place/El Lugar de Mujeres: Latin America and the Politics of Gender Identity." In M. Keith and S. Pile, eds., *Place and the Politics of Identity*. London: Routledge, 102–116.

Rajasingham-Senanayake, D. 2001. "Ambivalent Empowerment: The Tragedy of Tamil Women in Conflict." In R. Manchanda, ed., *Women, War and Peace in South Asia: Beyond Victimhood to Agency*. London: Sage, 102–130.

Ramet, S., 1990. "The Evolution of Yugoslav Nationalities Policy: Some Methodological Considerations." *Bradford Studies on Yugoslavia*, no. 15.

———. 1992. *Nationalism and Federalism in Yugoslavia, 1962–1991*, 2nd ed. Bloomington: Indiana University Press.

Rener, T. 1996. "State of the Art: Women's Studies in Slovenia." *European Journal of Women's Studies* 3: 167–171.

Richters, A. 1994. *Women, Culture and Violence: A Development, Health and Human Rights Issue*. Leiden: Leiden University, VENA.

Rich, A. 1983. "Compulsory Heterosexuality and Lesbian Existence." In E. Abel and K. E. Abel, eds., *The SIGNS Reader: Women, Gender and Scholarship*. Chicago: University of Chicago Press, 139–168.

———. 1994. "Compulsory Heterosexuality and Lesbian Existence." In *Blood, Bread, and Poetry*. New York: Norton, 23–75.

Ridd, R., and H. Callaway, eds. 1987. *Women and Political Conflict: Portraits of Struggle in Times of Crisis*. New York: New York University Press.

Roberts, H., ed. 1990. *Doing Feminist Research*. London: Routledge.

Rosenblum-Cale, K. 1979. "After the Revolution: Women in Yugoslavia." In I. Volgyes, ed., *The Peasantry of Eastern Europe: 20th-Century Developments*, vol. 2. New York: Pergamon Press.

Rothfield, P. 1990. "Feminism, Subjectivity and Sexual Difference." In S. Gunew, ed., *Feminist Knowledge: Critique and Construct*. London: Routledge, 121–144.

Roy, A. 1997. "Introduction: Cultural Studies, Violence and Femininity." *Women: A Cultural Review* 8 (3): 259–263.

Rubin, G. 1993. "Thinking Sex: Notes for a Radical Theory of Sexuality." In H. Abelove, et al., eds., *The Lesbian and Gay Studies Reader*. New York: Routledge.

Ruddick, S. 1989. *Maternal Thinking*. Boston: Beacon Press.

———. 1993. "Notes Toward a Feminist Peace Politics." In Cooke and Woollacott, 109–127.

Rukszto, K. 1997. "Making Her into a 'Woman': The Creation of Citizen-Entrepreneur in Capitalist Poland." *Women's Studies International Forum* 20 (1): 103–112.

Rus, V. 1971. "Sadašnji medjunacionalni odnosi u Jugoslaviji" (Contemporary Interethnic Relations in Yugoslavia). *Gledišta*, nos. 5–6: 761–769.

Rutherford, J. 1988. "Who's That Man?" In R. Chapman and J. Rutherford, eds., *Male Order: Unwrapping Masculinity*. London: Lawrence and Wishart, 21–68.

Ryan, L. 1997. "A Question of Loyalty: War, Nation and Feminism in Early Twentieth-Century Ireland." *Women's Studies International Forum* 20 (1): 21–32.

Said, E. 1978. *Orientalism*. New York: Vintage Books.

Sajor, L. I., ed. 1998. *Common Grounds: Violence against Women in War and Armed Conflict Situations*. Quezon City, Philippines: Asian Centre for Women's Human Rights (ASCENT).

Sancho, N. 1997. "The 'Comfort Women' System During World War II: Asian

Women as Targets of Mass Rape and Sexual Slavery by Japan." In R. Lentin, ed., *Gender and Catastrophe*. London: Zed Books, 144–155.

Sander, H. 1993. "Prologue." In Stiglmayer 1993a, xvii–xxiii.

Sandoval, C. 1991. "Third World Feminism: The Theory and Method of Oppositional Consciousness in the Postmodern World." *Genders* 10: 1–25.

Sarkar, T. 1995. "Heroic Women, Mother Goddesses. Family and Organization in Hindutva Politics." In Sarkar and Butalia, 181–215.

Sarkar, T., and U. Butalia. 1995. *Women and Right-Wing Movements: Indian Experiences*. London: Zed Books.

Satish, D. 1997. Review of Sarkar and Butalia. In "Gender in the Making: Indian Contexts," special issue, *Thamiris* (Amsterdam) 4 (1): 195–199.

Savran, D. 1996. "The Sadomasochist in the Closet: White Masculinity and the Culture of Victimization." *Differences: A Journal of Feminist Cultural Studies* 8 (2): 127–152.

Schirup, C. U. 1991. "The Post-Communist Enigma: Ethnic Mobilization in Yugoslavia." *New Community* 18 (1): 115–131.

Schlegel, A., ed. 1977. *Sexual Stratification: A Cross-Cultural View*. New York: Columbia University Press.

Schott, R. M. 1996. "Gender and 'Postmodern War.'" *Hypatia* 11 (4): 19–29.

Segal, L. 1990. *Slow Motion: Changing Masculinities, Changing Men*. London: Virago.

Seidel, G., ed. 1988. *The Nature of the Right: A Feminist Analysis of Order Patterns*. Amsterdam and Philadelphia: John Benjamin Publishing.

Seidel, G., and R. Gunther. 1988. "'Nation' and 'Family' in the British Media Reporting on the 'Falklands Conflict.'" In Seidel, 115–128.

Seidler, V. J. 1994. *Unreasonable Men: Masculinity and Social Theory*. London: Routledge.

———. 1997. *Man Enough: Embodying Masculinities*. London: Sage.

Seifert, R. 1993. "War and Rape: A Preliminary Analysis." In Stiglmayer 1993a, 54–72.

———. 1996. "The Second Front: The Logic of Sexual Violence in Wars." *Women's Studies International Forum* 19 (1–2): 35–43.

Sekelj, L. 1990. "Yugoslavia, 1945–1986." *Sociology* (Sociologija: Journal of Yugoslav Sociological Association), Supplement for the XII World Congress of Sociology (in English): 65–85.

———. 1991. "'Realno samoupravljanje,' 'realni nacionalism' i dezintegracija Jugoslavije" ("Real Self-Management," "Real Nationalism" and the Disintegration of Yugoslavia). *Sociology* (Sociologija: Journal of Yugoslav Sociological Association) 33 (4): 587–599.

Sharoni, S. 1994. "Homefront as Battlefield: Gender, Military Occupation and Violence against Women." In M. Tamar, ed., *Women and the Israeli Occupation*. London: Routledge, 121–137.

Sharpe, J. 1991. "The Unspeakable Limits of Rape: Colonial Violence and Counter-Insurgency." *Genders* 10: 25–47.

Shetty. S. 1995. "(Dis)Figuring the Nation: Mother, Metaphor, Metonymy." *Differences* 7 (3): 50–79.

Sinha, M. 1995. *Colonial Masculinity: The "Manly Englishman" and the "Effeminate Bengali" in the Late Nineteenth Century*. Manchester, England: Manchester University Press.

Sklevicky, L. 1987a. "Konji, žene, ratovi: Problem utemeljenja historije žena u Jugoslviji" (Horses, Women, Wars. Problems in Establishing Women's History in Yugoslavia). In Sklevicky 1987b, 51–61.

———, ed. 1987b. *Žena i Društvo: Kultiviranje Dijaloga* (Woman and Society. Cultivation of a Dialogue). Zagreb: Sociološko društvo Hrvatske.

———. 1989a. "Emancipated Integration or Integrated Emancipation: The Case of Post-Revolutionary Yugoslavia." In A. Angerman et al., *Current Issues in Women's History*. London: Routledge, 93–108.

———. 1989b. "More Horses Than Women: On the Difficulties of Founding Women's History in Yugoslavia." *Gender and History* 1 (1): 68–75.

———. 1995. "Organizacija i Emancipacija" (Organization and Emancipation). *Kruh and Ruze*, no. 3 (Winter 1994–Spring 1995): 4–12.

Slapšak, S., ed. 2000a. *War Discourse, Women's Discourse: Essays and Case-Studies from Yugoslavia and Russia*. Ljubljana: Topos and ISH.

———. 2000b. "Yugoslav War: A Case of/for Gendered History." In Slapšak 2000a, 17–68.

Slim, H. 2004. "Relief Agencies and Moral Standing in War: Principles of Humanity, Neutrality, Impartiality, and Solidarity." In H. Afshar and D. Eade, eds., *Development, Women, and War: Feminist Perspectives*, A Development in Practice Reader. London: Oxfam, 195–211.

Službeni List. 1974. *Zakon o silovanju* (Law on Rape). Public document. Belgrade: Službeni List.

Smith, A. D. 1986. *The Ethnic Origins of Nations*. Oxford: Basil Blackwell.

———. 1988. "The Myth of the 'Modern Nation' and the Myths of Nations." *Ethnic and Racial Studies* 11 (1): 1–26.

———. 1991. *National Identity*. Harmondsworth: Penguin.

Smith, V. 1990. "Split Affinities: The Case of Interracial Rape." In M. Hirsch and E. Fox Keller, eds., *Conflicts in Feminism*. New York: Routledge.

———. 1998. *Not Just Race, Not Just Gender: Black Feminist Readings*. New York: Routledge.

Sofos, S. 1996. "Inter-Ethnic Violence and Gendered Constructions of Ethnicity in Former Yugoslavia." *Social Identities* 2 (1): 73–92.

Sollors, W. 1989. "Introduction: The Invention of Ethnicity." In W. Sollors, ed., *The Invention of Ethnicity*. New York: Oxford University Press.

Spasić, I. 2000, "Woman-Victim and Woman-Citizen: Some Thoughts on the 'Feminist' Discourse on War." In Slapšak 2000a, 343–358.

Spijkerboer, T. 1994. *Women and Refugee Status*. The Hague: Emancipation Council.

Spillers, J., ed. 1991. *Comparative American Identities: Race, Sex and Nationality in the Modern Text*. New York: Routledge.

Spivak, G. 1987. "Deconstructing Historiography." In R. Guha, ed., *Subaltern Studies*, vol. 5, *Writings on South Asian History and Society*. New Delhi: Oxford University Press.

Spyer, P. 2001. "Photography's Framings and Unframings: a Review Article," *Society for Comparative Study of Society and History* 43 (1): 181–192.

Stiglmayer, A. 1993a. *Mass Rape—The War against Women in Bosnia-Hercegovina*. Lincoln: University of Nebraska Press.

———. 1993b. "The War in the Former Yugoslavia." In Stiglmayer 1993a, 1–35.

Stockle, V. 1993. "Is Sex to Gender as Race Is to Ethnicity?" In V. Stockle, *Gendered Anthropology*. London: Routledge, 17–38.

Stojanović, S. 1972. "Od postrevolucionarne diktature do socijalističke demokratije: Jugoslovenski socijalizam na raskršću" (From Post-revolutionary Dictatorship to Socialist Democracy: Yugoslav Socialism on the Crossroads). *Praxis* 9 (3–4): 375–398.

Stoler, A. 2002. *Carnal Knowledge and Imperial Power: Race and the Intimate in Colonial Rule*. Berkeley: University of California Press.

Supek, O. 1994. "Women and Nationalist Conflict in Former Yugoslavia: War Rapes and Human Rights." Paper presented at the American Anthropological Association conference, Atlanta, Ga., November–December.

Taguba, Antonio. 2004. "Article 15–6 Investigation of the 800th Military Police Brigade." U.S. Army report into Abu Ghraib prison abuse. March 3. Available at http://news.bbc.co.uk/1/hi/world/americas/3684825.stm.

Taylor, D. 1993. "Spectacular Bodies: Gender, Terror and Argentina's 'Dirty War.'" In Cooke and Woollacott, 20–40.

Taylor, J. 1991. *War Photography: Realism in the British Press*. London: Routledge/A Comedia Book.

Theweleit, K. 1987. *Male Fantasies*, vol. 1. London: Polity Press.

———. 1993. "The Bomb's Womb and the Genders of War (War Goes on Preventing Women from Becoming the Mothers of Invention)." In Cooke and Woollacott, 283–317.

Thompson, J. 1991. "Women and War." *Women's Studies International Forum* 14 (6): 63–75.

Thompson, M. 1994. *Forging War: The Media in Serbia, Croatia and Bosnia-Hercegovina*. Wivenhoe Park, Colchester: Article 19, International Centre against Censorship, Human Rights Centre, University of Essex.

Toch, H. 1998. "Hypermasculinity and Prison Violence." In Bowker, 170–178.

Todorova, M. 1999. *Imaginarni Balkan*. Belgrade: Biblioteka XX Vek.

Turshen, M., and C. Twagiramariya, eds. 1998. *What Women Do in Wartime: Gender and Conflict in Africa*. London: Zed Books.

Twagiramariya, C., and M. Turshen. 1998. "'Favours' to Give and 'Consenting' Victims: The Sexual Politics of Survival in Rwanda." In Turshen and Twagiramariya, 101–117.

Uncaptive Minds. 1995–1996. Special issue on ex-Yugoslavia, 8 (3–4).

United Nations. 1993. Commission on Human Rights Inquiry, Attachment IX, Annex II—Report on Allegations of Rape. February 10.

———. 1994a. Commission of Experts' Final Report. Section IV: Substantive Findings (E: Detention Facilities; F: Rape and other Forms of Sexual Assault). United Nations Security Council S/1994/674, 27 May.

———. 1994b. Commission of Experts' Final Report. Annex IX—Rape and Sexual Assault. United Nations Security Council, S/1994/674/Add.2 (vol. 5), 28 December.

———. 1994c. Commission of Experts' Final Report. Annex IX.A—Sexual Assault Investigation. United Nations Security Council, S/1994/674/Add.2 (vol. 5), 28 December.

Unterhalter, E. 1987. "Women Soldiers and the Unity in Apartheid South Africa." In Macdonald, Holden, and Ardener, 100–121.

Valić Nedeljković, D. 1997. *Rikošet Reči* (Ricocheting Words). Belgrade: Media.

van Niekerk, M. 1993. "Ethnic Studies in the Netherlands: An Outline of Research Issues." SISWO (Amsterdam) *Research Notes* 1: 2–14.

van Tienhoven, H. 1993. "Sexual Torture of Male Victims." *Torture* 3 (4): 133–135.

Veljanovski, R. 1996. "Zaokret elektronskih medija" (The Turn in Electronic Media). In Popov, 610–636.

Verdery, K. 1992. "Comment: Hobsbawm in the East." *Anthropology Today* 8 (1): 8–10.

———. 1996. *What Was Socialism and What Comes Next?* Princeton: Princeton University Press.

Vickers, M. 1998. *Between Serb and Albanian: A History of Kosovo*. New York: Columbia University Press.

Vindhya, U. 2000, "Comrades-in-Arms: Sexuality and Identity in the Contemporary Revolutionary Movement in Andhra Pradesh and the Legacy of Chalam." In M. E. John and J. Nair, eds., *A Question of Silence? The Sexual Economies of Modern India*. New Delhi: Kali for Women, 167–191.

Vojnović, M. 1995. *Kobno osipanje srpskog naroda* (Fatal Dispersion of Serbs). Belgrade: Prometej.

Vranić, S. 1996. *Breaking the Wall of Silence: The Voices of Raped Bosnia*. Zagreb: AntiBarbarus.

Warner, M. 1996. *Monuments and Maidens: The Allegory of the Female Form*. London: Vintage.

Watson, P. 1993. "The Rise of Masculinism in Eastern Europe." *New Left Review* 198: 71–82.

Weeks, J. 1985. *Sexuality and Its Discontents: Meanings, Myths and Modern Sexualities*. London: Routledge and K. Paul.

West, L. A., ed. 1997. *Feminist Nationalism*. London: Routledge.

Winkler, C. 1991. "Rape as Social Murder." *Anthropology Today* 7 (3): 12–14.

Withuis, J. 1995. *De Jurk van de kosmonaute: Over politiek, cultuur en psyche* (The Dress of the Cosmonaut: On Politics, Culture and Psyche). Amsterdam: Meppel Boom.

Wittig, M. 1992. *The Straight Mind and Other Essays*. Boston: Beacon Press.

Wolchik, S., and A. Meyer. 1985. *Women, State, and Party in Eastern Europe*. Durham: Duke University Press.

Wood, L., and H. Rennie. 1994. "Formulating Rape: The Discursive Construction of Victims and Villains." *Discourse and Society* 5 (1): 125–148.

Yugoslavia 1945–1985. 1986. Belgrade: Federal Statistical Office.

Yuksel, S. 1991. "Therapy of Sexual Torture." Paper presented at the XI World Sexology Congress, Amsterdam, Netherlands, June.

Yuval-Davis, N. 1985. "Front and Rear: The Sexual Division of Labor in the Israeli Army." *Feminist Studies* 11 (3): 649–676.

———. 1987. "The Jewish Collectivity and National Reproduction in Israel." In Khamsin Collective, ed., *Women in the Middle East*. London: Zed Books.

———. 1989. "National Reproduction and the 'Demographic Race' in Israel." In N. Yuval-Davis and F. Anthias, eds., *Woman-Nation-State*. London: Macmillan, 92–109.

———. 1996. "Women and the Biological Reproduction of 'The Nation'." *Women's Studies International Forum* 19 1 (2): 17–24.

———. 1997. *Gender and Nation*. London: Sage.

Yuval-Davis, N., and F. Anthias. 1989. *Woman-Nation-State*. London: Macmillan.

Zajicek, A., and T. M. Calasanti. 1998. "Patriarchal Struggles and State Practices: A Feminist, Political-Economic View." *Gender and Society* 12 (5): 505–527.

Zajović, S. 1994. "Radjanje, nacionalizam i rat" (Birth-giving, Nationalism and War). *Žene protiv rata* 1 (August): 6–10.

Zalevski, M. 1995. "Well, What is the Feminist Perspective on Bosnia?" *International Affairs* 71 (2): 339–356.

Zalihić-Kaurin, A. 1993. "The Muslim Woman." In Stiglmayer 1993a, 170–174.

Žarkov, D. 1991. "The Silence Which Is Not One: Sexuality, Subjectivity and Social Change in a Feminist Rethinking of Research on Peasant Women." Master's thesis, Institute of Social Studies, The Hague, Netherlands.

———. 1994. Review of S. Drakulić, *Balkan Express: Fragments from the Other Side of War* (London: Hutchins, 1993). *Journal of European Women's Studies* 1 (1): 130–132.

———. 1995. "Gender, Orientalism and 'History of Ethnic Hatred' in the Former Yugoslavia." In P. Lutz and N. Yuval-Davis, eds., *Crossfires, Nationalism, Racism and Gender in Europe*. London: Pluto Press, 105–120.

———. 1997. "War Rapes in Bosnia: On Masculinity, Femininity and Power of the Rape Victim Identity." *Tijdschrift voor Criminologie* 39 (2): 140–151.

———. 2000. "Feminist Self/Ethnic Self. Theory and Politics of Women's Activism." In Slapšak 2000a, 167–194.

———. 2001. "The Body of the Other Man: Sexual Violence and the Construction of Masculinity, Sexuality and Ethnicity in Croatian Media." In Moser and Clark, 69–82.

———. 2002a. "'Srebrenica Trauma': Masculinity, Military and National Self-image in Dutch Daily Newspapers." In Cockburn and Žarkov, 183–203.

———. 2002b. "Feminism and the Disintegration of Yugoslavia: On the Politics of Gender and Ethnicity." In "Social Development Issues," special issue, *Women in Conflict and Crisis* 24 (3): 59–68.

———. 2004. *Working through the War: Trajectories of Non-Governmental and Governmental Organizations in the Balkans Engaged in Psycho-Social Assistance to Victims of War and Family Violence*. Utrecht: Admira.

Žarkov, D., R. Drezgić, and T. Djurić-Kuzmanović. 2004. "Violent Conflict in the Balkans: Impacts, Responses, Consequences." Background paper for UNRISD 2005 Report, *Gender Equality: Striving for Justice in an Unequal World*.

Zolić, H. 1986. "Razvoj republika i autonomnih pokrajina u periodu 1981–1985 godine" (Development of Republics and Autonomous Provinces in the period of 1981–1985). In *Jugoslovenska privreda izmedju stagnacije i razvoja* (Yugoslav Industry between Stagnation and Development). Belgrade: Institut ekonomskih nauka.

Zwerman, G. 1994. "Mothering on the Lam: Politics, Gender Fantasies and Maternal Thinking in Women Associated with Armed Clandestine Organizations in the United States." *Feminist Review* 47: 33–56.

INDEX

Abortion, 141; laws, 247 n.15
Abu Ghraib Prison, 166
Agency: annihilation of, 216; and empowerment, 222; feminist, 71; and intersections with gender, ethnicity, war, violence, 213; maternal, 71; political, 26; women's political, 58; and Yugoslav feminism, 213
Ajanović, Irfan, 61
Albanian women, as overreproductive, 20
Amnesty International, 117
Antinationalist feminists, 214
Armed body, 13; female, 203, 204; invisibility and absence of, 213
Australia, 194

Bacchetta, Paola, 227
Bakić-Hayden, Milica, 50
Bangladesh, 178
Bassiouni, M. Cherif, 133, 147, 236 n.17
Bernard, Cheryl, 148
Bhashin, Kamla, 172
Blagojević, Marina, 81
Bloul, Rachel, 148
Body: feminist theorizing of, 9; and intersections with gender, sexuality, ethnicity, nation, 2; male, 9; maternal, 66; metaphoric and material, 10
Bogović, Josip, 157
Boric, Rada, 214, 215
Bosnian refugees, 108, 110
Bosnian Serb forces, 7
Bourke, Joanna, 163
Brečić, Petra, 155, 166
Bringa, Tone. 148
Brownmiller, Susan, 85, 144, 147, 176
Butalia, Urvashi, 72, 173, 226

Catholic Church, 141
Center for Rape Victims, Bosnia, 134
Center for Women War Victims, Zagreb, 150
Children: from forced pregnancies, 154; terror against, 41
Ćirilov, Jovan, 37, 38
Civil war, 5
Cleiren, Tineke, 160, 161
Cock, Jacklyn, 220
Cockburn, Cynthia, 185
Collective victimhood: narrative of, 85
Colović, Ivan, 3
Committee of Mothers, 44–45
Connell, Robert, 162
Copelon, Rhonda, 170, 182, 187
Crary, David, 136
Croatia: Association of Catholic Doctors, 141; Krajina, 209; nation-state, 204; president of (Franjo Tudjman), 44, 49, 77, 102, 192
Croatian daily *Vjesnik,* 23
Croatian weekly *Danas,* 32
Culture, European, 198

Das, Veena, 174
Davis, Kathy, 9
Dayton Peace Accords, 5
De Alwis, Malathi, 71, 171

De Mel, Neloufer, 173
Deshpande, Satish, 227
Discursive space, 212, 216
Djurić-Kuzmanović, Tanja, 244 n.1
Drakulić, Slavenka, 27, 72–74, 76, 79, 136, 150, 246 n.10; 249 n.14
Drezgić, Rada, 4, 75
Duhaček, Dasa, 77, 78
Dutch women raped by Russian soldiers, 175

Easthope, Anthony, 163
El-Bushra, Judy, 223
Embodiment: as experience, 9; and intersections with sexuality and subjectivity, 9; symbolic, 201
Emmanuel, Sarala, 221
"Empire of sex," Sarajevo as, 96
Enloe, Cynthia, 69, 143, 163, 175, 224, 243 n.13
Ethnic: cleansing, 20, 98, 153; female body raped, 153; purity, 131; seclusion, 99
Ethnicity: ambiguous, 10; and collective identity, 214; conflicting, 10; contradictory, 10; and intersection with sexuality in rape of Muslim men, 160
Ethnicized communities, 165
Eurocentrism, 213
European Union, 48–49, 103, 117
Experts, United Nations Commission of, 6

Fe/male body, 10
Female body: conflicting meanings of, 12; sexual geography of, 68; as site of power and dominance, 9; symbolic functions, 11; symbolic meanings, 10; theoretical perspectives on, 8; undomesticated, 38; victimized, 85; Western feminism on, 9
Female subjectivity, feminist theorizing of, 80
Femininity, epistemological status of, 12
Feminism: in Croatia, 150; in Serbia, 77; in Slovenia, 77; South Asian, 173; South Asian Hindu, 78; and theorizing, 9, 212; in Yugoslavia, 77, 79. *See also* Nationalism
Folnegović-Šmalc, Vera, 145
Forced impregnation, 116, 124; of Croat women, 142; of Muslim women, 129, 138, 140, 142; of Serb women 129, 138
Forces, Bosnian Serb, 7
Forde, C. Daryll, 193
French TV, 205
Fuss, Diana, 9

Gendered war strategy, 143
Geographies of ethnicity, 116
Germany, 97
Griffin, Susan, 85, 176
Gunther, Richard, 193
Gutman, Roy, 144, 149

Haag, Pamela, 179, 182
Hayden, Robert, 6, 50, 154, 174
Heberle, Renée, 180, 182
Helms, Elissa, 185, 216
Herak, Borislav, trial of, 117, 134–36
Heritage of representations, gendered, 195
Heterosexuality, 9; and homosexuality, 10, 138; male, 95; and Muslim men, 158
History of ethnic hatred, 5, 102
Hoxha, Fadil, 21, 23–26, 28, 30, 32–33, 72
Hughes, M.Donna, 77
Humiliation, masculinized, 163
Huston, Nancy, 64

Iconography of submission, 65
Identity, European, 50
India, 171, 172, 226; and Hindutva Nationalist movement, 227

Innes, Catherine, 114
International War Crime Tribunal, 143, 147
Intersections: of gender and other collective identities, 181; of masculinities and homo/heterosexualities with ethnicity, 164
Iveković, Rada, 13

Jansen, Willy, 148
Jayawardena, Kumari, 171
Jeffrey, Patricia, 226
JNA (Jugoslovenska Narodna Armija), 202
Jones, Adam, 155
Jordan, Michael, 146

Karadžić, Radovan, 118, 137
Kašić, Biljana, 175
Kelly, Liz, 85
Kenya, 171
Kesić, Vesna, 150
Kohn, Elizabeth, 146
Koontz, Claudia, 220
Korać, Maja, 215
Krass, Caroline, 146
Krog, Antje, 177
Kulenović, Muradif, 137

Language: interpretation of rape, 179; Serbo-Croat, 27; as site of ethnic identity, 62
Latin America, 212
Litričin, Vera, 215
Lončar, Mladen, 155, 166
Lutz, Helma., 148

Macdonald, Sharon, 12
Maček, Ivana, 100
MacKinnon, Catharine, 149, 150, 181
Male body: and production of ethnicity, 156; and symbolic meanings, 10
Manhood: Albanian, 20; in the Balkans, 55; and hegemonic masculinities, 162; and heroic masculinity, 164; militarized, 123; and sexual potency, 119; and soldering in Serbia, 119; and virility, 120
Marcus, Sharon, 179, 180, 183
Masculinity: and colonialism, 163; competing forms of, 162; production of, 162; studies, 162
Maternal body, 13, 22, 24, 26, 45, 50, 58; as ambiguous category, 32; as marker of national territory, 69; self-politicized, 72; symbolic capacity of, 70
Maternal politics, 22, 58, 70, 79, 81; in Argentina's "Dirty war," 181; in Sri Lanka, 71, 173, 226
Mazurana, Dyan, 225
McKay, Susan, 225
Memory, masculinized, 163
Men, sexual violence against, 158
Menon, Ritu, 172
Mertus, Julie, 20, 177
Messerchmidt, James, 164
Metaphors: feminine, 70; maternal, 53
Mežnarić, Silva, 74, 152, 153
Mibenge, Chiseche, 172, 177
Milić, Andjelka, 78
Military skills, as addition to women's domestic skills, 195
Milošević, Slobodan, 4, 19, 87, 103–5
Mladjenović, Lepa, 215
Montenegrin women, rape of, 20
Mookherjee, Nayanika, 178
Morality, sexual, 94
Mostov, Julie, 154
Motherhood: and intersection of symbolic-geographic spaces, 69; and militarization, 79; as site of discursive struggle, 69
Mothers: false, 61; true, 63, 65; Tamil and Sinhalese, 71
Mujahideen fighters, 198
Multiple rapes, of Muslim women, 117

Munk, Erica, 149, 153
Muslim men, 129, 135; rape of, 158
Muslim women: trauma and shame, 130; virginity, 145

Nationalism: and antinationalist feminism, 217; and Bosnian feminism, 216; and collective identity, 213; and Croatian feminism, 214; ethnic, 11; and language, 62; as male enterprises, 216; as political force, 5; and Yugoslav feminism, 77
Nation-state, metaphor of, 214
Netherlands, 97
Niarchos, Catherine, 155, 176
Nikolić-Ristanović, Vesna, 77
NIN, 33, 34, 35

Opportunistic rapes, 153
Orientalism, 135, 148
Orthodox Church, Serbian, 141
Ottoman Empire, 120
O-ZONA: Assistance to Women in Crisis, 215

Pakistan, 172
Parliament, Bosnian, 59
Patriotic feminists, 214
Pedersen, Susan, 171
Penrose, Jan, 12
Peteet, Julie, 164, 165
Petovar, Tanja, 151
Petrović, Ruza, 233 n.1, 248 n.3
Phallic power, 165
Philosophy, Western, 12
Pintarić, Srećko, 55
Political platform, ethnically inclusive, 202
Popović, Srdja., 151
Power, Margaret, 227
Power: category of, 11; domains of, 11; relations, 10; and intersections of masculinity and heterosexuality, 164
Production of ethnicity, 10
Prostitution, in Sarajevo, 88

Radcliffe, Sarah, 81
Radio Wall, Sarajevo, 88
Rajasingham-Senanayake, D., 226
Rape, 39, 105, 116–17, 119, 129 (*see also* sexual violence); of Croat women, 132; denial of, 149, 251 n.17; homosexual, 138; intersections of gender and ethnicity in, 122; of men, 156; of Montenegrin women in Kosovo, 20; of Muslim men, 158; of Muslim women, 129, 132, 153; peacetime, 174; and race, 137; and savage resilience, 129; of Serb women, 30, 143, 151; and sexual assault, 150; as a war strategy, 98; as a war weapon, 196
Refugees, 53
Reisinger, Oto, 103
Rennie, Heather, 174, 176, 177, 179
Representational capacities, of the male and female body, 19
Rich, Adrienne, 9
Roy, Anita, 78, 226
Ruddick, Sara, 85
Rutherford, Jonathan, 164
Rwanda, 172, 222, 224

Sarkar, Tanita, 81, 226–27
Scotland, 56
Schott, Robin, 181
Seidel, Gill., 78, 193, 226
Seifert, Ruth, 178
Sekelj, Laslo, 6
Self: ethnic, 58, 138, 156; victimized, 86
Serbian daily *Politika*, 32
Serbian weekly *NIN*, 31
Serbs: as chief enemy, 203; as ethnic enemy, 185; and history of suffering, 210
Serb women, under-reproductive, 20
Sexism, 73

Sexuality: female, 68; misconceptions of, 161
Sexualized fe/male body, 10
Sexual objects, Arab Muslim Women as, 158
Sexual purity, 131
Sexual slavery, Japanese military system of, 147
Sexual violence: against men, 155, 158, 164, 165, 169; and intersections of gender and sexuality, 170; mass rape, 214. *See also* Women
Sharpe, Jenny, 163, 165, 171
Shetty, Sandhya, 70
Sinha, Mrinalini, 162
Slavonia, 201, 206
Slim, Valerie, 171
Slovenian independence, 43
Smith, Valerie, 85, 171
Social and physical spaces, 68
Socialist Federal Republic of Yugoslavia, Central Committee of the League of Communists of, 22
Socialist Yugoslav past, 201
Social practice, embodiment as, 9
Sodomy, 138
Soldiering, 64; in the Balkans, 227; female, 228; and rape, 123; and virility, 92, 120; and war, 65; and women, 224
South Asia, 212
Spasić, Ivana, 216
Spijkerboer, Thomas, 148
Spyer, Patricia, 89
Stern (German weekly), 196
Stiglmayer, Alexandra, 154, 160
Studies, (post)colonial, 11
Subjectivity, 9, 213; female political, 57, 79; political, 148
Suffering: collective, 209; grand narrative of, 205; narrative of ethnic, 41
Symbolic geographies, 12; and emasculation, 165

Taylor, Diana, 175, 181
Taylor, John, 89, 99
Thompson, Mark, 234 n.5
Tijanić, Aleksandar, 27, 28
Tijsen, Melanie, 160, 161
Tito's death, 21
Tradition, Christian, 52
Tudjman, Franjo, 44, 49, 77, 102, 192

United Nations, 7, 103, 117; Commission of Experts, 6, 133, 147, 155, 236 n.17; Resolution 1325, 222
UNPROFOR, 92, 94,
Ugresić, Dubravka, 217
Ustashe, Croatian army, 209

Victim: actual, 36; potential, 36
Victimhood, metaphors of, 215; symbolic, 102
Victimization, narrative of, 87, 228
Victimized body, 13
Vietnam War, 201
Violence, ethnic war and media war, 2, 5, 10, 85, 203
Vlahović, Jugoslav, 65
Vranić, Seada, 145, 149, 155
Vukovar, 211

Wall of Love, 54, 58–59, 60, 78–79, 103
War Crimes Commission, 133
Warner, Marina, 12
War rapes as marking ethnic boundaries, 154
Wartime committees, 44
White plague, 4
"Whore," use of the word, 27, 37–38
Withuis, Jolanda., 175
Women: Bosnian, 196; Croat, 196; Dutch communist, 175; in elite military guards unit, 194; Jewish, 175; Muslim, 116, 198; as political force, 76; as potential brides, 195; political innocence of, 216; sexual violence

Women (*continued*)
against, 116, 214; Sri Lankan Sinhalese, 71; as symbolic reproducers of nation, 69; Tamil Tiger militant, 173; and will to violence, 226
Women in Black, 87
Women soldiers: beauty of, 192; bodies of, 201; Croat, 202–3, 211; Muslim, 196, 199, 201; Serb, 208
Wood, Linda, 174, 176–77, 179
Yugoslavia: feminist discourses of disintegration of, 212; International Criminal Tribunal, 177; Socialist Federal Republic of, 1; Yugoslav National Army, 30
Yuval-Davis, Nira, 69

Zalihić-Kaurin, Azra, 145
Zlatković, Jelena, 74
Zolić, Hasan, 20

Dubravka Žarkov is an associate professor at the Institute of Social Science, The Hague.

Library of Congress Cataloging-in-Publication Data
Žarkov, Dubravka, 1958–
The body of war : media, ethnicity, and gender in the break-up of Yugoslavia / Dubravka Žarkov.
p. cm.—(Next wave)
Includes bibliographical references and index.
ISBN 978-0-8223-3955-7 (cloth : alk. paper)
ISBN 978-0-8223-3966-3 (pbk. : alk. paper)
1. Women in mass media—Former Yugoslav republics.
2. Women and war—Former Yugoslav republics.
3. Yugoslav War, 1991–1995—Women. 4. Kosovo (Serbia)—History—Civil War, 1998–1999. 5. Mass media and war—Former Yugoslav republics. 6. Ethnicity—Former Yugoslav republics. 7. Nationalism—Former Yugoslav republics. 8. Former Yugoslav republics—Ethnic relations. I. Title.
HQ1715.5.Z37 2007
949.703082—dc22
2007008328